DATE DUE

Global Banking Strategy

Global Banking Strategy

DEREK F. CHANNON
Professor of Strategic Management and Marketing
Manchester Business School

JOHN WILEY & SONS
New York · Chichester · Brisbane · Toronto · Singapore

British Library Cataloguing in Publication Data

Channon, Derek F. (Derek French)
    Global banking strategy.
    1.   Banking
    I.   Title
    332.1
    C458
    ISBN 0 471 92031 2

Typeset by Acorn Bookwork, Salisbury
Printed and bound in Great Britain by
St Edmundsbury Press, Bury St Edmunds

Contents

To
S and M who kept me company
during much of the early draft of this book
and who kindly listened without interruption
but provided inspiration.

Preface

This book was scheduled to be delivered well before it was finally finished. For this I sincerely apologize to its original sponsor, IRM. However, if it had not been late I might well have missed some of the dramatic changes that have occurred in bank strategy since the mid 1980s. Further delays in the subsequent reviewing process have also enabled me to revise the manuscript to incorporate the early results of the crash of 1987, as well as the 'Big Bang' in London and the internationalization of the yen, which have helped to demonstrate further the effects of a fully integrated global market place. Chapter 4, of which the title has been slightly modified in the light of recent events, has continuously been extended although the predictions within the chapter have consistently been held to—only the timing and sequence of events have been modified to reflect reality.

In the past several years the financial services industry has been in a state of dramatic transition. When the idea for this research was originally put to my friend Michel Ghertman, then director of IRM, at the beginning of the 1980s, the banking industry was already in a state of rapid change. It was also faced with the massive problem of the developing country debt burden, born out of the cumulative effect of the first and second oil shocks. Since the crisis of 1982, the industry has partially accommodated this problem although the overall possibility of a massive financial crisis has perhaps increased and the world lives on a delicate knife edge which may have been sharpened by the events of October 1987. Partly to reduce the problems of the debt crisis, but also due to deregulation and securitization, the period since 1982 has seen a further dramatic transformation of the banking industry from its traditional intermediation role to that of a dealing orientation. Moreover, while the work started by looking at the strategies of the leading commercial banks it has finished by being forced to consider the positions of a wider group of players, including the leading investment banks and brokerage houses, which as a result of the changes described have also been forced to internationalize and diversify their product market-scope. I hope this book has captured in part these new transformations which have important implications potentially, not only for bankers, but also for public policy-makers and society at large.

In writing the book I have been helped immensely by bankers and financial institution executives in many countries. IRM sponsored research to be conducted by myself and my research assistants in the major countries of Western Europe including the UK, Germany, France, Holland, Belgium and Italy, in the Far East, notably Japan and Hong Kong, and in the USA and Canada. I should like to thank all those bankers from central banks and major commercial banks who gave so freely of their time and confidence in helping me and my assistants undertake the basic research for the book.

Unlike much of my previous work in the area of strategic management, I have tried to paint a macro picture of a dynamic industry rather than just focusing on the strategies of individual institutions. This latter type of approach is to be found more in the cases contained in *Bank Strategic Management and Marketing* which formed part of the essential background research for the present study. At the same time, however, a number of non-mutually exclusive generic strategies are identified and illustrated with examples in Chapter 9.

I should also like to thank my research assistants who provided so much of the work which I have used. These included Anant Vijay, who worked with me on the strategies of European banks, Makoto Showda who provided an understanding which I could not otherwise have obtained of Japanese financial institutions, and Sally Falshaw who worked on banks from all the major countries.

Finally, I must thank IRM, who sponsored the original project. I hope the result has been the development of a research base which could not have been anticipated at the start of the project and which has important consequences of particular signifiance for bankers, supervisors and politicians for the furture.

While all those listed above have given so freely of their time and assistance in the development of this work any errors and omissions remain the responsibility of the author and for these I sincerely apologize.

DEREK F. CHANNON
Boston, October 1987

CHAPTER 1

The Evolution of Multinational Banking

1.1 THE BIRTH OF INTERNATIONAL BANKING

Perhaps the earliest attempt to create a truly global bank was that of the Barclays Bank group in establishing Barclays Bank (Dominion, Colonial and Overseas) through the amalgamation of the Colonial Bank, the Anglo-Egyptian Bank and the National Bank of South Africa. Against the wishes of the Bank of England, which insisted that Barclays DCO, as the new bank became known, should not be an integral part of Barclays Bank itself, this first major international bank was created. Predominantly a retail banking business operating large branch networks in South Africa, Nigeria and other colonies of the British Empire, the new bank used its sterling area base as a foundation. The concept of the bank was to remit all surplus funds to London from where they could be redirected as required to other subsidiaries within the sterling area.

Unfortunately, Barclays DCO was ahead of its time in a number of respects. It was not created to service multinational corporate accounts; it was based on what proved to be the wrong currency and the free inter-country trade of the Empire was to prove illusory in the post-war period when decolonization became the norm and the Empire gave way to the much more decentralized British Commonwealth, many members of which opted to operate outside the sterling area.

1

The scope of the British Empire, coupled with the fact that London was a traditional key financial centre, led to the creation of other specialist London-based banks usually serving specific geographic areas and the colonies within them. Thus, Grindlay's Bank specialized in the Indian subcontinent, the Chartered Bank focused on the British colonies of the Pacific Basin and the Standard Bank of South Africa was concerned with providing banking services throughout Southern Africa, most of which was part of the British Empire. These banks provided local retail banking services to the colonists and also supported trade between the colonies and the United Kingdom. There were also a few banks which specialized in non-colonial territories, such as the Bank of London and South America (BOLSA), which specialized in providing trade and local banking services in the countries of Latin America. The French banks, to a lesser degree, provided similar services to the colonies of the French Empire, notably in North and West Africa.

These colonial banks were not strictly multinational banks but rather were institutions created to provide local banking services within specific territories or regions and to facilitate trade with the mother country. Further, they tended to provide retail, rather than mainly wholesale, banking services. With the exception of Barclays, they were also structurally unusual in that their head offices tended to remain in London or Paris while their centres of operations were based in the territories in which they specialized. The institutions were, however, in some cases large, powerful banks in their own right.

In addition to the development of the 'colonial' international banks a number of major banks did establish international branches. These were centred upon the major international financial centres, such as London and New York, and were primarily concerned with trade finance and raising international capital. The need to provide worldwide services for bank customers was thus limited since there were few multinational corporations attempting to manage their affairs on an integrated global basis. Each major financial centre was largely independent of others and activities were mainly concerned with the need of the local domestic market.

1.2   THE DEVELOPMENT OF MULTINATIONAL BANKS

The development of modern multinational banks with a global perspective, and primarily operating in countries where they possess no political affiliation, is a much more recent phenomenon, dating back to the late 1960s. During this period, many US industrial corporations had begun to diversify geographically. While many European companies had also expanded overseas, these moves, like those of the London-based banks, had largely been to the territories of earlier empires. The US companies, by contrast, expanded into the developed economies, especially of Western Europe. By this time improvements in systems and communications also allowed the new multinationals to operate with much more centralized structures than the European corporations which had earlier created subsidiaries in the colonies. These ran as far more autonomous units than the overseas subsidiaries of the new US multinationals.

As the US corporations spread abroad, they turned to their domestic banks to provide them with the specialist corporate services they needed. In Europe, where branch-based banking for both retail and corporate accounts was the norm, the banks were not specialized in corporate banking. By contrast, the large New York—and to a lesser extent, Mid-Western banks—constrained by US bank regulations, had in large part evolved as essentially corporate banks with few, if any, retail customers. Some such as Citibank, Chase Manhattan, Manufacturers Hanover and Chemical had small retail businesses within Manhattan, but others like J. P. Morgan, while clearly commercial rather than investment banks, had no retail operations and specialized in meeting the banking needs of large corporate clients.

The US banks based in the far west were much more akin to the Europeans. In the state of California, where statewide branching was legal, Bank of America, Security Pacific, Wells Fargo and the forerunner of First Interstate were all large, multibranch operations. As a consequence their emphasis tended to favour retail rather than corporate business and their organization structures centred on the branch and geography, rather than customer type, which was to emerge as the predominant organisational determinant on the East Coast.

As their corporate clients established themselves overseas, therefore, the large corporate banks, led in particular by Citicorp where the chairman, Walter Wriston, identified the opportunity, moved to escape the constraints of domestic US banking law and expanded overseas. In 1960, fewer than ten US banks had overseas branches, and total foreign assets amounted to less than $4 billion. By the end of 1977 over 100 US banks had established overseas branches and outstanding assets were $257 billion of which over $230 billion were claims against borrowers outside the USA[1]. The need to develop an overseas presence was accentuated by a series of regulatory constraints imposed within the USA. US controls on the flow of capital overseas, imposed from the early 1960s through the interest equalization tax, the Voluntary Foreign Credit Restraint Program and restrictions on direct foreign investment, virtually closed the New York market and made US-based international operations increasingly difficult. The Federal Reserve's Regulation Q, imposing a ceiling on the level of interest paid on bank deposits, also encouraged US multinationals to hold surplus funds earned overseas in London, where the Eurocurrency markets were developing, rather than repatriating them to New York. To gain access to these dollar funds and to maintain close relations with their US-based multinational clients, the main corporate banks in the US thus became increasingly multinational in their own operations. Commercial banks however, remained, lending- and transaction-based intermediaries as the Glass–Steagall Law prevented them from entering securities markets within the USA.

The major US money centre banks began to expand their overseas branch networks, opening new offices in existing and emerging financial centres and later in major trading cities around the world. Initially few of these offices were full branches and in many countries there were restrictions on granting full banking status. In such countries banks opened representative offices, or in some cases formed local subsidiaries, these units often being upgraded to full branches when local regulatory authorities permitted. Some countries, such as Australia, Canada

[1]S. Frowen, *A Framework of International Banking*, Guildford Educational Press, Guildford, 1979, p. 32.

Table 1.1   Financial centres with more than 50 international Banks 1987

Europe	North America
Belgium	USA
France	
West Germany	*Latin America*
Italy	Mexico
Luxembourg	Bahamas
Netherlands	
Switzerland	
United Kingdom	
Asia	
Hong Kong	
Japan	
Singapore	
Australia	

and Sweden, kept out the multinational banks until very recently, but gradually the world deregulated, leading to the spread of multinational banking. This is illustrated in Table 1.1 which shows the number of major countries in the world with more than 50 multinational banks present.

By the mid 1970s a number of major US banks had established significant international 'networks' of branches and offices. These units, however, tended to operate largely as autonomous offices with only limited integration. While the US multinational banks initially focused on servicing their existing and emerging US multinationals, local branches were soon to attack the indigenous markets in which they were located as well. Initially the banks sought to provide services to host country multinationals but, where possible, soon extended to cover all forms of domestic large and medium corporate accounts, and selected individuals. By the mid 1980s they had not only expanded their coverage to a global scale in many cases but, by the introduction of electronic banking, the networks had begun to be linked by global integrated communications systems. The early leaders in multinational banking had also been joined by many new competitors from the US regional banks, anxious to preserve their relations with their own customer base in the USA, more and more of whom required international services; by the leading investment banks who developed their international arms in response to the globalization of the main capital markets; and by a number of non-banks, such as brokerage houses, which offered a similar set of financial services to multinationals as did the various types of banks.

1.3   THE EMERGENCE OF THE GLOBAL CAPITAL MARKET

The development of US multinational banks similarly forced the large banks in other countries, noticeably Western Europe and Japan, to evolve in a similar manner, both to service indigenous multinationals and to penetrate apparently attractive overseas markets. By the late 1980s, therefore, there were several hundred major commercial, investment and trust banks with international presence. Only a few of these, however, could be really considered to be global in orientation, although there was a clear trend towards globalization from amongst the large US money centre commercial and investment banks and a few major European commercial banks plus, as the focus of financial power shifted to the East, the leading Japanese financial institutions. The primary thrust of multinational banking also remained focused on the market for corporate banking services, although by the mid 1980s there was also a trend in a few leading institutions to move towards the development of global strategies for retail banking.

Concurrent with the development of US international banking, the Eurodollar market was expanding and evolving rapidly. The international capital market had developed initially after the sterling crisis of 1957 had led to restrictions being imposed on the use of sterling bills for the use of international trade between non-UK residents. The London Bill, a traditional vehicle behind much of the world trade, thus abruptly ceased to play a major trading role. The London merchant banks, determined to remain a force in international trade, were therefore forced to seek an alternative vehicle to sustain their position. At the same time the deterioration in East–West relations meant that the Eastern Bloc countries were anxious not to place on deposit in the USA any dollar revenues earned from international trade. They were, therefore, prepared to accept lower interest rates on deposits placed in the relatively more politically secure banks of Western Europe. Other US overseas creditors too, anxious to avoid the interest rate ceiling effect of Regulation Q, were prepared to leave dollar credits outside the United States. The Eurodollar market was thus created by a meeting between a financing need on the part of the British merchant banks and a source of dollar deposits based outside the USA.

In its early years the new Eurodollar market was principally a wholesale market, dominated by the London merchant banks and providing them with the facility to offset each other's fund surpluses and deficits. The market was small and operated as a limited adjunct to the London discount market. However, a sustained period of trade deficits by the US economy led to the market expanding rapidly. In addition, the Federal authorities imposed restrictions on the export of investment dollars to curb the rapid growth in US outward investment. As a result, US companies were forced to seek overseas sources of finance and they turned to the emerging Eurodollar market in London[2].

The ceiling on deposit interest rates imposed in the USA by Regulation Q also encouraged US corporations with surplus dollars earned overseas to locate their funds abroad where no interest rate ceiling applied. This added to the funds available in the Euromarkets and ironically, to some extent, encouraged US domestic banks to enter the market for deposits to support domestic lending within the USA. By the end of the 1960s the early domination of the British merchant banks which had pioneered the market had been superseded by the arrival of the major US banks in London to tap into the Euromarket for their own purposes.

As the banks began to expand their international branch coverage, new centres for offshore currency markets began to emerge in a variety of locations as financial authorities provided attractive environments for relatively unrestricted operations. London

[2]D. F. Channon, *British Banking Strategy and the International Challenge* Macmillan, London, 1977, p. 108.

continued to remain the leading international banking centre. However, unlike most national markets, the Euromarkets were not subject to exchange controls and other forms of restrictions, such as bank reserve requirements, restrictions on interest-rate movements and controls over money supply and credit. This lack of official restriction encouraged the rapid expansion of the market, first in London, and subsequently in other centres around the world, notably Hong Kong, Singapore and New York. For depositors, anonymity proved a major attraction despite the fact that there was no depositor protection in the form of a lender of last resort. As the recently retired chairman of Citibank, Walter Wriston, commented at the International Monetary Conference in London in 1979, the Euromarkets had emerged because of 'national attempts to allocate credit and capital'. However, Mr Wriston went on to argue that 'National borders are no longer definable against the invasion of knowledge, ideas or financial data'[3].

By 1980, the Eurocurrency market had grown to $941 billion and it was already the main international capital market. During the 1980s the market had undergone a further revolution as a consequence of deregulation, leading to a growing integration of the international market and the leading national capital markets, deregulation and the increased securitization of all forms of assets. A more detailed discussion on the development of this global integration is given in Chapter 2 which explores the linkage between the capital markets and the development of multinational banking.

1.4   THE GROWTH OF THE FOREIGN EXCHANGE MARKET

During the early 1970s exchange rates also became less stable. As a result, companies involved in international trade began to require new services in foreign exchange management and in information for dealing with currency fluctuation and political risk. The companies turned to the emerging multinational banks

---

[3]L. Sandler, The final days of offshore banking, *Institutional Investor*, June 1984, 62.

to provide these services. As a result, the foreign exchange markets expanded rapidly, although as shown in Chapter 3 these markets increasingly became remote from the market for trade finance funds. As more and more multinational corporate treasuries came to realize that getting their companies' funds in the right currency, in the right country at the right time, the central treasury became a potential profit centre. Moreover, the leading multinational banks increasingly traded on their own book in the forex markets. In addition, investment capital flows added to the volume as deregulation and the removal of exchange controls led fund managers to diversify their portfolios around the world. The combined effect of corporate treasuries and banks, coupled with the increase in international portfolio investment had led to massive growth in the size of the foreign exchange markets. This had also added greatly to currency instability and made the management of fixed currency exchange rates a virtual impossibility for individual governments. Moreover, it had also made exchange control an increasingly difficult policy to implement. Ironically, however, from 1985, attempts had been made by the leading industrial nations to move back towards an era of controlled exchange rates. While initially this policy had appeared to meet with some success, political disagreements between the USA and the leading trade surplus nations of Japan and West Germany, were to lead to devastating consequences in the crash of 1987.

1.5   THE IMPACT OF THE OIL CRISIS

By the early 1970s therefore three critical interrelated factors were emerging. Multinational banks were learning to operate on a global basis, an unregulated international capital market was developing and the flow of funds across national borders was sufficiently great to destabilize fixed exchange rates. Then in 1973 came the first oil shock.

The development of multinational banking was given a sharp boost by the first oil shock. The intermediary role of the private multinational banks was rapidly expanded by the main oil-producing countries placing their surplus funds with them.

Similarly, the surpluses created in the main OPEC countries led to corresponding deficits in the main industrialized countries, and especially in the lesser developed economies dependent for their energy needs on imported oil. These countries, to finance the extra costs of imported oil, turned increasingly to the commercial banks for funds to cover their balance of payments deficits. The first oil shock thus led to a rapid expansion of the international capital market and in particular, the role played by the banks in recycling the funds accrued by the oil producers. In addition it also led to growing instability in the global foreign exchange market.

Further, while the early focus of international banking had been to supply the funding needs of the major multinationals, the financing of balance of payments deficits by the commercial banks transformed their own asset structures. The private corporation customer increasingly gave way to demands from governments or state-owned enterprises for funds to cover budget deficits or to develop large infrastructure or natural resource developments. As shown in Chapter 5, the resulting increase in sovereign risk lending created the 'Debt Bomb' which threatened the downfall of the international banking system in the early 1980s and subsequently led to factors underlying the crash of 1987 which threatened the return of the world economy to a new great recession like that of 1929.

1.6   THE IMPACT OF TECHNOLOGY

Technology has been instrumental in the development of global banking. The two major technological factors have been first, the development of an efficient and speedy world communications network and second, the evolution of computer technology. Developments in communications and computer systems have made it possible to operate a centralized banking operation with linked computers. This has led to a rapid acceleration in information and money transfers, allowing banks and corporations dramatically to improve their cash management capability onto a real-time basis. The development of global dealing or transaction centres in different time zones has also caused national or regional banking systems to be increasingly integrated into one global financial system.

Technology had also been a major force behind the trend to deregulation. Alternative delivery systems, the unbundling of some services, the rebundling of others, the development of new service innovations and the like would not have occurred but for the dramatic improvements in information technology. These new ways of doing traditional business created pressure for deregulating the traditional barriers that existed between different classes of financial institution. As a result, whereas it was possible to consider the different players such as commercial banks, investment banks, brokerage houses, retailers and the like as operating in different market sectors as recently as five years ago, these differences are increasingly seeming artificial. By the mid 1990s the major institutions from all sectors and from the leading nations can be expected to be in head-to-head competition with one another in an environment where technological skill will be of paramount importance in gaining competitive advantage.

Technology has also changed the fundamental cost structure of the banking industry. Substantial economies of scale available to high-technology banks have resulted in an increased consciousness of the value of high market share and led to a growing concentration of power in larger institutions. This trend has also encouraged the mergers and acquisition of smaller institutions, and the formation of strategic alliances between institutions in an effort to match the scale economies available to the larger competitors.

The technology-driven integration of world financial markets linking equities, securitized debts, foreign exchange and new instruments such as futures and options has also compounded the volatility risk of violent movements between both product and geographic markets. Such volatility has been exacerbated by the development of computer-based trading techniques which were instrumental in triggering the dramatic Wall Street crash of 1987.

1.7   THE EVOLUTION OF US MULTINATIONAL BANKING

While the major US money centre banks initially moved abroad to service their major corporate clients and to tap into the emerging Euromarkets, they were soon to offer their own brand of commercial banking to the indigenous corporations of the main developed economies. Faced with competitors which were traditionally branch-based, full service banks, lending primarily on overdraft, and unable to provide specialized corporate banking services, the US banks found it relatively easy to penetrate large corporate accounts in Western Europe. Only in West Germany, where the relationship between banks and corporate customers was much more close, did the US banks find market penetration difficult. By contrast in the United Kingdom, Scandinavia, the Benelux and France, the major US multinational banks found it relatively easy to penetrate the large corporate market by their more aggressive marketing approach and the offer of international banking services and medium-term finance rather than overdraft facilities.

A critical difference between the US bankers and those of Western Europe was in their manner of servicing the corporate account. Concentrating initially on providing an integrated service to European indigenous multinationals which matched that provided to their major domestic accounts, the US commercial banks used a structure composed of specialist account executives, devoted exclusively to corporate banking. While not investment bankers, these account executives were trained to make commercial loans, especially over a period of time, and to evaluate the creditworthiness of corporate customers on an ongoing cash flow basis. Moreover, since they were specialized in corporate customer service, the US banks were better suited than their European competitors in understanding the banking needs of industrial customers. They were also able to focus on a relatively small group of customers or prospects, by contrast to the branch manager of a European bank who was expected to offer the full range of the bank's corporate and consumer services to all categories of customer both personal and corporate, within the geographic coverage of his individual branch, as well as to administer his branch.

Most importantly, the American banks brought to Europe a proactive stance to selling banking services. Traditionally in Europe, bankers had been trained not to be proactive in selling. Rather, customers were expected to approach the bank to obtain financial services and especially loans. At that time, credit assessment tended to be undertaken on a 'gone' basis, namely the bank assessed its risk in terms of what would happen if a client were forced to go into liquidation. The US banks' competitive evaluation on an ongoing business basis based on cash flow, or the projected capability of a client to repay capital and interest, was revolutionary in Europe.

Further, the concept of direct selling of loans was similarly alien to the nature of traditional European banking practice. For many years therefore, major British and European banks were not even prepared to use the terms of 'selling' and 'marketing' in training executives from these banks to compete against the US banks. Instead the phrase 'business development' was coined as a respectable terminology for use in attempting to convert traditional branch bankers into effective competitors with the US commercial banks. Even with training, however, European branch bank systems were not well equipped to provide dedicated corporate banking services. Individual bankers remained extremely reluctant to cold canvass call on corporate clients and the banks did not have specialist corporate banking services fully developed. The banks were also organized primarily by geography rather than by customer and had no knowledge of profitability by service or by customer, but only by branch.

This compared with the tactics of the leading US multinational bank. In 1974, Citicorp had established its World Corporation Group (WCG) to provide a specialist service to worldwide multinationals. Under this system a global account manager (GAM) was appointed to act as the coordinator for all the bank's services at the central office of a worldwide account. Initially, some 460 such accounts were identified worldwide, only about half of which were based in the USA. With an account load, including prospects, of only some ten accounts, a GAM was responsible for ensuring that the array of commercial bank services provided to each institutional customer around the world was profitable. In addition, the GAM was expected to develop, in conjunction with other local account officers servicing the account at other Citibank locations around the world, an annual profit plan for the customer. This would detail the expected demand for loan, deposit and fee-based services to be taken from Citibank in each location in which the relationship would operate. The end result would be an annual customer profitability plan for the customer, subdivided by geography to show where the profits would be earned. In this way, it was possible for the GAM to gain approval for trade-offs. For example, a loss might be acceptable in Country A, if it contributed to extra profits in Country B and an overall improvement in global account profitability. A major multinational with this system might thus be serviced by up to 30 local account officers around the world, each working for the World Corporation Group in Citibank and reporting, not only to their own country managers, but also to the GAM responsible for the account worldwide. These multinational accounts were thus provided with a range of specialized services such as multicurrency lines of credit and loans, foreign exchange and deposit facilities, all across national or even regional boundaries as well as 'integrated global financial advice'[4].

Vital to the operation of this type of organization was the need to develop a system of profitability measurement by customer and by service. In Citicorp, and later in other major US multinational banks, such a system was developed by the mid 1970s. While not perfect at this time, such a system enabled the banks that had such management information systems to develop product and customer strategies which unbundled individual services for customers and allowed trade-offs to be made against a background which formally understood the implications for overall account profitability. By contrast, even by the mid 1980s, this understanding of account or service profitability was extremely badly developed in the main European banks. As one general manager for a major British clearing bank put it recently when describing correspondent banking services: 'I believe I am losing money on half the services I am offering—the only trouble is I don't know which half'[5].

The fundamental approach to corporate customers of the US multinational banks, especially those from New York, was reflected in their organization structures. By the mid 1970s

[4]John P. Rudy, Global planning in multinational banking, *Columbia Journal of World Business*, Winter 1975, 821.
[5]Private research, 1985.

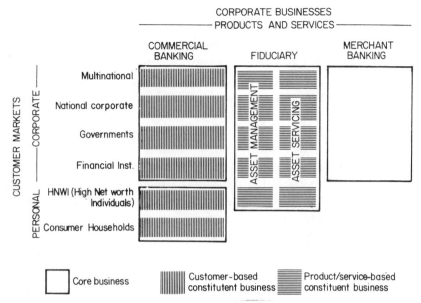

Figure 1.1   Citibank corporate structure mid 1970s
Source: John P. Rudy, Global planning in multinational banking, *Columbia Journal of World Business*, Winter 1975. Copyright © 1975. Reprinted by permission of the Trustees of Columbia University in the City of New York

Citicorp was therefore organized in a quite different way from a traditional European-based bank. The primary division in Citicorp was by customer as shown in Figure 1.1. 'Corporate' accounts were divided into four key clusters: namely 'multinationals', where a specialist organizational unit serviced key corporate accounts on a global basis; 'national corporate' which serviced other corporate accounts on a local national basis; 'governments', which serviced states and state-owned enterprises; and financial institutions which serviced relationships with correspondent banks and other financial institutions. At this time consumer banking and investment banking were much less important in Citicorp although, as described later, these activities were to become significant areas for future growth, with the latter area in particular leading to a further major amendment to organization structure.

Each of the main conceptual blocs had 'strategic weight, a goodly measure of strategic independence and future promise, yet was based on line experience. Each was distinct from the organisational structure, though it was natural to expect that none should stray too far from the organisation's image'[6]. Each of the main generic business categories identified in Citicorp's scheme, therefore, had a worldwide application that could be developed into strategic concentration on particular customer segments and products as well as specific geographical areas. The multinational customer group could be serviced on a global basis which other groups would tend to handle by attacks on chosen geographic targets. Ironically, in its reorganization of institutional banking in 1980, Citicorp abandoned the successful WCG structure, only to have largely to replace it in 1984 as relationship positions with leading multinationals began to decline.

While the Citicorp system of the 1970s was the leading edge of the US multinational bank attack on international markets, other major US banks attempted somewhat similar tactics. Focusing on the market for international and multinational corporate banking services, the major US commercial banks during the 1970s rapidly expanded their network of overseas branches.

Initially the banks opened offices in the leading financial centres of Western Europe, London, Frankfurt and Paris. A branch or representative office was also usually established in the other major economies of Western Europe and some presence, often by acquisition or by subsidiary formation, was established in Switzerland. Specialist shipping branches were often added in Greece. Outside Europe, strong networks were built in the developing financial centres of the Pacific Basin, including Singapore, Hong Kong and Tokyo with Malaysia, Indonesia, Korea, and the Philippines following later. In the late 1970s and early 1980s mainland China and Australia became the focus of attention. Bahrain also succeeded Beirut as a possible centre to service the Gulf states. The multinational banks also built strong networks in the main countries of Latin America, with a strong presence particularly in Brazil, Mexico, Venezuela and Argentina. The regulatory constraints imposed by the US authorities also spawned the development of offshore booking centres in a number of low-tax, favourable environments in the

[6]Rudy, op. cit., p. 20.

Caribbean including Panama, the Cayman Islands and the Bahamas. These centres emerged as important booking centres for Euromarket transactions arranged in New York until deregulation took place there. These locations were also important centres for flight capital from unstable political environments in Latin America which formed a substantial component of the sovereign risk lending made to these countries and for 'money laundries' for money generated from the lucrative, but illegal, drugs trade between the USA and Central America. Notably absent from the development of global branch networks were the continent of Africa and the Eastern Bloc countries, although a number of the banks had opened representative offices in Moscow and had trade centres in Vienna.

Having established their primary country networks by the mid 1970s, the leading multinational banks extended their coverage to lesser countries during the late 1970s and early 1980s as shown in Figure 1.2. At the same time there was a trend, lasting until the early 1980s, to increase branching to include other large cities in the major developed countries such as the UK, West Germany and Japan. Many of these branches were subsequently closed, however, following failures to achieve adequate account penetration and successful counter-attacks by indigenous banks as these learned how to compete with similar account officer systems to those used by the Americans. There was also a growing awareness of the cost of excessive branch operations in the light of increased competition by other US and foreign banks in most markets.

Nevertheless, the New York banks, in particular, came to rely increasingly on earnings from abroad. The percentage of earnings of the major US commercial banks derived from overseas operations expanded rapidly during the 1970s. This trend was especially true for the New York banks, where overseas earnings by the late 1970s represented well over half the total. This was also the case for other major US domestic banks keen to penetrate corporate markets. However, the Mid-Western banks, inhibited by the especially restrictive Illinois banking laws, were less able to cope with the move to multinational operations and overseas earnings remained a relatively small element of their total profits. The West Coast money centre banks, although less

Figure 1.2 Global office networks of leading U.S. money centre banks 1987 (excluding subsidiaries).

	EUROPE									FAR EAST & AUSTRALIA								LATIN AMERICA & CARIBBEAN							NORTH AMERICA		REST OF WORLD			
	UK	France	W. Germany	Switzerland	Netherlands	Belgium	Italy	Spain	Other	Japan	Hong Kong	Singapore	Australia	Phillipines	Thailand	Korea	Other	Brazil	Mexico	Argentina	Venezuela	Panama	Bahamas	Other	USA	Canada	UAE	Bahrain	USSR	Other
Bank America	4B	B	4B	B.R	B	B	R	R	6B	4B	2B +R	B	R	B	B	2B	11B, R	2B	R	7B	R	B	–	10B, R	H	R	R	–	R	2B
Chase Manhattan	2B	B	B	R	R	–	B	B	4B, 3R	B	B	B	R	B	B	B	5B, 2R	R	R	R	R	B	B	12B, 3R	H	–	5B	B	–	28B, 5R
Citicorp	6B	B	B	4B	2B	2B	3B	2B	5B, 4R	4B	9B	2B	6R	2B	R	2B	13B, 2R	12B	B	5B	3B	4B	B	31B 2R	H	–	2B	–	–	B, 2R
First Chicago	2B	B	3B	B.R	–	–	2B	B	2B, 3R	B	B	B	R	B	–	B	2R	R	R	R	R	B	–	B	H	2R	R	–	–	–
First Interstate	B	–	R	–	–	–	R	R	B	B	B	R	B	R	R	B	B, 2R	R	R	–	R	–	B	B.R	H	–	–	B. R	–	B, 4R
Manufacturers Hanover	3B, 2R	R	6B, R	B	–	–	2B	2B, R	5B, 2R	2B	B	B	R	B	R	B	B, 4R	2R	R	B.R	R	–	–	3R, B	H	–	–	R	–	4R, B
J. P. Morgan	2B	B	2B	B	–	2B	2B	B	–	B	B	B	R	–	–	B	B, 2R	R	R	B	R	B	B	–	H	–	–	B	–	5R
Bankers Trust	2B	B	R	R	–	–	B	B	–	B	B	B	–	B	R	B	B, 3R	2R	R	B	R	B	B	2R	H	–	–	B	–	4R

Key: B = Branch; R = Representation Office; H = Home country

Source: Annual Reports

dependent upon multinational operations, were more successful in building their overseas interests.

While the concept of a 'Global Network' became important, the banks which successfully exploited it were few and were those which developed services which could make use of the network and which were managed in a coordinated manner. Failure to organize for the delivery of global services was to lead later to questioning of the establishment of some branches and to network rationalization by the late 1980s.

An increasing number of US regional banks joined the early multinationals during the late 1970s and these, coupled with the emergence of European and Japanese multinational competitors, led to intense competition for a relatively narrow international customer base which was growing in sophistication, and needing fewer and fewer traditional corporate banking services. As a result by the late 1980s the first signs of a major shakeout were clearly present in the banking industry. Nevertheless, by the early 1980s most major money centre banks had endeavoured to build global branch networks. Focusing initially on the major capitals of Western Europe and the leading multinational centres, few were prepared to recognize the cost of such systems and that the changing pattern of multinational bank usage would permit only a small number of institutions to be really profitable in providing services to large multinational clients, irrespective of their country of origin.

During the 1980s increasing rationalization of global networks by many US multinational banks occurred. Further, with domestic deregulation, excessive competition and serious problems brought on by sovereign risk lending, many banks turned their attention back to expansion within the US market. Nevertheless the rapid development of the US banks during the 1970s, coupled with the development of technology, especially for global funds transfer and later for all forms of global trading, meant that by the late 1980s global, as distinct from international, or even multinational banking services had clearly developed. Moreover, these services were different from traditional lending- or transaction-based services and embraced new markets such as swaps, options and futures as well as some integration of the debt and equity markets. Multinational banking had arrived, led by the US banks, and with it a global capital market, a global foreign exchange market and a growing integration of the main national economies of the world.

1.8   THE EUROPEAN RESPONSE

As the American banks began successfully to rampage through most of their corporate markets, the European banks developed their strategic response. The main banks in West Europe had been slow to develop their multinational networks except where they had colonial connections as with the British, French and Dutch banks.

In the early 1970s, in France three of the four largest banks, Crédit Lyonnaise, Société Générale and Banque National de Paris (BNP) were all publicly owned. The fourth—and the largest—bank, Crédit Agricole, was mutually owned and was at this time primarily a bank dedicated to the agricultural market, taking in deposits from farmers and others in rural areas and lending mainly for agricultural needs.

Each of the main French commercial banks, despite their ownership, operated independently. Moreover, the government ownership and attitude had inhibited the development of international banking in France. Further, changes in French law in 1966 brought about the removal of traditional demarcation lines between investment and commercial banking, thus allowing the state-owned banks to develop as full service banks, adding merchant banking and related banking services as well as commercial banking. Initially, the international strategy of the main French banks had been to develop consortium relationships, rather than follow the Americans and develop global branch networks. Thus Crédit Lyonnais initially chose to operate through Europartners, BNP with Société Financière Européene and Société Générale in the European Bank International Consortium (EBIC). Crédit Agricole did not begin to develop its international presence until the late 1970s. Although these banks initially tended to join consortia, French banks later aggressively began to expand their own global networks. By the mid 1980s the three leading banks were well established around the world. The

French banks had also modified their organization structures away from the system of all customer-class branches towards the adoption of specialist corporate divisions dedicated to service the needs of large corporate customers.

There were a number of reasons why consortium banks initially proved a popular strategic option for the French and other major European banks[7]. Firstly, banks became members of consoritia in order to complement their own activities. Secondly, consortium banks could provide some services, especially for multinational corporations, that individual domestic banks could not. For example, membership of a consortium gave banks a closer relationship than that of a correspondent bank in countries where the individual bank might not have network cover. This was clearly the case for French, German and some British banks in the early 1970s before they had established their own overseas networks. Thirdly, the consortium route offered smaller banks the opportunity to enter into the international markets where on their own they would not have the financial or managerial resources to be effective competitors. Fourthly, consortium bank participation allowed banks to generate specific new skills, such as specialization in particular geographic or product market areas such as energy. Fifthly, by pooling the participants' knowledge of particular markets, the consortium was able to provide detailed information that would not normally be available to individual banks. Finally, it was suggested that the consortium banks, being more like merchant banks in their operation, could act in a more entreprenurial manner than their traditionalist, commercial bank parents.

As a defensive measure against the invasion of the major US banks, many of the leading European banks initially formed themselves into consortia. These European banking clubs, ABE-COR, EBIC, Inter Alpha and Europartners, whose memberships are shown in Table 1.2. evolved various forms of cooperation and joint ventures in locations where the partners were not individually represented, such as New York and Hong Kong.

These early banking clubs, as with most consortium banks,

---

[7]A. A. Weissmuller, London consortium banks, *Journal of the Institute of Bankers*, August 1974, 207.

Table 1.2   Leading European consortium bank participations 1975

Bank	Estab-lished	Participants	Holding	Home country
European Banks International Co. (EBIC)	1973	Amsterdam-Rotterdam Bank	14.3	Netherlands
		Banca Commerciale Italiana	14.3	Italy
		Creditanstalt Bankverein	14.3	Austria
		Deutsche Bank	14.3	W. Germany
		Midland Bank	14.3	UK
		Société Générale de Banque	14.3	Belgium
		Société Générale	14.3	France
Orion Bank	1970	National Westminster	20	UK
		Chase Manhattan Corp.	20	USA
		Royal Bank of Canada	20	Canada
		Westdeutsche Landesbank	20	W. Germany
		Credito Italiano	10	Italy
		Mitsubishi Bank	10	Japan
Banque de la Société Financière Europèene	1974	Algemene Bank	12.5	Netherlands
		Banca Nazionale del Lavorno	12.5	Italy
		Bank of America	12.5	USA
		Banque Nationale de Paris	12.5	France
		Banque de Bruxelles	12.5	Belgium
		Barclays Bank International	12.5	UK
		Dresdner Bank	12.5	W. Germany
		Sumitomo Bank	12.5	Japan
Midland and International Banks	1964	Midland Bank	45	UK
		Toronto Dominion Bank	26	Canada
		Standard Chartered Bank	19	UK
		Commercial Bank of Australia	10	Australia

Source: D. F. Channon, *British Banking Strategy and the International Challenge*, Macmillan, London, 1977, pp. 170–6

however, proved to be a transitory and unstable stage in the development of multinational banking. A number of reasons were apparent for the failure of the consortium bank strategy. Firstly, the rapid growth of the global banking market led many of the participants to rethink their initial defensive posture and to pursue their own policies of international network development. This often brought the partners into competition with their consortium investments. Secondly, many consortia were established without clear objectives and no in-built mechanisms to resolve potential conflicts between the partners. Thirdly, the consortium banks suffered from serious managerial problems. The top management positions in these banks tended to rotate between nominees of the partners and much of the management was seconded from the parent banks. Conflicts of interest between the needs of the consortium bank and that of parent institutions could thus cause divided loyalties amongst management[8].

As a result, most of the consortium banks formed during the early and mid 1970s had tended to disappear. In most cases they had been bought out by one of the major partners and had become wholly owned subsidiaries. Consortium banks still existed but their role had been much diminished. They did, however, form an important intermediate step in the development of many multinational banks, especially those from Europe and Canada. They were also important in helping some of the major Japanese banks to internationalize.

Lacking a colonial background as the result of the First World War, major German industrial companies were slow to develop international operations. As a result the leading German banks had no significant reason to develop an overseas network. By the early 1970s they had not established overseas branches. The largest bank, the Deutsche Bank, did not operate any overseas branches, preferring to make use of subsidiaries, associates and consortium operations. In 1973, however, the two other leading commercial banks, Dresdner Bank and Commerz Bank, had actively begun to develop their international networks. The failure of a consortium-bank-based strategy subsequently led the Deutsche Bank to break its links with EBIC and to open its own branches in the leading financial centres in the world. The Deutsche Bank, using the close relationships it enjoyed with leading German companies based on its own equity investments and those held on behalf of other investors, was then quick to develop its overseas business. The bank was successful in capturing much of the overseas business of emerging German multinationals. The Deutsche Bank and other leading German banks also used their large placing power in the Eurobond market to build strong positions in lead management and participation for bond issues in the emerging international capital market. By the late 1980s the major German commercial banks had become international rather than global in their operations. They were not, however, strong multinational players and in large part were

---

[8]D. F. Channon, *op. cit.* pp. 181–3.

Figure 1.3 Global office networks of lending European Banks 1987 (excludes subsidiaries).

	EUROPE									FAR EAST & AUSTRALIA								LATIN AMERICA & CARIBBEAN							NORTH AMERICA		REST OF WORLD			
	UK	France	W. Germany	Switzerland	Netherlands	Belgium	Italy	Spain	Other	Japan	Hong Kong	Singapore	Australia	Phillippines	Thailand	Korea	Other	Brazil	Mexico	Argentina	Venezuela	Panama	Bahamas	Other	USA	Canada	UAE	Bahrain	USSR	Other
ABN	B	5B,R	5B	3B	H	3B	3B	2B	8B	3B,R	2B,R	B,R	B,R	–	–	B	8B	B,R	–	R	–	B	–	13B	9B,R	3B	3B	R	–	45B
AMRO	B,R	B	–	–	H	B	–	–	–	B,R	B	B	R	–	–	–	2B,3R	–	–	–	–	–	–	–	B,3R	–	B	–	R	R
BNP	B	H	5B	R	B	4B	B,2R	2B	3B,7R	2B	B,R	B	6B	B	R	B	3B,6R	2R	R	B	R	B	–	B,R	5B,R	–	R	–	R	5B,5R
Barclays	H	O	O	O	O	O	O	O	8O	O	O	O	O	O	O	O	6O	O	O	O	O	–	O	10O	O	O	O	O	O	21O
Commerz Bank	B	B	H	O	–	2B	–	2B	R	2B,R	B	–	R	–	R	–	R	2R	R	R	R	–	–	–	4B	R	–	R	R	3R
Credit Lyonnais	2B	H	3B	2B	–	6B,R	2B,R	6B	2B,3R	2B,R	B,R	B	R	B	R	B	B,6R	2R	–	R	R	–	–	B,R	6B,4R	R	R	–	R	3B,7R
Credito Italiano	B	R	R	R	R	–	H	–	–	B	R	–	–	–	–	–	B	R	R	B	R	–	–	–	B,2R	–	–	–	R	R
Deutsche Bank	B	B	H	–	–	B	B	B	R	B,R	B	B	R	–	–	–	R	B,R	R	B	R	–	–	B,3R	B,R	R	R	R	R	2R
Lloyds Bank*	H	5B	6B	B	B	B	B	23B	15B	B	B	B	–	–	–	B	B,4R	21B	R	B	R	4B	–	76B,R	7B,R	O	B	B	R	–
Midland Bank	H	B	–	B	R	–	B,R	B	2B	B	B	B	R	B,R	R	B	4R	R	R	B	R	–	–	2R	B	–	–	–	R	–
NatWest Bank	H	O	O	O	O	O	O	O	2O	O	O	O	O	–	–	O	O	R	O	B	–	–	O	–	O	O	–	O	O	–
Société Generale	5B,R	H	B	–	2B,R	–	2B	–	2B,7R	2B,R	B,R	B	–	B	R	B	3B,6R	2R	R	B	R	–	–	R	3B,3R	–	R	B,R	R	B,4R
Swiss Bank Corp	B,2R	R	–	H	–	–	–	R	–	B,2R	B,R	B,R	2R	–	R	–	–	–	R	R	R	R	–	B,2R	4B,2R	–	–	B,R	R	4R
Union Bank Switzerland	B	–	–	H	–	–	–	R	R	B	–	B	R	–	–	–	–	2R	R	R	–	–	–	B	3B,2R	3R	R	R	R	5R

Key: 0 = Office (undesignated); B = Branch; R = Representative; H = Home Country; * = includes some country specific subsidiaries & BOLSA
Source: Annual Reports

heavily biased towards German-orientated business. By contrast to the British, French, and to a lesser extent the Dutch banks, the leading German commercial banks still had only weak international networks, as shown in Figure 1.3.

The major British commercial banks had all pursued an active international development strategy. Barclays, building upon its original overseas bank, Barclays DCO, was early to open branches in the world's leading financial centres. In 1961 an office was started in Zurich, in 1965 a new subsidiary was opened in California and representative offices were opened in each of the major financial centres. In 1971, following the purchase of all outstanding shares in Barclays DCO, the group reorganized and renamed the former colonial bank Barclays Bank International. This new subsidiary became the bank's international division and rapidly expanded its global coverage, concentrating largely on the corporate banking market. Unlike other British banks, Barclays did not participate strongly in consortium operations but rather relied on the independent development of its international network. In 1984, the bank also moved to integrate its worldwide banking operations fully by dissolving the differences between the parent domestic-orientated bank and Barclays Bank International, to form a unified global bank. Subsequently, with the deregulation of the London market in 1986, Barclays had also invested heavily to build up the strongest British commercial bank presence in investment banking with the creation of Barclays de Zoete Wedd (BZW).

By contrast, the Midland Bank had traditionally adopted a policy of not establishing a direct presence in countries where it maintained a close correspondent bank relationship, acting for such correspondents in the London market. In the early 1960s, however, it became apparent that this policy was likely to fail as major international banks began to establish their own presence in London. As a result, Midland strongly adopted a consortium bank strategy. It led the way in helping to establish the first true consortium bank, Midland and International Banks Ltd, in conjunction with the Commercial Bank of Australia, the Standard Bank (later part of Standard Chartered Bank Group) and the Toronto Dominion Bank. Similarly, Midland linked with the Amro Bank, Banque de la Société Générale de Belgique and the

Deutsche Bank to form the European Advisory Committee as the forerunner to creating specialist corporate banks to cover the United States, Latin America, Asia and the Pacific Basin. The consortium policy began to change in the early 1970s, however, and belatedly, Midland began to establish its own international network. In 1974, the bank reorganized to create an autonomous international division and a rapid programme of overseas branch openings followed.

The other two major British commercial banks, Lloyds and National Westminster, adopted strategies intermediate to those of Barclays and Midland. Lloyds bought out the National Provincial Bank's shareholding in their joint venture international bank, which initially gave them a limited overseas presence, mainly in Western Europe. This bank, renamed Lloyds Bank (Foreign), became the main international subsidiary. In 1971, Lloyds made its main international move with the purchase of the British Bank of London and South America (BOLSA), the British overseas bank with established branch networks in a number of countries in Latin America. In 1974, all Lloyds international interests were merged and renamed as Lloyds Bank International and this was followed by a programme of rapid global network expansion. Lloyds, like the Midland, was not, however, really seen as a global strategy player but rather as a regional specialist operator. Unfortunately the bank's specialization in Latin America was subsequently to cost it dear as a result of the developing country debt crisis.

The National Westminster Bank, lacking any historic international presence following the sale of the National Provincial's overseas interests and the very limited international activities of the Westminster Bank, had to start from the beginning. While participating to a limited extent in a number of specialist consortium banks, National Westminster's main thrust came from an aggressive campaign of establishing new branches and representative offices in all the main financial centres and in other, mainly industrialized countries, which offered potential banking opportunities. In particular, the NatWest had focused on the US market but concentrating on the New York market and adjacent states rather than following the herd and attacking the Californian market. However this early conservatism was later to prove a benefit as NatWest escaped the lightest from the problems of sovereign risk debt and by the late 1980s had emerged to overtake Barclays as the largest and most profitable British bank group.

By the mid 1980s all the main European banks had developed their international banking activities and profits from overseas operations had become a substantial component of group totals. By contrast with domestic banking, however, in most cases overseas activities were substantially less profitable and in many countries, notably Japan, and to a lesser extent the USA, it had proved extremely difficult for the European banks to achieve an adequate return on investment.

The most significant investments made by the non-US banks had been into the United States. Many had purchased local US banks, notably in California where the possibility of statewide branching seemed especially appealing to the branch-banking-orientated Europeans. Unfortunately this appeal was to prove illusory and in one case disastrous. All the major British banks purchased US bank subsidiaries, four of them in California. With the exception of the Standard Chartered Bank, which purchased a clearly positioned middle market specialist institution, Union Bank, most of the other investments proved disappointing[9], or in the case of the Midland Bank disastrous. Midland purchased a majority stake in Crocker Bank, the fifth largest bank in the state, yet initially made no attempt to intervene in the management of its newly acquired investment. In the event, Crocker proved to have serious problems due to loans to Latin America and the California agricultural market. These led to the reporting of substantial losses. Only when the scale of these losses became apparent did the Midland act to take over the management of its US subsidiary. In February 1986, despite a series of capital injections, the bank was forced to sell Crocker to its Californian rival, Wells Fargo, although Midland retained the former subsidiary's non-performing Latin American debt portfolio. To provide the necessary provisions against these loans Midland was later forced to sell off more of its assets, as well as to seek new

---

[9]Foreign banks in America—presence before profit, *Euromoney*, August 1984, pp. 80–1.

capital, thus effectively eliminating the bank as a global player. Lloyds Bank, too, sold off its poorly performing Californian subsidiary to Sumitomo Bank. While other banks had not experienced such difficulties few had achieved a satisfactory performance from their entrance into the US market.

1.9   THE ERA OF THE RISING SUN

In line with the rapid expansion of the national economy and the relatively recent strong trend for major industrial corporations to develop international investments, in the 1980s the main Japanese banks had begun to emerge as formidable international competitors. In the international capital markets, the Japanese banks overtook the American banks as the largest international banking presence. In 1986, Japanese banks accounted for over half the total rise in the Bank for International Settlements area banks' lending. At the same time American banks international balance sheets actually fell. Throughout 1986 the Japanese banks competed aggressively amongst themselves for asset growth and much of this activity took place via their London-based branches. During 1986 Japanese bank cross-border lending from London grew by 40 per cent, compared with 10 per cent for British banks and a decline of 10 per cent by American. As a result, by the end of 1986 Japanese banks had established a clear lead in the international banking market with a 32 per cent share of international assets compared with 19 per cent for US banks and 8 per cent for French banks[10].

In line with their growth in assets, since the late 1970s the main Japanese city banks and long-term credit banks had been rapidly expanding their overseas networks. By the late 1980s these institutions had established branches in all the major financial centres. They had been closely followed by the trust banks. By comparison with the US multinational banks, however, the Japanese still had weak global networks in the late 1980s as shown in Figure 1.4 and had made little impact in local domestic markets. However, the banks were becoming important

[10]*Bank of England Quarterly*, May 1987, 241.

	EUROPE									FAR EAST & AUSTRALIA								LATIN AMERICA & CARIBBEAN							NORTH AMERICA			REST OF WORLD		
	UK	France	W. Germany	Switzerland	Netherlands	Belgium	Italy	Spain	Other	Japan	Hong Kong	Singapore	Australia	Phillippines	Thailand	Korea	Other	Brazil	Mexico	Argentina	Venezuela	Panama	Bahamas	Other	USA	Canada	UAE	Bahrain	USSR	Other
Bank of Tokyo	2B	B	3B	–	–	B	B	2B	2R	H	7B	2B	2R	B	B	2B	8B,4R	R	R	7B	R	B	–	4B,R	7B,4R	2R	R	B	–	8R
Dai Ichi Kangyo Bank	B	R	B,R	–	–	–	R	R	R	H	B	B	2R	–	R	B	B,5R	R	R	R	R	B	–	–	3B,3R	R	–	R	–	R
Industrial Bank of Japan	B	B	2R	–	–	–	–	R	–	H	B	B	2R	–	R	–	5R	2R	R	–	–	R	–	–	2B,5R	R	–	R	–	R
Long-term Credit Bank	B	R	R	–	–	–	–	–	–	H	B	B	2R	–	R	–	5R	2R	R	–	–	R	–	–	2B,2R	R	–	R	–	–
Mitsubishi Bank	B	R	B,R	R	–	B	R	R	–	H	B	B	R	R	R	B	5R	–	R	R	R	–	–	–	4B	R	–	R	–	2R
Mitsui Bank	B	R	B,R	–	–	B	–	R	–	H	B	B	2R	R	B	R	5R	R	R	R	–	B	–	–	4B,R	–	–	R	–	–
Sumitomo Bank	B,R	R	B,R	R	–	B	B,R	2B,R	2R	H	B	B	R	–	R	B	5R	–	R	R	R	B	–	–	5B,2R	R	–	R	–	3R
Tokai Bank	B	R	2B	R	–	–	–	R	–	H	B	B	R	R	R	B	4R	R	R	–	–	–	–	–	3B,R	R	–	R	–	R
Fuji Bank	B,R	B	B,2R	–	–	B	R	R	–	H	B	B	2R	–	R	B	B,6R	R	R	–	–	–	–	2R	5B,3R	R	–	R	–	R
Sanwa Bank	B	R	B,R	–	–	B	R	–	–	H	5B	–	2R	–	R	–	B,4R	–	R	R	–	B	–	–	5B,2R	R	–	R	–	–

Figure 1.4 Global office networks of leading Japanese banks 1987. Key: B = Branches (includes Agencies); R = Representative Offices; H = Home Country Offices:

Source: Annual Reports

players in the capital markets and they threatened to become very important institutions in multinational banking by the end of the 1980s. In addition to the banks, the leading Japanese brokerage houses were also emerging as dramatically important global players.

Traditionally, until the end of the 1960s, the Ministry of Finance (MOF) maintained very strict controls over the multinational activities of Japanese banks and only the Bank of Tokyo was allowed to branch overseas. This bank was primarily concerned with foreign exchange and trade transactions rather than longer term lending. While the Bank of Tokyo had remained a leading overseas Japanese bank, its relatively weak domestic position and short-term funding orientation had caused it to lose market share as the City banks and long-term credit banks had been allowed to expand abroad. The Bank of Tokyo had, however, a long experience of overseas operations and as a consequence had developed the most extensive international staff of any Japanese bank. This was an important factor in the early development of the multinational capability of Japanese banks since most did not have a well-developed international management structure, making it especially difficult for them to penetrate local indigenous banking markets except in connection with Japanese-related business.

In the early 1970s, the MOF began to allow Japanese banks to develop overseas, led by the major city banks—the leading commercial banks in Japan—and the long-term credit banks, and especially the Industrial Bank of Japan (IBJ). This latter bank held a special position within the Japanese banking structure. Originally a publicly owned institution, the IBJ was privatized by the post-war occupation administration. Nevertheless, the IBJ maintained an extremely close relationship with government and its representatives sat on the tripartite major industry committees of the Ministry of International Trade and Industry (MITI) which had been responsible for helping to set the pattern of post-war industrial structure development in Japan.

The IBJ, together with the Long-Term Credit Bank of Japan and the Nippon Fudosan Bank, provided long-term funds for industrial fixed investment and for working capital, directing their loan portfolios to a substantial extent into sectors favoured by MITI for industrial development. Based to some degree on the model of close relationships with large corporate accounts established by J. P. Morgan and the Deutsche Bank, IBJ internationalized when MITI and major Japanese corporations believed overseas expansion was desirable. In particular, IBJ was involved in overseas project finance, especially for raw material and energy projects, which could provide the resources necessary to support the Japanese economy.

Unlike the main City banks, the IBJ was not a part of a major industrial group and hence maintained a strong direct corporate client list which cut across those of the leading City banks. These institutions tended to be central units in the leading Japanese industrial groups as described in Chapter 4. Again, in the 1970s the MOF began to permit the City banks to expand overseas, partly to support the international moves of their group affiliate companies and partially as a means of expansion.

During the late 1970s and early 1980s, the Japanese banks began rapidly to develop their overseas presence. The main thrust of this overseas effort, like that of European banks, had been to establish a position in the United States. Like the British, the Japanese banks had, in particular, opted to enter the market in California by acquiring local banks and growing from this base. Thus Sanwa Bank was one of the earliest arrivals and had purchased several local Californian banks—Hacienda Bank, Golden Gate Bank and First City Bank—to create the Golden Gate Sanwa Bank. The bank nearly quadrupled its branch network in 1986 with the purchase of Lloyds Bank's $3 billion asset Californian subsidiary and was the second largest Japanese bank in the state. The Bank of Tokyo purchased California First Bank to become the largest Japanese bank in the state with over 100 branches in 1987. In August 1983 Mitsubishi Bank also bought into the crowded California market when it purchased BanCal Tri-State Corp, owners of the Bank of California, making Mitsubishi the third largest Japanese bank. This acquisition also gave Mitsubishi operations in the state of Washington and Oregon as a result of grandfather clauses permitting the three state activities. Other major Japanese bank positions in California included Mitsui Manufacturers Bank owned by Mitsui Bank; Tokai Bank of California owned by Tokai Bank, Dai-Ichi Kangyo Bank of

California and Sumitomo Bank of California owned by the Dai-Ichi Kangyo Bank and Sumitomo Bank respectively. By the end of 1986, therefore, the major Japanese City banks were the leading international banking competitors in the California market, with an estimated 13 per cent of the market and assets of over $67 billion, an increase of 32 per cent on 1985[11].

The most controversial move, perhaps, by the Japanese banks was the purchase by Fuji Bank in 1983 of the Chicago-based Walter E. Heller & Co[12]. A non-bank, the Heller purchase gave Fuji access to the finance company's 10,000 customers in 49 cities throughout the United States and an asset base of $.5 billion. With the strong trend towards deregulation in the United States, Fuji hoped this purchase would place the bank in a strong position for nationwide banking. Overall, North America accounted for some 30–35 per cent of Japanese banks' foreign business in 1984, while for most of the banks, overseas operations made up some 15–20 per cent of overall activities.

From their early bridgeheads in the US market the Japanese banks had initially sought to pick up trade-related business between the USA and Japan, helping Japanese and US companies tap the New York and Tokyo capital markets respectively. Expanding from a Japan/US trade bank was, however, difficult and individual banks had with greater or lesser degrees of success sought to develop niche positions. Thus Mitsubishi Bank, using its triple A credit rating, had with very fine rates penetrated the US municipal and state debt guarantee market. Fuji Bank had backed the issuance of debt to finance student loans. Long-Term Credit Bank had issued irrevocable letters of credit to guarantee public utilities debt while Sumitomo Bank had also provided substantial guarantees for public financing. The Industrial Bank of Japan, by contrast, was growing rapidly by the provision of long-term fixed rate funds for capital investment—the bank's domestic speciality—backed by parent bank guarantees[13].

---

[11]*American Banker*, 10, September, 1987, 22.
[12]Walter Heller had also been evaluated by Midland Bank as a prospective acquisition but had been rejected in favour of Crocker.
[13]D. Lake, Beefing up US Banking Share without muscling in, *Euromoney*, May 1986, 36–9.

By 1987, the Japanese banks in the USA had emerged as the leading foreign banks and were slowly but surely increasing their penetration of the corporate market. At the same time the Japanese banks were looking forward to the possible demise of the restrictions of Glass–Steagall, with a view to competing with the Japanese securities firms such as Nomura, Yamaichi and Daiwa who were rapidly making their presence felt on Wall Street.

In addition to North America, the Japanese banks had expanded rapidly in the main financial markets of Western Europe and especially in London and Switzerland. While these two countries represented the main thrust of the Japanese institutions in Europe, the banks were actively expanding their networks in the main cities of the larger European countries. Overall, Europe accounted for around 25 per cent of Japanese banks' international operations in 1984[14].

In London and Switzerland the focus of attack for the Japanese banks was the area of investment banking and the securities markets. Still to a degree inhibited by domestic regulation in Tokyo, London enabled the Japanese banks to engage in virtually all aspects of the Euromarkets. With aggressive pricing and a growing level of innovation the Japanese banks were gradually rising in the ranks of Euromarket lead managers to challenge their own securities companies and the leading American commercial and investment banks. By 1987, rapid asset growth had clearly established the Japanese banks with the highest market share of the London international market. In the 10 years from 1975 to 1985 they accounted for more than a third of the total growth in London-bank-based international liabilities and their share increased from 13 to 31 per cent. Most of this business growth was, however, supplying funds to their own offices overseas and principally to head offices in Tokyo, where the funds were lent on to domestic borrowers[15].

The other major area for Japanese bank expansion had been in

---

[14]K. Rafferty, The new global push of Japanese banking, *Institutional Investor*, March 1984, 197.

[15]International banking in London, *Bank of England Quarterly*, September, 1986, 373.

the Pacific Basin which was the fastest growing market and one where profitability was high. The banks had all established significant operations in Hong Kong, and for most banks Asia represented some 15–20 per cent of their international business.

By contrast, Japanese bank exposure elsewhere was limited. The banks had some exposure in Brazil as a result of Japanese company involvement and the presence of a substantial Japanese community in the country. Africa, India and the Middle East were relatively very unimportant areas for the Japanese banks, however.

By 1987 the Japanese City and Long-Term Credit Banks had become important players in international banking and they made up half of the world's top 25 banks as measured by deposits or assets. Moreover, with an extremely high domestic saving rate, a strong balance of payments surplus and the growing internationalization of major Japanese companies, the Japanese banks were expected to continue to grow in importance while the yen was beginning to challenge the dollar as the principal world currency of exchange.

1.10   THE INVASION OF THE NEW COMPETITORS

The initial development of multinational banking was largely due to the major commercial banks moving overseas to service their increasingly international corporate customers. However, those customers had grown in sophistication and had challenged the traditional intermediation role of the commercial banks as the providers of funds. Rather corporations had sought for and found a wider and wider mix of financing alternatives in an increasingly global market as a consequence of new technology, major product innovation and the arrival of new competitors to the large banks from organizations such as investment banks and securities houses.

By the late 1980s the sophisticated corporate treasurer could trade his entire financial position on a 24 hours a day basis via terminal systems linked to and similar to those used by the banks. Investment banks and brokerage houses could issue securitzed debt instruments which tapped virtually any capital market, in any currency, and these instruments could be traded on a global basis with arbitraging possibilities between any one of an ever widening array of financial alternatives.

As a result, while this work is primarily concerned with examining the strategies of major multinational commercial banks, in the future the leading multinational financial institutions will be drawn from a wider group of sources. These will include the leading brokerage houses, primarily from the USA and Japan, the major US investment banks, some of which already have non-bank parent companies, a number of leading insurance companies and a growing number of non-banks which have diversified into the financial services industry. By the mid 1990s, as discussed in Chapter 9, the strategies of the major banks and these new competitors will be in direct competition with one another in a largely deregulated world. Deregulation will also have often been forced reluctantly upon individual national regulatory authorities by the pressure of global events beyond their control.

1.11 CONCLUSION

The period since 1960 has seen the emergence of multinational banking and the development of a deregulated global capital market. This was pioneered by the major US money centre banks who moved to establish international branch networks to support the overseas expansion of their own corporate customers, to escape the constrictions of US bank regulations and to tap into the emerging international capital market. The introduction of the US banks into the European markets in particular prompted an initially defensive response by the leading European banks. At first, these institutions attempted to join together into defensive clubs, but the aggressive approach of the US banks allowed them to penetrate, in particular, the indigenous corporate markets in Europe, except perhaps in West Germany.

Belatedly recognizing the changing needs of the corporate market, the Europeans then gradually substituted a direct presence in the major financial markets for their consortium representation. This was accentuated after the first oil shock when sovereign risk lending came rapidly to replace corporate lending as the main international loan activity and the size of the Euro-markets expanded to recycle the surpluses of the oil-producing countries. The Europeans were also inhibited in competing against the Americans by virtue of their geographically orientated organization structures compared with the customer-based structures of the US banks. Nevertheless, the Europeans primarily focused their counter-attack on the US market, opening a series of branches throughout the main financial centres and attempting to penetrate the US corporate banking market. In addition, a number of banks attempted to enter the US market, especially in California, by acquiring local financial institutions with a greater focus on retail activities but with only limited success.

More recently, the major Japanese banks have emerged as important and aggressive international banking competitors. Again, focusing on the US market, the Japanese banks had also attempted to gain penetration by acquisition, especially in the state of California. These banks, however, had not yet developed strong multinational capabilities for sale to third-country corporations. By contrast such banks enjoyed close linkages with Japanese companies and especially those from the large industrial groups of which the banks were key members.

By the late 1980s multinational banking had thus become commonplace. Market interpenetration was high in the industrial country markets except in Japan. Third-world markets tended to be relatively unimportant unless they were rapidly growing as with the countries of the Pacific basin. The industry had become extremely competitive as a result and this pressure had been compounded by the erosion of industry boundaries and the entry of new competitors such as securities houses and investment banks to provide alternatives to traditional banking services. Finally, deregulation and the impact of technology threatened to herald a future decade of rapid and traumatic change as the boundaries between institutions continued to blur and banks tried to modify their strategies to seek long-term distinctive advantage and avoid price-sensitive, low-differentiation service positions. The next decade of multinational banking threatened to see the development of a truly global capital market, serviced by a group of worldwide financial institutions only some of which had their origins as traditional commercial banks. The rest of this book is largely given over to describing this tranformation and its origins.

CHAPTER 2

The International Capital Market

2.1 THE EMERGENCE OF THE GLOBAL CAPITAL MARKET

Fundamental to the development of multinational banking has been the development since the late 1950s of the Euromarket. This unregulated market has become, in terms of size, number of bank, brokerage, governmental and corporate participants, critical in importance to the functioning of the international monetary system.

A Eurocurrency technically is any currency on deposit outside the borders of the home country of that currency and beyond the control of its regulatory authorities. Such deposits are therefore created when currency is transferred to a bank or other organization outside the home country as a payment for goods or services or as a straight transfer of funds. The latter area is actually of considerable importance. For example, in the early years of the Euromarkets, an important source of funds was the Eastern Bloc which preferred to leave dollar funds obtained from trade or other sources on deposit outside the United States, for fear of sequestration. Similarly there has been a substantial flow of flight capital by rich individuals into the Euromarkets from high political risk countries or as a means of tax evasion. The classic picture of the bearer bond holder is thus that of the Belgian dentist. Although difficult to quantify, one confidential report from a major New York money centre bank has estimated that some $103 billion of flight capital flowed from 23 developing countries between 1978 and 1983. Over the same time period the same countries added \$381 billion in new debt, much of which quickly returned from whence it came, via the 'suitcase trade' in flight capital. In the main, however, the rapid growth in the size of the Euromarkets stems from the recycling of the Eurodollar surpluses accumulated by the OPEC oil-producing countries after the first oil shock in 1973. The development of the Euromarkets in size and currency is shown in Table 2.1. The market has grown at an average of around 20–30 per cent per annum except in 1972–73 when bank lending to non-residents grew by over 60 per cent. In the early 1980s there was a slowdown in market growth due to problems with repayments on sovereign risk lending. In the mid 1980s growth has returned although lending has centred on the interbank market, with the Japanese and Europeans helping to provide the funds needed to finance an apparently ever expanding US trade deficit. Most Euromarket deposits are taken and held in dollars. The growth of the Euromarkets in part has thus mirrored the movement of the dollar and the relative liquidity position of the USA.

Interest rates in the USA are set by the Federal Reserve in large part. By contrast, the rates prevailing in the Euromarkets are set by supply and demand. As a result, at times of tight domestic monetary policy in the USA, banks and companies based there have found it cheaper to borrow dollars overseas. The oil surpluses after 1973 were therefore largely placed by the oil exporters with US and leading European banks. Since these surpluses occurred in dollars, the Euromarkets swelled rapidly as the

Table 2.1   Eurocurrency market size (\$ billions)

	1972	1974	1976	1978	1980	1982	1984	1985	1986
Estimated size									
Gross	210	395	595	950	1515	2146	2352	2833	3560
Liabilities to non-banks	35	80	115	190	325	634	684	822	938
Liabilities to central banks	25	60	80	115	150 ⎫				
Liabilities to other banks	150	255	400	645	1040 ⎭	1512	1668	2011	2622
Eurodollars as % of gross liabilities	78	76	80	74	74	79	80	88	87

Source: Morgan Guaranty Trust Co.

banks placed their surplus deposits through the market with new borrowers, often governments who needed the funds to support balance of payment deficits. Such lending was also dollar-based, irrespective of the domestic currency of the borrower, thus exposing loans to exchange rate risks related to the relative exchange rate of dollars versus domestic currencies.

During the late 1970s continuing US domestic deficits caused the dollar to lose value and the Euromarkets began to diversify somewhat into perceived stronger currencies. As a percentage of the gross market dollars, this declined to 74 per cent of the total, while Deutschmarks and Swiss francs became more popular. This trend reversed again during the early 1980s as the US banks became net takers from the international financial system to finance a growing and continuing US budget deficit.

2.2   THE MAJOR EUROMARKET INSTRUMENTS

At the core of the Euromarkets has been the interbank market. This has been concerned with dealing in offshore deposits and foreign exchange, and Eurocurrency deposits have formed an increasing element in the liabilities base of the multinational banks. Moreover, as the market has developed it has seen the creation of an increasingly complex array of financial instruments. In addition, from its initial base in London, the market has expanded to embrace a wide variety of different centres around the world. While London has remained the principal market, other markets have emerged as important. Leading centres have included New York, Paris, Luxembourg, the Bahamas and Caymans, Hong Kong, Singapore and Tokyo, with the latter centre, in particular, gaining in importance with the growth of Japan's trading surplus. The estimated size of international banking by centre is shown in Table 2.2.

As the market has evolved, a wide choice of financial instruments has developed. Deposits have been the most important instrument in the market and these parallel the turnover on the foreign exchange markets for spot and forward transactions for up to a year ahead. These deposits were traditionally lent out in form of syndicated loans, and these were arranged primarily by the major multinational banks.

Table 2.2   International banking analysed by centre

	End December 1986				Share of total market				
	Foreign currency lending to:		Domestic currency lending to non-residents	Total	1982 (%)	1983 (%)	1984 (%)	1985 (%)	1986 (%)
	Residents	Non-residents							
Gross lending of which:	752	2331	890	4107					
United Kingdom	242	665	50	957	26.9	26.6	24.3	24.5	23.3
United States Int. banking facilities		25	444	469	14.5	15.4	15.2	12.8	11.4
Japan	268	208	138	614	7.5	8.6	8.9	10.4	15.0
France	53	155	33	241	7.2	7.0	6.7	6.6	5.9
Luxembourg	27	138	3	168	4.3	4.2	3.7	4.0	4.1
Swiss trustee accounts				134[a]	3.9	3.4	3.7	3.7	3.3
Belgium	35	118	7	160	3.3	3.3	3.3	3.8	3.9
Canada	25	49	4	78	2.6	2.6	2.5	2.2	1.9
Netherlands	13	68	20	101	2.9	2.6	2.4	2.5	2.5
Switzerland	13	46	49	108	2.8	2.8	2.2	2.5	2.6
Germany, Federal Republic	3	42	116	161	2.8	2.5	2.4	3.1	3.9
Italy	25	52	6	83	1.7	1.6	2.1	2.1	2.0
Offshore banking centres		673	5	678	17.7	18.1	19.0	17.9	16.5

[a] End September 1986.
Source: *Bank of England Quarterly*, May 1987, p. 241

The Eurobond market developed after the deposit market and for many years was substantially smaller than that for syndicated loans. In the mid 1980s, however, a fundamental shift had occurred as investment banks, brokerage houses and some commercial banks had begun to offer new alternative bond-type instruments as alternatives to loans. As a result the 'bond' market had expanded rapidly in the form of new tradable instruments. Moreover, even traditional loans were being securitized to an increasing degree by commercial banks anxious to reduce their asset positions and so reduce the pressure on their equity bases. Traditionally the Euromarkets had developed with the multinational commercial banks dominating the segment for short-term deposits and syndicated loans while the bonds segment had been dominated by investment banks and brokerage houses such as Crédit Suisse First Boston, the leading bond issuing house and a joint venture between First Boston Corporation and Crédit Suisse, and Merrill Lynch. The major US investment banks such as Salomon Bros and Goldman Sachs had also extended their operations into the Eurobond markets from their already strong position as issuers of domestic US securities. In the past few years the market had also experienced major intervention by the leading Japanese brokerage houses led by Nomura Securities. Securitization had also caused many of the leading multinational commercial banks to endeavour rapidly to build up their investment banking capabilities so as to play a more powerful role in the bond markets. Despite the multinational banks' efforts, however, the market for each specialist instrument tended to be relatively concentrated with the top five institutions usually controlling around half the market. However, few commercial banks had, by the late 1980s established strong positions against the main brokerage houses and the US investment institutions.

Eurocurrency deposits are placed usually at a minimum size of $50,000. They can be placed at call or for fixed periods. Call deposits are made overnight or at seven days' notice and in a variety of currencies, although the dollar is by far the most important. Time deposits are placed for periods of 1, 3, 6 or 12 months in a variety of currencies. Sterling and dollar deposits can also be placed for longer.

The London banks have also issued certificates of deposit

(CD's) denominated in US dollars. Such certificates are issued in several forms. The most common are tap or straight CD's which are issued by a borrowing bank which wants to tap the market. Such certificates have a fixed interest rate and maturity between 1 and 12 months with the interest rate being related to LIBOR (London Inter Bank Offered Rate) and according to the issuing bank's credit rating. Floating rate CDs are usually issued with maturities of up to three years and pay a slightly higher interest rate than tap CDs. Such instruments are of greater interest to the Japanese and European banks and again are usually issued in dollars. Tranche CDs are issued with maturities of up to five years with a fixed rate of interest. Such certificates usually form part of a programme of issues by a bank up to a present limit of $100 million or more. Such CDs tend to be privately placed rather than offered publicly and, as such, are more like a bond than a bank CD. In 1981 Chemical Bank also introduced the Discount CD which were CDs offered at a discount to par.

In addition to conventional currency offerings, a number of Euromarket issues have been made in mixed baskets of currencies, the most important of which are SDRs (Special Drawing Rights) and the Ecu (European Currency Unit). The SDR was originally a composite currency developed for use between governments and the International Monetary Fund, and was composed of some 16 currencies with different weights based upon their share of world trade. As some of these currencies were themselves not very marketable, this inhibited the overall marketability of the SDR. As a result, the SDR was simplified in 1981, to contain only five currencies, each of which was actively traded, thus enhancing the overall marketability of the SDR.

The Ecu is a basket of nine EEC country currencies, each weighted according to its relative share of the combined gross national product of the EEC. The Ecu includes sterling even though the UK is not a member of the European Monetary System. Like SDRs, the Ecu can be quoted convertible with other currencies according to the weighted value of the exchange rates of the amounts of which it is composed.

Banks will quote interest rates on deposits dominated in Ecus or SDRs even though the initial deposit will be placed in one currency, usually dollars. This is because Ecus and SDRs do not themselves exist as currency units. The actual rate of interest would by calulated as a weighted average of the rates paid on the individual currencies within the cocktail. As a result of the mix of currencies it was expected that rates for Ecus or SDRs would not fluctuate as much as with single currencies.

During the late 1960s, and as an extension of the Euromarkets, an international bond market developed. The first bonds were issued in 1963 when interest equalization tax was introduced in the USA, leading to the closure of the New York capital market for international bond issues. The market grew rapidly, especially during the 1980s, and in 1986 new bond and Floating Rate Note (FRNs) issues had reached a record $220 billion, up 35 per cent on 1985. Issues of FRNs fell by 15 per cent, however, and the real growth was in fixed rate bonds which reached $172.4 billion. Issues of Eurobonds have also been growing faster than issues of foreign bonds on domestic markets and, in terms of both the gross amount raised and of trading turnover, the Eurobond market is now the third largest bond market in the world, after the US and Japanese domestic markets[1].

Such bonds are usually international bonds issued on behalf of a corporation, government or international agency such as the IMF. Issues are usually unsecured and issuers are required to have a good name or the backing of a strong, creditworthy parent. Subsidiary companies of nationalized corporations would thus normally obtain parent company or government guarantees. New issues are usually arranged by syndicates of international banks, with a lead bank or banks being responsible for organizing the syndicate. Such lead positions are a function of managerial skill and placing power and an important source of income for arrangement fees, compared with the increasingly thin spreads obtained from participations alone. By the mid 1980s Eurobond issues, which were traditionally issued in conjunction with leading international investment banks such as the major US and some British houses, were becoming targets for the major multinational banks and brokerage houses. The German and Swiss international banks were also powerful competitors in the Euro-

---

[1]Developments in international banking and capital markets in 1986, *Bank of England Quarterly*, May 1987, 237.

Table 2.3 Leading Eurobond bookrunners 1983–6

		1986				1985				1984				1983		
	Rank	No. of issues	amount ($bn)	Share (%)	Rank	No. of issues	amount ($bn)	Share (%)	Rank	No. of issues	amount ($bn)	Share (%)	Rank	No. of issues	amount ($bn)	Share (%)
Crédit Suisse First Boston	1	55	7.63	8.37	1	101	19.04	14.10	1	144	9.37	11.8	1	77	8.00	16.9
Deutsche Bank	2	49	7.55	8.29	5	75	7.70	5.70	3	94	5.78	7.3	2	85	6.09	12.9
Nomura Securities	3	62	6.86	7.52	8	61	5.03	3.73	9	54	1.98	3.5	13	24	0.95	2.0
Salomon Bros	4	33	5.03	5.51	4	67	7.83	5.80	6	75	3.54	4.5	9	31	1.06	2.2
Banque Paribas	5	44	4.12	4.52	10	55	3.34	2.47	17	38	1.20	1.5	23	18	0.45	1.0
Daiwa Securities	6	45	4.08	4.48	12	37	2.94	2.18	16	42	1.25	1.6	22	21	0.58	1.2
Morgan Guaranty	7	32	4.07	4.47	3	62	7.86	5.82	2	78	5.81	7.3	4	40	1.84	3.9
Morgan Stanley	8	34	3.42	3.75	6	63	6.42	4.76	5	87	3.62	4.6	6	36	1.61	3.4
Merrill Lynch	9	23	3.09	3.39	2	47	7.96	5.89	4	63	5.16	6.5	3	24	2.06	4.4
Nikko Securities	10	30	2.95	3.23	25	32	1.87	1.38	23	30	0.87	1.1	21	21	0.59	1.2
Union Bank of Switzerland	11	28	2.67	2.93	9	27	3.75	2.78	11	47	1.83	2.3	18	13	0.67	1.4
Yamaichi Securities	12	29	2.26	2.48	20	32	2.23	1.65	34	29	0.59	0.7	38	10	0.29	0.6
Goldman Sachs	13	15	1.90	2.09	17	41	6.22	4.61	8	41	2.06	2.6	11	25	1.03	2.2
Commerz Bank	14	30	1.75	1.92	17	32	2.38	1.76	19	21	1.01	1.3	10	22	1.04	2.2
S.G. Warburg	15	14	1.69	1.86	13	25	2.84	2.10	7	57	2.68	3.4	5	41	1.63	3.5
Morgan Grenfell	16	14	1.58	1.73	32	13	0.99	0.73	20	21	0.97	1.2	36	12	0.33	0.7
Shearson Lehman	17	11	1.46	1.60	15	16	2.49	1.85	12	28	1.65	2.1	25	9	0.43	0.9
Bankers Trust	18	10	1.36	1.49	16	25	2.42	1.79	33	18	0.61	0.80	76	3	0.05	0.1
L.T.C. Bank of Japan	19	12	1.35	1.48	35	11	0.82	0.61	–	NA	NA	NA	–	NA	NA	NA
Orion Royal Bank	20	23	1.35	1.48	11	51	3.00	2.23	15	37	1.28	1.6	16	21	0.80	1.7

Source: Euromoney

bond markets, along with leading US banks, merchant banks and those European commercial banks which had developed strong investment banking skills. In recent years the Japanese banks and securities houses had also begun to emerge as extremely important Eurobond issuers. Leading Eurobond issuers for 1983–6 are shown in Table 2.3.

Both public issues and private placements are made. In the first case, bonds are quoted on the London, Zurich, Luxembourg and, recently, Tokyo markets. The bonds are fully negotiable and are usually bearer designated, with no tax being deducted from interest payments. An active secondary market exists but, although the bonds are quoted on one of more stock exchanges, most trading takes place over the counter between banks.

Private placements are cheaper to issue because full advertising and issuing costs are not incurred. However, such placements are normally not quoted and hence there is no secondary market in such bonds. As a result, placed bonds normally carry a higher rate of interest to compensate for the loss of marketability. Bonds are issued normally in minimum denominations of $10,000 or equivalent in other currencies, although about 50 per cent of issues are in dollars. Maturities, which have tended to shorten, run from 3 to 25 years, although few have a life beyond 15 years. While the number of dollar issues still predominates, in recent years there has been a very rapid growth in European currency and yen issues. Yen issues seem most likely to grow in importance as a result of the internationalization of the Japanese currency.

As a result of rising inflation and volatility in interest rates, the concept of floating rate notes (FRNs) has developed. A growing number of Eurobonds were issued in the early 1980s paying variable interest rates. Such bonds had a similar maturity structure to conventional fixed rate bonds. The interest rate for FRNs was set relative to LIBOR, usually with a margin of around one quarter per cent over. The interest rate was applied for a specific period, usually 3–6 months, after which it was adjusted for the subsequent period based upon the prevailing LIBOR rate. FRNs grew rapidly in importance during the period of high interest rates, in the early 1980s, but with the return of lower interest rates flexible rate instruments tended to decline in importance and/or be prepayed from funds obtained by fixed rate bond issues.

During the mid 1980s substantial growth also occurred in note issuance facilities (NIFs), a further variant of the Eurobond. The volume of NIFs issued trebled in size to $9 billion in 1984. NIFs enabled borrowers to raise medium-term funds by issuing a series of short-term notes with a flexibility of draw down. Two basic forms of NIFs had developed. In the first of these a group of banks was invited to tender for any notes issued up to a predetermined maximum interest rate spread. Any notes not taken up were underwritten with the underwriters being committed to take up the excess or provide equivalent funds by issuing a credit. In the second method a note-placing agent was responsible for placing any notes issued, again with underwriters taking up any unplaced notes. The underwriting role was performed by banks which assumed the risk of having to lend at some future time, but these risks were not shown in their balance sheets. This was causing concern to some supervisory authorities who felt that such risks should be reflected in the measurement of bank capital adequacy.

In 1980, Merrill Lynch made the first issue of Eurocommercial paper. This was essentially a promissory note similar to a CD but issued by a corporation rather than a bank. The product was also similar to the commercial paper issued by corporations, mainly through brokerage houses, in the United States. US commercial paper had been available to Eurodollar investors since the early 1970s but the new issue was more suited to the Euromarket. Such an instrument could be issued in either interest-bearing or discount forms. In the former case, interest was payable on maturity of the notes, while in the latter, interest was discounted at the time of issue.

These Euronote facilities were designed to allow the borrower to raise medium-term funds by the issue of a series of short-term notes. Initially they tended to require underwriting which enabled borrowers usually to switch between multiple component facilities for the lowest cost of funds but at the cost of front end and commitment fees. Distribution of such notes was usually by a tender panel or a sole placement agency.

By 1985, however, a non-bank investor base developed for

Euronotes as an alternative to US Treasury bills. Swiss investors in particular were interested in such short-term instruments, especially when issued by top-quality corporate borrowers. As a result they were prepared to buy such issues at up to 60 points below the interbank bid rate, at about one-month maturity. At these levels the yield on Euronotes, while still above the US Treasury bill rate, was lower than the US commercial paper rate. An increasing number of US borrowers, therefore, were attracted to the Euronote market, leading to a rapid growth in the number of uncommitted Eurocommercial paper issues. In 1984 the proportion of non-underwritten facilities was just 3 per cent; this rose to about a third in 1985 but, in 1986, was over three-quarters, while the volume of facilities arranged grew to $70 billion, an increase of 40 per cent on 1985[2].

The multinational banks had also made heavy use of the Euromarkets to boost their capital adequacies. Banking supervisors had applied considerable pressure to ensure that adequacy ratios were enhanced. As a result, in the mid 1980s many of the leading banks based in the UK, USA, France and Germany had built their equity bases by increased retentions and by raising additional capital. The US and British banks had made heavy use of perpetual subordinated FRNs, while some US banks had issued FRNs where redemption was linked to the issue of additional equity, thus allowing the banks to count the funds as primary capital. Major French banks had issued FRNs for the first time, as well as capital instruments such as *titres participatifs* and *certificats d'investissement*. The market for these particular FRNs got into serious difficulty in late 1986, however, as Japanese banks, which had been primary buyers of such securities, withdrew from the market due to the thin terms available and the perceived risks of the issuers as a result of sovereign risk debt problems. Until Citicorp took the bold decision to reserve a substantial portion of its developing country risk exposure (see Chapter 5), few large multinational money centre banks around the world had found it attractive to raise substantial tranches of new equity capital.

The trend to FRN issuance had also affected the traditional

[2]*Ibid.*, p. 239.

Eurocredit market. Such credits were increasingly being traded between banks as a way of improving liquidity. For example, a loan taken on at, say ½ per cent over LIBOR could be sold to another bank at, say, 3/8 per cent, thus releasing the lending capacity in the selling bank for alternative opportunities without increasing the gearing ratio. Traded loans tended to be mostly concerned with the debt of quality borrowers. Trading of loans to troubled debtors was less common, although efforts were being made to package some developing country loans for sale at deep discounts, mirroring the 'junk' bonds market, which had emerged, trading in lower rated corporate paper. This trend had also led to the development of a secondary market and transferable syndicated loans were innovated, specifically designed to be traded in this new market. The development of a market for such troubled loans was instrumental in establishing a value for sovereign risk positions and had influenced large provisions for losses made by many banks after Citicorp's move in 1987.

The international capital market had also become much more diverse in terms of the currency of instruments and in pricing. Wide variations in exchange rates had led borrowers increasingly to consider alternative currencies to the dollar, with the yen and the Deutschmark emerging slowly as alternative reserve currencies. With the continuation of large US trade deficits and Japanese surpluses the 1990s seemed likely to show the eclipse of the dollar as a single world reserve currency and the emergence of perhaps a more stable multicurrency system. Similarly, pricing in relation to bases other than LIBOR had become more common. Bases such as LIBID (the London Interbank bid rate), LIMEAN (the mean of London Interbank bid and offer rates) and the US Treasury bill rate had all been used in recent years. In large part, this change in primary bases had reflected the market's concern about the creditworthiness of individual banks and currencies. It was thus expected that, in the event of a banking crisis, the spread between the bid and offer rates would widen sharply and some banks would have much greater difficulty in raising funds than would others. A further consequence had been that non-banks, such as good-quality corporations or governments, had been able to borrow at rates comparable or lower than those available to the banks themselves.

2.3   THE IMPACT ON MARKET AND INDUSTRY STRUCTURE OF THE NEW INSTRUMENTS

The growth of bonds, NIFs, FRNs and Euronotes indicated a marked shift in the structure of the international capital market. During the early 1980s there was a major shift from bank credits to marketable paper. This reflected the securitization of corporate and governmental lending, and the growing reluctance of the multinational banks to add assets to their balance sheets. For borrowers, the advantages of floating rate notes and, latterly, bonds, were that interest margins were usually lower than with bank credits; they could be arranged for longer maturities; and they were not easily withdrawn as a result of turmoil in the international capital market.

The trend to securitization had proceeded furthest in the United States where, by 1986, net borrowings in commercial paper and bonds by non-financial corporations represented around 80 per cent of the total, compared with less than 50 per cent in the early 1980s. Banks, brokerage houses and non-banks, such as retailers and automobile finance companies, were actively securitizing mortgages, automobile loans, consumer credit receivables and the like, all of which had traditionally been carried on the books of the issuing institutions. The same pattern was also emerging in the international capital market where, in 1986, securitized lending again accounted for over 80 per cent of gross new credit compared with around 50 per cent in the mid 1970s, as shown in Table 2.4[3].

For the multinational commercial banks the trend also changed their competitive position sharply. While securitization had effectively been started in the United States by the major Wall Street investment banks and brokerage houses building up the commercial paper market, the commercial banks were excluded from this process as a result of Glass–Steagall legisla-

---

[3]Rimmer de Vries, *Global Financial Change, World Financial Markets*, Morgan Guaranty Trust, December, 1986, p. 1.

Table 2.4   The securitization of international lending ($bn)

	1983	1984	1985	Jan.–Sept. 1986
Securitized financing	87	151	215	258
Bond issues	77	112	168	232
NIFs and similar back ups	10	29	47	26
Syndicated bank loans	67	57	42	40
Other back ups	3	11	11	7
Total borrowing	157	219	268	305
Securitized financing as % of total	55	65	80	84

Source: Morgan Guaranty Trust Co.

tion. This prevented the commercial banks from operating as principals in the US securities markets. The securitization of the Euromarkets, again led by investment banks and brokerage houses, was, however, open to the commercial banks which, due to deregulation, were able to operate investment banking subsidiaries in London. With the growing reluctance of banks to undertake syndicated lending due to a rising cost of funds, deposit mismatch and securitization, forcing lower margin spreads, coupled with difficulties in raising sufficient equity to cover a rising asset base, most of the major multinational commercial banks were actively endeavouring to build up their investment banking skills, and to securitize a growing part of their balance sheets. The development of investment banking within the commercial banks was not easy, however, due to the clash of cultures normally prevailing in the two types of institution, as discussed further in Chapter 6. Nevertheless some progress had been made by some commercial banks and this change in the market structure was a further indication of an overall trend towards a universitality in banking, and further interlocking of traditionally separated market sectors.

Competition had also intensified amongst investment houses and the leading multinational banks to produce innovative financial engineering product concepts which would be marketable yet reduce borrowing costs. During 1984 the most notable innovations had been in the arrangment of NIFs[4]. A further

---

[4]Developments in international banking and capital markets in 1984, *Bank of England Quarterly*, March 1985, 59.

development had been the introduction of multicomponent facilities which allowed the borrower to make drawings under any of a variety of facilities one of which was usually a NIF with a wide choice of maturities, currencies and interest rate bases.

While normally banks could choose not to renew a loan facility in the Eurodollar market, their flexibility had been severely constrained as a result of the rapid growth in country risk lending in the 1970s following the two oil shocks. As the debt had mounted, as described in greater detail in Chapter 5, debt reschedulings had increased dramatically and the multinational banks had, therefore, lost much of their traditional flexibility on the renewal of credit lines. Instead, the banks had been increasingly locked into their customers, forcing them to use bond instruments to modify their own liability positions.

In order to stabilize their lengthening asset maturities the major multinational banks had endeavoured to reduce their reliance on Eurocurrency deposits. To tie down the source of funds and the rates at which these would be available, the banks were forced to concentrate on medium- and long-term fund sources rather than the interbank market which was seen as too short-term to meet their needs. The Eurobond market thus provided two such sources through fixed rate bonds tied to interest rate swaps and by the direct issuance of floating rate notes.

Investment banks and brokerage houses in particular were also active in developing bond products for government and corporate borrowers. With this type of instrument, organizations with different credit ratings could exploit their relative advantages in different segments of the capital market. For example, in the fixed rate Eurobond market the difference between high- and low-rated borrowers could be some 200–300 basis points. In the market for floating rate notes by contrast these differences were likely to be no more than 100 basis points. The gap between these two spreads thus enabled participants to swap interest rates and both save money.

Normally, therefore, a bank would issue a fixed rate bond while a second organization like a BBB credit-rated company would issue an FRN for the same amount. The two parties would then agree to service the other's interest payments. The lowest rated corporate would also usually pay a small portion of the floating rate note interest, thus sharing in the gains it had made in obtaining fixed rate funds at a lower rate than it would have otherwise been able to do on its own credit rating. Typically, a bank might, therefore, end up with an all-in cost of funds half a per cent below LIBOR, less than it would pay on an FRN, while the corporation paid a lower fixed interest rate plus an additional 5/8 per cent, again much cheaper than if it had raised the money on its own behalf[5].

The use of currency and interest rate swaps had grown dramatically in the early 1980s and by 1986 it was estimated that over 80 per cent of all Eurobond issues had a swap transaction associated with them. The pricing and trading of swaps had therefore become the key drive in the Eurobond market. In 1984, it was estimated that interest rate swaps grew to around $80 billion up from about $20 billion in 1983 while currency swaps grew from less than $5 billion to nearly $15 billion[6], in 1985 fixed rate bonds issues reached $107 billion while in 1986 the market rose by 60 per cent to $172 billion[7]. Most of these issues involved swaps and by the end of 1986 the total outstanding was $300–400 billion, but as the future value of the dollar appeared more uncertain straight dollar-denominated swaps declined in popularity while demand for Deutschmark, yen- and Swiss franc-denominated instruments grew dramatically. Currency swaps also continued to grow sharply and by the end of 1986 were estimated to have reached $100 billion outstanding[8].

As a result of the growth in swaps many higher credit risk companies were no longer borrowing long-term fixed rate money from banks but borrowing at lower cost floating rates and then obtaining fixed rate money via a swap. Bank lending margins were thus being further eroded while their portfolio risk was increasing as they were forced to lend to lower rated companies in an effort to maintain spreads.

The greater volatility of interest and exchange rates during the 1970s and 1980s had also created demand for new instruments

---

[5]M. A. Seighart, Funding the banks, international capital markets, *Financial Times Survey*, 19 March 1984, p.v.
[6]*Economist*, International Banking Survey, 16 March 1987, pp. 20, 39.
[7]*Bank of England Quarterly*, May 1987, p. 237.
[8]*Euromoney*, Corporate Finance Supplement, January 1987, p. 6.

with which to hedge exposures. These instruments too, had tended to be in a form that was off bank balance sheets. The new instruments included the use of financial futures, forward rate agreements—a form of over-the-counter interest rate futures contract traded mainly by banks in London—and currency and interest rate options. These latter instruments gave buyers the right but not the obligation to buy or sell financial assets at a predetermined price thus limiting downside risk while leaving open upside potential in return for a specified initial premium[9].

As a result of the structural shifts in the Euromarkets, the relationship between loan credits and bonds was growing much closer. Whereas traditionally the two markets had been largely separated with the credit market being much the larger, by the mid 1980s securitization had led to a much greater role for the bond market and since 1982 bonds had tended to be a larger component of the international capital market than credits. By the mid 1980s the market appeared to have undergone a fundamental change from which it seemed unlikely to retreat.

The development of the market in interest rate and currency swaps, however, has played a key role in the integration of international and domestic capital markets. These instruments have enabled borrowers to explore both domestic and Euromarket financing possibilities for their funding requirements. Swaps have also led to a convergence of domestic and international bond yields and encouraged borrowers to seek solutions for profitable swap opportunities amongst less widely traded currencies, so increasing the use of currencies such as the Australian dollar, Canadian dollar and French franc in the international markets. As a result there has been a noticeable integration of the domestic and international capital markets around the world and a clear trend towards the development of a global capital market. The integration has also been facilitated by the process of deregulation that has gradually taken place in most industrialized countries and by developments in technology which have served to increase competition and reduce transaction costs while providing dramatic improvements in communication and linking international exchanges on an on-line, real-time basis.

[9]Recent innovations in international banking, *Bank of England Quarterly*, June 1986, pp. 209–10.

2.4   BANK STRATEGY—OPPORTUNITIES AND THREATS

The development of a global integrated capital market, the squeeze on bank margins due to perceived credit risks, higher costs of funds than competitors, securization, deregulation and technology have had a marked effect on the strategy of multinational banks. Some of the changes are dealt with at length in later chapters but a summary of key changes and the opportunities and risks these have brought is perhaps useful at this point.

The major commercial banks which sought to adopt a multinational strategy in the 1970s have been drawn inexorably into the development of the global capital market. As that market has evolved so too has the strategy of the international banks. Securitization has led to the rapid extension of off-balance-sheet exposures in order to reduce prices for credit and minimize the requirements for additional, expensive equity capital. In order to participate in these new securities-dominated markets, commercial banks, where regulation has permitted, have added securities-dealing capacity, usually by acquisition and investment banking, to become universal banks. For their part brokerage houses, investment banks and some non-banks have attacked the traditional markets held by the commercial banks by innovating new financial instruments and by globalizing their own operational activities.

Moreover as deregulation has proceeded and developments in technology have speeded communication and transaction times, the blurring of traditional market boundaries has led to the emergence of 24-hour trading in the array of new instruments amongst the main financial centres and all the main global competitors. Heavy investment in information technology, dealing capacity and communication networks to build global trading capability has therefore also become a prerequisite for strategic success for those organizations determined to participate in the new market.

The impact of the investment needs required to build brokerage and investment banking capability and technological superiority has meant that only those organizations of sufficient size to afford such commitments are emerging as the global players. For most institutions the global game is not viable and they must adjust to niche strategy positions.

For the large institutions, therefore, the key opportunity of being a dominant competitor in the rapidly developing global market seems especially attractive. Yet it is fraught with difficulty. Success will largely be dependent on being able to develop and retain key individuals and to sustain technological leadership. Moreover the risks are high. Off-balance-sheet exposures and the speed of dealing make managerial control especially difficult and few oranizations have incumbents in senior management positions experienced in the new market place, or systems of information able to provide reliable management controls. For the safety of the world economy it is to be hoped that the pursuit of global strategies by individual corporations in such a market of accelerating volatility does not result in a possible collapse at electronic speed.

2.5 THE MAJOR FINANCIAL CENTRES

2.5.1 *London*

The three key financial centres of the world are London, New York and Tokyo. Traditionally London has been the leading international centre while New York has been a primary source of innovation especially in capital market instruments. Tokyo, until the past few years, while enjoying a strong domestic market has been tightly regulated by the Ministry of Finance and hence has been slower to develop as an international centre. This position is now changing rapidly as further deregulation occurs in both the United States and Japan to herald the development of the so-called level playing field as in London where brokerage houses, commercial banks and investment banks can all compete with one another without artifical constraint. This is illustrated in Figure 2.1 which shows the differences in permitted activities for different types of institution which still prevail.

Thus, for example, in London domestic and foreign banks can underwrite corporate securities in London but not in Tokyo or New York. Securities companies, domestic and foreign, can deal in foreign exchange in London and New York but not in Tokyo. Securities companies in London may hold a banking licence but

Activity		(1) US Bank Holding Co	(2) Japanese City Bank	(3) UK Clearing Bank	(4) US Securities Firm	(5) Japanese Securities Firm	(6) UK Merchant Bank
Banking License	NY	YES	YES	YES	S	S	S
	LO	YES	YES	YES	YES	YES	YES
	TO	YES	YES	YES	NO	NO	NO
Dealing in Corporate Securities	NY	NO	NO	NO	YES	YES	YES
	LO	YES	YES	YES	YES	YES	YES
	TO	S	NO	S	YES	YES	YES
Foreign Exchange Dealing	NY	YES	YES	YES	YES	YES	YES
	LO	YES	YES	YES	YES	YES	YES
	TO	YES	YES	YES	NO	NO	NO
Dealing in US Treasuries	NY	YES	YES	YES	YES	YES	YES
	LO	YES	YES	YES	YES	YES	YES
	TO	NO	NO	NO	YES	YES	YES
Dealing in UK Gilts	NY	NO	NO	NO	YES	YES	YES
	LO	YES	YES	YES	YES	YES	YES
	TO	NO	NO	NO	YES	YES	YES
Dealing in Japanese Gov't bonds	NY	NO	NO	NO	YES	YES	YES
	LO	YES	YES	YES	YES	YES	YES
	TO	YES	YES	YES	YES	YES	YES
Trust Bank	NY	YES	YES	YES	S	S	S
	LO	YES	YES	YES	YES	YES	YES
	TO	YES	YES	YES	NO	NO	NO
Account at the Central Bank	NY	YES	YES	YES	S	S	S
	LO	YES	YES	YES	YES	YES	YES
	TO	YES	YES	YES	YES	YES	YES

Type of Institution

YES = Full license permitted.
NO = Not generally permitted.
S   = Permitted only through special purpose companies, such as a 50 percent owned affiliate or a nonbank bank.

NY = New York.
LO = London.
TO = Tokyo.

Figure 2.1 International financial centres—permissible activities by type of institution
Source: Federal Reserve Board of New York Quarterly Review, Spring 1987, 3, New York

not in Tokyo and only under certain circumstances in New York. Over time it is to be expected that these differences will disappear and deregulation will be essentially complete in the next few years in the principal markets, leading to an integrated global financial services market place.

By 1987, London had clearly developed as the leading international financial centre in the world. Although both New York and Tokyo exceeded London as domestic markets, London has historically been the centre of the international capital market and had been fundamental in the development of multinational banking from servicing the needs of individual corporations to them becoming critical ingredients in the world financial system. As a result, the range of investment instruments on offer, and the sophistication of the market made London difficult to beat. London was the birthplace of the Eurocurrency markets and despite the relaxation in New York, London had maintained its early lead and still had over 23 per cent of international lending and was the major centre for new issues, although Tokyo in particular had been gaining market share in recent years and overtook New York in 1986 as an international finance centre in terms of volume.

As the leading Euromarket centre, London provided active markets for all the convertible currencies: namely US dollars, Deutschmarks, Swiss francs, French francs, Japanese yen, Dutch guilders and Belgian francs as well as sterling. Deposits in any of these currencies could be made for any time period from overnight to 12 months. Interest rates were related to demand and were linked to domestic interest rates, the volume of foreign transactions in that currency and the position of central banks. London tended to set the interest rates in the Euromarkets which were usually fixed in relation to LIBOR. This rate was independent of, but linked to, the sterling domestic interest rate.

The Japanese banks had been particularly active in building their market share in London during the 1980s. They increased their share of the international loans market to 32 per cent in 1985 and their market share had risen by over 50 per cent from 1980. Much of this growth was in interbank claims on overseas banks and investments. By the end of 1985 Japanese bank's international assets were 40 per cent more than those of British banks and 50 per cent more than the American banks in London[10].

The British capital market did not provide a significant market in foreign bonds due largely to the imposition of tight exchange controls which remained in force until 1979. These controls essentially resulted in a closed market for foreign investors in an effort to stop the outflow of sterling. These restrictions also inhibited the development of a sterling-based Eurobond market. Moreover, those issues that had been made in sterling tended to carry options, exercisable by the holder, for interest and/or principal to be paid in a foreign currency, usually dollars or Deutschmarks. For Eurobond issues other than sterling, however, London was, until 1985 when it was overtaken by Tokyo, the leading primary and secondary market and was the major world centre for Eurobond trading. Over 400 Eurobond issues were listed on the London Stock Exchange but most transactions took place in the over-the-counter market maintained by the major banks in London.

Within the City of London nearly 500 banks, both domestic and foreign, operated. This number had increased considerably since the early 1970s despite the substantial cost of operating in the London market. In addition there were over 20 merchant banks; 11 discount houses; some 20 finance houses; and over 200 stockbroking firms active in the market[11]. Also, London contained a substantial number of commodity brokers, licensed deposit takers, building societies, insurance companies and brokers.

The future of London as the leading international financial centre seemed assured, due to its time zone position and also as a consequence of the growing importance of global dealing for not only foreign exchange but also equities and debt securities. London's advanced deregulation also ensured the maximum level of competition between all forms of financial institutions. With the securitization of lending, the birth of a global electronic equity market and a major foreign exchange market, London allowed commercial banks, investment banks, brokerage houses

[10]*Bank of England Quarterly* op. cit. March 1986, pp. 67–8.
[11]*Ibid.*, p. 379.

and other forms of market maker all to compete in all market sectors, unlike the current position in any other financial centre. Increasingly, the linkage between all forms of financial instrument will grow, leading to a dealing-orientated environment where dealing is done on an electronic exchange. To avoid artificiality between the different market sectors, open access to all competitors will become imperative and regulators will be unable to seperate them if they wish to maintain efficient markets. The position of London and the way it has developed seem likely to force similar deregulation in other leading centres in the Far East and New York.

Deregulation in London reached its peak in October 1986 with the Big Bang which removed the restrictive practices of the London Stock Exchange and led to a dramatic increase in competition as commercial and investment banks, both domestic and foreign, rapidly absorbed most of London's traditional stockbrokers and jobbers to dominate the market. Meanwhile, the traditional floor-based exchange in a few months gave way to electronic trading of both domestic and international equities.

2.5.2   New York

The New York market is the largest and most diversified capital market in the world. With no exchange controls, the US markets have actively encouraged the entry of overseas participants and borrowers. New York is the most important capital market although subsidiary markets also operate in Chicago, Los Angeles and San Francisco. The US market centres are, however, closely linked via an intense network of correspondent relationships. The US market has been at the forefront of securitization. Brokerage houses and investment banks pioneered the development of the US commercial paper market as an alternative to conventional term lending. Since that time a variety of financial activities have been converted into tradable paper including real estate mortgages, automobile loans and the like. A substantial pressure towards securitization has been the development of money market rate interest payments on a variety of bank and savings and loan institution deposits. These funds have needed to be invested in tradable instruments while at the same time the banks have wanted to keep their own asset balances in check due to worries about funds mismatches and difficulties in raising new equity. The techniques for securitizing domestic credit have been transferred to the international capital markets by US brokerage companies and the specialist investment bankers trading in the Euromarket.

A market for CDs denominated in US dollars is made in the USA by its banks. These are held outside the US, primarily in London. Purchasers of these Euo CDs tend to be US multinationals, bank trust departments, money market funds and institutions holding overseas dollars. In addition a wide variety of tradable bond and note instruments has been developed also based in dollars. The Eurodollar bond market is the largest of all the Eurobond markets in terms of amounts issued per annum. In the primary market some $10 billion on average has been issued per annum although this has been rising in line with the growing securitization of the bond market. The majority of new issues have usually been managed by syndicates of international investment banks and brokerage houses located in the principal financial centres. Borrowers have tended to be both US and other multinational corporations.

The market for Eurobonds is unregulated and new issues are not registered with the Securities Exchange Commission or registered on other US domestic stock exchanges. UK residents are not normally allowed to purchase Eurobonds in the primary market except when such issues are made as private placements. By contrast, the secondary market for Eurobonds is very active. The corporate bond market in the US is the largest in the world with respect to both borrowers and investors. Eurobonds are also quoted in many foreign stock exchanges. Most dealing, however, takes place through bank over-the-counter markets in the new international financial centres.

The New York market is also critical in the grading of bond issues. Three agencies rate individual corporations on a regular annual basis. This organizations, Standard & Poors, Moodies and Fitches, issue ratings on new and existing bonds on a regular and directly comparable basis. Bonds rated in the top four categories (AAA, AA, A and BBB) are regarded as eligible for bank investments and are therefore known as bank quality bonds.

The US markets have also been instrumental in the development of futures markets. By buying financial futures an investor can buy an interest rate contract which locks in a known rate of return. Thus, if he expects future interest rates to fall he could sell forward, while if he expects rates to rise he would do the converse. Three major futures markets have developed, the Chicago Board of Trade, the International Monetary Market (IMM), a division of the Chicago Mercantile Exchange, and the New York Futures Market (NYFM). The futures currency markets of the IMM and NYFM offer similar facilities to the forward foreign exchange markets but differ in their manner of operation. Major participants in these markets are commercial banks dealing in foreign exchange, and multinational companies anxious to hedge against exchange risks. On the IMM market eight currencies are traded, while on the NYFM this was restricted to five. On these markets, contracts were made for quarterly delivery in contrast to the foreign exchange markets where forward contracts can be made for variable time periods. Transactions are also of fixed sizes equivalent to $50,000 and $100,000 compared with the possibility of making contracts for odd amounts in the foreign exchange markets. This diversity of markets, however, provides opportunities for arbitraging between them.

At the end of 1986 there were more than 250 foreign banks operating in the USA. The assets of these banks exceeded $500 billion and constituted nearly 20 per cent of US banking assets. This figure was somewhat inflated by the fact that the largest participants—the Japanese banks, with assets of $245 billion and a total market share of 8.7 per cent of banking assets—booked most of their Western hemisphere loans in their US branches.

Japanese banks were by far and away the most dominant group of foreign banks, accounting for nearly half the total assets and commercial loans outstanding at foreign banks. The Japanese accounted for 20 per cent of all commercial and industrial loans outstanding to US addresses and between a quarter and a half of standby LCs and guarantees associated with US municipal bond offerings.

In addition to the Japanese banks, the big four Japanese securities dealers were emerging as a powerful threat to the domestic securities houses. Since 1984, the Japanese had rapidly expanded their historically small offices, encouraged by the US authorities eager to find sources of finance to cover the US budget deficit. By 1986, Nomura and Daiwa Securities had been so successful that they were recognized by the Federal Reserve Bank of New York as primary dealers in government securities, entitling them to trade directly with the Federal Reserve and recognizing them as competitors equivalent to the leading US institutions. The Japanese were also building their market share positions in other markets.

New York was, however, still regulated by the Glass–Steagall Act which prevented commercial banks from full participation in the securities markets, although loopholes had been established to allow some banks to operate in the commercial paper market. Whilst some traditionalists sought to maintain this increasingly artifical barrier between commercial banking and investment banks and brokerage houses, events in the international capital markets seemed destined ultimately to sweep this restriction aside.

2.5.3 Tokyo

The Japanese capital markets have emerged rapidly in importance since the beginning of the 1980s. The Japanese domestic market has traditionally been very active in both commercial paper and bonds, however, the increase in Japan's trading surplus coupled with deregulation has stimulated considerable growth in the Tokyo market as an international centre. The banking system as described in Chapter 4 has been historically closely linked to the corporate market, although with securitization coming to Japan and the cash surpluses accumulated by Japanese companies, bank lending has declined sharply.

The bonds issued by foreign corporations, international institutions and sovereign states denominated in yen have been designated as Samurai bonds. While very small in terms of the total of bonds traded domestically, the Samurai bonds have become important in a global perspective, and in terms of new issues, the Japanese market is the fourth largest for foreign bond issue after Switzerland, the USA and West Germany.

All early issuers of Samurai bonds have been international

agencies such as the World Bank. The first corporate Samurai bond was issued to Sears Roebuck in 1979. Bonds are issued in both bearer and registered form but can be readily converted from one to the other. Interest is paid semi-annually with maturities of 10–15 years. New issues are strictly monitored and controlled by the Ministry of Finance and the Bank of Japan.

In the primary market, new issues are arranged by the leading securities companies, Nomura, Nikko, Daiwa and Yamaichi. Non-resident investors are allowed to purchase only 25 per cent of new issues in the primary market. This restriction does not hold in the secondary market, however, and about 50 per cent of bonds are held by foreign investors. The slow growth of the Samurai market was due to restrictions on issues such as a minimum A rating, a two-month lead time to issue to clear underwriters' terms and conditions and a full prospectus.

Much more recently the Shogun bond market was opened with the issue by the Bank of Tokyo of $300 million for the World Bank in August 1985. These bonds were denominated in foreign currencies but issued in Japan. By early 1987 15 such issues had been completed but only two of these had been for pure corporate names. The relatively thin market for Shogun bonds was due to the reluctance by many Japanese investors to take positions in foreign currencies at a time of rapid appreciation of the yen.

Much of the growth in the Euroyen market had therefore come not from an increase in demand for yen but from swap deals. These were bond issues in which the borrower raises yen at low long-term interest rates and swaps the proceeds immediately for another currency, usually US dollars. Because of the bureaucratic restrictions imposed by the Ministry of Finance, Japanese bond underwriters found themselves at a disadvantage in matching the speed of Euromarket dealers in London. As a result much of the Euroyen bond growth had occurred via the London subsidiaries of Japanese underwriters. In addition, in London the Japanese banks were not precluded from participating in securities activities.

As a result of US pressure the Japanese capital market was being opened at a speed which surprised many observers. From December 1984 foreign corporations, state and local governments and government agencies with a credit rating of A or better were authorized to issue Euroyen bonds in a similar way to Samurai bonds and restrictions on the number and size of issues were eased. Foreign institutions were also allowed to act as lead managers for the first time.

In 1985, withholding tax on Euroyen bond issues by Japanese residents was abolished to encourage Japanese corporations to issue Euroyen bonds. Later in the year the market was broadened to include substantially more Japanese corporations by relaxing credit standards for domestic issues. FRNs zero coupon bonds and dual currency issues were also permitted for non-resident borrowers. Late in the year overseas subsidiaries of Japanese corporations were also allowed to issue Euroyen bonds under the same criteria as their foreign competitors. Late in 1986, a Japanese offshore market was also established and by mid 1987, 181 Japanese and foreign banks had applied for licences to open offshore accounts.

Interest rates on large time deposits were also freed from government control, leading to a rapid growth in CDs, money market certificates, acceptance credits and short-term government bonds. Moreover this was a first step towards a policy of complete interest rate freedom as prevailed in London and New York.

A number of foreign commercial banks were also allowed to establish securities affiliates thus breaching the traditional barrier between banks and securities houses. Led by Citcorp, with its purchase of the London securities house Vickers da Costa which had a seat on the Tokyo exchange, other US banks such as Chase, Security Pacific and Morgan Guaranty swiftly followed. Similarly European banks with a universal banking tradition were also active. Japanese banks, still excluded from their own securities market, were endeavouring to seek similar concessions for their London-based merchant banks also to open offices in Japan. Further since 1985, nine foreign banks had been granted permission to establish trust banking subsidiaries in most cases with the active encouragement and support of the Japanese trust banks, so allowing them to participate in the huge domestic market for managed funds. By the use of swaps the leading Japanese City banks had also managed to change their capital base to obtain long-term funds, traditionally the historic preserve of the long-term credit banks whose special status was under active review.

Despite this widespread and rapid deregulation in the Japanese market more changes were anticipated. These included removals of control of interest rates on small deposits including those taken by the Post Office, a key source of government funds in Japan; the creation of corporate bond and commercial paper markets; and the opening of the Stock Exchange to general membership and the removal of fixed commission rates[12].

Despite these moves, which had been welcomed by European and US authorities, there were still considered to be many restrictions on foreign financial institutions operating in Tokyo. Firstly, it was not felt that non-Japanese firms were given equal treatment; for example, only a limited number of seats were given to foreign firms on the Tokyo Stock Exchange, and foreign banks tended to be excluded from syndicates allowed to bid for Japanese government debt. Secondly, regulatory policies still prohibited foreign institutions from operating in some markets, such as brokerage firms from the foreign exchange markets, while regulatory and administrative rigidities in the money markets inhibited foreign competition. Third, foreign companies found it extremely difficult, if not impossible, to acquire financial institutions in Japan although Japanese banks in particular, had, in part, developed their overseas interests by acquisition, especially in the USA. Fourth, unlike in most financial centres, foreign banks had little or no access to the cheap retail deposits enjoyed by the Japanese banks, but rather were obliged to bring in funds from abroad or use the underdeveloped local wholesale market. Finally, and most important, there were substantial invisible barriers to foreign firms operating in Japan caused by the policy of the Ministry of Finance of operating via the difficult-to-interpret method of 'window guidance'. This informal method of obtaining concurrence with central policy from the financial institutions was considered to be the most difficult supervisory system for foreign organizations to understand in the world[13].

[12]*Financial Times* Survey, Japan banking finance and investment, 16 February 1987, p. 1.
[13]E. Gerald Corrigan, A perspective on the globalisation of financial markets and institutions, Federal Reserve Bank of New York, *Quarterly Review*, Spring 1987, p. 6.

As a result only 79 foreign banks operated in Japan by 1987, most of these trading at a loss, while even the most profitable earned only a meagre return on assets. While this represented a substantial increase on the numbers operating in the early 1970s it was small compared with the presence of non-indigenous institutions in London or New York.

The build-up of the Japanese trade surplus, which in turn had sharply increased the availability of investable funds, had, however, led the authorities to relax the rules on foreign entrants into the market for investment advice and management. In 1986 a new law was introduced covering all aspects of investment advice and discretionary investment management. By April 1987, 35 non-Japanese companies had been granted licences to establish investment advisory operations and 25 had applied for discretionary investment management licences.

Similarly foreign participants were being allowed to enter the rapidly growing securities trading market. The number of foreign-owned securities companies licensed to operate in Japan grew from 10 in 1984 to 36 by early 1987 and was expected to reach 50 by the end of that year. Membership of the Tokyo Stock Exchange, however, remained elusive and had led to an embarrassing row between the British and Japanese governments in early 1987, with threats to withdraw licences granted to Japanese institutions in London unless British firms gained greater access to the Tokyo market. The securities bureau of the MOF was expected to pressurize the exchange to admit more foreign members in 1988 as most Japanese major stocks moved to screen-based trading and more space became available. Commission rates on the exchange also remained fixed and, as Tokyo trading volumes had grown to around 70 per cent of those of New York, with only 93 full members compared with more than 600 in New York, brokerage profits in Tokyo were especially attractive. Further, these profits were being used to fuel the penetration of the leading Japanese brokerage houses in London and New York.

However, the securities industry and the banks remained divided by Japan's equivalent of the US Glass–Steagall legislation, Clause 65. The MOF recognized that ultimately the traditional barriers which prevented the development of financial conglomerates in Japan would have to be removed but the different bureaux within the ministry jealously guarded the historic privileges of their constituents. Rather the strategy of the MOF was to expand the areas where different groups of institutions could compete equally. As a consequence banks and securities companies by 1987 were competing in newly developed areas of the market such as the underwriting and sale of government bonds, trading in bond futures, CDs, acceptance credits and yen-dominated commercial paper[14].

Tokyo, by 1987, was clearly moving towards establishing itself as the third key link in the global capital market. Much deregulation remained to be implemented before it was as free as London but clearly, despite the conservative attitudes of many in the MOF, Japan was expected to shift towards an open system. How the MOF would itself evolve to try and maintain its traditional managerial role over the Japanese economy remained an interesting and open question.

2.5.4 Paris

Paris has evolved as an important centre for the Euromarkets. Although smaller than London, Paris is one of Europe's major markets for Eurodollar call and time deposits. In 1986 French banks held foreign assets of $241 billion compared with $957 billion held by UK-based banks, $469 billion for US-based institutions and $614 billion for Japanese banks. The French domestic market has been severly restricted by regulations, although the Euromarket has been able to expand much more rapidly. Since the mid 1970s, the French-franc-denominated Eurobond market has declined in importance. In the early 1970s French franc bonds were significant, being surpassed only by bonds denominated in dollars and Deutschmarks. From the mid 1970s, however, the French market was essentially closed as a result of government regulations. The market reopened in 1978 but until the mid 1980s remained severely restricted. New issues were closely monitored by the French monetary authorities which required approval over the timing of any new issues.

[14]C. Jones, Dismantling business, *The Banker*, June 1987, pp. 44–9.

Franc issues were sold on a secondary market operated by the banks operating in the main European financial centres and especially on the London and Luxembourg exchanges. The tight regulations imposed by the French government without doubt inhibited the development of Paris as an international financial centre. This became recognized in the mid 1980s and France was embarking on a policy of rapid deregulation similar to some extent to the developments in London. In 1986 the French franc Eurobond market was reopened to public and private French and foreign borrowers. Swaps and convertible bonds were authorized but not FRNs initially. In December 1985 a commercial paper market was also permitted. In late 1987 full-scale deregulation was scheduled along the lines of the Big Bang in London and the major state-owned French banks were to be denationalized. The timetable for denationalization was however, put back as a consequence of the October 1987 crash.

2.5.5 Luxembourg

Luxembourg has emerged as an important Eurobond market place and Eurocurrency deposit centre. This has been encouraged by the local government's flexible attitude towards international banking. Many international banks have therefore established in Luxembourg. This has been especially true of the leading German commercial banks, which have traditionally used Luxembourg as the front for their Euromarket operations because they have not been required to provide the reserve requirements which would have been the case if they had opted to operate the same facilities in West Germany.

After London, Luxembourg was the second centre for secondary trading in Eurobonds. Little primary issuing occurred, however. Because the major German banks were discouraged by official reserve requirements which inhibited the flow of capital into the country, they had established Luxembourg subsidiaries to provide their primary vehicles for operating in the Euromarkets. The Eurodeutschmark bond market was, therefore, operated out of Luxembourg in both primary and secondary market forms.

While most Eurobonds were listed on the Luxembourg stock exchange, most transactions took place over the counter of the international banks. The size of the Eurobond market was some fifty times bigger than that of the domestic market. Luxembourg had, however, been losing ground to London due to the latter's greater diversity and superior dealing facilities. This trend was perhaps accelerating as the bond markets and the foreign exchange markets moved more to a dealing mode and a number of leading German banks switched their primary Euromarket operations to London.

2.5.6 Switzerland

Switzerland consists of a federation of 26 centres operating within a federal constitution. Zurich is in the main financial centre although both Geneva and Basle have emerged as significant secondary centres. As a rule, inward and outward investment are deregulated. However, because of the attractiveness of the economy, financial inflows have occasionally exceeded outflows, resulting in official constraints such as charges on Swiss franc deposits or a tax on non-resident purchases of Swiss securities.

The Swiss capital market is active in both local and foreign bonds and shares. The stock exchange is the second largest in Europe after London while the foreign bond market exceeds that of New York. Foreign bonds are the largest components of new issues on the Swiss capital market. Moreover, the Swiss market accounts for some 40 per cent of the total world market for foreign bonds. In addition, the major Swiss banks are major issuers of short-, medium- and long-term Eurocredits which are denominated in Swiss francs.

Foreign bonds are denominated in Swiss francs and issued by non-Swiss corporations, governments and international agencies. Japanese companies have been particularly important issuers of Swiss franc bonds. Foreign borrowers are, however, carefully vetted and only the best risks find it easy to tap the Swiss capital market. Lenders are, therefore, assured as to credit risk, while borrowers gain international prestige by being allowed to participate in the market.

While there is no primary Eurobond market in Switzerland, due to opposition from the central bank, there is an active market in secondary trading. A wide range of Eurobonds denominated in currencies other than Swiss francs is actively traded on the Swiss stock exchanges as well as over the counter in banks and licensed security traders. The major Swiss banks are very active in the primary Eurobond issuing market as lead managers and syndicate participants. The placing power of the banks has been especially important in gaining these lead positions. A very significant proportion of Eurocurrency issues have ended up as securities held in the investment portfolios of Swiss banks.

2.5.7   Hong Kong

Based on a free market economy, Hong Kong was one of the most open capital markets in the world. There was no exchange control, dealing costs were low and no withholding taxes applied. This flexibility had led to a rapid growth in the number of financial institutions in the market, despite the threat hanging over the Crown Colony caused by possible changes resulting from a return to rule by the Peoples Republic of China in the mid 1990s.

There was an active market in Hong Kong of Eurocurrency call and time deposits which were subsequently placed through Sinapore and other Euromarket centres. Maturities were normally for terms from two days to two years and no minimum set amount applied. A market for Hong Kong dollar Eurobonds was initiated in 1977. These bonds were in bearer form with interest payable annually in Hong Kong dollars and free of withholding tax. The market has been of limited importance due to the weakness of the Hong Kong dollar. A secondary market in other currency bonds was maintained in Hong Kong, however, and more transactions were handled than in any other Asian financial centre.

2.5.8   Singapore

The financial centre in Asia was Singapore until the mid 1980s. Flexible government policies to encourage the growth of an international financial services industry had led to substantial international banking development in Singapore. The country had also encouraged the development of the Asia dollar market—the local equivalent of the Eurodollar market. This market was for short-term loans and borrowings in any convertible currency, and an international market for the issue of medium- and long-term bonds in any convertible currency. Much of the trading volume in the market took place between Singapore and Hong Kong.

The Asia dollar market was originally established by the Bank of America, encouraged by the government, in 1968. The bank established an Asian Currency Unit (ACU) of which there are now more than one hundred. The ACUs in Singapore accept both overnight and long-term deposits from a few days up to 12 months. The majority of such deposits are placed in US dollars. There is no fixed minimum amount to deposits but the usually accepted minimum is $25,000 per transaction or its equivalent. Rates in the Asian dollar market are somewhat more competitive than in the domestic market, thus creating arbitrage opportunities.

Apart from the government's incentives to develop the market, Singapore has a substantial time zone advantage. It provides a vital link between the Euromarkets in Japan and San Francisco and those in London and Western Europe. Singapore can start its day dealing with Tokyo and San Francisco and at the end of the day can hand over to London, Frankfurt and Zurich to help generate the 24 hour a day global markets in foreign exchange and securities dealing.

2.5.9 Offshore Centres

In addition to the major capital markets, during the 1970s a number of offshore Euromarket centres developed. These centres, usually located in low- or no-tax areas where the authorities had created a favourable environment for banking, became important booking centres for Euromarket transactions. Most of the arrangements for such transactions, however, were still made in London or New York. As the market has moved increasingly towards the issue of bonds and away from syndicated credits, the position of these offshore centres has tended to decline. Thus the volume of international bank lending out of the USA doubled from 1981 to 1983 and grew by 90 per cent in Singapore and by 30 per cent in London. By contrast, in the offshore centres of the Bahamas, Bahrain, the Cayman Islands, Luxembourg and Panama, lending to non-residents only grew by 14 per cent[15].

In part the decline in offshore centres has been due to the regulatory authorities in the major centres becoming more flexible. While regulations constrained the development of multinational banking, the banks were motivated to set up offshore centres where their operations were uninhibited. Arrangements could still be made in the major centres but transactions, the component of a deal subject to supervisory control, were conducted in offshore centres. By the early 1980s most authorities had come to recognize this and had decided that they would move to flexibilize their approach rather than lose total control of the global deregulated market.

In the United States, therefore, the opening of International Banking Facilities (IBFs) led to a substantial return of business to New York from the offshore centres of the Caribbean. The trend towards the established centres has also been compounded by events which have demonstrated that the multinational banks and the global capital market are not wholly remote from political intervention. In 1979, therefore, market confidence was rocked when the US authorities froze assets in US bank branches worldwide held by the Iran government and its agencies. Similarly, in 1983, the Philippines authorities blocked the deposits in Citibank's branch in Manila, many of which were interbank deposits. As a result of these incidents and the collapse of banking affiliates in secondary centres such as Luxembourg and Panama, where there was no adequate lender of last resort, banks have come to recognize that the lack of any form of supervision in an unregulated market can be dangerous. Some supervision has, therefore, been seen as desirable and hence the trend back to the established centres where central banks, while not controlling the market, can act to stop dangerous practice which might lead to instability and a fatal loss of confidence.

[15]L. Sadler, The final days of offshore banking, Institutional Investor, June 1984, p. 61–66.

2.6 CONCLUSION

In the past 25 years, concurrent with the development of multinational banking, a worldwide deregulated capital market has emerged. Based initially in London, it has evolved as a global market linking the world's major domestic capital markets and essentially creating an interlocking financial system which is no longer controllable by any individual government or nation. Key players in this market have been the multinational banks, investment bankers and brokerage houses which have both participated in the market and helped to shape it. The development of the capital market and multinational banking have therefore gone hand in hand, being mutually dependent.

The development of multinational banking strategy also owes much to the two oil price shocks of the 1970s which led to a dramatic extension of the role of the private sector banks in the international financial system and transformed the size and scale of the market. In the 1980s the development of the Japanese trade surplus has similarly led to the growing internationalization of the yen and the emergence of Japanese financial institutions as key players in the global capital market. The yen has begun to rival the dollar as the leading reserve currency while Tokyo has emerged as the world's third key financial centre.

In the deregulated environment, the international market participants have also proved to be extraordinarily innovative, with the creation of a remarkable array of monetary and near monetary instruments. In the past few years there has been a fundamental shift in the market away from conventional bank lending and towards the introduction of more marketable securities such as commercial paper, swaps and floating rate notes. This trend has led to much closer links being forged between the bond and syndicated credit markets. Volumes have also tended to increase sharply due to additional trading.

There has also been a fundamental effect on competition, with commercial banks, investment banks and brokerage houses now, where regulations permit, in direct competition with one another where once each operated in carefully segregated sectors of the market. Further integration can be expected in the future linking the foreign exchange, financial futures, bonds, loans and equities markets to some extent in a form of global exchange. In this new deregulated market the active institutions will be able to interchange between the various sectors of the market via swaps and the like to create and almost infinite array of possible financial instruments. The implications of this for the regulatory authorities are dramatic. No longer will individual governments be able to control their exchange rates or isolate their financial markets from the rest of the world. Attempts to do so will only transfer action to countries or centres outside the control of individual governments. As a result monetary policy will increasingly need to reflect the wishes of the participants in the global capital market rather than the national desires of specific national governments, leading to a growing commonality in national fiscal and monetary policies.

For those concerned with monitoring the banking systems new checks and balances need to be developed not merely on a national but on a global basis to monitor the impact of securitization and off-balance-sheet risk. Moreover, the authorities will need to embrace not only banks but other key players in the system such as brokerage houses, and increasingly, large multinational corporations which can also act as banks yet not be subject to the same regulatory guidelines. Regulators will also have to consider not merely their own domestic environments but the position of their own institutions within the global market place to ensure that a similarity exists with the regulatory position in the global financial centres. The days of national isolation created by regulatory walls are over.

CHAPTER 3

Multinational Banking and the Foreign Exchange Market

3.1 THE FOREIGN EXCHANGE MARKETS

The growth of multinational banking and the development of the global capital market occurred concurrently. At the same time a third element in the emergence of the world financial system had been the changing pattern of the foreign exchange market. This, too, has exhibited massive growth which increasingly has not been related to world trade but rather has been the result of shorter term speculative movement, as much based on sentiment as economic factors. The foreign exchange market has also served as a bridge to the international capital markets as the flow of international investment has increased, with the multinational banks providing an important interface function.

As with the capital markets, the foreign exchange markets has also moved from a tightly regulated system, sustained by the central banks of the leading industrial countries supporting one another to maintain fixed rate parities, to a deregulated market. However, in the late 1980s efforts were in hand for the major industrial nations again to seek to stabilize international exchange rates within agreed bands. The build-up of offshore funds brought on by the growth of multinational business, improved treasury management and cumulative deficits built up especially by the United States, together with a growing volume of international investment, however, has meant that an ever larger pool of funds, not subject to central bank control, could be moved for or against a chosen currency, according to sentiment and perceived relative risk. This flow of funds had grown from a stream in the 1960s to a torrent in the 1980s, making it difficult, if not impossible, even for groups of central banks, acting in concert, to hold the line on a particular currency even when they wished to for any length of time. This has led to the collapse of the system of fixed exchange rates and introduced the era of floating exchange rates despite the recent efforts of the central banks to return to a more stable system. This chapter explores the development of the foreign exchange markets, describes their current working and explores the linkages with the international capital market.

3.2   THE BRETTON WOODS ERA

In 1944 at the Bretton Woods Conference, the International Monetary Fund (IMF), was established by the leading Western countries with the objective of ensuring that the member states would manage their exchange rates and balance of payments in a responsible manner. The new fund was charged with supplying funds as and when necessary to assist the central banks in this task according to the quotas of funds each goverment agreed to contribute to the new institutions. These funds would be made available by subscriptions by member states and from borrowings made by the IMF itself. Member states also agreed to make their currencies convertible and to maintain their value at fixed rates relative to gold.

In the immediate post-war period the need to restore the war-ravaged economies of Western Europe made convertibility impossible. A series of offset arrangements was therefore made to handle the balance of payments deficits and surpluses incurred by the member states. Between 1950–8 this was achieved by the European Payments Union, which superseded a series of earlier arrangements.

In 1958, an attempt was made to restore convertibility as the European economies recovered. This, however, exposed problems which had been hidden by the previous offset arrangements. The principle of convertibility meant that funds in the foreign exchange market could move from currency to currency or into gold, so placing pressure on the central banks to maintain their parities by buying or selling currency or gold. In particular some currencies, such as that of West Germany, were seen to be undervalued while sterling and, to some extent, the dollar were overvalued. These latter currencies were the two main reserve currencies. The need for adjustments in the fixed rates of exchange led to pressures being exerted on individual currencies or moves in and out of gold. In 1960, for example, there was a gold crisis, in 1961 the Deutschmark was revalued and sterling came under pressure to devalue.

Such pressures led the central bankers to produce the First Basle Agreement, which accepted that speculative movements of funds would not force individual countries to deviate from agreed exchange rate policy. While the volume of funds in the open market at this time was relatively small in relation to the combined resources of the central banks, there was still enough pressure to cause a series of rapid crises by moves against sterling and the dollar and a rising demand for gold. To alleviate this pressure, the USA, UK, Germany, France, Italy, Belgium, Holland and Switzerland (members of the Group of Ten) established the Gold Pool, to centralize their dealing in gold. The Pool was managed by the Bank of England which sold gold as necessary to support sterling and the dollar, the supply of gold being provided by the Pool member states on an agreed quota basis. The Pool members also bought gold when market conditions justified.

Continued pressure on sterling and the dollar made it obvious that IMF funds might be inadequate against a concerted run on either of the major currencies. It was therefore agreed, in 1962, to establish the General Arrangements to Borrow under which the Group of Ten would make extra loans available to support sterling and the dollar. These arrangements were later modified to cover the currencies of all the member states. The US Federal Reserve also established a system of swaps of currency between the US Central Bank and others. These funds could then be used to intervene in the foreign exchange markets to support the dollar. Prior to 1961 the Federal Reserve had not operated in the foreign exchange markets and held no foreign currency which could be used for intervention purposes.

The swap arrangement was thus necessary in 1961 when the dollar was under pressure relative to the Deutschmark. The Federal Reserve held no Deutschmarks with which it could intervene in the market. An informal swap was therefore made with the Bundesbank to provide Deutschmarks which the Federal Reserve could sell to relieve pressure on the dollar. The success of this venture led the Federal Reserve subsequently to establish a series of formal swap arrangements with all the main central banks and the Bank for International Settlements (BIS). The swaps could also work in the other direction, with the Federal Reserve providing dollars to be used by other central banks. The Bank of England was to make frequent use of these arrangements over the years in regular defences of sterling.

The role of sterling as a central reserve currency came under increasing pressure during the 1960s as a result of decolonization and the declining position of the UK economy. A sterling crisis in 1964 forced the Bank of England to arrange for a second Basle Agreement under which an extra $500 million dollar swap arrangement was made to be followed later with a $3 billion line of credit from 11 central banks and the BIS[1]. The continuing pressures on sterling were seen as being due to the large overseas holdings of sterling held by individuals and governments. At times of weakness therefore, there were large sums which could be placed into the foreign exchange markets, adding to the pressure on the currency. A formal agreement was therefore reached with the Group of Ten to insulate the UK from the sale of these large overseas sterling balances. In 1968, the UK thus agreed with specific countries that they would hold a fixed percentage of their reserves in sterling against a guaranteed exchange rate. These arrangments remained in force until 1976 when sterling again came under great pressure and IMF standby credit of $3.4 billion were agreed, followed by a series of

---

[1]B. Teur, *International Monetary Corporation 1945–70*, Hutchinson University Laboratory, London, 1970, pp. 261–2.

medium-term credits from the BIS and 11 central banks, to protect the UK against withdrawal of the Sterling Balances[2].

While the 1966 arrangements provided temporary respite for sterling, the second Arab-Israeli war led to a move into gold and the pressure on sterling returned, leading to devaluation in 1967. As a result, market pressure switched to other currencies while the price of gold continued to rise until, in 1968, a crisis was reached when the gold pool was disbanded and a two-tier pricing system for gold was introduced. Under this system gold transactions between central banks took place at a fixed price while in the free market the price of gold was allowed to float.

By the late 1960s, continued weakness of the US economy and a growing trade deficit led to a rapid rise in the size of the pool of funds available to the emerging Euromarkets. As indicated in Chapter 1 this period coincided with the first phase of modern multinational bank development by the leading US money centre banks. At the same time there was also a fear that there might be a shortage in short-term international liquidity. It was proposed therefore, that a new international asset be established. The French, who had converted much of their foreign reserves into gold at the fixed rate agreed between central banks, favoured an increase in the fixed price of gold, but this was strongly opposed by the US which recognized such a move as a devaluation of the dollar. Eventually in 1969, Special Drawing Rights (SDRs) were created as a new form of IMF borrowing. Downward pressure on the dollar and upward pressure on the Deutschmark continued, however, and in 1971, at the Smithsonian Conference in Washington, a further currency realignment was made. This was to be the last international attempt to maintain the principle of convertible fixed exchange rates.

In 1969, the heads of state of the governments of the EEC had agreed to move towards a common monetary system, leading to total integration of the European currencies into a common unit by 1980. The plan also determined to reduce the trading margin tolerances permitted between the European currencies, with the central banks intervening in the markets, using the currencies of the community, to maintain relative parities. This system, which

[2]J. Walmsley, *The Foreign Exchange Handbook*, Wiley, New York, 1983, pp. 56–68.

came to be known as the Snake, allowed individual currencies to move in the market by up to plus or minus 2.25 per cent against other currencies of the community and up to 4.5 per cent against non-community currencies, such as the dollar. While the Snake initially included all the member states of the community when it started in 1972, there was an immediate run on sterling, forcing the British government to withdraw from the system after only seven weeks. In addition, despite the dollar devaluation in 1971, pressure switched back to the US currency again in the face of combined US balance of trade deficits. As a result in March 1973 the US government decided to float the dollar.

3.3 THE EMERGENCE OF THE FLOATING RATE MARKET

The US move was initially expected to be of only temporary duration as previous floats by various governments had been. After an initial period when rates rose or fell, a floating currency was expected to find its own level before the re-establishment of a new fixed rate. However the outbreak of the Third Arab-Israeli War led to the first oil shock. The Arab oil producers, in order to put pressure on the West, suddenly raised the price of crude. While this resulted in a massive revision in the flow of world funds it also threw the foreign exchange markets into turmoil. Like sterling before, the French franc was forced to drop out of the European Snake as the markets moved against countries dependent upon heavy imports of OPEC crude oil. As a result, therefore, what had been expected to be a temporary floating of the dollar turned into the beginning of a new era.

The floating of exchange rates effectively turned the international markets into a form of short-term commodity trading game. The Swiss banks, apparently in the belief that they could obtain an especially favourable position, moved heavily into foreign exchange dealings. However, casualties also soon occurred. Union Bank of Switzerland was forced to sustain an estimated loss of $150 million in 1973 while Westdeutsche Landesbanke Girozentrale lost $105 million[3].

[3]Channon, *British Banking Strategy*, p. 119.

In June 1974, however, the West German bank I. D. Hersatt collapsed with massive foreign exchange losses of some $500 million. The West German authorities moved to close the bank, but handled the situation badly by announcing their intention while the New York market was still trading. This resulted in a number of spot forex transactions being incomplete, potentially transferring part of the Hersatt position to innocent banks with which it had been trading. While the responsibilities in the Hersatt affair were subsequently resolved, it led to a tightening of supervision by the central banks, and the creation of a committee on banking regulations and supervision led by the BIS, in an attempt to reduce the risk of similar failures in the future. The first oil shock thus led to drastic realignments in international financial values as most Western industrialized countries moved into deficit to fund their oil purchases. The IMF established an oil facility in 1974 to help recycle the surpluses now created in the OPEC countries to those countries in deficit. Much of this role was ultimately undertaken by the major multinational banks as described in Chapter 5. The first oil shock, however, also dramatically increased the pool of funds which were on relatively short-term deposit in the Euromarkets. These funds also moved rapidly from currency to currency, via the foreign exchange markets, making it virtually impossible for central banks to maintain long-term fixed exchange rates as the flow of funds in the market was far higher than the reserves available to the authorities. The era of floating rates had begun.

As it became clear that floating rates would remain, adjustments were necessary in the definitions of the SDR and the European Unit of Account. A currency basket definition of the SDR was introduced in 1974, while the EEC introduced a similar type of definition for the European Unit of Account in 1975[4]. The IMF Articles of Agreement also needed to be changed, since floating exchange rates were contrary to its constitution. At the Jamaica Agreement in 1976, therefore, a Second Amendment to the IMF Articles legalized floating rates. The new agreement also abandoned a fixed price for gold which was removed as a vehicle

---

[4]Walmsley, op. cit., p. 63; see also J. J. Polak, The SDR as a banker of currencies, IMF Staff Papers, December 1979, IMF, Washington.

for intercurrency parity. Gold prices had tended to rise sharply due to the uncertainties introduced as a result of the first oil shock.

A third of the gold holdings of the IMF were either returned to its members or sold at auction, with the profits from the proceeds of the sale being used to benefit lesser developed country members of the fund. These gold auctions took place between 1976 and 1980. The US treasury also sold part of its own gold holdings, but other countries actually began to buy gold. Thus while the US and IMF were attempting to break the link between gold and international currency values, this policy was not universally adopted by others and France, in particular, which had been an active holder of gold, revalued its holdings at market prices to boost its reserve position. Other countries followed suit, and a number of them used their revalued holdings as collateral for loans.

The main funds flows from the OPEC countries found their way into dollars and sterling, providing an initial boost to both currencies. In 1976, however, under a Labour administration, the UK moved into a serious balance of payments deficit. A rapid run on sterling occurred as OPEC surpluses held in London moved to dollars and the pound fell sharply. This led to the provision of further IMF Standby Credits and medium-term support through the BIS.

Since 1976 each periodic political and economic crisis had seen rapid movements in any currency—with the flow of funds being so great and so rapid that the monetary authorities had found it increasingly difficult to do anything other than iron out temporary disorderly markets. The markets had become global, with the speed of money movements accelerating rapidly as a result of improvements in dealing technology.

While underlying economic factors, such as the balance of payments, relative international productivity, wage rates, the level of inflation and success in international trade were key to the exchange rates of individual currencies, the foreign exchange markets had also demonstrated substantial short-term fluctuation largely unrelated to these longer term economic trends. Thus in addition to the traditional economic factors every major political event had also triggered rapid shifts in the market.

Major international political events, such as the overthrow of the Shah of Iran, the second oil shock, the election of a Conservative government in the UK, the US hostage crisis in Iran, the threat of Muslim Shi-ite extremists in Saudi Arabia, the Soviet invasion of Afghanistan, the Polish crisis between government and workers, the election and subsequent attempted assassination of President Reagan, the death of President Sadat of Egypt, the socialist polities of President Mitterand, had all led to rapid and major shifts in the values of individual currencies or gold. Moreover, such movements had tended to become increasingly violent, as the volume of the foreign exchange markets had grown sharply compared to both the level of world trade and that of the sum of official reserves.

3.4   THE DECLINE AND FALL OF THE DOLLAR

During the early 1980s the dollar sharply increased in value against other major currencies. At the same time, however, the US trade deficit had begun to grow as exports fell due to the uncompetitiveness of US industry and a rising flood of imports, especially from the Far East. By 1985 it had become clear that the dollar was becoming dangerously overvalued. As a result, in September the central banks of the five leading industrial nations, meeting in New York, agreed to try and orchestrate a smooth decline in the value of the dollar. In addition, the US sought to keep its domestic economy growing and to reduce interest rates.

Initially the Plaza accord, as the agreement between the central banks became known, appeared to work smoothly. The dollar began an orderly decline as the views of the central banks became known and they intervened collectively in the foreign exchange markets. However, as 1986 wore on the orderly retreat became increasingly to look like a rout as the markets moved massively against the dollar and in favour in particular of the yen and the Deutschmark, as shown in Figure 3.1

Although the central banks intervened increasingly in the market to try and stabilize the dollar's decline the markets themselves found little to be optimistic about. By mid 1986 the

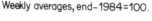

Weekly averages, end–1984=100.

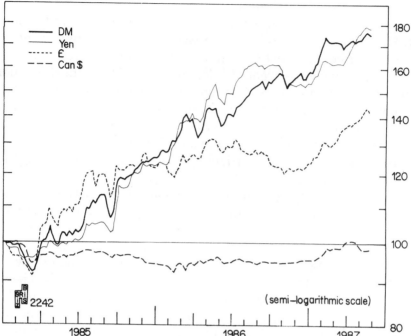

Figure 3.1 Bilateral exchange rates of selected currencies against the dollar (1984–7)
Source: BIS

dollar exchange rate against the Deutschmark, the Swiss franc and the yen had depreciated by over 60 per cent from their levels 15 months previously. Moreover, the decline appeared to be continuing, as the politicians seemed unable to act with economic coordination.

Following the relative failure of an economic summit in Japan in May 1986, the value of the dollar actually rebounded for a short period, appreciating by up to 10 per cent against the yen. By June, however, the collapse continued, falling another 13 per cent against the yen by August 1986. The upward movement of US interest rates and somewhat more encouraging prospects for the US domestic economy stabilized the rate against the yen, but failure to get agreement in Europe for concerted central bank action led to continued decline against European currencies and especially the Deutschmark.

Better US trade figures brought another short rally in October 1986, when in a period of three weeks, the dollar recovered by over 5 per cent against the yen and the Deutschmark. An agreement announced between the Japanese and US authorities that they would cooperate on foreign exchange issues and that the adjustment in exchange rates between the dollar and the yen had gone far enough, helped to stabilize the yen/dollar rate until late December 1986. Against the major European currencies the dollar continued to fall in late 1986 and for the first time the dollar fell below 2 DM.

Pressure continued into 1987, in particular as German and Japanese interest rates began to rise and the governments of these countries declined to reflate their economies or show adequate signs of reducing their trade surpluses. In addition each month seemed to bring yet another increase in the already record levels of the US trade deficit. By the end of January 1987 there had been a further collapse in the dollar which fell to 1.77 DM and to 150 yen, a fall of over 12 per cent since mid December. At this point, ahead of a meeting between the finance ministers and central bank governors in late February, the major central banks intervened collectively to support the dollar. Improved trade figures and a decline in German and Japanese interest rates helped to calm the slide. The finance ministers also announced the Louvre agreement to cooperate closely to create stability in the exchange markets around the levels then prevailing.

Initially the markets believed that the new Louvre agreement had established target bands within which currencies could trade but that significant movements outside these targets would act as a trigger for central bank intervention. In late March, however, US officials denied the existence of such targets and further pressure mounted against the dollar. Despite heavy concerted central bank intervention, by March the dollar had fallen to less than 150 yen for the first time.

A communique issued by the Group of Seven countries' prime ministers after their meeting in Washington in April 1987 confirmed the cooperation announced at the Louvre meeting earlier. This did little to reassure the markets, however, and the continued growth of the Japanese trade surplus, the accelerating US trade deficit, fears of US protectionism and a trade war led to further declines in the dollar. The rate against the yen fell to 138 by the end of April and then pressure switched to the European currencies, with the dollar dropping to DM 1.76 in early May.

During the summer of 1987, the dollar remained weak but relatively stable. Then in October, following the disagreement between the US and, in particular, the German authorities, the US indicated that unless the Germans were prepared to reflate, they would not act to defend the dollar. As a result Black Monday occurred on 19 October 1987 as the New York Stock Exchange crashed.

In the following weeks the dollar again came under pressure, falling to 133 yen and 1.65 DM. Meanwhile, US politicians vacillated on measures to be taken to cut the soaring US deficit. The world's foreign exchange markets looked on in despair. In the short period from early 1985 to the autumn of 1987 the dollar had fallen by some 60 per cent of its value against the yen and the Deutschmark.

3.5   THE IMPACT OF THE FOREIGN EXCHANGE MARKET ON ECONOMIC DEVELOPMENT

Traditionally the foreign exchange markets had been linked to world trade and movements occurred between exchange rates based on long-term differences in industrial productivity and national inflation rates. As individual countries gained or lost competitive advantage, exchange rates adjusted relative to other countries. Such adjustments occurred relatively slowly and could in part be managed by central bank intervention. Substantial devaluations, or revaluations of individual currencies, could be announced by government decree and usually consisted of a few percentage points. During the 1970s, one major impact of the move to floating exchange rates was the decoupling of the foreign exchange markets from underlying trade and economic positions and the conversion of the market into a giant global casino as a growing number of banks and non-banks took positions against the market the central banks were attempting to set.

The dramatic changes in the value of the dollar demonstrated how the foreign exchange market could transform the relative economic and competitive positions of countries in a very short time. Further, such changes, while partially linked to underlying economic fundamentals, were clearly more influenced by sentiment and political actions, since the rate of change of an economy itself did not match the speed of change in markets. Moreover the speed of both the rise and the decline of the dollar during the 1980s also demonstrated the extreme difficulties for central banks, even acting in concert, to control relative exchange rates.

The speed and amplitude of the changes in the value of the dollar also appeared to be accelerating in both time and amplitude. This is illustrated in Figure 3.2 which shows the real bilateral exchange rate movements against the dollar for selected

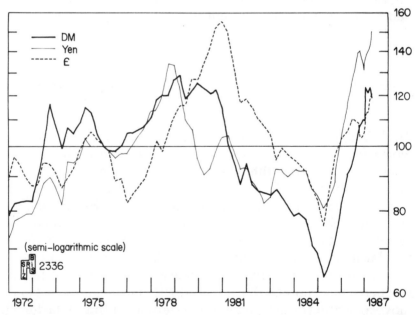

Figure 3.2   Real bilateral exchange rate movements 1972–87 (fourth quarter 1975 = 100). (*Note*: Data prior to September 1986 are quarterly averages; thereafter monthly figures are shown.)
Source: BIS (Adjusted on the basis of movements in relative unit labor costs.)

currencies since 1972. During the 1970s, despite the two oil shocks, the relative exchange rates between the dollar and other currencies did not change violently. The maximum amplitudes of the swings in relative value were of the order of 20 per cent and the rate of change, apart from 1973, was gradual.

During the 1980s, the rate of change and the scale had changed dramatically. In the early 1980s, the dollar exchange rate appreciated dramatically as a result of the rising US budget deficit being supported by the reinvestment of the Japanese trade surplus and capital flows from other industrialized nations. Then, from 1985, came the depreciation of the dollar as central banks and governments moved to correct the overvaluation of the dollar. However, in both cases, the size of the changes in value were much more than during the 1970s, at up to 50 per cent over a very short period.

Such volatility in the value of individual currencies had a serious negative effect on economic development. The relative competitive positions of individual countries were transformed at a pace which left no opportunity for countries to manage economic adjustment by changing the structure of their econo-mies. As a result, huge economic and social costs were incurred. In addition, governments were being forced to adopt short-term changes in monetary policy in order to meet the needs of the foreign exchange markets, rather than long-term rational econo-mic policies. The intervention by central banks also provided an automatic loser for speculators to play against. As a result huge sums of taxpayers' money were spent attempting to smooth exchange rate changes against an enormous growth in specula-tive funds in the markets.

The rapid changes in exchange rates also had substantial destabilizing effects at the level of the individual firm or indus-try. The impact of changing rates on different industry cost structures varied substantially, causing major losses or gains in markets according to the extent and direction of the impact. However, for most industries the speed of the changes had meant that it was not possible to adjust gradually. Moreover, while markets could be rapidly lost, it had proved much more difficult to recapture lost positions when exchange rates had swung in the opposite direction. Eastman Kodak, for example, estimated that its pre-tax profits were depressed by \$3.5 billion between 1980 and 1985 when the dollar was appreciating. While the fall in the dollar boosted earnings per share by 60 cents in 1986, the company's lost share of market outside the USA had proved much more difficult to recover[5].

Moreover, there were no signs that the volatility was likely to slow down. Indeed there seemed every likelihood it would increase, as companies, which perhaps traditionally had not bothered to cover exchange risks, were forced to enter the market, so adding further volume. Further, an increasing number of companies was also emerging as active speculators to join the banks and financial service institutions.

As a result, in addition to the relatively violent amplitude of annual swings in foreign exchange values, there had also been a strong trend for short-term currency movements on a daily basis. This high degree of short-term exchange rate volatility is illus-

Table 3.1   Daily variability of selected dollar exchange rates[a]

	Deutsch mark	Japanese yen	£ sterling
	Monthly figures		
1982 (averages)	3 (0.66)	4½ (0.76)	2 (0.59)
1983 (averages)	2 (0.55)	1 (0.52)	1½ (0.53)
1984 January–July (averages)	3 (0.66)	1 (0.42)	2 (0.55)
August	3 (0.71)	– (0.50)	2 (0.60)
September	7 (1.41)	– (0.43)	7 (1.19)
October	4 (0.74)	1 (0.40)	4 (0.70)
November	3 (0.84)	– (0.41)	2 (0.83)
December	– (0.51)	– (0.30)	1 (0.49)
1985 January	1 (0.48)	– (0.31)	5 (0.71)
February	3 (1.21)	4 (0.70)	6 (1.09)
March	7 (1.07)	2 · (0.54)	8 (1.48)
April	11 (1.30)	3 (0.67)	14 (1.53)
May (1–5)	6 (1.39)	– (0.45)	1 (0.92)

[a]Variability is measured by the number of days on which exchange rate changes exceed 1 per cent. Figures in brackets are the standard deviations of day-to-day percentage changes in exchange rates.
Source: BIS, Annual Report 1985, p. 146

[5]Companies and currencies, The Economist, 4 April 1987, p. 83.

trated in Table 3.1, which shows two measures of daily exchange rate movement. The first indicates the number of days in each month since August 1984 on which rate movements had exceeded 1 per cent. The second measure shows the size of the standard deviation of the daily exchange movements from their average day-to-day movement. The figures actually show only the changes from day to day at noon each day and therefore probably understate total volatility, in that even greater movement could take place within a 24-hour period. Clearly, by comparison to 1982 and 1983, the most recent period had recorded a substantial increase in volatility, especially for the dollar and sterling. In 1985, the Deutschmark/dollar and dollar/ sterling rates reached extremely high measures of volatility. In April 1985, for example, day-to-day movements of the dollar/ Deutschmark rate exceeded 1 per cent on half of the working days and those of the dollar/sterling rate on two-thirds of the working days[6]. This short-term volatility in the markets had continued in 1986–7 and again the amplitude of the swings was actually increasing with a resulting increase in cross-trading, as these markets had proved less volatile than trading against the dollar.

3.6   THE SIZE OF THE FOREIGN EXCHANGE MARKET

A major irony of the fact that the foreign exchange markets were wreaking havoc with national economic policies and industrial structures was that, until recently, there was little information available to the supervisory authorites on the nature and make up of the market. In an attempt to improve their knowledge, the central banks in the United States, Japan and the UK conducted a coordinated survey of the markets in April 1986 in London, New York and Tokyo.

The first global estimate of the market occurred in 1977, when the volume of daily trading in London was estimated at $29 billion, compared to $24 billion in Germany, $18 billion in Switzerland, $9 billion in Amsterdam, $8 billion per day in New York and $5 billion in Paris. This indicated a market size of

[6]BIS, 55th Annual Report, pp. 146–7.

around $80 billion in 1977, compared with total world reserves of $318 billion in 1977 and total developed country reserves of $180 billion[7].

The 1986 study of the three main financial centres revealed that daily trading volume in these markets alone averaged nearly $200 billion. In the largest market, London, daily trading was around $90 billion, in New York $50 billion and in Tokyo, $48 billion. These figures excluded double counting arising from interbank dealings within each centre, but not that arising from transactions between banks in different centres. Adding back estimates for trading in other significant trading centres such as Frankfurt, Paris, Amsterdam, Zurich, Singapore and Hong Kong, would indicate a daily trading volume globally of $300–$500 billion. By contrast, at the end of 1986, total world non-gold reserves were $509 billion while developed country reserves were $314 billion. Foreign exchange reserves for the developed economies totalled $218 billion.

The Bank of England survey gave the first clear picture of the position in the London market. In New York and Tokyo, however, where similar surveys had been undertaken in 1983, a very rapid rate of growth was observed. Volume in New York had nearly doubled and was up ten times on the 1977 figure. Volume in Tokyo had quadrupled since 1983. Over the same period growth in world trade, reflected in the import values of industrial countries, had risen by less than 30 per cent. While part of the growth in foreign exchange volume was thus trade-related and another part due to the integration and cross-border flows of funds of the capital markets, a large part of the volume gains in the foreign exchange markets was due to speculation, in particular by the leading financial institutions.

3.7   THE FOREIGN EXCHANGE MARKET PARTICIPANTS

Apart from the major multinational banks and investment houses, other key players in the foreign exchange markets were

[7]H. Giddy, Measuring the world foreign exchange market, Columbia Journal of World Business, Winter 1979.

the specialist money brokers. These latter organizations, for example, handled 43 per cent of transactions in London. Much of their activity, however, was arranging business between banks (42 per cent of gross activity), or through other similar brokers abroad (41 per cent). Despite the heavy use of broker inter-mediaries, the banks were the primary participants in the foreign exchange market, with interbank activity accounting for over 90 per cent of all transactions in London and New York.

An increasing number of non-banks had, however, entered the market, including other financial institutions, such as pension funds and insurance companies. A growing number of multina-tional corporations, while historically active via banks, had also entered the markets themselves, and had established their own in-house dealing rooms. As a result, around 10 per cent of transactions were with non-banks in London and New York. In Japan, however, the percentage was much higher at 30 per cent. This was due to the rapid growth in speculation undertaken by many cash-rich Japanese corporations from the mid 1980s.

During the 1980s, however, there had been a notable increase in the volume of transactions undertaken by non-bank financial institutions. This growth was occurring as the relationships between short- and long-term capital, money and securities markets expanded and as deregulation broke down the bound-aries between banks and non-banks. In the USA, where the differences between the various types of institution had eroded most, many non-banks had moved into the traditional bank markets and in particular many had begun to operate their own foreign exchange dealing operations.

The New York Federal Reserve thus noted that many non-bank financial institutions had begun to offer one or more of the following facilities[8].

(i) Providing foreign exchange services to portfolio investors and borrowers in the United States and abroad. Package deals, which accommodated customers' foreign exchange needs, stemming from underlying securities transactions, had become especially prevalent. Thus fully hedged commercial paper was

[8]Giddy, *op. cit.*, p. 39.

available to foreign borrowers wishing to raise funds in the USA but avoiding foreign exchange risk.

(ii) Meeting corporate foreign exchange needs related to mergers and acquisitions of foreign assets.

(iii) Using long-term foreign currency swaps to bring together borrowers and/or investors with different currency interests.

(iv) Arbitraging to profit from price discrepancies occurring between the interbank market and the International Monetary Market where foreign currency futures are traded.

(v) Positioning in size on the International Monetary Market to speculate on currency movements both for customers and on their own books. Commodities houses managing investment funds had thus shifted part of their portfolios into foreign exchange. They had then applied the same analytical techniques to estimate changes in currency markets that they had done for years in the commodity markets. Some participants were also using spread trading techniques on foreign currencies, hoping to take advantage of distortions in historical price relationships between two currencies.

(vi) Positioning in the foreign exchange swap market.

(vii) Offering foreign exchange options contracts to customers.

(viii) Several non-bank financial institutions had established full dealing operations to support their foreign exchange activities. A few quoted rates but not usually consistently nor did they maintain reciprocal lines with banks, conducting operations through banks, brokers and sometimes the International Monetary Market.

By contrast, multinational corporations were traditionally relatively small players in the market, accounting for only about 1.5 per cent of total activity. A study in the late 1970s by the US Treasury found that 55 per cent of large multinationals did not speculate in the foreign exchange markets. However, during the 1980s a growing number of multinational corporations had established their own dealing rooms. Moreover, the volatility in exchange rate movements meant that more companies were finding that getting corporate funds in the right place, the right currency at the right time, was increasingly important to determining overall corporate profitability. For example, a typically aggressive treasury placed the company's entire cash and liquidity position into a cocktail of currencies each day, irrespective of the corporation's actual global currency position. By measuring performance against a selected cocktail of currencies the treasury was able to measure its performance in terms of lowering or raising the corporation's cost of borrowed funds. The proactive treasury management mode of such a central treasury was, nevertheless, still relatively rare in Europe by the late 1980s although growing in significance. In the United States, however, important changes in accounting principles meant that balance sheet translation gains or losses produced by exchange rate changes were to be shown in a separate component of stockholders' equity rather than in current earnings as had been the case under the previous rules. The growing amplitude of exchange rates shifts could therefore transform earnings statements based on changes in the value of overseas assets but with no real effect on cash flow. As a result many US companies felt compelled to protect themselves against wide swings by hedging balance sheet exposure with outright forward contracts. From 1981 therefore management focused on the management of transaction and economic exposure[9].

Companies had also become more sophisticated in risk management techniques. In response to greater market volatility some engaged in a spot transaction rather than an outright forward contract, and followed this by a swap. While the end result was the same the speed of the market made the spot deal easier to price and such a contract could be made to eliminate exchange rate risk while the swap could be done more slowly as rates tended to be less volatile. This technique mirrored that used by the banks to offset outright forward contracts done by customers[10]. Despite the development of a range of new foreign exchange market products, the majority of transactions remained simple.

However, a growing number of multinationals were managing their foreign exchange positions aggressively. These firms tended to trade actively on an intraday basis and at times took

[9]M. D. Andrews, Recent Trends in the US Foreign Exchange Market, Federal Reserve Board of *New York Quarterly Review*, Summer 1984, p. 40
[10]*Ibid.*

aggressive positions to take advantage of short-term exchange rate movements. This could lead to a heavy volume of spot and swap transactions with the latter being used to roll over positions coming due. Some corporations were even reported to quote prices on occasion. Overall, therefore, there was a clear indication that more multinational corporations were using their central treasuries on a proactive basis rather than as an operational scorekeeper[11].

A growing number of companies and banks were also forming specialist trading companies which not only operated in the foreign exchange markets but also integrated forward to manage both ends of a trade deal as well as just offering financial services. New trading companies had been established by major manufacturing multinationals which had the lion's share of world trade, such as General Electric, Rockwell International, General Motors and Control Data, in part to offset the problems of the lack of credit from LDCs by offering counter-trade opportunities.

These new trading companies in the USA in part mirrored the major Japanese trading companies which not only dominated imports and exports into and out of Japan, but were gaining an increasing share of third-world trade. The top nine Japanese traders also dominated the Tokyo foreign exchange market and were major providers of trade finance in their own right. The trading companies were very aggressive operators, often operating rates for trade finance well below those offered by banks on the expectation they would still make a profit by handling the totality of a trade deal. By 1983 these companies held some 10 per cent of all world trade[12].

The foreign exchange market, however, remained dominated by the leading multinational banks. Although regulations differed from country to country, these institutions did take positions as well as operating for customers, and profits from foreign exchange trading had become an important source of earnings for many of them, as shown in Table 3.2. Since the international debt crisis, and with the growth of competition, however, the

[11]Ibid.
[12]D. Miles and R. Goldsberg, *Sears World Trade Inc. Case Study 91-584-021*, Harvard Business School, Boston, USA, 1983, pp. 13–15.

Table 3.2   Multinational bank revenues from foreign exchange operations ($ million)

	1984	1985	1986
Citicorp	258	358	412
Chase Manhattan	119	173	222
J.P. Morgan	30	173	230
Chemical Bank	61	102	103
Barclays (£m)	84	113	123
National Westminster (£m)	70	44	110

Sources: Annual Reports

multinational banks had reconsidered their positions on active foreign exchange trading to take better account of relative risks and rewards. During the early 1980s many large banks adopted a high-volume approach to the market, taking open positions in the spot market which were put on and closed out in the space of a few hours as traders sought profits from short-term activities. In part this activity was undertaken to avoid exposure risks in highly volatile markets where taking long-term positions was unacceptably risky. However, profits from short-term trading had become increasingly difficult to obtain as margins had been eroded due to increased competition as more and more banks and a growing number of non-banks had begun to trade in a similar manner. Moreover, advances in dealing room technology had speeded up dealing and reduced information-based competitive advantages which still prevailed at the beginning of the 1980s.

Some banks had also reduced their activities due to the large balance sheet exposure involved in granting the interbank credit lines needed to entice such levels on activity. The rapid collapse of Continental Illinois Bank and the subsequent run on Manufacturers Hanover in 1983 as banks withdrew credit lines demonstrated the nervousness of the interbank market. The costs of operating a large dealing room had also escalated and with a limited pool of top-quality dealers in world markets, the cost of good dealers had climbed rapidly. Moreover, such individuals tended to 'burn out' quickly as a result of the pressure and speed of the market. To support the dealers, banks were also forced to invest heavily in back-up hardware and software and back office systems and people to cover the ever growing volume of transactions. The close linkage of the foreign exchange market to changes in world events also meant that banks needed ever faster access to news data covering economic, political and social developments. These trends which had emerged in the foreign exchange markets by the early 1980s were also appearing in the securities and bond trading markets in the late 1980s as these, too, moved towards a global trading structure and relationships between the markets increased.

By 1983 in the New York market it was found that banks were less willing to undertake volume for its own sake and had reduced short-term position-taking. Instead some banks had begun to emphasize longer term strategic positions. Some had taken a more conservative profile in the interbank market and there had been an increase in the use of brokers. In 1983 the proportion of interbank spot transactions performed through brokers increased to 56.2 per cent from 54.2 per cent in 1980. This enabled banks to cut back on expensive dealing staff and back-up facilities, to manage positions better and to limit reciprocity[13].

Instead of straightforward volume trading in foreign exchange the banks were moving increasingly to new areas of dealing. Such new areas included foreign exchange futures, currency swaps and foreign exchange swap positioning. In the face of these activities many banks had become more involved in trading in financial futures on the International Monetary Market (IMM) via brokers or their own subsidiaries. The turnover of the IMM, most of which occurred in Chicago, had grown rapidly, with average daily volume up from $1.1 billion in 1980 to $2.3 billion by 1983. Yen and Swiss franc futures growth had been particularly significant. The IMM had therefore become a further source of liquidity for the foreign exchange market while traditionally it was seen as offering an opportunity for arbitrage. As a result the IMM and the interbank market had become much more closely linked so reducing arbitrage possibilities.

---

[13]M. D. Andrews, Recent Trends in the US Foreign Exchange Market, *Federal Reserve Board of New York Quarterly Review*, Summer 1984, p. 42.

	Forward	Futures
Size of contrast	Negotiable	Standard
Delivery date	Negotiable	Standard
Deal method	Private, usually telephone	Usually open outcry on market floor
Commissions	Negotiable	Flat rate for small deals; otherwise negotiable
Security	Credit risk assessed case by case	Margin required
Clearing	Direct settlement with counterpart	With clearing corporation
Regulation	Self-regulated or by central banks	In US by commodity Futures Trading Commission
Delivery	Over 90% delivery date	Less than 1% delivery
Price fluctuation	No limit	Daily limit set by exchange
Liquidity	Provided by banks, corporations	Provided by banks, corporations and individuals
Leverage	Nil	Very high

Figure 3.3   Comparison of futures and forward markets
Source: J. Walmsley, *The Foreign Exchange Handbook*, Wiley, New York, 1983

The IMM futures market started in seven currencies in 1972. In 1974 trading in gold futures was added. The standard futures contract and the forward exchange markets are compared in Figure 3.3. Whereas with most forward foreign exchange contracts terms were agreed with the expectation that the contract would be delivered, futures contracts were rarely delivered. Instead dealers would tend to close out positions by a sale or purchase before contracts matured.

The move to swaps positioning was considered to be more conservative than spot positioning as interest rate differentials did not tend to move as quickly as spot rates. More attention was therefore devoted to swaps and specialist traders were increasingly devoted to this activity whereas traditionally dealers handled both spot and swap transactions[14].

3.8   THE MAKE UP OF THE FOREIGN EXCHANGE MARKET

The foreign exchange market consisted of three kinds of activities: spot, swap and outright transactions. Spot deals were settled within two working days of taking place, outright deals were forward deals due for settlement at a future date. In New York, a 1980 study by the Federal Reserve indicated that 64 per cent of trading was spot, some 6 per cent was outright forward and the remaining 30 per cent was in the swap markets[15]. By 1983 there had been a slight shift with spot trading making up to 63.4 per cent of transactions compared with 33.2 per cent for outrights. In London, 73 per cent of transactions were spot, with almost all the balance being represented by forward contracts. Less than 1 per cent of total turnover was represented by forward maturities of more than one year. New foreign exchange instruments such as foreign currency options or futures were relatively insignificant, accounting for under 1 per cent of total business[15]. The low utilization of these new instruments may, however, have been understated, as such transactions were often conducted via bank subsidiaries not included in the central bank's surveys.

[14]*Ibid.*, p. 42.
[15]The market for foreign exchange in London, *Bank of England Quarterly*, September 1986, 380–1.

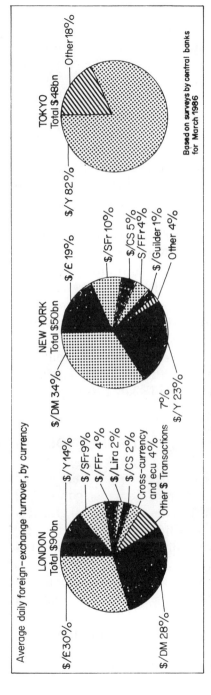

Figure 3.4   FX trading volume by currency in leading financial centres
Source: Bank of England; Federal Reserve Bank of New York; Bank of Japan. Reproduced from *The Economist*, 21–27 March 1987, Survey of International Banking p. 34, London

The main currencies traded in the foreign exchange markets were the US dollar, the Deutschmark, yen, sterling, the Swiss franc, the Canadian dollar and the French franc. Detailed statistics worldwide were unavailable on the relative volumes of each main currency, but in New York in 1980, it was indicated that the main currencies other than the US dollar were the Deutschmark which accounted for 32 per cent of volume, sterling (23 per cent), the Canadian dollar (12 per cent) and the yen (10 per cent). Since 1977, the yen had increased in importance, overtaking the Swiss, Belgian and French francs, and the Dutch guilder.

By 1986, the yen in particular had increased in trading importance in New York, to account for 23 per cent of volume, as shown in Figure 3.4, while the role of sterling had declined to 19 per cent. In London, the sterling/dollar market was the largest volume at 30 per cent. However, Deutschmark/dollar volume was 28 per cent while yen/dollar trading represented 14 per cent. Tokyo was still largely a dollar/yen market, and little trading was undertaken in other currencies. In all the major markets in 1986, the overwhelming volume was trading in the dollar versus other currencies. There was very little trading in cross-currencies, although by 1987 there were indications that this was growing, as the currency markets felt increasingly uncomfortable with the declining dollar as the world's key reserve currency.

3.9   THE WORKINGS OF THE GLOBAL MARKET

The world's foreign exchange markets were not wholly open and were constrained by different exchange control policies operated by specific countries. The development of global communication systems, linked by satellite and/or land line communications systems had, however, meant that global cash management systems were becoming commonplace. The major capital markets around the world were able to operate, more or less, on a continuous basis 24 hours a day via time windows to one another. The market started at 9.00 a.m. each day in the small New Zealand market, which opened in time to catch the end of the previous night's market in New York. Two or three hours later, Tokyo opened and caught the end of the West Coast US market. This was followed an hour later by the markets in Hong Kong and Manila and half an hour after this, by Singapore. The Middle Eastern centres opened after this, but the market slowed down at this point, as dealers waited to see how the European markets opened. Zurich, Paris and Frankfurt opened an hour before London and before Tokyo closed, allowing the European dealers to assess how the Japanese market had been working, as the dealers there closed out their positions. The New York market opened at midday London time, and positions were passed westward as London closed. After New York, there was somewhat of a gap in the market as the West Coast market in San Francisco tended to be a satellite of New York. Passing positions westward from the USA was therefore difficult because the New Zealand market was too small to pass large positions on and the Tokyo market was still not highly diversified outside the dollar/yen market[16]. The deregulation of Australia meant that a new market had opened in Sydney which would help to bridge the gap, while the rapid internationalization of Tokyo would further extend the global marketplace.

The foreign exchange market had been at the forefront of the technological revolution that was increasing the 'dealing' element of all areas of the international banking and capital markets. While there had been dramatic growth in the foreign exchange markets, all forms of trading had shown similar trends. In Eurobonds, the issue volume had climbed sharply since the early 1980s; trading in US government securities had grown dramatically by the late 1980s and overseas investors had become major purchasers; the market for global equities where shares were quoted on the major financial centre exchange had also begun to develop[17].

This growth was partially due to the dramatic growth in the number of electronic dealing terminals. In 1980, Reuters had installed 20,000 terminals, by 1985 this had risen to 53,000; Telerate terminal installations had grown from 3000 to 14,000 over the same time, while the number of Nasdaq terminals had grown to 125,000[18].

[16]Walmsley, op. cit., pp. 7–8.
[17]Euromoney, October 1985, 286.
[18]Euromoney, October 1985, 286.

To gain an edge, banks and foreign exchange traders had invested heavily in new hardware and software systems. New systems development remained rapid and the lifecycle for dealing-room technology was short and getting shorter. Dealing rooms had also been getting bigger, integrating more and more markets in the same trading area. With the deregulation of the London market, in 1986 Barclays de Zoete Wedd moved to a new room containing space for nearly 600 dealers, Midland Montague had 610 positions, while Shearson, Lehman operated the largest dealing operation in Europe with 750 places. The largest dealing room in the world was Merrill Lynch's three-storey trading centre in New York, with 1245 positions. This rapid growth in dealing-room size was made necessary by the advent of screen-to-screen dealing systems like Nasdaq, Instinet, Reuters and CATS which permitted deals in a growing range of securities and instruments to be undertaken in seconds. As a result, margins had thinned drastically, making it necessary to increase volume and market share in order to maintain profitability. At the same time, the new large dealing rooms were rapidly shifting markets away from physical exchanges towards electronic networks[19].

The costs of equipping the modern dealing room were massive. By the late 1980s the average cost for each position was £75,000 to fit out, while the lifecycle of the average dealing room had shortened to three years. In addition, in London, the average dealer cost £100,000 in salary and overheads. Rents in London were around £50 per square foot and even higher in New York and Tokyo, with the average dealer taking up 60 square feet of space. As a result, each dealer had to generate £130,000 of profit to break even[20]. To be successful, therefore, dealers relied less and less on commission trading and more and more on taking open positions. In foreign exchange this was relatively attractive, since dealers could often position against central banks, leaving taxpayers ultimately to pick up the cost. However, as markets had diversified, market-makers had not always found it easy to score against one another. After 19 October 1987, few market-

[19]Euromoney, Information Technology Supplement.
[20]Euromoney, Information Technology Supplement.

makers had broken even, let alone made profits. Nevertheless, in the foreign exchange markets actively trading banks had made a significant percentage of overall profitability from position-taking in the markets.

The needs of the successful dealer were threefold. Firstly he needed a system to handle deal capture. Dealers, or their support staff, input details of each deal to the system and needed readily accessible data on their current portfolio, exposure, position and so on. They needed to be able to monitor customer limits and produce a variety of management reports. The more sophisticated software systems could also produce confirmations of deals automatically, generate telexes to the counter-party, analyse portfolio profitability and so on.

Secondly, dealers needed easy access to a series of external information services. The problem therefore was how to provide such access without cluttering the dealer's desk with keyboards and screens. To solve this, sophisticated switching software had been developed which allowed a number of in-house and external information services to be accessed from a single keyboard at the dealer's workstation without any log on procedures. The dealer then pressed a button to get the service he wanted. An alternative approach made use of high-speed broadcasting of all the relevant data from a central data base.

The dealer also needed a series of calculation aids to assist him in spotting dealing opportunities, to calculate yields, cross-rates, values to maturity and the like for each transaction. Currently most such aids were sold as stand-alone software packages but these were becoming increasingly integrated into total systems. New integrated packages also linked to external on-line services such as Reuters or Telerate, enabling positions to be automatically updated[21].

Overall the investment in information-processing capabilities in the foreign exchange markets had been a key reason for increased volume and the development of the integrated, continuous global market. The increased pace of technical change, coupled with the developments in loan securitization, the options and futures markets, commodities trading and the

---

[21]S. Heath, Decision aids for the dealing room, *Banking Technology*, June 1985, pp. 23–4.

development of a screen-based global equities market opened a vast panorama of possible financing choice and dealing opportunities for banks, brokers, corporations and other traders. In the future even higher investment was anticipated, and active research into artificial intelligence systems was expected soon to result in even more complex dealing systems.

The rising cost of hardware and software development had led to a drive for volume and a decline in margins. In addition it had led to a potential serious increase in risk. Any dealer could potentially bet the bank in a few minutes. As a result, some bank managements were actively trying to contain risks by developing improved risk management techniques. These were increasingly being used on an intraday basis to check the exposure positions of individual dealers, to see how far over agreed trading limits individual dealers were exposed. J. P. Morgan for example set amounts by which individual dealers in specific currencies could exceed their end-of-day limits during the trading day. Chase Manhattan, by contrast, did not theoretically allow dealers ever to exceed end-of-day limits while Manufacturers Hanover allowed its dealers to go from one to five times over position limits, depending on the individual dealer and the market[22].

In addition, there was a strong move to the adoption of global, rather than local or regional limits. This permitted centralized hedging of open positions and required on-line global reporting. Bankers Trust had thus adopted a global limits position in 1987. By contrast, Citicorp remained decentralized, and allocated local limits to dealers on the basis of historic performance, although the sum of the limits provided remained less than the bank considered it could afford to lose[23].

3.10   THE RELATIONSHIP WITH THE CAPITAL MARKETS

There was a close relationship between the foreign exchange markets and the capital markets. This had also been increasing as a result of securitization and deregulation. Provided spot and

---

[22]International banking survey, The Economist, 21 March 1987, p. 34.
[23]Ibid.

forward markets existed for a currency, an exposure could be readily hedged in either market. For example, the treasurer of a German multinational expecting a future payment in sterling but needing dollars to pay a creditor in the United States could borrow sterling against his future receivable. These funds could be converted into dollars to pay the US creditor. As an alternative the treasurer could take a forward contract to sell sterling against the dollar in the foreign exchange market, against his future sterling revenue. He could then borrow dollars against the foreign exchange and again pay his creditor. The choice of which of these routes to use would be a function of the costs of each.

Central banks would therefore intervene in the foreign exchange markets either directly or via the money markets, to influence one or the other. Pure intervention in the foreign exchange markets would occur when a central bank bought or sold a foreign currency against its indigenous currency in the spot or forward markets. Other forms of intervention might include the use of exchange controls or changes in reserve requirements. Sales and purchases of currency by a central bank generally had some influence on the spot market. However, if market sentiment was still in favour of moving contary to the position of the central bank, the reserve positions were inadequate to resist such sustained pressure for long.

An intervention by an outright forward purchase tended to have an immediate effect on the margin between forward and spot rates. Further, such a move did not immediately affect central bank reserves until the contract matured. The Bank of England attempted to reduce the discount margin on forward sterling by such a move during the 1964 and 1967 sterling crises, but lost heavily when devaluation actually occurred. A swap intervention affected both the spot and forward market rates. In this case, the bank sold spot and bought it back forward. Foreign exchange swaps had been used regularly by the Swiss National Bank to manage domestic liquidity, since the size of this market was small compared with the foreign exchange markets, allowing the relative weight of the central bank to have an effect.

Central banks could also influence exchange rates by operations in the money markets by a similar variety of methods. Modification to existing official interest rates was the most obvious method. An increase in domestic interest rates, relative to those of other currencies, usually increased the exchange rate, whereas a decline had the opposite effect. Operations in the money markets were the other major method. By the sale or purchase of paper in the markets, central banks could influence the cost positions of the banks. The degree to which such an influence occurred was a function of the reserve ratio applied in each country. For example, consider a situation where a 5 per cent reserve ratio was required. The withdrawal of one million of cash from the system by the central bank would force a bank to buy extra official paper. This would reduce its reserve ratio by one million and effectively shrink the bank's lending capacity by 20 million, if it were to maintain its required reserve ratio of 5 per cent.

However, the continued volume growth of the foreign exchange markets threatened the impact of central bank intervention. Increasingly, therefore, the intervention of central banks was dependent upon influencing the psychology of the markets rather than dominating actual trades.

3.11 CONCLUSION

The growth of the Euromarkets and multinational banking in the main international money centres, coupled with a massive volume growth in the foreign exchange market and rapidly improving global communication networks, had led to the development of a 24 hour a day, global foreign exchange market. This had become linked to the domestic and international money markets, making it increasingly difficult for central banks and governments to insulate national policy from international pressures. The increased velocity of international money flow brought on by improved electronic distribution systems had led to increased volatility in both the long- and short-term exchange rate markets. By the late 1980s the power of central banks effectively to intervene in the foreign exchange and money markets to stabilize positions or to maintain exchange rate positions had been severely eroded, if not made impossible, except in the short term.

In no small part the expansion of the foreign exchange markets had been due to the development of multinational banks. By the end of the 1970s, these organizations were operating increasingly on a volume basis in the short-term spot market in a manner which had nothing much to do with world trade which was static or in decline. The market in international currencies thus became a speculative market like any commodity, influenced not merely by economic factors, although these tended to apply over the long term, but increasingly by political, social and phychological factors. The increased difficulties in maintaining rational economic management at the national level could therefore, in part, be attributed to the pursuit of profit objectives by the multinational banks. However, the short-term nationalistic position adopted by individual governments and their central banks could not be excused. To some extent, therefore, any multinational bank which failed to optimize its own position would have failed managerially in what had become a fiercely competitive environment, exacerbated by a growing number of non-bank financial and non-financial institutions entering it and by the development of parallel markets such as the IMM.

The plea of the Japanese Export Trade Organization for a stable world system of exchange rates based on nations cooperating to carry out macroeconomic management such that exchange rates might reflect economic fundamentals rather than speculation, market psychology and short-term profit-seeking, seemed remote in the late 1980s. However, the avoidance of future massive shifts in currency values, such as had occurred with the dollar in the 1980s, was essential for global economic stability. Given the volume of money in the foreign exchange markets, the growing number of bank and non-bank players, and the increasing number of financial instruments available, improved understanding and control of markets seemed essential. Yet it was not until 1986 that the Bank of England conducted the first official survey of the largest foreign exchange market in the world. With the continued development of 24-hour global high-technology trading and increased reliance on open positions for profits by the banks, it should be an urgent priority for supervisory authorites to cooperate on a global basis to clamp down on speculative

pressures which threaten the world economy, and to stop con-
tinually seeking local national advantage. The probability of
achieving such cooperation regrettably seems remote.

CHAPTER 4

The Banking System and Industrial Development

4.1 INTRODUCTION

The banking industry plays a major role in the process of industrial development. Differences between the relative economic successes of different countries have, in part, been attributed to ways in which the role of banks varies in the process of industrial investment. A number of critical studies have been issued on the role of banks, especially in the UK, which as an industrialized nation has recorded by far the worst case of relative industrial decline in the period since the end of the Second World War. During the same period, by contrast, the Japanese and West German economies have experienced a dramatic turn round from war-ravaged economies to becoming leading industrial nations.

While it is not possible fully to develop a causal argument which clearly demonstrates the superiority of one system over another it does seem that the banking system prevailing in a country has had an important impact on industial structure development. This chapter seeks to explore the role of the banking industry on economic development in industrialized countries and compares and contrasts the systems working in the UK and Japan in particular. It concludes with briefer views of the position in the USA and West Germany, which are somewhat intermediate to the contrasting positions of the other two countries.

In 1977, a Committee to Review the Functioning of Financial Institutions, under former Prime Minister Harold Wilson, was established to examine criticisms that the poor British post-war economic performance was at least partially due to failures in the financial system. The Wilson Committee reported after three years and after taking extensive evidence from industry, trades unions, financial institutions and others. The findings of the committee were that there was little evidence to support the premise that the financial institutions had failed to provide the funds required for industrial investment.

Subsequently, in 1981 a further report was published on bank lending to industry from a study group established by a Member of Parliament, Michael Grylls. This report concluded that the banking sector had lent too little to industry and argued strongly in favour of a greater supply of long-term funds, more liberal attitudes to corporate debt levels and a redirection of bank funds from the personal to the corporate sector. These criticisms echoed the findings of G. T. Edwards in his works with J. C. Carrington[1].

The conclusions of the Grylls study group provoked a detailed response from the Committee of London Clearing Banks. This argued that the views advanced by critics of the bankers were incorrect due to the use of incomparable statistics, that the financial systems of lending in each of the various countries were actually becoming increasingly similar, and that the critics had failed to understand the differences in the financial industry structures in each country. In practice, it was argued that the systems in Germany, France and the UK were actually very similar after corrections for statistical and structural differences although it was accepted that Japan was substantially different[2]. Interestingly, in an earlier work D. Vittas and R. Brown had actually noted substantial differences between the banking systems in these countries and their relationships with industry[3].

---

[1]G. T. Edwards and J. C. Carrington, Financing Industrial Investment, Macmillan, 1979; see also G. T. Edwards, *How Economic growth and inflation happen*, Macmillan, 1984
[2]D. Vittas and R. Brown, *Bank Lending and Industrial Investment*, Banking Information Service, London, 1982.
[3]D. Vittas et al., Banking and systems abroad, Committee of London Clearing Banks. Evidence to the Wilson Committee, London, 1978.

Significant differences in the methods of loan assessment between banks of various countries have also been observed[4].

4.2   THE PATTERN OF ECONOMIC DEVELOPMENT

The key factors which drive economic development are shown in Figure 4.1. The demographics, attitudes, values and size of population, the relative international cost of raw material resources, exchange rates, productivity and technological position all influence the direction and ability of an economy to change relative to its competitors. The four key internal forces, however, are also primary factors. The financial institutions, which include banks and other financial intermediaries, are one of these forces. The following sections consider in some detail the cases of the development of the post-war British and Japanese economies.

At first sight there are some close similarities between the two. Both are island nations, both are short of raw materials although

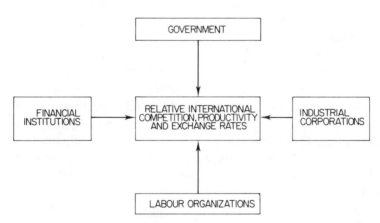

Figure 4.1   The forces determining rational industrial development
Source: Adapted from M. E. Porter, *Competitive Strategy: Techniques for analysing Industries and Competitors*, Free Press, New York, 1980

[4]K. Fubara, *Lending Procedures of the Commercial Banks in USA, UK, Japan, Germany and France*, Centre for Business Research, 1983.

Britain, as a result of finding oil in the North Sea, has become a net energy exporter, while energy deficiency has been a major problem for the Japanese. By contrast, Japan, with an indigenous population of about twice that of the UK, has enjoyed a larger domestic market to provide a base for the products of industry. Both nations, however, have needed to export to survive, taking in low-value raw materials, transforming them into finished goods and living largely off the intervening value added.

4.3   THE UNITED KINGDOM

4.3.1   The Role of Government

In the UK in the post-war period there has been a series of stable governments. However, power has fluctuated periodically between the two main political parties, Tory and Labour. The right of centre Tory Party has favoured a capitalist approach with deregulation, a free market economy based on competition and with private enterprise fulfilling the leading economic role. The socialist Labour Party has favoured much greater state participation, national ownership of major sectors of the economy, with periodic threats to nationalize all major industrial corporations, or at least to move to power sharing between management and unions, severe restrictions on outward investment, planning agreements with government and directed investment of savings into industrial sectors identified by government. This centralist-decentralist, socialist-capitalist dichotomy has tended to occur within the British economy every five to ten years. The success of Mrs Margaret Thatcher in winning a third successive term for the Tory party in 1987 was unprecedented in UK politics for over a century. Both parties have also attempted to spend their way out of recession or, when the economy became overheated, to apply financial constraints often in the face of exchange rate pressure. Extensive use of demand management has therefore characterized post-war British monetary policy with the use of credit controls and short-term interest rate changes being common.

This policy of 'stop-go' has, in particular, damaged industries with long-term capital cycles such as automobiles, consumer durables and the like[5]. Moreover, the threat of nationalization and public sector intervention has tended to exacerbate the problems of the economy for Labour administrations, leading to a loss of confidence in the international money markets, a severe erosion of the exchange rate and the need to adopt recessionary policies. One consequence of these policies was that interest rates in the UK had tended to remain high relative to corporate profits compared with other leading industrialized countries. Moreover the profitability of British enterprises was consistently lower, further discouraging investment, as shown in Figure 4.2. A further major difference between the UK and other developed economies was the high level of public spending on social welfare. As a result of such severe policy fluctuations, government failed to provide a stable environment where any form of industry, privately owned or public sector, could plan rationally for a long-term future. It is interesting to note that the relative stability of government for Britain during the 1980s was yielding the country its fastest economic growth and relative improvement in productivity and corporate profitability for many years.

Since the mid 1960s, recognition of the dysfunctional effects of stop-go macroeconomic policies led both major parties to experiment with national planning. These attempts were, however, badly implemented. The only significant attempt took place in 1968. Under the Labour administration of the time, the National Plan commenced with an assumed growth rate and businesses were asked to plan on the assumption that this growth rate would be achieved. Unfortunately, private sector companies did not believe, or accept, this growth rate projection and hence largely ignored the Plan. Public sector authorities such as the Central Electricity Generating Board were, however, asked to invest to meet the projected demand pattern and hence substantial overcapacity in power generation was built into the

---

[5]See, for example, D. F. Channon, *The Strategy and Structure of British Enterprise*, Macmillian, London, 1973, Chapter 4.

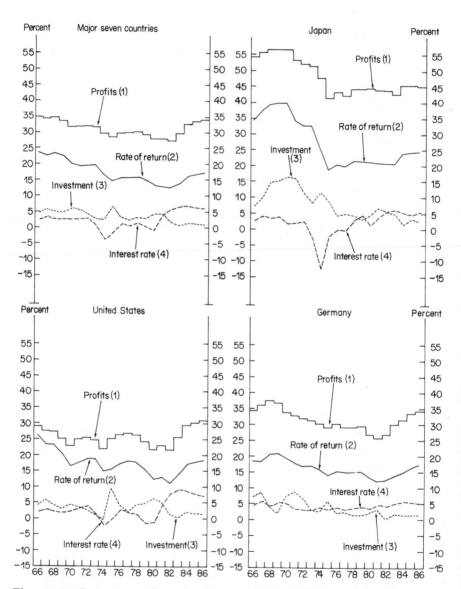

Figure 4.2 Company profits, rate of return and investment in manufacturing (1) Gross operating surplus as a percentage of gross value added (2) Gross operating surplus as a percentage of gross capital stock (3) Growth of real gross capital

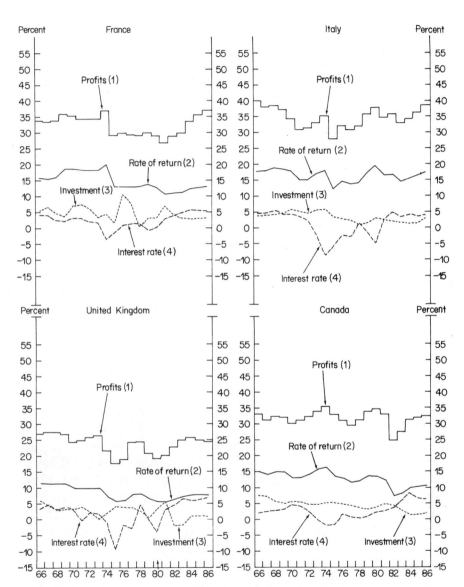

stock **(4) Long-term government bond yields less the rise in consumer prices.**
(*Note*: OECD estimates and forecasts from 1985 onwards.)
Source: *OECD Economic Outlook* December 1985, France

economy. Moreover, the Plan, rather than being based on rational economic analysis, was developed from political objectives.

Part of the infrastructure of this planning phase in the UK economy survived. In particular, the National Economic Development Council (NEDC)—a tripartite body composed of representatives of government, industry and the trade unions, but excluding the financial institutions—continued to exist through various changes of government. The NEDC itself had a small, permanent secretariat, the National Economic Development Office (NEDO), and beneath this, a series of small, industry-specific development committees had been created. The NEDC and the small EDCs, while composed of representatives of government, industry and unions, had no power to implement any policies. Rather, the EDCs could only undertake research, usually of an international, comparative nature, and make recommendations for change within an industry sector. While the NEDC and the EDCs had proved a useful forum for discussion between three of the four key groups it had not been an interventionist planning unit, as for example, the Ministry for International Trade and Industry had been in Japan. Indeed by the late 1980s the NEDC and most of the small EDCs were under severe threat as the Tory Party moved even further away from state intervention and opted to design macroeconomic policy without specific consultation with either industry or the union movement.

In the UK, the primary responsibility for economic management had traditionally rested with the Treasury, not the Department of Trade and Industry. The Treasury had largely practised demand management, manipulating the pressure for short-term demand in the light of government economic objectives. These were, in turn, largely set for political impact and based on a balance between the level of the balance of payments, exchange rate and the level of unemployment. The long-term development of industry had little political importance and, therefore, received little weight in economic decision-making, not least because the Treasury had little practical knowledge or interest in microeconomic variables. During the 1980s the primary concern of government had been to reduce the level of inflation. This had been achieved largely by controls over the money supply, resulting in high interest charges, a sharp run down in manufacturing industry, especially in the older traditional sectors, and a rapid growth in unemployment. These policies had been extremely painful but inflation had been reduced, industrial restructuring had occurred largely as a result of international market forces, and the economy was moving rapidly towards being largely high-value-added industry and service sector based.

Where direct intervention with industrial structure had been undertaken it had largely been for ideological and political purposes rather than economic reasons. Thus nationalization had been extended in the post-war period to cover much of transportation, utilities, steel, and some loss-making sectors of the economy such as automobiles, aerospace and computers. The 1980s had similarly seen successive Conservative governments adopt an aggressive policy of denationalization or privatization. This had two interesting effects. First, it had stimulated improved productivity in privatized industries and second, it had dramatically spread share ownership within British society, as most nationalized enterprises were sold off at a substantial discount.

Government expenditure on research and development in the UK had been relatively high. By contrast with Germany and Japan, however, where such research was largely directed towards commercially viable industry sectors, in the UK spending tended to be focussed in the defence sector, such as aircraft, where the UK had no hope of a volume market based on its own requirements. There had been little strategic investment into futuristic industry sectors selected as being critical for industrial restructuring into the growth industries of the future. North Sea oil investment had perhaps been an area where government funds had been used to try and revitalize the ailing shipbuilding industry to build rigs and the like for offshore exploration. By contrast, heavy investment or subsidies to support losses had been made in traditional industries like steel, railways, coal and shipbuilding in order to support continued employment. These subsidies had been withdrawn during the 1980s, leading to a dramatic shrinkage in capacity and substantial job losses in these sectors. While the residual capacity was turning in profits, the Conservative government forced dramatic disinvestment in these traditional industries, but completely failed to help build new growth industries in their place. To be fair, however, government policy in the 1980s had successfully stimulated the emergence of a new generation of small, entrepreneur led businesses which had provided a valuable contribution to lowering unemployment. However, in terms of helping to create global strategic advantage in specific sectors UK government policy had a negative rather than positive effect.

Summarizing, the force of government in the UK had been orientated to the short term rather than the long term. It had been marked by periodic policy reversals due to the conflicting objectives of the two main political parties. Policy had also been dominated by the Treasury practising short-term demand management and had shown little regard for the impact on long-term industrial structure.

4.3.2   The Role of Organized Labour

Organized labour is the second major force affecting relative economic development. In the UK, organized labour has tended to have a negative impact on industrial development. The structure of the British union movement was traditionally composed of a mixture of craft and general unions. These were often in competition with one another and it was normal for multiunion representation to occur at the workplace. Craft unions jealously guarded traditional work practices and thus tended to inhibit technical change which threatened to change their jobs. For example, in the printing industry direct input by journalists to computer typesetting machines threatened the National Graphical Association whose members traditionally set print by making lead plates. As a result, any attempt to introduce the new technology was bitterly resisted by the craft union. This was successfully achieved, however, by some groups in the mid 1980s, leading to a dramatic shakeout in labour and sharp gains in productivity.

Failure by unions to accept new technology had led to a reluctance on the part of management to invest in new plant. As a result British plants tended to be overmanned, beset by restrict-

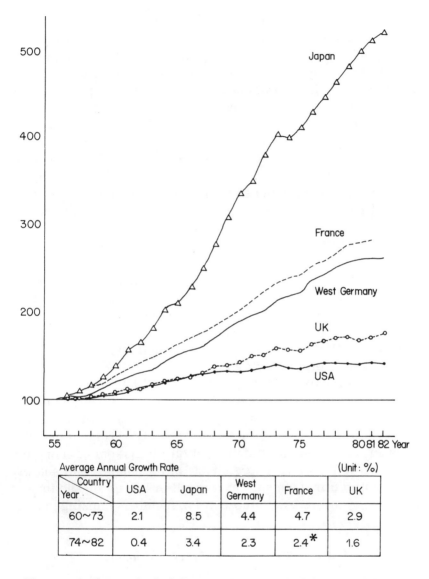

Figure 4.3   Changes in the labour productivity of major industrial countries (1955 = 100)

Notes: (1) Labour productivity represents GNP (or GDP) per employed person (except military personnel) (2)* Is from 1974 to 1981

Sources: USA, *Economic Report of the President, Survey of Current Productivity of the Labor Force; Bundesbank Monthly Report; Economic Trends; OECD National Accounts and Labor Force Statistics;* JETRO, *White Paper on International Trade,* 1983, p. 4

ive practices leading to lower relative international productivity and high labour cost. Details of the rate of change in international relative labour productivity are shown in Figure 4.3. Of the major developed economies only the USA had experienced lower overall labour productivity gain in the post-war period. The British case was worsened, however, by the fact that while the productivity gain had been low, hourly wages had risen sharply, especially during the 1970s. This had resulted in an overall substantial rise in hourly unit wage costs and corresponding loss in international competitiveness. While there was some debate as to whether this rapid rise in labour costs was the result of labour action or rising prices, there was no doubt that during the 1970s the effect had been a further loss of market share in world trade and substantial pressure on the exchange rate of sterling relative to other currencies. The relative exchange rate position of sterling had tended to weaken since 1970, although there was one period in the late 1970s when the return of a new Tory administration led to a temporary gain in the rate. British goods were also often seen to be of relatively poor quality compared with those of other industrial nations, thus exacerbating the relative productivity loss.

The Conservative governments of the 1980s had, however, substantially reduced the power of organized labour. This had occurred as a result of new labour laws which reduced union powers and increased internal democracy. Government had also removed the unions from consultation on matters of economic policy while the deflationary effects of its policies had sharply reduced union membership as a result of labour shakeouts and reduced any militarism in those union members remaining in jobs.

4.3.3   The Role of Industrial Structure

At the end of the Second World War the UK had the most developed industrial structure in the West outside the USA. Britain held a dominant world market share position in shipbuilding and was a leading supplier in industries such as automobiles, steel, chemicals and electrical engineering. Since then, British manufacturing industry had exhibited a remarkable

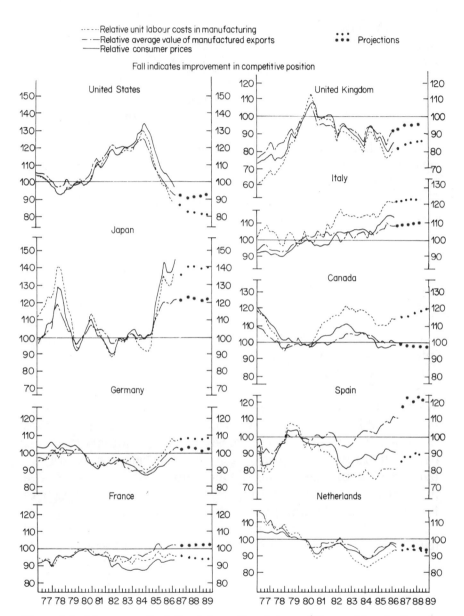

Figure 4.4   Measures of relative international competitive position (indices in US $ terms; 1980 = 100)
Source: OECD

decline and by the mid 1980s there was virtually no significant sector in which British industry held world market share domination. The relative decline of the strength of British manufacturing industry is illustrated in Figure 4.4 which shows the relative decline in manufacturing competitiveness relative to other major industrialized countries.

Although Britain remained the resident country of a substantial number of the world's leading corporations, many of these concerns had tended to diversify outside the United Kingdon where investment opportunities seemed better. By comparison with other industrial nations, the UK had generally exhibited the lowest rate of new investment, as shown in Figure 4.5, which also illustrates the dramatically greater investment rate which had been achieved by Japan over the same period.

To some extent the decline of UK enterprise could be attributed to managerial failures. In many cases, British company management was slow to adopt new managerial techniques, failed to invest in new technologies, did not face up to labour difficulties and exacerbated a class divide which segregated management from the workforce by a 'them and us' attitude. Interestingly, comparative models of similar firms within the same industry but with American, and more recently Japanese ownership, have shown that superior productivity performances are possible within the foreign-owned companies operating in the UK. While some British-owned and-managed companies have also been able to achieve significant productivity gains, overall there would appear to have been a lack of pressure for performance in many others. One impact of the laissez-faire policies of government during the 1980s has forced much of British industry to improve its productivity, while changes in labour law have reduced the power of organized labour and made it easier for managers again to control their businesses.

4.3.4 The Role of The Financial Institutions

In the post-war period, the UK had the most sophisticated system of financial institutions outside the United States, with a well-developed capital market, strong merchant banks and

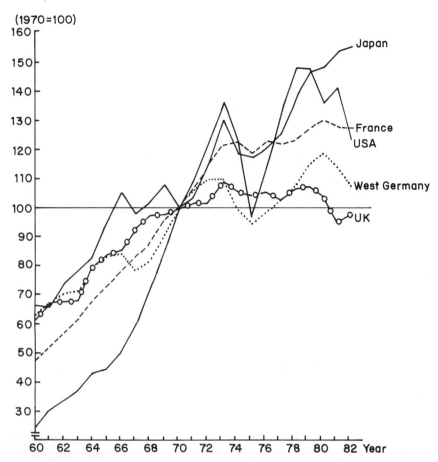

(1970=100)

Figure 4.5   **Long-term changes in gross fixed capital formation in the major industrial countries (1970 = 100)**
Note: **USA figures indicate private gross fixed capital formation: all others indicate gross domestic fixed capital formation**
Sources: USA, *Economic Report of the President, Survey of Current Business*; Japan, *National Income Statistics*; West Germany, *Bundesbank Monthly Report*; UK, *Economic Trends*; France, *National Accounts of OECD countries*; JETRO, *White Paper on International Trade*, 1983, p. 5

securities houses and an oligopolistic group of large commercial banks which were the major providers of loan funds for domestic corporations. Traditionally, however, the British Clearing Banks had tended to be retail in their orientation. Commercial lending was largely based on overdraft. Medium-term lending came to the United Kingdom largely as the result of the introduction of competition from the US multinational banks in the early 1970s and it was the introduction of these banks which largely reshaped traditional lending patterns in the UK. The American banks, with their use of specialized calling officers to cater for the needs of corporate clients, rapidly gained market share in the market for domestic sterling lending as well as becoming the major operators in the London international financial markets. By comparison with their British competitors, the Americans were seen as aggressive, innovative and specialist financial service providers to the corporate market.

Overdraft lending was not, however, truly short-term and normally was allowed to roll over on a regular basis. Nevertheless, long-term money in the UK was more difficult to obtain than in Japan or Western Germany where loan portfolios tended to be longer. A further difference with lending in the UK was that the main clearing banks tended to assess customer creditworthiness on a 'gone' basis rather than an ongoing one. This meant that they evaluated the position of a borrower assuming that he might be placed into liquidation. The ultimate asset value of a business was, therefore, important. By contrast, US banks in entering the UK market evaluated borrowers much more on their ability to repay any loans granted and were, therefore, much more concerned with monitoring corporate cash flow.

The British clearing banks had begun to diversify significantly after 1968. Before this time the structure of the industry had been remarkably stable since the 1920s when it consisted of the 'Big Five' large clearing banks and the 'Little Six' smaller largely retail and regionalized banks. In 1968 came the formation of the National Westminster Bank by the merger of the National Provincial Bank and the Westminster Bank, two members of the Big Five. Subsequently, Barclays merged with Martins and an attempt to merge these two with Lloyds was blocked by the Monopolies Commission.

After the structural upheaval of the late 1960s, the British banks began also to diversify their range of service offerings. All moved into credit finance and leasing and most attempted, by acquisition or internal development, to make a limited entry into the market for investment banking. By contrast with German universal banks, however, the British banks had remained weak in investment management and merchant banking. Thus, services such as advice on corporate financial structure, the arrangement of long-term capital issues of both debt and equity and advice on mergers and acquisitions was still usually provided by merchant banks. More recently, in the markets for Eurocurrency credits and notes, companies were turning increasingly to the large US investment banks, a number of major US money centre commercial banks with strong investment banking capabilities, to a number of European specialist investment bankers and to the large, multinational securities houses, such as Merrill Lynch and Nomura. This trend again illustrated how the traditional intermediary role of commercial banks was being eroded and that the historic boundaries between specialist sectors within the financial services industry were becoming increasingly meaningless.

The banks in the UK had also operated at arms' length from their customers. They had not held substantial equity positions in their customers, unlike the German—and to a larger extent the Japanese—banks. Similarly, bank managers were not trained in credit assessment to understand or evaluate the business of their customers in other than financial terms. This lack of understanding is perhaps one of the major criticisms that corporations have levelled against British banks and why they have tended to be more favourable to US commercial banks[6].

Long-term capital for equity investment in the UK had largely become the province of pension funds, both self-administered and professionally managed. There was little long-term lending, except for property investment, in the UK unlike in Japan or Germany. Other funds were long-term savings invested with specialist funds operated by insurance companies and commercial and merchant banks which also managed most non-self-administered pension funds. Commercial banks did not normally undertake long-term lending, except for mortgages, although the indigenous banks had increased their offerings of medium-term loans.

[6]See, for example, *Greenwich Research Associates Studies of the Market for Banking Services in Multinational Corporations*, Greenwich Research Associates, 1984.

In order to maximize the long-term earnings potential of pensioners and policy holders, there had been a strong trend on the part of the investment institutions to increase their holdings of overseas investments. Since 1979, when the UK government removed exchange controls, overseas investments by British institutions and individuals had risen sharply. There were two contradictory political arguments concerning this outward flow of capital. The first considered it was appropriate to invest overseas to provide a diversified spread of investments and to seek the best opportunities. Many companies shared this view and had also increased their activities outside the UK. The contrary view by the Labour Party was that much of this investment flow should be redirected back into British industry and in particular should be used to try and revitalize the domestic manufacturing sector and so create new employment opportunities.

While no strong evidence has emerged that the financial services industry has failed to provide adequate sources of long-term capital for industrial investment, both banks and other financial institutions have tended to adopt conservative investment policies. True venture capital has been short and fund managers have tended to invest for maximum short- and medium-term profitability rather than voluntarily supporting industrial redevelopment. This trend has indeed accelerated during the 1980s with the deregulation of the financial markets. Banks, too, by failing to understand the businesses of their customers have also perhaps not done all they could to assist in industrial development and structure change. Long-term, directed investment related to an objective, national strategic position has clearly not played a role in setting investment policy.

4.3.5 Summary

In the United Kingdom, government, unions, industrial management, and to a lesser extent the financial institutions, have not operated a consistent strategy. Rather, as a result in particular of frequent short-term government economic policy shifts, industry has not had an environment in which to work out a stable strategy. Further, the structure of organized labour has been harmful due to the presence of multiunion representation, and the differences between small craft and general unions. For its part, industrial management has been generally weak, especially amongst traditional long-established British corporations. Where new entrepreneurs have emerged they have tended to focus on the service industry sector rather than on manufacturing. By contrast, the financial services sector in the UK is sophisticated in many respects. However, corporate lending by the commercial banks has tended to focus on the short term, although competition from external multinational financial institutions has forced the banks to devote an increasing share of assets to medium-term lending. This pattern is to a degree now being threatened by the trend to securitization. Further, the banks have only in recent years been able to offer effective merchant banking services. Finally, the banks have, in large part, because of their hands-off posture in dealing with corporate clients, tended to be remote and lacking in understanding to the needs of business. Similarly, the long-term capital institutions have also favoured policies which have led to overseas investment being favoured over domestic. Overall, therefore, all the forces operating on the UK's indigenous economic performance have tended to be negative, or at best, neutral.

4.4 JAPAN

4.4.1 The Role of Government

By contrast to the UK, Japan has had the same political party in power since the return to civilian rule after the Second World War. Government has played a substantial role in the redevelopment of the Japanese economy in the post-war period. The close relationship between government and industry was established much earlier in the evolution of the Japanese feudal system which placed great emphasis on service to the nation, yet at the same time could tolerate great competition under a system of centralized control. Traditionally, in the post-Meiji restoration period, the Emperor was simultaneously Head of State, Head of Government, Highest Conqueror, Supreme Judge and Comman- der in Chief. Absolutism was the form of government during the formative years of the Japanese economy; the absolutism turned to militarism and after defeat in the Second World War to imposed democracy[7].

In the post-war period, therefore, under a Western-imposed democratic system, Japan elected the National Diet which in turn selected the Prime Minister. However, the power of the Diet was limited[8]. In particular, the management of the economy was seen as being too important to leave to politicians. Bureaucrats from the major ministries, which consisted of some of the very best and brightest of Japan's most educated individuals, had a sub- stantial influence in the management of the economy. In 1980, for example, 45,131 university applicants took the advanced civil service examination of which 1254 passed[9]. The best of these went to the Ministry of Finance (MOF), the Economic Planning Agency (EPA), and the Ministry of International Trade and Industry (MITI), the critical ministries in the management of the economy.

The main role of the EPA was to analyse the international and domestic economic position and to develop long-term policies for Japan in the light of this. The EPA which, unlike other institutions, was not associated with specific interest groups, was also not involved in routine policy-making. Further, the agency had no implementation powers. The role of the agency focused on a long-term perspective for the Japanese economy, compared with the short-term perspective of the MOF and the industry concentration of MITI[10]. During the 1960s the EPA had prepared the medium-term Economic Plan for Japan. Unlike the fate of the UK Economic Plan for the same period, prepared by the short-lived Department of Economic Affairs, the EPA plan emphasized consistency between macroeconomic targets and

[7]C. J. McMillan, The Japanese Industrial System, Walter de Gruyter, Berlin, 1984, p. 47.
[8]J. M. Shinohara et al. The Japanese and Korean experiences in management develop- ment, World Bank Staff Working Papers No 574, World Bank, 1983, pp. 14–15.
[9]S. Bronte, Japanese Finance: Markets and Institutions, Euromoney Publications, Lon- don, 1982, p. 137.
[10]Shinohara et al., op. cit., p. 15.

the projections of industry. Secondly, it highlighted the trade-offs between the rate of growth, balance of payments and the rate of inflation[11].

A series of plans was produced subsequently, each with an underlying slogan which tried to merge economic projection and political aspiration such as 'Doubling National Income Plan' or the 'Comprehensive National Development Plan'. While these plans were not exceptionally accurate they undoubtedly had an effect on business opinion and market expectations[12].

The main governmental ministry concerned with industry level planning was MITI. The ministry had been active in identifying problems within the Japanese economy and implementing policies for removing these. MITI was created in 1949 to promote the development and independence of the Japanese economy and, in particular, to stimulate international trade. Such trade was seen as the key to off-setting Japan's natural disadvantage of being a heavily populated island nation unable to feed itself and devoid of most important natural resources.

MITI worked closely with the private sector in the form of major corporations and trade associations. Unlike the macroeconomic perspective of the EPA, MITI worked at the microeconomic level and in considerable detail. The successful implementation of a strategy to rebuild Japan's industrial structure came about by the careful identification of strategic industries which were the nucleus for industrial development and exports. Initially, the task was to catch up with the West in heavy industries. MITI therefore encouraged mergers and coordinated investment and specialization via legislative powers and administrative 'guidance'. This was quite opposite to the conventional market economy approach of the USA. MITI thus favoured 'a new concept of income elasticity for the demand side and comparative technical progress for the supply side as a basis for development policy'[13].

In heavy industry, such as iron and steel, heavy engineering, shipbuilding, chemicals and automobiles, investment was made

[11]*Ibid.*, p. 16.
[12]G. C. Allen, *The Japanese Economy*, Weidenfeld & Nicholson, London, 1981, p. 39.
[13]Shinohara *et al.*, *op. cit.*, p. 20.

rapidly to build capacity and to improve productivity by the use of the most modern technology. Exports were supported by aggressive financing and marketing efforts, led by the Soga Shosha, the leading Japanese international trading companies. As a result of this policy of selective investment, Japanese industry achieved dramatic success in gaining market share in shipbuilding, steel, automobiles and the like.

MITI's policy of transforming the Japanese economy worked to reduce uncertainty for the private sector to invest. Japanese industry was, therefore, protected from external competition by a series of tariff and non-tariff protectionist devices while incentives were offered to develop selected sectors. MITI's two criteria for dynamic industries were high-income elasticity and a high rate of technical progress. To promote investment in such industries, MITI sought to modify factor prices. In addition MITI endeavoured to ensure Japanese industry adopted adequate scale economies by monitoring (without always achieving success), the investment plans of private sector organizations. This was especially difficult due to the industrial group structure which dominated much of Japanese industry, with each group wanting to participate in each key industry sector, resulting usually in at least six competitors per sector.

By the mid 1970s, however, other newly industrializing countries with low-cost labour, notably Korea, began to try and emulate Japan. In addition, the first oil shock forced a reappraisal of the validity of a national strategy based on high energy consumption industries. From this reappraisal came a policy of shifting the economy towards the growth of smaller enterprises, and an emphasis on high-value-added, rather than resource-intensive, production. MITI's mission thus became 'to find solutions to such pressing problems as industrial adjustment, the promotion of small and medium-sized enterprises, the development of local economies, protecting the environment, balancing population distribution, consumer protection and reducing the high level of prices'[14].

After the first oil shock, Japan increasingly planned to diversify its sources of energy. In some cases this meant playing off

---

[14]MITI, *MITI Handbook, 1981–82*, Tokyo, p. 13.

one country against another. This has been identified in the so-called ABC strategy (signifying Australia, Brazil and Canada), and supplemented with tactics such as stockpiling, developing new sources, and overseas joint ventures designed to increase overall capacity, so lowering raw material costs, in the light of a surplus of supply[15]. As a result, Japanese industry was able to increase the value-added component of its output relative to other nations. The success of these policies meant that the Japanese economy was much faster in coming out of the second oil shock in 1979 than any Western economy. The major trading companies had provided a key role in implementing this strategy, replacing other multinationals such as the oil majors in supplying the basic needs of Japanese industry.

For MITI, the primary mechanism for its intervention in the economy had tended to become a strategy of influence over industry exit and entry barriers. By using an intricate mix of tools, including administrative guidance, industry consensus, legislation, fiscal policy and financial support, MITI had reduced exit barriers in mature industries and entry barriers in high-value-added, high-technology sectors. With this strategy, MITI's direct involvement in industry overall had not needed to be extensive in sectors where Japan maintained an existing competitive advantage. Only where relative competitive advantage had been eroded had MITI felt it necessary to intervene to rationalize capacity or to transfer the low-value-added industries offshore to developing economies where low labour or raw material costs could be exploited with Japan supplying technology, high-value-added components and processing machinery for such businesses.

During the development phase of new industries, MITI also encouraged research and development by providing governmental support, assisted in the provision of bank funds and protected fledgling industries from overseas competition by operating formal or informal trade restrictions. When forced to liberalize, MITI had utilized bureaucratic procedures to delay such moves, using non-tariff mechanisms to make foreign penetration of the

---

[15]MacMillan, *op. cit.*, pp. 78–9.

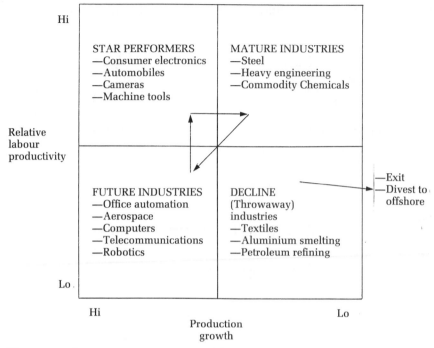

Figure 4.6   Japanese national competitive advantage matrix
Source: based on Horvath and McMillan, Industrial planning in Japan, *California Management Review*, Fall 1980, **16**, University of California Errad School of Business Administration, Berkeley, California

Japanese market difficult. At the same time MITI had taken steps to endeavour to increase domestic competitiveness.

MITI operated a portfolio approach, illustrated in Figure 4.6. Industries with high growth and high relative national productivity of labour were star performers. Such industries were growing profitably and, although 'profitable' in terms of generating national resource, might require the reinvestment of most of this resource to maintain their relative international competitive advantage. Such star industries included automobiles, consumer electronics and electrical machinery, machine tools and the like. These industries were, however, tending to be replaced by new electronics-based products and new industries based on new materials technology and information processing. Where such fledgling industries were identified, they were supported by a

variety of means including fiscal incentives, government spon-
sorship of research and development and protection of the
domestic market by a variety of tariff and non-tariff entry barriers. Those industries in the mature phase of the lifecycle
generated financial and labour resources. These sectors, such as
steel, heavy engineering and shipbuilding, which were in the
first post-war phase of the resurgence of the Japanese economy,
were approaching maturity in the 1980s. MITI thus encouraged
the release of the surplus human and capital resources tied up in
these businesses. Unlike a laissez-faire-based system, however,
MITI was extremely concerned to prevent an excessive growth in
unemployment on either a national or a regional level.

Where Japan had lost its competitive advantage, as in the
production of low-value-added products such as textiles or in
high-energy-using sectors such as aluminium smelting, MITI's
recommendation was to exit from the sector or to transfer it
abroad to an area with a superior relative labour, raw material or
energy advantage. The major trading companies had played a
leading role in the overseas transfer of declining industries,
bringing back to Japan the products of the projects for conversion
into high-value-added output. Thus, for example, Japan has
transferred offshore its high-energy-consuming aluminium
smelting industry to be replaced by a growing aerospace
industry.

The success of this strategy is illustrated in Figures 4.7 and 4.8
which show how Japanese exports had moved towards the
high-value-added and knowledge-intensive fabricating and
assembly industries and away from the commodity, capital-
intensive businesses that were the cornerstones of post-war
Japanese economic development. Figures 4.7 and 4.8 compare
the average annual growth rates of dollar exports and unit export
sales for basic raw material industries and fabricating and assembly industries achieved during the two five-year periods 1970–5
and 1975–80. Over the decade the rates of growth achieved by
commodity products in general showed a substantial decline.
Steel, for example, fell from an average growth in export value of
around 30 per cent over the period 1970–5 to less than 10 per
cent between 1975 and 1980. Similarly, fertilizers showed an
even more dramatic decline from an average of over 60 per cent

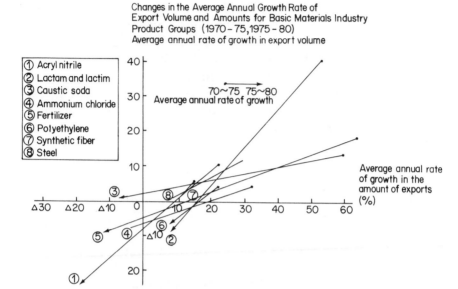

Figure 4.7   Japanese exit from low value-added industries
Source: MITI

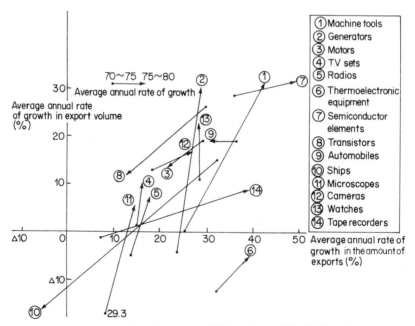

Figure 4.8   Japanese development of high value-added industries
Source: MITI

growth by value in the early 1970s to negative growth of about 10 per cent in the late 1970s. Similar patterns by volume and value can be observed in other undifferentiated commodity products. By contrast the reverse pattern is observed in the higher value-added products shown in Figure 4.8. Overall, MITI, by a policy of substantial intervention, had been instrumental in the double transformation of Japan's industrial structure, into a high-value-added, global export-based economy by the mid 1980s.

The third major government agency in the Japanese system was the Ministry of Finance (MOF). The primary function of the MOF was the preparation of the annual budget. It thus played a crucial role in governmental bureaucracy and also controlled the entire financial system, external financing, banking, the securities industry, social security and taxation. The MOF bureaucracy operated to achieve a balanced budget as a means of maintaining fiscal neutrality against political pressures. In 1965 this principle was abandoned to finance economic growth, but the MOF moved to retain rigid control over public expenditures to maintain monetary balance. Throughout the post-war period the MOF had been careful not to appear to promote overstimulation of the economy and had made sure that annual growth rates in the general account budget were kept well below estimated GNP growth rates[16]. In particular, the MOF favoured a low and stable interest rate policy to reduce corporate costs and so improve international competitiveness, thus stimulating investment. Government expenditure, as a percentage of GNP, had also been kept low and the MOF had, on occasion, moved to reduce taxation to prevent government revenues rising too fast as the result of GNP growth. This, in turn, had stimulated private savings, Japan enjoying the highest savings ratio of any industrialized country, these savings flowing through the banking system in particular, back to finance industrial investment. At the same time, however, adequate funding was made available for infrastructure development to provide the necessary background against which private sector industry could flourish. Interestingly, as Japanese trade surpluses had grown during the 1980s, leading, in particular, to political friction with the USA, the conservatism of the MOF was a cause of growing criticism

---

[16]Shinohara et al., op. cit., p. 18.

within and outside Japan. The MOF bureaucracy was even being attacked by its own minister in 1987, for blocking greater industrial growth and the stimulation of imports to help redress Japan's embarrassingly large trade surplus with the USA.

An important further factor in the Japanese system of industrial development had been the seeking of widespread consensus in decision-making. Planning by the main economic ministries involved extensive consultation between the civil servants and outside parties, notably organized by industry. Interestingly, by contrast with the British system of consensus-making, organized labour was not involved in the decision-making, but the financial sector was.

While seeking collective agreement was very much a national characteristic of the Japanese, the involvement of many in the decision process had meant that most sectors of government, industry and the nation had been able to adopt common goals. The process had involved the establishment of many deliberative councils at national and subsector level responsible for setting priorities and guidelines for policy formulation. The guidelines were, however, eventually set by the ministry bureaucrats with the councils merely debating them but usually coming to accept the broad principle. The councils did, however, allow the formation of a broad consensus around the bureaucrats' views which were ofter presented as 'visions'[17].

Visions could operate at any level of the economy— macroeconomic, sectoral or industrial—and usually contained a number of common elements. They first identified the problems of the current state of the Japanese economy and compared and contrasted these with the position in the leading Western industrial nations. They also tended to identify emerging trends and proposed solutions that would improve the economy. This process of careful and critical self-analysis, international comparison and solutions based upon relative strategic position were unique features of the Japanese system. By contrast in the UK, for example, economic planning tended to take place in isolation on a narrow, nationalistic basis rather than after consideration of the country's realistic, relative international position.

[17]Shinohara et al., op. cit., pp. 22–3.

The Japanese process had also been bottom-up in its approach, with new initiatives originating from the lower levels of the ministries, from officials actively involved with the detail of day-to-day operations. These proposals were then formally discussed at the various levels within the appropriate ministry before reaching the top, at which point they would tend to have the full backing of the ministry behind them. Coordination between and within ministries was, however, far from optimal due to the intense rivalry and factionalism between groups within the government party that existed within and between ministries, such as that in the MOF, between the securities and the banking bureau. The main disadvantages of the Japanese system had been a slowness in making decisions, especially if they involved substantial change in the existing system. The system also tended to protect the positions of vested interests.

4.4.2 The Role of Organized Labour

In the post-war period Japan had enjoyed the lowest strike rate, the best labour productivity gain, a high rate of acceptance of technical change and low unemployment. The reasons for this enviable record were not because Japanese workers were docile and lacked union representation but rather were based on a different, non-confrontational relationship between management and workers, compared with the position in Western countries.

Unlike the practice in the West, Japanese unions were based on the corporation rather than industry. The members of enterprise unions were those employees in the workforce who were permanent employees. About a third of all employees were unionized, but in larger firms the percentage was around two-thirds, while in firms of under 100 employees it was less than 9 per cent[18].

Labour cooperated in industrial structure development in Japan, largely because the system operated on the basis of mutual trust. Technology was not seen as a threat, but rather as an opportunity to improve productivity. Labour costs were fixed

[18]MacMillan, *op. cit.*, p. 183.

and workers could not be easily laid off and had to be continuously trained to improve their efficiency and productivity.

As a consequence, Japanese companies did not encourage labour mobility. By contrast in the West, especially in the USA, labour was seen as a variable cost and labour mobility was thus considered to be desirable. In the Japanese system, workers were integrated into the corporation and became essentially institutionalized. The corporation became not merely an employer but the centre of a family. The overall sense of consensus had thus seen the Japanese workforce cooperating with government and corporations in industrial development. As individuals, workers were committed both to the sense of national vision and to the long-term development of the specific enterprise to which they belonged. Unions, however, gained important concessions for their members. Similar basic pay and work conditions to management were granted but, in addition, unions had the legal right to direct involvement in all management committees making decisions relating to labour conditions. Firms with more than ten workers had to submit their work rules to the Labour Standards Office and clauses involving quick employee dismissal were not permitted in labour agreements[19]. This contrasted strongly with the British and American industrial relations systems, where workers and management were segregated and engaged in confrontational style collective bargaining rather than cooperation. Interestingly, in the new climate in the UK in the mid 1980s, Japanese firms such as Nissan establishing new subsidiaries in the UK had sucessfully negotiated similar one-union and flexible working arrangements with progressive British unions such as the Electricians' Union and the Amalgamated Engineering Union, much to the chagrin of the more traditionalist unions.

4.4.3   The Role of Industrial Corporations

There was close interaction between government and industry in the Japanese system. This occurred in many ways. Industry itself was organized into a series of powerful formal bodies, the most

---

[19]*Ibid.*, p. 181.

important of which was Keidanren. There is no real equivalent to Keidanren in the West—the Confederation of British Industry which would be the UK equivalent had by no means as much power and influence with government. Keidanren consisted of a federation of over 110 leading industrial associations crossing all sectors of the economy. Further, the largest firms were normally the leaders in each of these associations, unlike in the West, where larger corporations tended to operate outside industry associations which usually represented mainly the views of smaller competitors. Keidanren operated with a panel of 39 standing committees involving the most senior executives of the largest Japanese corporations. Each of these committees undertook detailed research on a broad range of issues including industrial structure development, fiscal policy and the like, and this involved substantial consultation and cooperation with government.

Corporate organization in Japan was also substantially different to the UK. In particular, the group membership syndrome, which pervaded so much of Japanese culture, had given rise to the development of a series of extremely powerful industrial groups around which much of the economy evolved. After the war the American occupation authorities broke up the former Zaibatsu groups which were seen as having played a leading role in the development of Japanese militarism. However, as the economy began to develop the former Zaibatsu groups began to reform. Although no longer formal organizations, the revised groupings still operated together, held shares in one another and met regularly to discuss areas of mutual interest for business and investment. These new groups tended to reform around a number of core institutions, including a general trading company, a major city bank and perhaps other important companies within the former Zaibatsu, such as Mitsubishi Heavy Industries from the Mitsubishi Group. By the early 1960s, therefore, the three main pre-war Zaibatsu—Mitsubishi, Mitsui and Sumitomo— had all at least partially reformed as large industrial groups, with a central President's Council to provide group guidance, as illustrated in Figure 4.9. In addition, three other powerful groups formed around the leading city banks of Fuji Bank, Sanwa Bank and Dai-Ichi Kangyo Bank. These too, included large trading

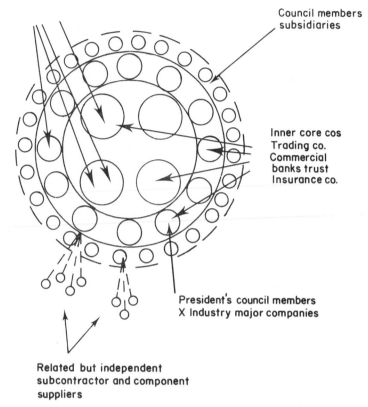

Joint venture/
group subsidiaries

Council members
subsidiaries

Inner core cos
Trading co.
Commercial
banks trust
Insurance co.

President's council members
X Industry major companies

Related but independent
subcontractor and component
suppliers

Figure 4.9   Japanese industrial group structure

companies, a trust bank and life and non-life insurance companies.

While these groups operated with different degrees of internal cohesion, they represented an extremely powerful force within the Japanese economy accounting for some 15.7 per cent of all national industrial assets in 1980. Overall, the position of the groups was somewhat more powerful than this, since in many cases they also performed the role of key customers for many of the smaller businesses supplying components and the like. Each such group thus embraced the activities of around 4000 companies which were formal members or directly associated organizations. Each group member company tended either to focus on a specific industry sector or to supply components and the like to a main company. Group companies did not themselves diversify into a wide range of product market sectors as their Western competitors tended to do. Further, each time a new product market sector was identified, for example office automation, a new subsidiary would be created to provide a specific focus on the new activity. Such a new subsidiary might be wholly owned by one of the principal companies within a group or its ownership and capital base could be provided by a number of group member companies. While the banks had been prime movers in the formation of post-war industrial groups in Japan, a number of other powerful groups had developed during this time. These tended to be in the newer industries, notably automobiles and electricals, which had developed rapidly. Such groups included Toyota, Matsushita, Nissan, Sharp and Sony. They were usually affiliated to a bank group, but operated largely independently and had themselves developed a series of relationships with subsidiaries, affiliates and suppliers.

The presence of these powerful groups within the Japanese economy meant that there was much easier coordination of industrial structure change, in that industries were relatively concentrated. There was a negative aspect to this system, however, in that each major group normally wished to maintain a presence in each key sector of the economy and to withdraw would imply loss of face. As a result, economic rationalization and concentration were difficult to achieve. However, it also illustrated why Japanese companies were such fierce international competitors because instead of one or two key participants in any markets, Japan was likely to field at least six. Moreover, in order to survive in the competitive domestic market, each of these competitors tended to operate efficiently by international standards, in order to remain effective competitors relative to their Japanese rivals.

4.4.4 The Role of the Banks

The domestic banking system in Japan had played an intimate and important part in the development of the economy in the post-war period. The relationship between the banking system and industry had been especially close in Japan. The major city banks were key members of the major industrial groups and traditionally up to a third of their loan portfolios were allocated to group member companies. In addition, the banks had been extremely close to government and would not undertake any major change in policy without prior consultation with the MOF. The Ministry had also kept a very tight rein on the financial system and had, until the mid 1980s, been reluctant to deregulate, by contrast with the more liberal attitude of the Bank of England.

The MOF historically encouraged saving by a fiscal policy which granted individuals tax exemption on bank deposits, post office savings and fixed income securities, up to a value of ¥14 million. This policy encouraged savings while stock dividends were taxed, making bank deposits a preferred savings medium. The banks in turn lent the money to industrial corporations for investment. Other savings went into life insurance and the Trust Banks where, since the early 1970s, there had been considerable growth, especially in pension funds. Unlike Western insurance and pension institutions, however, many of these funds were lent to industry for long-term investment rather than being placed into equities or property[20].

The MOF also tightly controlled interest rates and allowed companies to deduct interest payment to banks as an expense, whereas dividends had to be paid out of after-tax earnings. As a result, in the Japanese system, bank loan finance had traditionally been the cheapest method of providing funds for companies. This in turn led to deep relationships between banks and borrowers, to overgearing by Western company standards of company balance sheets and to a relatively weak market for securities. This reliance on bank lending forced companies to continue to borrow heavily to support the cash flow needed for growth. Driving for volume, Japanese companies thus increased in market share and thereby reduced costs as a result of scale economies. Those companies that did not grow fast enough to generate adequate profits to cover interest payments and to be

---

[20]K. Fubura, *Pension Funds in Britain and Japan*, unpublished members dissertation, Manchester Business School, 1983.

able to borrow more, became casualties or candidates for merger[21].

Traditionally, the structure of the banking industry was also specialized in Japan. There were 13 city banks, the largest of which were central to the leading industrial groups while the cthers were more regional in coverage[22]. These banks took in most of their funds base from the short-term money markets and personal deposits and lent to major companies on a short-term, three-month roll over loan, basis. By contrast, Japan had three long-credit banks, the most prestigious of which was the Industrial Bank of Japan, which lent to industry for long-term equipment investment. These banks had also been at the forefront of overseas project finance ventures to secure long-term natural raw material resources for Japan. Trust Banks undertook both long- and short-term lending, but tended towards more of the former as their funding base tended to be long-term trust and pension fund money. Small- and medium-sized companies were funded by local and sogo banks, but because loan demand had tended to be weak, these banks tended to place many of their deposits into the short-term money market. Special sections of the economy such as small businesses, agriculture and the fishing industries were serviced by special, semi-public, cooperative banks.

The multinational banks, by contrast with the UK, played little role in Japanese industrial development. At the beginning of the 1970s the few foreign banks operating in Japan enjoyed 3 per cent of domestic lending. By 1987 the number of foreign banks operating in Japan had increased to 79, but this group still only enjoyed around 3 per cent of domestic lending. Foreign banks thus found it extremely difficult to penetrate the domestic Japanese market, due to their lack of affinity to the major industrial groups and difficulties in obtaining access to low-cost domestic funds.

After 1973 and the first oil shock, the traditional heavy reliance on bank borrowing by major corporations became much less popular. The consequent rising level of interest rates,

---

[21]Bronte, op. cit., p. 4.
[22]See R. Hofheim Jr and K. E. Calder, The East Asia Edge, Basic Books, New York, 1982, Chapter 8. See also Bronte, op. cit., Chapters 2, 3, 4.

coupled with high gearing, caused many companies to make the reduction of interest payments a high priority. As profitability rose for those companies gaining a share in world markets, internal funding for new investments increased. In 1970, Japanese companies raised 34.5 per cent of their long-term fund needs internally. By 1980 this had reached 60 per cent. Net long-term loans for the banks fell over the same period as companies also paid off external debts. In addition, there was an increase in companies raising direct capital by the issue of equity and bonds, leading to a growing importance of the securities industry. In 1973 external funds raised by direct means were 10.4 per cent of the total, whereas by 1980 this had risen to 17.2 per cent[23]. The MOF also gradually allowed more Japanese companies to raise funds in the international capital markets, although it still closely monitored the flow of any such issues. Nevertheless, by contrast with the West, Japanese companies remained substantially more geared than Western corporations, less internally financed and much more reliant upon the banking system.

In the mid 1980s, however, Japanese companies became increasingly cash-rich as a result of their continued success in export markets. Bank lending slumped, and as many companies repaid outstanding loans, they themselves discovered the new game of 'Zaiteku' or financial engineering. In 1986–7 many major Japanese companies were acting as banks, taking positions notably in the foreign exchange market, and making the great majority of their net profits, not by making things, but rather by getting their surplus funds. It was this pursuit of Zaiteku profits that had largely fuelled the growth of the Tokyo foreign exchange market.

The banks, too, moved to expand their investment banking activities, especially outsids Japan, where they were not so constrained by the conservatism of the MOF. By the use of swaps, the traditional city banks, with a short-term fund base, were also extending their deposit maturities to more closely match those of the trust and long-term credit banks. As a consequence, and coupled with the increased pace of deregulation

[23]*Ibid.*, p. 5.

by the MOF since 1984, the Japanese banks were changing their traditional role as loan funds providers to industry, and beginning to look more like their Western competitors, although long-term client relationships remained the order of the day.

4.4.5   Summary

The rapid growth of the Japanese economy demonstrated a comprehensive effort at planned constant industrial structure evolution. Macroeconomic policies provided favourable conditions for economic growth by providing low-cost funds, low public sector demand and incentives for a high level of savings. The bureaucracy developed industrial policy on a comparative international basis, favouring industry sectors consistent with Japan's relative competitive position. Prior to the first oil shock when energy sources were cheap, policy favoured the development of heavy industry. After this time emphasis switched to high-value-added and low-energy-using sectors domestically, and the investment in overseas projects to gain long-term, secure bases of raw materials or the export of high-energy-using industries such as paper and aluminium smelting. New industries were protected until they were viable, helping to convert import substitution industries into export industries and creating a broader industrial base. By the late 1980s Japan was well positioned to achieve dominance in the new high-value-added industries which would form the basis of a growth industrial economy in the early part of the twenty-first century and was emerging as the key player in the global financial services industry. This was not the result of laissez-faire policies, but a carefully developed strategy aimed at achieving dominant competitive advantage against key Western competitors. The successful implementation of such a strategy was based on the essential cooperation of the key forces in industrial development.

The state agencies cooperated closely with the organized private sector and ensured collaboration between companies in the private sector with selective research investment and the like. While organized labour was not directly involved in the process, the method of organizing by enterprise unions, the lack of resistance to new technology introduction as a result of the permanent employment principle, and the use of corrective measures to prevent income disparities, meant that the labour force gained consistently from industrial restructuring. The labour force thus adopted positive attitudes to such change. Finally, the domestic banking system, in particular, played a distinctive role in the process, by acting as the essential financial intermediary in the collection and reallocation of savings to the corporate sector, consistent with the overall agreed policy on industrial structure evolution.

4.5   THE USA AND WEST GERMAN SYSTEMS

The post-war evolution of the US and West German systems had been somewhat intermediate to the relatively extreme positions of the UK and Japan. Like Japan, West Germany had undergone a dramatic improvement in its industrial performance since the end of the Second World War. From a destroyed economy at the beginning of the 1950s, West Germany had grown to the size of France and the UK by 1960. Japan passed German GNP in 1968, but since then the Federal Republic had maintained its position as the third largest industrial economy. By 1981, West Germany accounted for over 9 per cent of world trade and held international resources equivalent to 11 per cent of all world reserves[24].

The German economy had, however, suffered since the second oil shock at the end of the 1970s. While the country recovered well after the first oil crisis, with export-led growth and a rising exchange rate, the early 1980s revealed that the economy had not adjusted its industrial structure as well as the Japanese. The country was still over-reliant on heavy industries offering relatively undifferentiated products such as steel and heavy chemicals, which were also high in energy consumption. In addition, Germany had invested strongly in its traditional engineering sector where capital equipment, automobiles and precision engineering were produced and sold on a quality

[24]M. Stocks, West Germany: a structural forecast to 1990, Economist Intelligence Unit, London, 1983.

rather than a price basis. While the performance of Germany remained good it had not kept up with that of Japan. Nevertheless, by the late 1980s, West Germany maintained a strong balance of payments surplus and the Deutschmark continued to gain against the dollar and sterling.

Examining briefly each of the internal economic forces, governmental policy in Germany had been consistent throughout the post-war period, despite changes of government. This had been due, perhaps, to a system of proportional representation which had prevented the introduction of radical shifts in economic policy. Both major political parties had favoured a mixed economy and a modern social welfare state and, during the latter part of the 1960s, actually formed a coalition government. There had also been general agreement on fiscal policy, with tight control of inflation remaining a consistent goal. Stop-go policies, with sharp bursts of reflationary spending followed by dramatic deflation, were not attempted while interest rates were kept low. Unlike Japan, however, the German government had not been interventionist in planning the economy. Rather, government had relied on the working of the free market economy and an evolutionary process of industrial structure change.

Industry thus faced a stable, low-interest-rate environment in which to operate. West German companies, however, were very slow to diversify and failed in particular to modify the overall industry structure to fit the post-oil crisis as the Japanese managed to do. The role of organized labour in Germany had generally been positive to industrial development. The structure of trade unionism, ironically suggested by British trade union advisers after the war, tended to eliminate many of the disadvantages of the British system of craft and general unions, in favour of universalist industry unions. By law, unions were allowed to appoint members to the supervisory board in German corporations and hence were involved in structural decision-making. In addition, faced with serious labour shortages, the Germany economy had made extensive use of migrant workers who could potentially be repatriated if necessary as a buffer to shield domestic workers from unemployment.

The large universal banks in Germany, like those in Japan, enjoyed a very close relationship with corporations. The Deutsche, Dresdner and Commerz banks were founded during the

Second Reich to provide a full range of services to industrial corporations. After the fall of the Third Reich, the main banks were broken up, the Deutsche Bank, for example, was initially divided into ten separate institutions but later, like the Japanese Zaibatsu, reformed during the 1950s. Unlike their Japanese counterparts, the German banks were also strongly involved in equity finance, both for their own portfolios and those of their customers. They also dominated the market for corporate lending. The banks had thus exerted a substantial influence on the development of the major industrial companies in West Germany and thereby industrial structure. Unlike in Japan, however, this power had not been tempered by an over-riding state strategy for industrial development.

The development of the German economy had been encouraged by a stable political environment, relatively positive labour relations, and a close relationship between banks and industrial corporations but hampered by an overall national industrial strategy and a reluctance by major corporations to diversify into major new industry sectors or to internationalize their activities.

By contrast, the United States had seen its home markets penetrated sharply by overseas competitors, notably the Japanese, and seen a substantial decline in its world market share positions. Overall productivity gains in the US had been low, as had industrial investment and R & D spending. Overall, international competitiveness had declined sharply, although not as much as in the UK. Fortunately, the USA had not been as dependent upon imports as the other nations, although the two oil shocks had resulted in serious balance of payments deficits to pay for imported oil. These had been exacerbated by a growing problem of public sector budget deficits, caused in particular by increased defence expenditure, which by the late 1980s had converted the USA into the world's largest debtor nation with a growing dependence on the continued recycling of the Japanese trade surplus to fund the debt.

Government in the USA, irrespective of which of the two main political parties had been in power, had consistently favoured a capitalist, free market economy. National planning along the lines of Japan had therefore not been attempted. There had thus been few efforts to protect domestic industries from overseas attack or to ease exit strategies from declining industries or entry strategies to build positions in new industries, except perhaps via the funding of defence-related research. Since the Second World War, however, the bureaucracy in the USA had increasingly moved to inhibit natural corporate evolution by imposing conflicting conditions on industry. Moreover, recurrent government deficits had forced up interest rates and reduced the supply of funds available to industry for new investment. Excessive public spending had also exacerbated the rate of domestic inflation by comparison with Japan and Germany. This, in turn, had led to reduced savings and a movement away from monetary instruments. Anti-trust policies had also reduced industrial efficiency by attacking market domination achieved by superior business performance and had prevented mergers, which might have improved industrial efficiency and reduced costs. Finally, government in the USA had taken a national, as distinct from international stance. There had been no international trade policy other than a relatively naïve free trade position. This had been exploited by the Japanese and only belatedly had the US authorities tended to become exasperated enough to threaten retaliation by the introduction of selective trade barriers.

By and large, industry in the USA had been extremely innovative in transforming itself to new structures to meet the challenge of industrial change. This had not been a function of a centrally planned transformation but rather a Darwinian survival of the fittest, fuelled by entrepreneurial skill and backed by stock market pressure. However, there had been a strong trend in the USA towards short-term profit maximization in order to meet the demands of investment managers, thus potentially sacrificing the long-term future of whole industry sectors.

The union–management forces in the USA had also tended to be relatively negative, although the class divide discernible in the UK was not strongly present in the USA. Nevertheless, the pattern of industrial relationships had clearly been confrontational, and many companies had made great efforts to avoid unionization in any form for fear it would have a negative effect on profitability.

The USA had a sophisticated system of financial institutions. By contrast with Japan, the securities markets were extremely well developed and a strong trend in the USA had been towards the securitization of corporate lending. The equity markets in the USA were also well developed. The commercial banks had traditionally been divorced from the securities market due to regulatory constraints. However, unlike the UK banks these organizations, notably those based in the major money centres, again as a result of regulations which had inhibited interstate branching, had tended to focus on large corporate accounts rather than retail business. They had, therefore, tended to devise products and services well suited to the needs of corporate clients and to service those needs with specialist officers well trained in corporate banking, by contrast with, especially, their UK competitors, and less so their Japanese ones. The brokerage houses and investment banks, and indeed some commercial banks, had actively promoted alternatives to straightforward loans via the commercial paper market and the international capital markets which had been restricted by the regulatory authorities in Japan.

Overall, therefore, the development of industry structure in the USA had relied extensively on pure evolutionary influences and had not been planned. Government had probably played a negative role in this evolution, although some of the constraints imposed by regulation may well have had beneficial side-effects in developing a positive attitude to supporting corporate accounts amongst financial institutions.

4.6   CONCLUSION

The causes of industrial development are not simplistic. Many forces are at work and these may be operating in a positive or negative manner. These forces may vary in relative strength and can reinforce or neutralize one another. To achieve superior economic performance it is important for the vector of these forces to be working in the same direction. In the case of Japan this has been basically true, while in Britain the opposite has been largely the case. This is not to say that a centrally planned system is superior but rather that the forces in each of the main areas should operate a consistent policy. In the case of West Germany, and the USA, the position has been somewhat

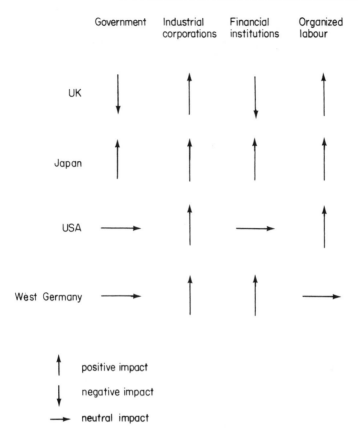

Figure 4.10 Relative force diagram of industrial development

between the two extremes, with some forces positive, while others are negative or neutral, as indicated in Figure 4.10.

The role of the financial institutions in economic development is almost certainly underestimated in most countries. The provision of the necessary financial resources is an essential component in economic development. The strategy of these institutions, and their objectives, thus can make a significant difference to the provision of these funds. Careful understanding of the role of each of the key forces should therefore be made, especially by governments, to ensure that a consistent strategy can be designed for industrial structure development, rather than relying on these forces to evolve by chance or subject to the 'he who shouts loudest' syndrome. Further, it is not appropriate to shout 'unfair' when one system, such as the Japanese, outperforms another, like the USA, by adopting policies not used by the other party but equally open to it.

CHAPTER 5

The Debt Bomb—Defused or Detonated?

5.1 INTRODUCTION

During the 1960s as the industrial economies of Western Europe, North America and Japan flourished, the developed world became increasingly dependent upon cheap Middle Eastern oil as the basic form of energy to drive their industrial output. Domestic coal and oil production was substantially more expensive than the 10–20 cents per barrel production costs of Gulf crude. Although world prices covered taxes paid to host and importing governments, and were set to reflect higher cost production fields, oil nevertheless became the critical source of world energy so creating a degree of vulnerability which was suddenly invoked by the Organization of Petroleum Exporting Countries (OPEC) on the third outbreak of the Arab-Israeli war in October 1973.

Linked by a common desire to defeat Israel, the main Arab producers moved to apply pressure on the governments of the West by forcing up the price of oil. Between October 1973 and January 1974 therefore the price of Saudi Arabian light, the standard Gulf crude, rose by over 400 per cent.

Until this time the global balance of payments system, after the period of post-war recovery, had settled into a relatively stable pattern during the 1960s and early 1970s. The major Western economies taken as a whole had grown and operated trade surpluses. Individual countries had performed better or worse than others, leading to periodic currency adjustments. The IMF support system, however, seemed adequate to handle these aberrations and in general the sustained growth in world trade had led to a continuous improvement in living standards. By contrast, the non-oil-exporting developing countries ran steady deficits on their current account balance of payments. The sum of these deficits was of a similar size to the total surplus achieved by the developed economies and overall was relatively small in terms of the global economy.

Broadly speaking, the main role of the international financial system was to recycle the developed country surpluses to the developing economies. This was achieved by the provision of aid and soft loans for development provided directly by individual governments and via the World Bank.

In addition, there was a steady capital flow from the developed to the lesser developed countries (LDCs) via the private sector, as multinational corporations made direct investments. While there was some debate about the merits of such direct investment, there was no question of the ability of the system to cope with the level or financial flows. The emerging multinational commercial banks played little or no role in the funding of balance of payments deficits. Some two-thirds of the LDCs external debts were thus owed to official sources, with the remaining third being debt owed to suppliers as well as to banks. Indeed comprehensive data covering loans by banks in the Bank of International Settlement's (BIS) reporting area or by US banks, including their foreign branches, were not even collected until the late 1970s—well after the first oil shock. During the 1960s bank lending to the LDCs had consisted largely of trade finance, a few term loans to governments often in conjuction with IMF stabilization programmes and a small amount of project finance, frequently guaranteed by third parties[1].

5.2   BUILDING THE BOMB

The first oil shock radically transformed the balance of world capital flows. In 1974 the OPEC countries achieved a dramatic

---

[1]*World Financial Markets*, Morgan Guaranty Trust Co., February 1983, p. 2.

increase in foreign exchange receipts to $105 billion, as shown in Table 5.1. Despite an increase in imports to $50 billion as a result of higher prices and also a surge in purchases, they achieved a current account surplus of some $55 billion. The great majority of this surplus was achieved by the Gulf States of Saudi Arabia, Kuwait, the United Arab Emirates and Iran.

The size of the transformation in the international balance of payments forced many oil-importing countries to seek assistance to cover their balance of payments deficits. The OPEC nations provided some limited relief. An official recycling facility was established by the IMF to which OPEC countries subscribed $2 billion. In addition loans were made to the World Bank of a further $2.25 billion and direct grants of $2.50 billion were provided to individual developing countries.

The majority of OPEC funds, however, were not used to support the developing economies. Some $6.50 billion was provided in direct loans to help fund the deficits created in Japan, Canada and leading European nations. A further $4.75 billion was directly invested in the developed economies, notably in equities and real estate in North America and the United Kingdom. The majority of the surplus was, however, held in liquid form. Some $10.50 billion was placed in bank deposits and

Table 5.1   Estimated OPEC revenues and their use in 1974

	$ billions
Foreign exchange receipts	105
Imports of goods and services	−50
Current account surplus	55
Liquid investments	37
Dollar bank deposits and government securities in the United States	10.50
Sterling bank deposits and government securities in the United Kingdom	6
Eurocurrency deposits	20.50
IMF oil facility	2
Loans to World Bank and other international institutions	2.25
Grants and loans to developing countries	2.50
Direct loans to Europe, Japan and Canada	6.50
Direct investments, real estate, etc.	4.75

Source: Morgan Guaranty Trust Co.

invested in government securities in the United States while $6 billion was similarly placed in sterling balances and investments in the United Kingdom. The remaining $20.50 billion was placed with the major multinational banks as short-term Eurocurrency deposits, largely in dollars.

The United States and United Kingdom thus financed all or most of their increased current account deficits caused by the increased price of oil by capital inflows from the oil producers. In the case of the United States there was actually a substantial net capital inflow of some $6.50 billion. To reduce deficits further the developed economies also substantially increased their prices for manufactured goods. As a result the net effect on the developed economies was substantial but not dramatic. Their cumulative surplus disappeared but overall they were not forced into significant deficit.

The brunt of the impact of the OPEC price rise was transferred to the oil-importing developing economies. These countries suddenly found themselves with serious balance of payments deficiencies and faced a difficult choice in coping with the crisis. Three major alternative options were open to them[2]. First, governments could finance the deficits by borrowing and running down reserves in the hope that the deficits would be temporary. Second, they could restructure their economies to reduce their dependence on oil and other imports while stimulating export or import substitution using reserves and borrowing to support themselves during the restructuring. Finally, they could deflate to minimize borrowing by limiting imports and reducing domestic demand.

While dome deflation occurred in the Western economies, and Japan in particular adopted the option of restructuring, the choice for many developing economies was more difficult. Some opted to build their industrial structures to reduce their dependence on imported manufactures but still faced a growing bill for energy imports. Others attempted merely to fund their deficits, hoping the problems would be short-term. Accustomed to a relatively high rate of growth and rising living standards during

---

[2]T. Killick, Euromarket recycling of OPEC surpluses: fact or myth?, *The Banker*, January 1981, pp. 15–23.

the 1950s and 1960s, and faced with rising expectations from rapidly growing populations, it is perhaps not surprising that those countries with access to the capital markets should choose to borrow to cover their deficits so as to sustain growth. For a third group of countries, including much of black Africa and parts of Asia, lack of access to the capital markets, plus a slowdown in aid from the developed countries, exacerbated already desperate levels of poverty. Those countries with access to the capital market turned increasingly to the commercial banking sector rather than to official financial institutions. The official institutions would have been unable to cope with the scale of the problem in any event as the basis for IMF funding was the main industralized economies and especially the United States. The governments of these countries, facing their own internal economic problems, were unwilling and politically unable to build the finances of the official bodies to allow them to undertake the task of recycling. For their part, the oil producers showed little inclination to place their newly acquired wealth with them or the World Bank. Borrowers, too, were not keen to take funds from the IMF. Any such monies provided from these sources were usually given as part of reconstruction packages which were politically unpopular amongst the populaces on the receiving end. Such packages were usually deflationary, increased unemployment, lowered economic growth and raised domestic prices: none of which was politically desirable.

By contrast the multinational banks were themselves receiving a massive inflow of liquid funds from the OPEC countries in the form of Eurocurrency deposits and were anxious to lend them. It was these deposits which were then recycled to those countries in deficit. This included many of the industrialized countries and indeed the bulk of sovereign risk lending was to industrial nations. These countries, however, were able to step up exports to cover the cost of borrowing and rarely did their exports to debt servicing ratios reach dangerous proportions. In addition, however, the banks funded many of the large deficits incurred by the newly industrializing non-oil developing countries. Later such lending was to be extended to the high-absorption oil producers, as the initial surpluses generated from higher priced

oil turned to deficits in the wake of ambitious industrial development projects. A dramatic growth in sovereign risk lending thus
took place from 1974, casting the multinational banks in a new
role and converting the Euromarkets into the principal world
capital market. Publicly announced Eurocurrency bank credits
arranged in 1974 totalled $28 billion, up from $23.50 billion in
1973, while the estimated size of the Eurocurrency market
increased by over $30 billion[3].

In 1979 the current account deficit of the non-OPEC developing countries grew by some $8 billion to around $34 billion.
More than three-quarters of the deterioration was accounted for
by nine countries including Argentina, Mexico, Peru, the Philippines and Turkey. Brazil was also emerging as a critical borrower, being virtually devoid of indigenous oil reserves. To
cover the increased deficit commercial bank credits again
expanded sharply and lending to non-OPEC LDCs rose to 39 per
cent of Euromarket lending, up from 22 per cent in 1974, as
shown in Table 5.2. Prospects for the non-oil developing econo-

Table 5.2 Growth of the Euromarkets and LDC lending
($ billions)

	Eurocurrency Bank Credit to:		
	All countries	Non-OPEC LDCs	%
1972	6.8	1.5	22
1973	21.9	4.5	21
1974	29.3	6.3	22
1975	21.0	8.2	39
1976	28.8	11.0	38
1977	41.8	13.5	32
1978	70.2	26.9	38
1979	82.8	35.4	43
1980	77.4	35.1	45.3
1981	133.4	45.3	34.0
1982	85.0	41.5	48.8
1983	74.2	32.9	44.3
1984	112.6	39.7[a]	35.3

[a]Includes bond issues in addition to bank credits.
Source: Morgan Guaranty Trust Co.

[3]World Financial Markets, Morgan Guaranty Trust Co., 21 January 1975, pp. 4–5.

mies were also not promising as the industrial nations moved into recession, bringing pressure on commodity prices—the principal exports of the developing economies. Financing of deficits remained relatively easy, however, as the OPEC surpluses continued to flow into the commercial banks and needed to be lent on. Sovereign risk lending proved an easy way of utilizing the funds. Moreover the popular belief, emphasized by Walter Wriston of Citicorp, that governments could not be bankrupted, made credit assessment superficial and little attention was paid to ensuring that good use was made of the bank funds provided. The fundamental seeds for creating the debt bomb were thus already in place by the end of 1975.

5.3 ADDING THE EXPLOSIVE

Between 1972 and 1979 the figures for annual bank lending via the Eurocurrency market expanded 12 times. Credits to non-OPEC LDCs by contrast rose by 23 times. The Euromarket was thus at first sight highly effective at meeting the financing needs of the non-oil developing countries over the period. In practice, however, Euromarket funding was extremely selective with only a relatively small number of countries actually receiving substantial funds. Sub-Sahara Africa and much of South East Asia, notably those countries with a low income per capita and large populations, were virtually excluded from the market as a consequence of their perceived low credit rating.

In contrast, loans to the developing economies of Latin America achieved predominance. Loans to Argentina, Brazil and Mexico alone accounted for around 83 per cent of net Eurocredits. As shown in Table 5.3 the five largest net borrowers listed accounted for 99.7 per cent of the recorded net total debt at the end of 1979. Net flows were not the same as gross since non-oil LDCs were also significant depositors with the banks and to some extent the banks were actually relending the LDCs' own assets. Moreover, those countries given favourable access to the international capital markets in the late 1970s had taken advantage of their position to borrow more funds than they actually needed. In this way they actually increased their international

Table 5.3   Gross and net Euromarket lending to non-oil LDCs, 1979 ($ billions end 1979)

	Gross	Net
Middle East	8.2	7.8
Asia	33.1	6.5
Africa	14.0	4.7
Latin America	103.5	65.1
All non-oil LDCs	158.8	68.5
Of which the five main borrowers:		
Argentina	13.1	5.4
Brazil	36.9	28.8
Liberia	6.8	4.4
Mexico	30.7	22.5
S. Korea	10.3	7.2
	97.8	68.3

Source: BIS Annual Report 1979–80

reserves, reinvesting the surplus back into the market. For much of the time during the 1970s additional borrowing was also encouraged because real interest rates were significantly negative. Rising levels of inflation could therefore be funded by borrowings costing less than the inflation rate, making such support extremely cheap. From the mid 1970s to the onset of the second oil shock in 1979 outstanding bank loans to the 21 principal LDC borrowing nations grew at an average annual rate of more than 30 per cent. US bank credit to this same group from domestic and foreign branches similarly increased at an average rate of over 21 per cent.

By the late 1970s the early OPEC surpluses caused by the first oil shock had largely disappeared, contrary to most forecasts. Few had thought it possible for the OPEC nations to spend so heavily but imports had risen dramatically for ambitious, often ill-founded projects, military hardware, luxury goods and the like. By 1976, most industrial countries were back in surplus while many oil producers were in net current account deficit. By the end of 1978 the net oil surplus had fallen to $7 billion, most of which was accounted for by Saudi Arabia, the largest oil producer, with a small population and a relatively low absorption capability. Other nations with larger populations, such as Nigeria and Iran, were again in deficit.

Apart from the rapid growth in higher priced exports to the oil-producing nations, the industrial countries had also maintained a balance of trade surplus in their dealings with the non-oil-producing nations. In addition, they maintained a surplus in trade with the Eastern Bloc nations. The economic turn around in the industrialized nations was also achieved not only by increased volumes of higher priced exports but also by a rapid adjustment to higher energy prices through improved technological efficiency in reducing oil demand. Between 1974 and 1984 the demand for oil products in the main industrial countries fell by almost 40 per cent in volume terms.

The burden for the higher price of oil was therefore almost wholly transferred from the industrial nations to the non-oil developing economies. Moreover, as these countries turned increasingly to the international capital markets to finance their deficits, the scale of the rising debt mountain climbed rapidly for the major multinational commercial banks. BIS reported bank claims on the non-oil developing economies grew from $35 billion at the end of 1974 to around $122 billion at the end of 1978. The bulk (38 per cent) of the cumulative OPEC surpluses which over the period between 1974 and 1978 had amounted to some $157 billion had been placed as deposits with the major multinational banks[4]. The initial heavy investments in US and British government securities proved increasingly less attractive while property and securities investments grew in importance.

By the end of 1978, therefore, the first oil shock had largely been absorbed by the industrial nations. Inflation and an unexpectedly high capacity for absorption had virtually eliminated the overall level of the OPEC surpluses and the industrial nations had largely recovered into an overall net surplus by increasing exports to OPEC members, to the non-oil LDCs and to Eastern Bloc countries. The overall deficit in the world economy was therefore being absorbed by the non-oil developing countries and certain Eastern Bloc nations. This deficit had been financed in large part by commercial short- and medium-term bank loans through the Euromarkets and funded by short-term

Table 5.4   LDC debt service Burden

	Annual disbursements[a] ($ billions)	Debt service ($ billions)	Ratio (%)	Debt service ratio (%)
1972	15.5	8.7	56.1	10.1
1973	21.8	11.8	54.1	9.5
1974	26.2	14.1	53.8	7.1
1975	35.8	15.9	44.4	7.9
1976	41.6	18.8	45.2	9.5
1977	50.8	24.6	48.4	10.2
1978	69.9	37.6	53.8	14.2
1979	82.0	47.5	57.9	15.7

Source: Laulan, op. cit.

deposits from the OPEC nations. The cumulative size of LDC debts was also rising to the point where the repayment of original loans and interest was proving an increasing burden to the countries in terms of their debt-servicing capability, as shown in Table 5.4.

With hindsight it can be argued that building the debt bomb inside the multinational banks was an act of foolishness. It is certainly true that prudence was not as great as it should have been and that loan credit assessment and monitoring were not undertaken as rigorously as they might have been. Moreover, there was a herd instinct at work where banks piled on assets to maintain their world rankings in assets growth. However, the rapid increase in sovereign debt exposure by the commercial banks was not entirely of their own making. Firstly, the banks were actively encouraged to undertake an enhanced role in recycling the OPEC surpluses by the monetary authorities acting at least in part in concert to mitigate the impact of high oil prices on the world economy. Secondly, there was no real alternative since the funds available to official institutions such as the IMF and World Bank were wholly inadequate to undertake the task.

The scale of the risk from sovereign risk borrowing was also not clearly understood. Surprisingly, perhaps, no accurate statistics were collected within countries by individual supervisory bodies or by the Bank for International Settlements on a global basis. The BIS for example did not begin to collect data on the international business of banks in Europe, the US, Canada, Japan and branches of US banks operating in the offshore Eurocentres in the Caribbean and the Far East until 1976. Prior to this time the BIS statistics only covered the claims and liabilities in foreign currency of international banks operating in Europe—the original core of the Euromarket. The new figures, however, still failed to take account of the maturities of outstanding debt commitments[5].

This omission began to be corrected in 1978 when the bank included figures for bank lending on a country-by-country basis broken down by maturity structure. These statistics, however, still failed to account for risk transfer. For example, if a British bank lent money to the branch of a German bank located in Brazil the risk would be counted as Brazilian although the loan might be guaranteed by the German parent, thus making the risk actually German. The BIS figures also did not break down lending into specific sectors such as government or private sector.

The control system problems of the supervisory banks were mirrored inside the banks themselves. In many cases overall exposure to countries and corporations was badly measured. Few banks possessed fully integrated data bases which produced accurate, up-to-date, reporting of exposures throughout bank networks. While some aggregate country exposure levels were monitored in many banks, relative risk exposure between sectors was again not known. Most banks' reporting systems merely reflected the requirements laid down by their national supervising authorities. Further, country risk measurement was poorly developed. While some rating agencies, such as Business International, had begun to produce measures of relative risk, the actual difference in interest rates in the Euromarkets between high- and low-risk countries was seldom more than 1 per cent. Moreover, many bankers over-rode their own credit assessment units to continue lending. As one large multinational bank

[5]P. Montagu, Clear picture of debts emerging, *Financial Times* World Banking Survey, 11 May 1981, p. iv.

general manager put it in describing the development of the bank's exposure in Brazil: 'I flew over the Mato Grosso and saw the scale of all those natural resources and knew they were good collateral for lending'[6]. Indeed many banks, at the time, believed that sovereign lending was virtually risk-free.

Finally, the presence of apparently ongoing negative yields made lending to cover cash flow deficiencies popular. All the time such negative yields existed borrowing was encouraged. Interest and principal in such periods were repaid by taking out further borrowings based on the collateral of rising capital resource values which rose in line with inflation. While the availability of bank finance thus helped to sustain economic activity much of the lending was on a false foundation. It could be sustained only as long as governments put off the unpleasant business of tackling world inflation[7].

In this way the development of the international debt crisis mirrored the worldwide property-induced secondary banking crash in the early 1970s, when banks lent into the property market around the world. The borrowing companies also did not have the cash flow to support interest and principal payments, expecting to repay both from sales of property which was rising in value at a greater rate than the cumulation of interest and capital repayments. This market collapsed when property values ceased to rise, leading to runs on secondary banks around the world and creating a major financial crisis in the early 1970s. The international debt bomb similarly came to cast its enormous shadow over the multinational banking industry with the delivery by OPEC of the second oil shock in 1979.

5.4 PRIMING THE BOMB

In 1979, as their surpluses were eroded, OPEC met and decided again on a sharp rise in the price for crude oil. The spot price of crude oil more than doubled in price from $11 to $24 a barrel. Further increases followed in 1980, lifting crude prices to a peak

---

[6]Personal Interview, UK Clearing Bank, London, 1981.
[7]The economic scene: a global perspective, *Bank of England Quarterly*, December 1983, p. 535.

of over $35 a barrel, before falling back in 1982 as the Western economies moved into deep recession and the demand for crude fell sharply. At the same time inflation accelerated.

However, the response by the developed economies to the new crisis was not the same as with the first oil shock. Firstly, most governments recognized that there was no simple long-term trade-off between unemployment and inflation. Whereas after the first oil shock some governments had endeavoured to spend their way out of difficulty, it was now seen that the fight against inflation had to take priority. This policy was accentuated by the election of right-wing governments in the USA, the UK and West Germany. These new regimes, recognizing the difficulties of curbing government expenditure, adopted monetary constraint policies as a way of getting inflation under control. As a result price rises due to the higher cost of oil did not spread through the economy to the same extent and, more importantly, money and real wages also grew less rapidly with the result that both corporate profits and fixed capital formation held up better than after the first oil shock[8].

Secondly, the new price rise finally convinced the developed country governments that high-price energy was there to stay. This view was confirmed when, in 1980, the Shah of Iran's regime was overthrown, and following the resulting Muslim Fundamentalist revolution, war broke out between Iran and Iraq. As a result oil supplies from both countries were disrupted. Rising prices, plus uncertainties about continued supply from politically unstable Middle East, thus encouraged increased measures towards oil conservation and the development of alternative energy sources. These had a major effect on reducing the demand for oil by other Western economies, as shown in Figure 5.1.

The second oil shock again produced immediate large surpluses for the major OPEC nations. Their terms of trade recorded an improvement of 46 per cent in 1980 over 1979 and their surplus increased by $56 billion to $164 billion. The aggregate deficit of the major industrial countries rose to $33 billion but, in relation to their economies, the increase of $22 billion and $12

[8]BIS 51st Annual Report, 1981, p. 34.

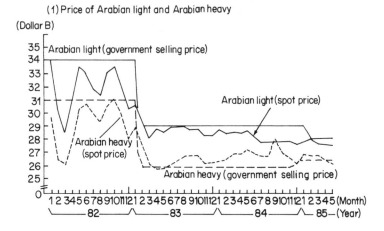

(1) Price of Arabian light and Arabian heavy

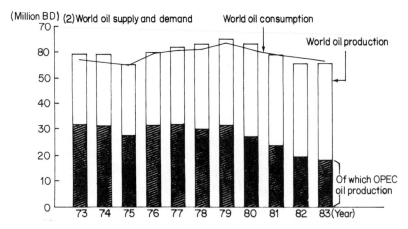

(2) World oil supply and demand

Figure 5.1 The world oil situation
Note: Spot prices are those from the middle of each month
Source: MITI White Paper on International Trade 1985

billion respectively in the trade deficits of the non-oil developing countries and the smaller developed countries were substantially larger[9].

Unlike in 1974–5, however, the developed countries were not able to improve their terms of trade with the rest of the world. This was due to the fact that the industrial countries did not go

[9]BIS 51st Annual Report, p. 78.

into recession until the latter part of 1980 and in addition the terms of trade with non-oil developing countries were declining as commodity prices also initially increased. The use of monetary policies aimed at controlling inflation, however, soon began to depress the industrial economies.

In addition to adopting monetary policies domestically, the monetarist Western regimes applied the same constraints to the international financial institutions of the IMF and World Bank. By contrast with the policies of providing at least some funds for institutional support after the first oil shock, no new IMF arrangement such as the first and second oil facilities was created nor were special SDRs created. Indeed two years of delay, caused mainly be reluctance by the US authorities, preceded the 1980 ratification of a 50 per cent increase in IMF quotas[10].

Governments in deficit were therefore forced to the multinational banks for funds. The banks thus absorbed the new OPEC surpluses and lent them on. Moreover, the good loan loss experience on sovereign risk lending after the first oil shock deluded many of the banks into continuing to believe that the probability of default was extremely low or non-existent. In addition, despite the introduction of monetarist policies and an economic slowdown, the banks believed that growth in world trade would almost inevitably continue, as it had done for the past 20 years, so allowing borrower nations to grow their way to servicing their debts. The emerging globalization of the international banking market also increased competition for asset volume growth between the growing number of multinational banks, leading to inadequate or improvident credit assessment and too fine spreads for the level of real risk being taken on.

As a result of the banks' complacent attitude to sovereign risk and intensive competition, lending to the developing countries continued to grow rapidly after the second oil shock at over 20 per cent per annum. In particular lending continued to be concentrated heavily amongst the largest borrowers and especially Argentina, Brazil and Mexico. The nine largest US banks were particularly aggressive in their lending to these countries with loans rising between the end of 1979 and mid 1982 at

[10]*World Financial Markets*, op. cit., February 1983, p. 4.

average annual rates of 30 per cent, 15 per cent and 35 per cent respectively.

Much of this increase was in short-term credits, reflecting the misguided view that such loans were less risky than long-term facilities. In practice this rapid build-up of short-term debt actually increased the borrowers' and ultimately the banks' vulnerability. Thus, any sudden reduction in the willingness of banks to roll over such facilities could potentially generate a crisis, making it impossible for the banks to withdraw their funds readily. The deep recession which gripped the industrial countries led to a decline in import demand especially of raw materials. This was also fuelled by Japan, which actively encouraged overinvestment in many high-capital-intensity, high-energy-consumption, raw materials. Commodity prices for resources other than oil thus fell. At the same time, as a result of monetarist policies, interest rates rose dramatically, leading to a further serious deterioration in the debt-servicing capability of the developing countries. Further, as inflation came under control in the developed economies, the reverse yield gap of the late 1970s turned into high real interest rates. The new OPEC surplus also quickly disappeared, with a swing of $110 billion in only two years, while the combined current account deficit of the 21 leading LDC debtor nations rose from an annual average of $30 billion in 1979–80 to nearly $65 billion in 1981–2. This represented an effective jump from 12 per cent of their exports in 1979 to 23 per cent in 1982.

The continued rapid build-up in debt, coupled with stagnant export growth, pushed the average major LDC outstanding debt to over 170 per cent of their exports. This was more than 40 percentage points higher than the ratio for the second half of the 1970s. At the same time high interest rates and shortening debt maturities caused the total debt service ratio to rise from 50 per cent in 1979 to 75 per cent in 1982. The problems were especially acute for the major Latin American countries where the average debt service ratio had reached 125 per cent by 1982.

In 1979, the first real warning that the debt bomb was built and that country risk exposure could explode with massive consequences came with the downfall of the Shah of Iran and his replacement by the Muslim Fundamentalist movement of the

Ayatollah Khomeini. The new revolutionary regime seized American hostages and the American government in turn froze all Iranian assets held by US banks around the world. Chase Manhattan Bank, as agent for $500 million credit raised by Iran in 1977, found itself as a result of the asset freeze unable to execute the request of the Iranian central bank to transmit due payments to the members of the loan syndicate. Members of the syndicate were polled by telex and by a simple majority the loan was called in and declared to be in default. This move was an embarrassment to non-US bank syndicate members whose governments were not in dispute with Iran, as the declaration of default could theoretically have forced them to call in other Iranian credits under cross-default clauses in the loan agreements[11]. In the event, the Iranian crisis was shortlived in that the US asset freeze was lifted and Iran, with its large overseas deposits, maintained its credit position. Nevertheless, the prospect that a sudden event could trigger a major crisis in the souvereign risk borrowing market began to cause many banks to review their lending policies.

5.5   THE POLISH CRISIS

In March 1981, towards the end of a bleak winter of political unrest and imposed martial law, the military government of Poland announced that it was seeking to defer repayment of $7.5 billion due to Western banks and governments that year. This amount was much larger than any previous rescheduling operation which had typically been in smaller, low-income developing countries such as Zaire, Sudan and Jamaica. Moreover, Poland's total borrowings were over $24 billion and repayments scheduled for 1982 and 1983 were similarly earmarked at $7.1 and $4.3 billion respectively. The main lenders to Poland were the European banks, US banks since 1976 having kept their exposure flat. The European banks, notably from Germany and France, had been encouraged to keep trade going and had there-

---

[11]P. Montagnon, Aftermath of Iran, *Financial Times* World Banking Survey, 11 May 1981, p. v.

fore considerably expanded their exposure. In the spring of 1980, the Polish government had proposed a further $500 million loan and were only able to raise about half this amount. Government economic policies and food subsidies were also seriously questioned by the bankers. As a result the Gierek regime abruptly raised food prices, leading to widespread strikes and the creation of the Solidarity movement[12]. This in turn led to a state of martial law, and the subsequent call for a rescheduling.

The problem of Poland was further complicated in that it was not a member of the IMF. As a consequence any rescheduling negotiations would have to take place without the support of the IMF, which would usually carefully examine a country's economic position and recommend a package of austerity measures designed to stabilize the situation. In such circumstances, banks designing a rescheduling agreement would do so in the knowledge that the government concerned had already given some sort of guarantee to correct future cash flow and the balance of trade.

In addition, the Polish request came at a time of tense East–West relations. The Reagan administration in the USA was imposing sanctions on the Soviet Bloc following the Russian invasion of Afghanistan. It was also strongly opposed to the introduction of martial law in Poland, seeing this as almost tantamount to a further Russian invasion, designed to crush the increased freedom in the country which had been seen with the emergence of the Solidarity trade union movement.

In the event agreement was reached in the summer of 1981 to reschedule the Polish debt. Ninety-five per cent of the payments due for 1981 were to be deferred till 1986 at a higher interest rate and in addition the Poles were charged a 1 per cent rescheduling fee. However, the crisis had a knock-on domino effect on the other countries of Eastern Europe. The banks suddenly began to reverse their lending policies, not only on Poland but on all the centrally planned economies. The problem of Poland was swiftly transferred to the other countries in the Eastern Bloc as banks around the world moved to reduce their exposure. As bank credit lines came up for renewal or loans matured they were not

[12]R. Ball, Poland's economic disaster, Fortune, 7 September 1981, p. 47.

rolled over or renewed. Instead the Eastern Bloc countries, irrespective almost of their economic state, were virtually excluded from the Euromarkets. Commenting critically on the approach of the bank loan syndication departments, Kit Mc-Mahon, then deputy governor of the Bank of England, added: 'Indiscriminate enthusiasm on the part of the salesman may have moved to encourage borrowers to take on commitments they were ill-equipped to shoulder when the going became more difficult. Now, however, there is a danger that we might see the reverse'[13].

East Germany and the Soviet Union were short of foreign exchange, but still were able to borrow with most of the $4.8 billion in new credits to the Eastern Bloc going to these countries during 1981 and early 1982. The Soviet Union drew heavily on its deposits with Western banks early in 1981 but made up these balances again later by substantial sales of gold[14]. Elsewhere, new deposits by Western Bloc countries were cut to a trickle. Romania, with $6.3 billion in commercial bank debt, announced it was facing a foreign exchange crisis and would have to reschedule its debt. Hungary, the model Eastern bloc economy, lost in a few short months practically all the foreign deposits it had taken the country years to build up. In a classic case of a bank confidence run, the country lost $1.1 billion in deposits during the first three months of 1982, reducing reserves to $374 million[15].

The fact that the main Eastern European countries were not members of the IMF made the problem worse. Instead of being able to turn to the IMF for assistance and a stabilization package, the Eastern Bloc countries were caught in the midst of a full-blown confidence crisis with no real institutional back up. In order to calm the position the BIS, in conjunction with the central banks of the UK, West Germany and France, agreed to launch a lifeboat in an effort to stop the run on the National Bank of Hungary. Noticeably absent was the USA, which because of the Reagan administration attitude to Eastern Europe might not

---

[13]P. Fallond and D. Shirrett, The betrayal of Eastern Europe, *Euromoney*, September 1982, p. 26.
[14]BIS 53rd Annual Report, p. 123
[15]Fallon and Shirrett, *op. cit.*, p. 19.

have been able to participate and in the event, therefore, the US Treasury was not asked to help.

The stabilizing action of the central banks brought some short-term relief to the market. While the panic scramble by the banks to cut their lines reduced, the long-term sentiment that during the late 1970s had been highly favourable to country risk lending had clearly reversed by the end of 1981. Already a stream of developing countries were coming to the banks to seek rescheduling agreements. As confidence drained the problems increased and whole regions, rather than individual countries, were becoming affected. Suddenly the enthusiasm of the loan syndication departments of the major banks, which had built the debt bomb, had evaporated. Instead, the managerial level involved in providing stabilizing credits was that of the chief executive officer of the major multinational banks as, together with a growing number of the central bankers, they moved to prevent a global crisis of confidence. For such a crisis would not merely affect the borrowing nations; it could rapidly translate into a run on the major lenders, the multinational commercial banks themselves, precipitating the collapse of the international financial system. The stark potential consequence of an explosion of the debt bomb now became obvious.

5.6   THE MEXICAN CRISIS

While the number of countries needing to reschedule grew rapidly in 1981, the first expectation that the debt bomb might explode occurred in 1982 when one of the markets leading borrowers, Mexico, faced an economic crisis which was to threaten the entire banking system. In 1981, Mexico, with large proven oil reserves and four years of rapid economic growth, was a favourite with the banks in the syndicated loan market.

Public sector debt, which was $19.6 billion in 1976, rocketed to $65 billion in 1982 with the private sector borrowing a further $20 billion. Pemex, the state-owned oil monopoly, had been a particularly heavy borrower to develop oil and gas reserves with foreign debt rising to over $20 billion, up nearly 700 per cent from five years previously. In June 1981, faced with a world glut of oil, Mexico was forced to cut its oil price by $4 a barrel and oil earnings for the year fell to $12 billion, instead of an expected $15 billion. At the same time, interest costs were rising as rates moved up, reflecting increased inflation in the industrialized countries. Mexico's debt-servicing charges increased by $2.5 billion to about $6 billion in 1981, causing the country to borrow more to cover outstanding interest on existing loans. At the end of the year the current account deficit was $13 billion and extra borrowings of $14 billion had been made to cover the shortfall.

However, a falling demand for oil, a sharp decline in oil prices, the continued high interest rates, plus the collapse under a burden of foreign bank debt by one of Mexico's largest corporations, Gruppo Alpha, threatened this position by early 1982. In early February, the central bank had allowed the peso to be devalued from a rate of 27 to the dollar to a new rate of 38.50. A series of minor devaluations followed, due to a massive increase in capital flight out of the country and to speculative buying of the dollar. By the end of July the peso rate against the dollar was 48.50. On 5 August, three banks at Mexico City International Airport ceased trading. At a hastily convened press conference the Finance Secretary, Jesus Silva Herzog, announced that the peso would be allowed to float as the government could not sustain the current exchange rate. In addition a two-tier exchange system would be introduced with a 'preferential rate' of 49.50 to the dollar, which would apply to exporters and importers of essential goods and services and for companies with outstanding dollar loans. All other transactions were to be subject to the market place. By the end of the next day the rate was 80 pesos to the dollar. Major increases also occured in the prices for government-produced goods and services, including gasoline and basic foodstuffs[16].

The new exchange rate if anything encouraged capital flight. Special establishments sprang up on the US side of the border with Mexico to sell pesos to US tourists at 90 to the dollar, while Mexicans were crossing the border to buy dollars at any price[17]. On 13 August, the government introduced exchange controls

[16]A. Robinson, The end of the illusion in Latin America, Euromoney, September 1982, pp. 77–82.
[17]Many patients, little medicine, Euromoney, March 1983, p. 36.

and all dollar accounts were frozen in a belated effort to stop the haemorrhage as billions of pesos flooded out of the country. President Jose Lopez Postillo then arranged $3.9 billion of emergency finance from the US government and central banks, requested a 90-day moratorium on public sector principal repayments, and applied to the IMF for an extended funding facility.

In April, an austerity package had already been introduced to cut government spending, while public sector prices were increased in an effort to reduce ths overall level of the public sector deficit from 12.5 to 9.5 per cent of GDP. Public and private sector imports were also cut by $3 billion. All public sector construction not linked to production was stopped, interest rates were to be related to external rates while the exchange rate would be modified to reflect the underlying competitiveness of the economy.

The August crisis in Mexico, as with the Eastern Bloc crisis the previous year, caused the banks to move rapidly to draw back their credit lines. This time, however, the problem was much worse because of the overall size of the Mexican loans and the number of banks involved. Some 1400 banks, many of them smaller institutions like the US regional banks, had bought Mexican exposure. These institutions did not possess sophisticated country risk exposure units. They had joined in the sovereign risk market as a result of the marketing efforts of the multinational bank syndication units, which had packaged the large loans and actively promoted them throughout the banking system. Now many of these institutions wanted to get out, to cut their lines or write off their losses.

Instead, they were to be forced to remain in and even to increase their exposure in order to hold the banking system together. Despite the intervention of the IMF, progress on re-establishing liquidity for Mexico was extremely slow. The scale of the crisis, however, became clear at the September meeting of the IMF in Toronto when Finance Minister Herzog told journalists that Mexico would repay no principal on its public sector foreign debt until the end of 1983. In addition the Mexicans appeared to suggest that they were ready to include $6 billion of interbank deposits in with the $80 billion of public and private sector debt. This caused havoc amongst the bankers, threatening a liquidity crisis in the international interbank system, as banks moved to pull back their money from other banks. Heavy pressure was put on the Mexicans by OECD-country central bankers and Mexico withdrew any talk of freezing interbank lines[18]. Nevertheless, the psychological shock of a potential default and the threatened termination of interbank liquidity brougnt home to the bankers the nature and scale of the debt bomb which now hung over the continued existence of the entire international banking system. In November 1982 the initiative was seized by Jacques de Larosiere, Managing Director of the IMF, who summoned a meeting on Mexico's principal private bank creditors in New York. At the meeting, de Larosiere presented the bankers with what some regarded as an ultimatum, saying in effect that the IMF would not present a package to its board without the banks also being prepared to put up new money. In all, de Larosiere was looking for $6.5 billion to be committed by the banks by mid December, of which $5 billion was to be new money. Such a demand was unprecedented and a total change of policy on the part of the IMF towards the creation of commercial bank credits[19].

Meanwhile the exchange rate had continued to decline. In November the Mexican government decided to open money exchanges on its side of the US border to compete with those on the US side. However, the competition on rates between the exchanges on both sides of the border placed the peso under even greater pressure and the exchange rate fell to around 150 pesos to the dollar in the black market.

On 1 December, Miguel de la Madrid succeeded as President. The new government moved to an even sharper dose of austerity. The peso was allowed to float freely and rose to 150 to the dollar. Price controls were lifted on all but basic foods. Value-added tax was raised to 15 per cent on most products and 20 per cent for luxuries, all in an effort to cut back inflation.

A Mexican default was thus avoided and, supported by the main central banks, the major commercial banks were reluctantly armtwisted to mount a rescue operation and subscribe to a

---

[18]A. Friedman, *Financial Times* World Banking Survey, 9 May 1983, p. 1.
[19]P. Field, D. Shirrett and W. Ollard, The IMF and central banks flex their muscles, *Euromoney*, January 1983, pp. 35–44.

new jumbo loan of $5 billion, coupled with access to a $3.8 billion IMF facility. 'We naturally wanted to get back what we put in during the boom years', one American banker said. 'We were assured we would not if we did not help now. There was no choice really. We can only hope the jumbo doesn't turn into a white elephant.' Similarly a British banker added 'it's true we had no choice, that's what is troubling me more. We got an ultimatum from the Bank of England—come in or get out. That precedent could mean more for the future of banking than a Mexican default'[20].

The IMF package for Mexico differed little from the April 1982 self-imposed austerity measures. The public sector deficit was to be reduced from 16.5 to 8.5 per cent in 1983, 5.5 per cent in 1984 and 3.5 per cent in 1985. The main implication of this was to be a massive rise in unemployment. Already estimated at 10–11 million or 40 per cent of the workforce, a further 4 million Mexicans were expected to lose their jobs by 1985 as a result of the austerity policy.

While the Mexican crisis was thus contained, new potential trouble spots began to erupt throughout Latin America. These involved not only small borrowing nations, but the major debtor nations of Brazil and Argentina.

5.7　LATIN AMERICAN DEFAULT?

Brazil, the largest economy in Latin America, had followed a development strategy that maximized public and private investment but with little regard to the economic and financial costs. The result had been an ambitious series of massive infrastructure, import substitution and natural resource projects carried out by a growing number of private and state-owned corporations. The cost of this programme had been covered by high taxes, compulsory savings and heavy domestic and international borrowing.

Between 1979 and 1982 this strategy was badly hit by three key changes in the external environment. First, Brazil was

[20]Many patients, little medicine, op. cit., p. 31.

heavily dependent upon imported oil and the second oil shock was largely responsible for a 45 per cent decline in the country's terms of trade. Secondly, like Mexico, Brazil suffered as a result of the sharp rise in international interest rates. Thirdly, the global recession caused a major drop in Brazil's exports in 1982.

By the end of 1982 Brazil's foreign debt was around $90 billion. In September 1982 an austerity programme had been introduced which raised the legal reserve rate from 35 to 45 per cent; almost no credit was available for private companies in the domestic market; dollar allowances for travel were slashed from $2000 to $100 a head; and a 25 per cent tax was imposed on dollar purchases. Government investments were frozen and further restrictions cut import capacity by 38 per cent. Then, after national elections in November 1982, Brazil went to the IMF with a debt rescheduling plan.

In mid December, Brazil found itself unable to meet $100 million in loan payments. The BIS coordinated another emergency bridging loan of $1.5 billion from the central banks of the United States, UK, France and Germany. In January 1983 the government reached agreement with the IMF on a three-year economic programme aimed at sharply improving Brazil's balance of payments performance, to create a trade surplus of $6 billion in 1983 and $8 billion in 1984. This was to be made possible by a series of mini devaluations running at least 1 per cent per month above the rate of domestic inflation. In addition Brazil was expected to improve its energy self-sufficiency and, together with additional conservation measures, this would lead to reduced oil imports. Domestic demand was also to be constrained again, leading to reduced imports. The public sector deficit was expected to reduce from around 14 to 8 per cent in 1983 and 6.5 per cent by 1984 while the growth in money supply was to be strictly controlled. Most controversial was the imposition of wage controls to prevent rises above the level of inflation.

To support this policy the IMF provided an extended facility of SDR 4.2 billion. Further, on 20 December 1982, Brazilian officials met with over 100 major creditor banks in New York to reveal their needs from the private banking sector. These included a new jumbo loan of $4.4 billion and the extension over eight years of 1983 medium- and long-term principal repayments which would turn $4 billion of 1983 payments due to foreign banks into new loans. A roll over of some $9 billion of trade related short-term debt was also required. Finally, the Brazilians asked the banks to renew all interbank credit lines, or re-establish them at the level prevailing at the end of June or December 1982, whichever was the higher. With great reluctance the banks were forced to stay in to support the Brazilians or run the risk of another major default.

The third largest Latin American borrower, Argentina, had fallen out of favour as a result of the Falklands war. By the end of 1982 foreign debt had reached some $42 billion with some $15 billion of this falling due and clearly unpayable. As one banker described it, Argentina is 'an enigma wrapped in a disaster enfolded in a God-damned mess'. Defeat in the Falklands war swept the ruling military Junta from power together with the Economy Minister Roberto Altmann, who had gained the confidence of some Western bankers. The new democratically elected Alfonsin regime was forced to turn to the IMF for assistance.

A rescue effort was undertaken with a bridging loan from the IMF and the banks. Argentina's public sector debts were also rescheduled, with much reluctance and great difficulty. The problems were compounded by Argentina's failure to get its rate of inflation under control, which was around 180 per cent at the end of 1982.

Elsewhere throughout the continent similar problems occurred. Bolivia, Chile, Columbia, Ecudor, Panama, Peru, Uraguay and Venezuela all needed to seek help. Wherever possible the banks reduced their exposure, but in most countries they were forced to accept long-term rescheduling. Debt-service ratios had reached impossible levels by the early part of 1983. The IMF, therefore, in conjunction with the major central banks, by a mixture of coercion and cajoling of both sovereign governments and multinational banks, was forcing politically unpleasant austerity packages down the throats of the Latin American countries whilst ensuring the banks maintained the minimum levels of liquidity to these countries to prevent the debt bomb exploding.

5.8   THE DEBT BOMB DEFUSED?

During 1983 and 1984 the policies imposed by the IMF began to take effect, especially in the two largest debtor nations, Brazil and Mexico. In addition interest rates declined from their peak and world trade expanded rapidly after the decline of the early 1980s, while in real terms oil prices declined sharply. In particular the US economy grew strongly, which coupled with the rising value of the dollar and a massive expansion in the level of the US current account deficit, led to a flood of imports notably from the Far East but also from the debt-troubled nations of Latin America. As a result the major debtor countries moved from deficit to trade surplus, sufficient to cover their increased debt-service costs. None, however, had reached the stage when they could roll over existing debts in a normal way or raise new money in the capital markets. Indeed bank lending to the LDCs fell significantly.

The aggregate current account deficit of the sixteen leading LDC debtor nations fell from nearly $55 billion in 1981 to about $12 billion in 1984. The turn round in trade balance had been even more dramatic with the sixteen countries, lifting their combined trade surplus by over $56 billion. Imports, in particular, were slashed in many countries as a result of restrictive controls on wages, money supply and the like, coupled with currency devaluations and import quotas. The pattern in 1984, however, was a return to export growth stimulated, in particular, by strong US demand. Mexico's exports rose by over 10 per cent, while Brazil's were up by over 21 per cent on 1983. Other countries also reported improvements, making it possible for many to earn enough virtually to cover their interest payments.

Improving economic conditions also helped to arrest capital flight which had been a major cause of the loss of liquidity for many countries. In most of the major debtor nations it was estimated that up to a third of the loans provided by the multinational banks and institutions rapidly left these countries as flight capital to end up in private banking accounts in no or low-tax havens. The decline in flight capital, in conjunction with the growth of trade surpluses, had assisted many countries to rebuild their foreign exchange reserves. Mexico's reserves were over $7 billion by the end of 1984, the equivalent of eight months' imports, and dramatically higher than the $800 million at the end of 1982. Brazil, too, had experienced a substantial improvement with reserves also over $7 billion from only $3 billion in early 1983. Debt growth had also slowed to a more sustainable pace. The external debt of the seven largest Latin American borrowers grew by around $16 billion or 5.3 per cent in 1983 and by a similar amount in 1984[21].

These improvements in performance were initially a cause of considerable optimism in many banking quarters. Further grounds for comfort came from the forced acceptance by Argentina of a tough IMF package. With an annual inflation rate which touched 1500 per cent in September 1984, due in large part to the Alfonsin government's seeking to maintain real wage levels by indexation, Argentina had been reluctant to accept the austerity package designed by the IMF. Self-sufficient in food and energy, Argentina seriously considered a planned default. In practice four Latin American countries led by Mexico and Brazil provided portions of a stopgap loan to prevent such a policy.

Further massive pressure was applied by Latin American finance ministers, economists from the IMF, commercial bankers and officials from the developed economies to persuade Argentina that such a default was unacceptable. In the event Argentina took its IMF medicine and in the fourth quarter of 1984 a deflationary package was put into place.

By mid 1985, therefore, the main debtor countries had been provided with long-term debt rescheduling packages by the banks, as shown in Table 5.5. Some optimistic commentators thus believed that the debt bomb had been defused and stability had been restored to the international monetary system.

Not only were the main debtor nations apparently improving but the slowdown in bank lending to LDCs, coupled with a sharp increase in the primary capital bases of the banks, had reduced their exposure to LDC debts. By the end of 1984, the cross-border claims of US banks on developing countries had declined from a

[21]G. Hector, Third world debt: The bomb is defused, *Fortune*, 18 February 1985, pp. 26–7.

Table 5.5   Major commercial bank reschedulings, 1985

	Amount ($bn)	Years covered	Maturity (years)	Interest margin	New credit ($m)
Argentina	16	1982–85	12	1⅜	4200
Brazil[a]	54.3	1985–91	16	1⅛	–
Ecuador	4.3	1985–89	12	1⅜	200
Mexico	48.7	1985–90	14	1⅛	–
Philippines	5.8	1983–86	10	1⅛	925
Venezuela	20.75	1983–88	12½	1⅛	–

[a]Brazil figures not yet confirmed.
Source: *Financial Times*, March, **29**, 1985, p. 6

peak of 186 per cent of primary capital at the end of 1982 to 141 per cent. The ratio of such claims on Latin American countries had fallen from 120 to 93 per cent. Both ratios were thus below the levels prevailing in 1977–8—the first years for which such statistics were collected[22].

5.9   OR MERELY DELAYED?

While clearly the situation had improved since the dark days at the end of 1982, there were still grounds for arguing that the debt bomb had perhaps only been delayed. For while there had been improvements in the performance of some countries, this had not been universal. In addition, the better trade performances of Brazil and Mexico were heavily dependent on the continuation of the growth in US import demand and, in the case of Mexico, a stable price for oil. Secondly, the adjustment of domestic balances had not kept pace with improvements in the external accounts and inflation remained rampant in most of the countries of Latin America.

The IMF also cautioned against overoptimism. Success could only be achieved if a number of factors remained stable. First, there could be no return to expansionary policies on the part of the debtor nations. Otherwise the debt ratios would not fall and even with continued austerity the ratios would be no better than

[22]Morgan Guaranty Trust Co., *International Bank Lending Trends*, July 1985, p. 8.

in 1980. Secondly, the agreed rescheduling packages merely postponed the cost of servicing, they did not eliminate the cost. Finally, the best scenarios for improvement rested on the assumption that the trade-weighted exchange rate of the dollar would fall by 5 per cent a year in real terms after 1987, industrial countries would continue to grow at 2.5–3 per cent per annum till 1990 and real interest rates would gently decline.

Adjusted for population gains, the 2.6 per cent GDP growth in Latin America in 1984 actually represented a mere 0.2 per cent increase in per capita production. Indeed economic performance based on this measure fell in twelve of the nineteen countries in the region. Such growth was also wholly inadequate to reduce the massive unemployment throughout the region and was 9 per cent below the level achieved in 1980. Living standards in the region had shown no improvement, and in some countries the imposition of IMF packages had led to drastic falls in real incomes, adding to political unrest and demands for debt repudiation.

Prior to 1982 the Latin American nations had managed to borrow more money each year than they paid out in interest and dividends. Since 1982 the effect of the rescheduling and the drying up of bank credit lines meant that the region had experienced a massive capital export flow to the creditor nations. This amounted to $18.4 billion in 1982, $30.1 billion in 1983 and $26.7 billion in 1984. Moreover, these capital outflows were expected to continue through at least the mid 1990s until the Latin countries had reduced their average debt to exports ratio down from the 325 per cent level in 1984 to around 200 per cent. As a result, for the rescheduling to be successfully accomplished, living standards would need to be continually kept down while unemployment would remain high.

The governments had also failed to contain inflation and many countries had not met the levels set under the terms of their IMF agreements. While indexation shielded some of the effect of high inflation, there was a serious political risk that austerity and unemployment would lead to a middle-class backlash as well as building up revolutionary pressure amongst the poor. The economic forecasts of the bankers were thus based essentially on a series of favourable macroeconomic outcomes and paid little attention to political pressures. 'Somehow', as one US banker put it, 'the conventional wisdom of 200 million South Americans sweating away in the hot sun for the next decade to earn the interest on their debt so that Citicorp can raise its dividends twice a year does not square with my image of political reality'[23].

5.10   THE BAKER SOLUTION

In a sharp turn of direction James Baker, the US Secretary of the Treasury, introduced to bankers, assembled for the IMF/World Bank meeting at Seoul in October 1985, a new interactive package to deal with the threat of the debt bomb. The new package, rather than relying on draconian austerity, aimed to improve the position of a number of major debtor LDCs by promoting economic growth. Although the debtor nations would be expected to continue IMF fiscal and monetary reform, they would also introduce 'supply side' policies such as those advocated by the World Bank. These included encouraging inward direct investment, liberalization of foreign trade, tax reform and the development of competitive market economies, where subsidies and controls which inhibited competition and protected inefficiency were gradually eliminated. Funds would also not be provided to countries with a high level of capital flight, in an effort to ensure that money would be put to work to improve the LDC economies rather than being redeposited in banks abroad.

The Baker proposals were initially to apply to fifteen middle-income countries which were major debtors and unable to borrow directly from the capital markets. Most of these countries were based in Latin America. In mid 1985 these countries had an exposure to all BIS banks of $273 billion, some 35 per cent of which was owed to US banks and 86 per cent of borrowings were accounted for by the Latin American countries, as shown in Table 5.6. Large borrowers such as South Korea, which still had access to the capital markets, were not included in the proposals.

Under the Baker solution, the World Bank and other development banks such as the Inter American Development Bank,

---

[23]L. Glynn, Is the Latin debt crisis over? Don't kid yourself, *Institutional Investor*, May 1985, pp. 84–90.

Table 5.6   Debt burden of potential Banker Plan recipients (December 1986)

	All BIS banks 1985	US banks July 1985	UK banks Dec. 1985	IMF June 1985	World Bank June 1985	Out-standing claims Dec. 1986
Latin America						
Argentina	26.9	8.0	3.4	1.6	0.6	40.4
Bolivia	0.7	0.2	0.1	0.1	0.2	3.9
Brazil	77.2	24.0	9.3	4.2	4.3	78.6
Chile	13.4	6.7	2.1	0.8	0.3	12.5
Columbia	6.8	2.8	0.8	0.0	1.8	12.9
Ecuador	5.0	2.2	0.7	0.3	0.2	5.8
Mexico	71.6	26.4	8.7	2.7	3.2	76.3
Peru	5.5	2.2	0.7	0.7	0.6	14.7
Uruguay	2.0	1.0	0.4	0.2	0.1	3.1
Venezuela	25.0	10.7	2.8	0.0	0.1	22.9
	234.1	84.2	29.0	10.6	11.4	271.2
Other						
Ivory Coast	2.6	0.5	0.3	0.6	0.8	7.7
Morocco	4.5	0.9	0.4	1.1	0.9	14.1
Nigeria	8.4	1.7	2.4	0.0	0.6	18.1
Philippines	13.1	5.4	0.4	0.7	1.9	22.9
Yugoslavia	9.9	2.4	1.7	1.9	1.8	16.9
Total	272.6	95.1	35.5	14.9	17.7	350.9

Source: Morgan Guaranty Trust Co.

would increase their lending to selected countries to improve industrial structure, competitive composition and foreign trade. As a result, the World Bank and other development banks were expected to increase their lending by a net $20 billion by the end of 1989. This new lending would require a sharp reorientation away from large projects and towards the private sector.

At the same time, commercial banks were expected to increase their overall exposure of some $270 billion by a similar $20 billion of new money. This actually represented a decline in real terms, but still constituted a reverse of the banks' policy of virtual withdrawal from the market for LDC lending. It was proposed that a new 'superbank' might be created to handle the new money put up by the commercial banks, with creditors

receiving votes in the new institution proportionate to the funds
they provided. The new institution would be run by executives
from the biggest creditor banks and would replace existing bank
syndication arrangements. Working in conjunction with the IMF
and World Bank, the superbank would aim to streamline new
banks, negotiate new loans to the LDCs or reschedule existing
credit lines[24].

While the banks cautiously welcomed the Baker Plan they
were also extremely reluctant to increase exposure to countries
which had not agreed terms with the IMF. Indeed the degree of
welcome given to the plan tended to vary in proportion to the
level of bank exposure, with those banks with the greatest
exposure being most enthusiastic.

Many other problems with the plan were also identified by the
banks. Firstly, they noted that the reduction on overall LDC
exposure had been caused by smaller banks withdrawing credit
lines or writing off LDC loans. These banks were not anxious to
increase their exposure again, implying that for the plan to work
the larger banks would have to take up the risk. While the
heavily exposed US banks could be expected to take up their
share together probably with the British and French, there was
little evidence to suggest that the German, Swiss and, especially,
Japanese, banks would willingly shoulder their portion of the
burden.

Secondly, the reluctance of the large banks to participate in the
plan was natural since they were concurrently being pressurized
by their indigenous regulatory authorities to improve their
capital adequacy ratios. Moreover, the Baker Plan requested that
the banks give LDC borrowers the softest terms possible to
facilitate the countries' repayments problems. The banks then
feared that by granting such terms, loans might be downgraded
by bank supervisors, thus exacerbating the pressure on them to
generate additional equity.

Thirdly, there seemed little likelihood that the World Bank or
the IMF would be able to provide any guarantees on new loans,
as these institutions would not wish to give up their own scarce
lending capacity for such a purpose. Moreover, governments

---

[24]*Economist*, 19 October 1985, p. 88.

were not being asked to increase the exposure of official export credit institutions to LDCs. Indeed there was pressure in both the US and the UK for cutbacks in such areas of public expenditure.

Fourthly, the change in position by the Reagan administration was largely due to concern over the political stability of Latin America, caused by deep poverty. Moreover, there was substantial pressure in the US Congress against significantly increasing the capital base of the World Bank.

Fifthly, the Baker Plan applied only to a limited number of countries. It provided no relief for the desperately poor, unbankable countries of black Africa or those nations outside the IMF such as Poland. Finally, despite the brave objectives there was no guarantee that the new funds would escape wastage due to the corruption and capital flight that had characterized earlier lending to these LDC countries.

5.11   THE CITI TAKES A HIT

By mid 1987 the early doubts concerning the Baker Plan for resolving the LDC debt problem had become reality. The countries themselves had not achieved the ambitious growth targets expected of them. A collapse in the price of oil in 1986 had hit the oil exporters like Mexico while similar terms of trade losses in other commodities, such as beef and cereals, had affected countries like Brazil and Argentina. As a result all the major problem countries had experienced a deterioration in their debt to export ratios. The average ratio of exports of the ten principal Baker countries rose from less than 265 per cent in 1982 to 385 per cent in 1986. Similarly despite declines in interest rates and lending spreads, the average ratio for the ten of scheduled interest payments to exports remained above 30 per cent—too high to provide the funds necessary for investment to stimulate internal growth[25]. Moreover, the rapid expansion of the US trade deficit made it increasingly difficult to expect that the US could long continue to absorb increased LDC exports while Germany

[25]LDC Debt Realities, World Financial Markets—June–July 1987, Morgan Guaranty Trust Co., pp. 1–11.

and Japan showed little inclination substantially to stimulate their own domestic economies.

Few of the countries had also made the changes envisioned in the plan to their domestic economies. There had been little denationalization of often inefficient state-owned enterprises, only limited effort to improve the investment environment for overseas corporations and the financial markets of the Baker countries remained closed, underdeveloped and heavily regulated. At the same time many of the austerity plans introduced in conjunction with the IMF had collapsed, while domestic inflation rates had soared.

Similarly, the banks, rather than providing the funds called for to support the Baker Plan, had actually reduced their net exposure. In 1986, BIS reporting banks provided some $3 billion in new money but this was some $2.8 billion less than repayments of existing loans and decreases in balance sheet outstandings due to charge-offs and loan sales and transfers to non-banks. Banks also began actively to pursue debt swaps as a further way of reducing their exposures.

Official funds from governments and institutions such as the World Bank and the IMF were also well below the figures projected by the Baker Plan. In 1985 and 1986 net lending by governments was only $2.1 billion compared with an average of $5.2 billion in 1983–4. Lending by international organizations also dropped to around $4.5 billion, well short of the $6.5–7 billion estimates made at the time of the Baker initiative. Indeed in 1986, the IMF, the supposed central player in managing the global debt problem, actually made a net reduction in its lending to the Baker countries.

To prevent a default the banks were therefore forced to agree to extensive renegotiations, reschedulings and roll overs against a background of growing militancy by the debtor countries. Faced with the harsh political choice of continued domestic poverty or paying the interest on overseas bank loans, many countries began to impose conditions which limited the scale of their overseas commitments. In 1985, Alan Garcia Perez, the President of Peru, announced that in future no more than 10 per cent of export earnings would be devoted to servicing overseas debts. In 1986, Mexico squeezed its creditor banks to stretch out its $44 billion of existing loans, obtained a new loan of $6 billion, at least $250 million of annual interest savings and further contingency lines, dependent upon the rate of internal growth and the value of exports. Then, in March 1987, Brazil, the largest debtor nation, declared an interest moratorium on $68 billion of outstanding foreign private sector debt.

Against this growing background of the Baker Plan failing one bank decided to expose the fragile myth that sovereign risk loans were still good. At a dramatic press conference on 19 May 1987 John Reed, the 48-year-old chairman of Citicorp, announced the result of a board decision reached earlier that morning to begin to take the hit of the overhanging debt bomb. Reed announced that Citicorp was establishing a $3 billion reserve against bad LDC loans, thus establishing around a $2.5 billion loss for the second quarter of the year—the largest single quarter loss in banking history.

This bold move had been carefully planned and executed. The Federal Reserve and the US Treasury had been forewarned as had the Securities and Exchange Commission and the credit-rating agencies. The regulatory authorities in London and Tokyo were also advised, while personal letters were delivered to the presidents of the leading debtor nations. In the half-hour or so before the press announcement, Reed and his colleagues also advised other senior bankers in the major US money centre banks.

As a result of the move Citicorp established a reserve of some $3.5 billion or 26 per cent against its outstanding LDC debt portfolio. The bank intended to use this reserve in part to cover any losses that might be incurred by reducing exposures via debt for equity swaps and loan sales. In addition Citicorp intended further to strengthen its balance sheet by issuing a substantial tranche of new equity.

The reaction to the Citicorp move within the international banking industry was swift and dramatic. A week later Northwest Corp, the 24th largest US bank, increased reserves against LDC loans by $200 million. The following day Chase Manhattan increased reserves by $1.6 billion[26]. In the UK, NatWest Bank,

---

[26]Jaclyn Fierman, John Reed's bold stroke, *Fortune*, 22 June 1987, p. 20.

the least exposed to LDC debt, announced it was reserving for over a third of its developing country loans. Other British banks were forced to follow suit as best they could. In the US and Europe some banks such as the Bank of America and the Midland, with already weakened capital adequacy due to established loan losses, faced dramatic cuts in shareholders' equity if they attempted to match Citicorp. However, banks everywhere were faced with growing pressure from the stock market and regulatory authorities to make allowances.

While the Citicorp move opened up the reality of the debt bomb to the banking system, in itself it did nothing to resolve the issue. While Citicorp might be able to extricate itself with creative measures such as loan disposals and debt swaps, the problem of financing the economies of Latin America and the developing world remained.

5.12   THE MEGA DEBT BOMB

In April 1985, the USA became a net debtor nation just five years after it had been the largest net creditor with overseas assets of over $140 billion. By the beginning of 1987 the net overseas debts of the USA had grown to $240 billion and the pace of the growth was still accelerating. Never had any country seen such a position of financial strength eroded so rapidly. By 1990 it was estimated that the US debt mountain would be around $700 billion or over eight times that of Brazil.

Some obervers believed the transformation of the US debt position would prove to be the 'dominant event in world finance in the 1980s[27]. Others were less concerned, noting the underlying strength of the $4 trillion US economy and the fact that, unlike the LDCs, US debts were denominated in its own currency. Indeed since 1985 the dollar had fallen by over 48 per cent against the yen and 42 per cent against the Deutschmark.

Despite this rapid depreciation in the value of the dollar, the USA had found it relatively easy to attract overseas funds, especially from Japan, to cover its mounting trade deficit. In

[27]L. Glynn, Uncle Debtor, *Institutional Investor*, May 1987, p. 142.

1986, foreign purchasers acquired some 40 per cent of new US Treasury bonds. In early 1987, overseas portfolio investment had bought heavily into US corporate bonds, mortgage securities and equities.

Nevertheless, while the US had managed to attract the surplus funds of other nations, it was gradually moving to a position where it was dependent on their continued flow. As a result the freedom of manoeuvre of the Federal Reserve and the Treasury was slowly being constrained to account for the wishes of foreign investors. Moreover, the continued decline in the value of the dollar was persuading Japanese investors to look for alternative investment opportunities. Indeed, while up to 1986 the US deficit had been covered by capital inflows from private investors, the multinational banks had been forced to pick up a growing volume of Treasury bills in order to prevent an even stronger run on the dollar. To stop further dramatic falls in future, therefore, it was expected that US interest rates might be forced to rise, so increasing the threat of inflation and industrial recession. In addition, with the freedom from exchange controls, there was the added fear that US investors might also flee from the dollar and into yen, Deutschmarks or other hard currencies. In early 1987, the finance ministers of the Group of Seven leading industrial nations agreed to act in concert to smooth any further decline in the value of the dollar and to act to stabilize foreign exchange rates within broad, unpublished bands. Urgent steps were also expected of the US government to reduce the level of the deficit. However, as the US moved towards further presidential elections short-term moves which might plunge the economy into recession seemed unlikely as long as the flow of overseas funds to finance the deficit remained viable. Political gain seemed once again to triumph over economic rationality.

The growing weight of the US deficit was therefore adding itself to the existing LDC debt bomb by mid 1987. This new threat, moreover, placed the US authorities on the horns of a dilemma. In order to reduce the US deficit some correction in the US balance of trade was essential. In particular, the markets of Latin America had been a traditionally important market for US goods. However, in order to service their own debts, the countries of the region were themselves being forced to achieve balance of payments surpluses. Traditionally these had arisen largely as a result of access to the US market.

By 1987 the current account surpluses being achieved by West Germany and Japan dwarfed the OPEC surpluses of the first and second oil shocks. These surpluses were being used to fund the growing US deficit which was largely caused by overspending by government and consumers on current account rather than on new investment. As a result of its widening trade imbalance, pressure was therefore growing within the USA for protectionist measures, which if implemented could threaten the LDCs and even many industrialized nations. Moreover, the growing burden of debt servicing further threatened the capacity of the US economy to grow and so support imports. The new mega debt bomb, thus threatened not only the international banking system but potentially the entire world economy, making the debt crisis of 1982 seem like only a forerunner to the main event.

5.13   DETONATION?

On Black Monday, 19 October 1987, the Dow Jones industrial average collapsed by 22.6 per cent on a trading volume of 605 million shares as investors panicked to sell their equity holdings. The scale of the collapse made the Great Wall Street Crash of 29 October 1929, when the market fell 11.7 per cent, seem almost trivial. As the chairman of the New York Stock Exchange put it, the market was close to meltdown. Chasing the time zones around the world, the great fall in stock prices was repeated in each main trading centre in turn. The great bull market of the 1980s had ended with a vengeance.

The causes of the crash in equity prices went back to the fundamental nature of the mega debt bomb. In Japan, domestic bond yields had increased sharply in 1987 while yields on equity, already low, had fallen substantially further as the Nikkei Dow had continued a dizzy climb and price earnings multiples had risen to over 60. The resulting reverse yield gap clearly indicated that either interest rates had to fall or share prices had to tumble. At the same time Japanese institutional investors were being encouraged by the MOF to buy US government bonds to finance the American deficit. As interest rates around the world rose partially in response to rising Japanese domestic rates the value of US bonds fell and this was compounded by the steady collapse of the US dollar versus the yen.

On 14 October, the US announced a larger than expected trade deficit of $15.5 billion, indicating that the deficit was apparently still rising with the politicians in Washington showing little or no resolve to get it under control. Moreover, showing his disapproval of a rise in West German interest rate, US Treasury Secretary Baker indicated that he would permit the dollar to float down against the Deutschmark rather than try to maintain its position in line with the value set by the Louvre Accord.

This was a clear signal that US interest rates would have to rise and/or the dollar would fall sharply. Both of these prospects were unattractive to investors, and foreign investors, in particular, dramatically withdrew their support. As a result the value of shares crashed as markets moved to correct the yield gap between bonds and equities. At the same time the dollar came under pressure against the major currencies of the yen and the Deutschmark although initially not in as spectacular a way.

With the crash of 1987 had the mega debt bomb finally detonated, leaving the world to face a massive economic slump reminiscent of the early 1930s? Many of the signs were similar. The earlier crisis was triggered by a similar collapse in equity markets, which in turn led to major corporate failures. These induced failures amongst the banking industry and severe deflation, protectionism and unemployment.

The 1987 collapse in equities found the banking system probably in worse shape than in 1929 as a result of the already large volume of overhanging country risk debt. In addition, in the USA, many regional banks in the Mid-West and Texas faced severe financial difficulties due to the collapse of the US farm sector and the fall in oil prices, which had severely reduced the loan-servicing capability of their customers engaged in agriculture and energy.

As a result of the crash many corporations, especially in the USA, were expected to be in difficulties. During the 1980s, many companies took on substantial increases in the level of debt in their balance sheets. This was especially true of the growing number of highly leveraged management buy-outs which had occurred since the mid 1980s. Should interest rates rise significantly many such companies were expected to have difficulties in servicing their debt. Moreover, the fall in the value of corporate gross assets could well trigger loan repayment clauses as collateral values would be inadequate to meet bank requirements. To meet debt and interest repayments therefore some companies were expected to go bankrupt while others might be forced to try and sell off businesses or divisions or clamp down on investment. There seemed a strong probability therefore that bank loan losses would rise sharply while investment would reduce, leading to recession.

This was expected to be compounded by the actual losses incurred by individuals as a result of the crash. Discretionary spending seemed likely to be sharply reduced, thus lowering consumption. In the United States it was estimated that the crash wiped some $550 billion off household portfolios and that consumption might be immediately reduced by around 1 per cent[28]. Moreover, as recession bit, unemployment could be expected to rise, again triggering bank loan losses from the massive growth in retail credit developed by banks around the world during the boom years of the 1980s.

The ingredients for a major slump clearly were all present. Whether the depth of such a recession was likely to be extreme depended upon how well the politicians and central authorities were able to restore investor confidence. Initial US moves to cut the budget deficit by $23 billion for 1988 were regarded as wholly inadequate and US politicians would have to realize that they could no longer live in economic isolation if world recession were to be avoided. Similarly Japanese politicians would have to understand that their country's very economic success in the post-war period now meant they had to pick up the economic ball from the USA if the world was to avoid a return to the dark days of the 1930s. The markets of the world waited for the politicians to act. If they did not the markets would themselves determine the issue and the mega debt bomb would have been detonated.

---

[28]P. Wilser, What the crash means for Britain, *Sunday Times* 25 October 1987, p. 79.

5.14 CONCLUSION

The two oil shocks caused a fundamental shift in the financing of the developing economies. Instead of seriously affecting the industrial nations the discontinuity of the sharp rises in the price of oil was transferred to the lesser developed economies by many of the multinational banks recycling the OPEC surpluses. These surpluses in turn were rapidly eroded with the high-absorption oil producers moving quickly from surplus to deficit.

The holders of the OPEC surpluses placed the bulk of their funds in investments in the developed economies, thus alleviating their capital outflow caused by higher oil prices, and in short-term Euromarket deposits with the multinational banks. During the 1970s the banks, often encouraged by their central banks, recycled many of these funds to cover the balance of payments deficits of those lesser developed economies which enjoyed access to the international capital market. For those countries which did not, such as the nations of Sub-Sahara Africa (with the exception of oil-producer Nigeria), and the poorer nations of the Pacific Basin, the two oil shocks proved disastrous. Deprived of Western aid, which was severely cut back, and with the World Bank similarly kept short of funds, these nations emerged in the 1980s as a cause for international crisis measures as over 150 million people suffered from hunger and malnutrition. For the bankers, however, such countries were largely unbankable.

At the end of the 1970s and during the early 1980s the banks continued to lend vigorously and without apparent concern to the major LDC debtors, notably those of Latin America, lured by apparently attractive profits on low-cost, recycled funds and deluded by the false premise that sovereign states cannot go bankrupt. In a highly competitive marketplace there was no shortage of takers for these assets and spreads did not reflect in any way the potential risks. Following the second oil shock the party was soon to prove to be over. By their profligate lending, the banks had fashioned the debt bomb which now threatened to explode and destroy the international banking system.

Following a series of false alarms after the fall of the Shah and the collapse of the Polish economy, the bomb threatened to explode when Mexico, closely followed by Brazil, Argentina and the other countries of Latin America, indicated they needed to reschedule their debts. A complex series of negotiations followed, coupled with the introduction of IMF-sponsored austerity packages. The banks were forced to maintain credit lines to the insolvent nations rather than adopting the herd instinct of retreating completely from providing support.

However, by the mid 1980s the role of the multinational banks in providing funds to LDCs had turned from feast to famine. In the 1970s they played an important intermediation role. Unfortunately, however, the funding was far too indiscriminate, partly as a function of intense competition, as a result of inadequate credit assessment and due to a lack of adequate regulatory monitoring. The funding provided by the multinational banks, while partly to finance industrial development, was initially provided to assist these countries in the face of oil-related balance of payments deficits. Even when funding was project-related, seldom was the viability of individual investments adequately assessed. Moreover, many of the funds were lost due to corruption and capital flight. As a result, as an element in the economic development of the LDCs the multinational banks provided funds but did not give adequate guidance or monitoring of their use. Nevertheless, only when the debtor countries were obviously in trouble did banks attempt to reduce their exposure. This was done in a similar indiscriminate manner with whole regions or continents suddenly finding they were no longer creditworthy. Without the benefit of hindsight, many of the problems that have developed have their roots in managerial failure to observe basic banking practices. Let us hope the losses now being incurred by major money centre banks will bring home to top managements the need always to observe such principles in future.

The major central banks and governments of the industrialized nations were also partly culpable for the ensuing disorder. They did not intervene, allowing market forces to work, not really appreciating that finance market access did not just slow down for a country—it stoped dead with a credit run, just like a confidence crisis in a bank. Only when such a run became obvious did the central banks step in as the BIS did to rescue the

National Bank of Hungary or the IMF did to force through a support package for Mexico. Moreover, the regulators demonstrated inadequate knowledge of what was developing in the international capital markets. Further, the official agencies often seem to have tried to enforce economic solutions which have failed to account for political reality. Finally, the developed nation governments, while generous, have not really provided appropriate funding or, in the case of Japan and Germany, adequately opened their markets to ensure global economic development and long-term political stability.

While some progress had been made to build global economic cooperation between governments and central banks, the inability of politicians in particular to recognize the development of the globally integrated financial market had led to a potential return to the great depression. The crash of 1987, induced by the US government's parochial misunderstanding that Japanese investors would not continue to provide the funds needed to cover profligate US domestic spending policies, would hopefully focus the minds after the 1988 Presidential election.

CHAPTER 6

The Changing Nature of Corporate Banking

6.1 THE PURSUIT OF THE MULTINATIONAL CLIENT

The rationale for the development of multinational banking owed much to the growing overseas expansion of industrial companies, especially those based in the USA. As the major US companies became multinational they increasingly needed a new range of banking services which linked together their operations as they gradually diversified throughout the world. The process of multinational corporation development has been well documented[1]. Initially, companies tended to open markets by exports, followed by the establishment of a sales subsidiary, then product assembly and, ultimately, full-scale manufacturing. At first such production tended to be for local markets, but, more recently, many industries have begun to design and produce products for global markets, producing at one or more sites servicing the world.

Where substantial volume economies of scale existed, regional integration occurred at first as with the automobile industry where an organization such as Ford of Europe, for example, initially designed and manufactured cars for the European market, producing bodies in Germany and the UK, engines in Belgium and the UK, and small-car assembly in Spain. These transfers of components led to the need to minimize financing

[1]See, for example, D. F. Channon and R. M. Jalland, *Multinational Strategic Planning*, Macmillan & Amacon, London and New York, 1979, Chapter 1.

costs by integrating the finance functions on a regional basis. The regional finance unit could thus operate in a series of different financial markets, manage exchange risk by netting overall exposure, operate leads and lags management, taking account of different exchange controls, raise currency in various markets according to cost and the like.

As the automobile industry and others moved to global strategies, so the need to manage corporate funds on a worldwide basis had also developed. This had been assisted by the development of improved global communication systems which had increasingly allowed central corporate treasuries to keep a close check on overall corporate cash and working capital balances around the world, so as to minimize funding costs within a given level of currency exposure.

Providing for capital needs had also become increasingly international as a result of the growth of the global capital market. For large multinational corporations, locations, currency and instruments had become more flexible and the routes to achieving a particular financial position could involve a complex sequence of steps. For the largest corporations there had also been the gradual development of a global equity market in the past few years.

Initially, during the early 1970s, central treasuries of the large US multinationals had little understanding of the international foreign exchange or money markets. Policy guidelines for subsidiary or area cash pool organizations tended to operate only in dollars, with little concept of netting or a balanced global currency perspective based on operational needs. With the growth of the main US money centre banks as multinational institutions themselves, treasury executives were suddenly being offered advice and systems which enabled them to maintain much closer control over the day-to-day operational management of corporate financial resources. The growing volatility in the foreign exchange markets also emphasized the need to understand and control the impact of currency rate changes. Further, as European banks countered the attacks of the US multinational banks in Europe by vigorously pursuing the US corporate market, competition increased sharply. Large multinationals found themselves able to play off one bank against another and to cut interest rates to the bone by operating a pool of international banks.

Moreover, the treasurers increasingly questioned the use of services provided by their bankers, partly as a result of individual banks beginning to target customer and product area segments and specializing to offer good and/or cheap specific services to selected customer groups. In addition, many corporations recruited their senior treasurers from the banking industry. Such new appointments were usually expected to reduce the overall cost of bank services. Growing intensity of competition, coupled with the size of credit needs of large multinationals, meant that such treasuries often used many banks as suppliers. In order to gain competitive advantage, therefore, each bank would try to gain favour by providing the best innovation. The large multinationals thus had less and less need of routine banking services. Indeed, some large multinationals by the late 1980s possessed virtually all of the capabilities of the banks. For example, British Petroleum's specialist finance subsidiary provided virtually a full range of banking services. It was an active trader in the foreign exchange markets, managed the group's financial resources, had engaged in Eurobond issues and arranged mergers and acquisitions, traditionally areas of investment bank expertise.

Moreover, whereas the standard bank intermediary product was a loan, the large multinationals, in the light of the oil shocks and bank exposure to sovereign risk lending, found their own credit ratings were superior to those of their bankers. As a result, ironically facilitated by some commercial banks which had developed their investment banking divisions, together with the major investment banks, the multinationals turned increasingly to the commercial paper markets and other flexible bond instruments such as Floating Rate Notes (FRNs) and swaps as their main source of non-equity funds. While initially this market was mainly used by US-based corporations, increasingly the sophisticated corporate banks and service companies brought the same service to non-US multinationals, hedging the foreign exchange risk of dollar borrowings where necessary.

Nevertheless, up until 1983, the major international banks, excluding the Japanese, had specific target lists of leading multinational corporations which they wished to lend to. Margins in the large corporate market were therefore squeezed to a very fine level. While large corporations maintained, in many cases, several hundred bank relationships with perhaps 30–40 lead banks, it was only those banks enjoying lead positions which tended to enjoy profitable relationships. One exception to this was that in difficult currency areas, such as Latin America, banks able to provide lines of credit, which other banks could not, also could develop a profitable relationship based on a specialist secondary lead bank position. Multinationals thus tended to develop a series of different types of bank relationships. Lead banks provided large lines of credit at competitive prices, but in addition provided a wide range of additional fee-based services and tended to be the primary conduits for transactions between corporate subsidiaries. Secondary relationships were those where banks provided specialist services in a specific geographic or product area. Such relationships were also profitable, provided the institutions did not expect automatically to use such a connection to develop into a lead bank position. While this might be a desirable objective for a bank, the trend in the USA since the late 1970s had been to reduce corporate lead bank relationships. The third category of bank could be classified as a 'me too' institution and had little distinctive product or geographic superiority. Such organizations provided back-up, or poorly used facilities for multinationals, as a marketing expectation in the hope of getting into a lead bank position. Finally, a number of local banks executed local services for individual subsidiaries in specific countries or provided limited financial services or credit lines at corporate or regional centres. Such organizations were generally profitable but their main sources of income tended to come from middle market accounts rather than large multinationals.

In one of its regular studies of 388 leading US multinationals, Greenwich Research Associates found, in 1982, that the most important factors in deciding to use a bank as a lead institution were its competence in operating global multinational relationships, high calibre of account officers, and the extent of the bank overseas branch network[2]. Those banks that had invested

[2]Greenwich Research Associates, *North American Multinational Banking, 1982; Report to Participants* (Greenwich, Conn., 1982).

in providing these facilities and skills succeeded with multinationals but many institutions were unable or unwilling to make such expensive levels of commitment. Citibank, for example, when operating its World Corporation Group Structure, appointed a global account manager to lead a team of 20–30 officers around the world to service a large multinational . This level of commitment was much higher than that provided by most multinational banks.

In Citibank, such a global account manager had responsibility for no more than 8–10 accounts including prospects[3]. Similarly, J. P. Morgan also maintained extremely close relationships with its customers, with highly trained account officers with very limited client case loads and a system of maintaining such officers on the account for a considerable time, rather than changing them frequently as was the case with many European banks[4].

Ironically, in 1980 Citibank abandoned its focused strategy on worldwide multinationals and turned instead to a structure which widened the number of companies subject to account profit planning, but on a geographic region rather than global basis. By 1984, this structural change had clearly resulted in a decline in relationships with worldwide multinationals, the GAM profit measurement system had lost its bite, and Citibank was therefore forced to think again. This led to the re-establishment of a similar system to the earlier structure, which endeavoured to optimize the profitability of relationships on a global basis, rather than settling for the narrower concept of country profit maximization.

The Greenwich study found also that frequent officer turnover was a major reason for a decline in client bank relationships. Other important factors causing a loss of relationships were uncompetitive loan pricing and a lack of attention being paid by account officers to the company's needs in both home and overseas markets. European banks, in particular, had suffered by comparision with the best US commercial banks, in terms of the quality of account officers, the frequency of their turnover, their lack of training as corporate bankers and too large a client list.

[3]D. F. Channon, Citicorp 'A' Case, *Bank Strategic Management and Marketing Casebook*, Wiley, 1986.
[4]*Ibid.*, J. P. Morgan Case.

Typically, for a leading European bank with an account relationship structure in operation, accounts loads would be up to 20–30 customers and prospects. In many cases, however, European banks in their home markets still serviced large corporate clients through branch managers, rather than by the use of specialist corporate bankers. This was a further reason why large multinationals usually reported that the calibre of the account officers of large US multinational banks was superior to that of their European competitors. The US account officers were not only trained to be international corporate bankers but also operated with greater decision-making discretion, whereas their European counterparts often did not possess the same level of corporate banking skills, being primarily trained as generalists, were national rather than international in orientation, and finally needed the approval of superiors to a greater degree in granting large credit lines. Moreover, the average account officer turnover in European banks was also two years or less, thus making it difficult for officers to develop a close relationship with corporate treasurers. A further structural defect for the Europeans was that there was often difficulty in coordination between the international and the domestic networks, because the organization of the bank was primarily by geography rather than by type of client. Many European banks were recognizing these deficiencies in their servicing of large multinational accounts by the late 1980s. Some had taken steps to correct the problems but few had adjusted their recruitment, training and reward systems effectively to match the US banks within their domestic organizations. Ironically, outside their home countries, however, their corporate account service tactics closely mirrored the Americans, using specialist account officers often recruited from their US competitors. Domestically the differences in structure were therefore largely based on political rather than practical considerations.

Factors leading to improvements in bank relationships were the provision of overseas local currency credit, innovation in tailoring services to the needs of the customer, and more competitive loan pricing. Successful niche strategy banks with particular geographic coverage, such as Standard Chartered Bank Group or Lloyds Bank International, could thus capitalize on their ability to provide local currency facilities in difficult political-economic areas such as Latin America or the Middle East. The importance of innovation in bank services was growing rapidly in the late 1980s as the multinationals turned increasingly away from straightforward lending and more towards securitized debt instruments. While competitive pricing was clearly important, it was rarely the case that price alone could lead to the development of a lead bank position. In the event of lower market prices being offered, it was normal that lead banks would be given the opportunity to meet such prices. They could usually defray such extra costs against the wider range of collateral fee-based business they conducted for large clients. Despite a trend towards unbundling of bank services, a lead bank relationship usually provided adequate opportunities for such a bank to make a satisfactory return. However, to maintain their lead bank positions, the major banks were being increasingly forced to be innovative in providing overall cheap sources of funds, mainly from securitized instruments, developed by their investment banking subsidiaries. Moreover, the breadth of knowledge required of good account managers was expanding to embrace both investment and electronic banking skills. As a result, the traditional account officer, focused on the sale of loans, was giving way to the more sophisticated concept of the relationship manager, charged with developing a deep relationship with his or her clients, and not merely with the corporation's finance function. Such individuals, while not necessarily technical experts in all aspects of corporate banking, were expected to understand their customers' businesses sufficiently to recognize proactively problems which might be solved using the bank's offering of financial services products and to call in technical experts in such services as and when appropriate.

6.2   THE DATA BASE PROBLEM AND BIG IRON SOLUTIONS

Unfortunately, for many banks, especially the Europeans, suitable internal control systems which enabled them to measure the profitability of overall client relationships or that of specific services were still not available by the late 1980s. As a result such banks were often pursuing large multinational corporate clients more as a matter of faith than economic conviction, expecting that by gaining a share of the potential loan volume of such accounts, the relationship would become profitable. This pursuit of volume, however, was often not only misguided but, because such banks usually failed to provide the necessary level of calling officer coverage or skill, usually unobtainable. Bank accounting systems, notably in Europe, were based on the needs of traditional branch bank economics. Under such systems most European banks had been extremely slow to develop cost structures for individual services. Instead they had relied on offering an overall bundled package of services to both individual and corporate clients. Moreover, banks contained a series of separate systems, each segregated from the other. Hence a loan customer might do forex transactions, place deposits, use letters of credit, have different subsidiaries operating through various branches, while the bank would have no real way of tracking the total of such a range of service usage except by time-consuming and laborious manual checks. As a result, banks found it extremely difficult to assess either individual product or customer profitability.

The traditional system worked effectively as long as clients wanted to purchase bundled services. Multinational clients, however, with growing purchasing sophistication, had begun to demand unbundling of the multiple range of services offered by banks, creating a serious problem as banks did not know the cost of individual services or the demands for services for each customer. Further, European banks in particular had relied for their overall profitability on the traditional bank intermediary role as gatherers of deposits from small savers which could be lent out to large corporations and others at a profitable margin. As these margins had come under increasing pressure, due to the higher cost of deposits and lower prices for loans, banks had been more concerned to generate fee-based income. However, relationship executives did not possess the account information with which to pursue such a selective product market strategy.

Profitability in such banks was, however, relatively well understood at the branch level, but because bank accounting systems did not contain integrated data bases they could not be interrogated to provide suitable management information on services and specific customers with which to set and guide marketing strategy. The recognition of the need for superior management information on customer and service usage was growing amongst European banks by the mid 1980s. Many were, therefore, making extensive use of external consultants, largely drawn from the major accountancy companies, to upgrade their management information, accounting and control systems. Even within the USA, it was estimated that only a fraction of the 14,000 odd commercial banks had created fully integrated data bases which enabled service and customer segmentation to be undertaken in such a way that the location of profits and losses amongst groups of customers and services could be clearly identified[5]. As superior management information was made available to banks so, increasingly, they had begun to operate with focused strategies, in line with new trends in the fast-moving market for banking services.

While, as a generalization, European banks were weak in developing integrated data bases, the Scandinavian banks were notable exceptions. The banks in Finland and Sweden had been the first to automate their back office operations and to operate a fully truncated system for paper-based services. As a result in Sweden, for example, paper was truncated as soon as it reached the banking system. Thus checks were electronically entered into a comprehensive system at the teller terminal which was fully on line. The check did not then travel to a central clearing house but remained with the institution receiving it, irrespective of which bank it had been drawn on.

The Scandinavian banks had spent heavily on building integrated data bases. Skandinaviska Enskildas Banken, the largest Swedish bank, was considered to be a leading institution. The bank had introduced an integrated data base for retail banking in the late 1960s, while a system for corporate and international business came on stream in the late 1970s. The system gave management quick access to information on an account's foreign

---

[5]Salomon Brothers, *Technology and Banking. A Path to Competitive Advantage*, May 1985.

exchange trading, capital markets activities, corporate checking accounts, loans, cash management services and domestic and international funds transfers. Essential data in the system, such as forex and funds transfers, all operated in real time. Such a system not only took a considerable time to develop but was expensive and SE Banken estimated that 14 per cent of its operational budget in 1984 was spent on new technology. Other Scandinavian banks spent similar amounts but these were largely seeking to catch up[6].

The lack of a segregated data base for wholesale business had also made it very difficult for most banks to offer the comprehensive range of electronic banking products that was coming to be demanded by many corporate treasurers. They were demanding increasingly real-time, on-line information on their domestic and/or global funds position. This could mean up to several hundred data inputs to be synchronized, often from a number of banks and increasingly on a global basis, to provide the requisite information. Unless the banks' computer systems were fully linked, therefore, the provision of such services was expensive or impossible. As a result, the development of such global transaction systems favoured a few large banks with an integrated global network of their own. However, as a rule, the larger the network of the bank, the more complex and expensive it was to build an integrated data base system. The problem was therefore especially acute for the large, essentially retail-orientated branch network banks in Western Europe. In the United States the Bank of America, with over 1000 branches in the State of California, faced similar difficulties. The bank therefore was committed to spending some $500 million a year until 1990 to update its systems. By contrast, however, Citicorp was the leading spender, with an estimated annual outlay of $850–900 million in 1985 and this spending was more efficiently split between retail and corporate banking sectors.

6.3 GAINING TECHNOLOGICAL ADVANTAGE

Citicorp was seeking to gain technological pre-eminence, spending almost twice as much as Bank of America, and accounting for

[6]J. W. Gilligan, The computer race at the big banks, *Euromoney*, June 1985, p. 300.

10–11 per cent of technology spending by the US banking industry in 1985. The banks' share of technological spending was also expected to rise to 14–15 per cent of industry spending by 1990.

Such heavy expenditure on technology was, however, confined to a few major banks and was seen to be emerging as a critical source of competitive advantage. As a result, Salomon Brothers reported that the largest 35 US banks were increasingly outperforming smaller US banks. From 1981–5 these large institutions had spent $16.2 billion on computer and telecommunications systems. This was $2.1 billion more than the expenditure of the other 14,000-odd US banks combined. Between 1986 and 1990 it was expected that the big banks would spend a further $40 billion and almost double the spending predicted for the rest of the industry. Technology expenditure, moreover, accounted for over 10 per cent of total industry operating expenses in 1985 and more than half of all estimated discretionary expenditure[7].

The availability of an integrated data base potentially transformed the method of operation of a bank. Using software packages to interrogate the data base from smart terminals, an executive could explore an entire account relationship throughout the range of services and locations operated by the bank. Similarly, banks could review their exposures by geographic region or industry. Each service could also be tested for price elasticity, or sensitivity analysis could be used to check the impact of alternative marketing strategies. Corporate and retail customers who cost the bank money could also be identified and purified from the system, or converted to profitability by the use of alternative delivery systems, pricing or extra volume.

J. P. Morgan, for example, had been early to see the value-added capability of developing such an integrated data base. The bank's Global Exposure System (GES) kept track of Morgan's worldwide credit exposures. At the end of each month the GES computers could print out a one-page summary of the bank's balance sheet, providing a position report on all areas of operations including loans, foreign exchange, swaps and bullion trad-

---

[7]Salomon Brothers, *Technology and Banking: The Implications of Strategic Expenditures*, May 1987.

ing. To support this picture, up to 7000 pages of detailed back-up information for management and control were also available.

All Morgan operations around the world could tap into the system for information on 75,000 client names and some 35,000 credit facilities. The massive GES data base was configured to enable Morgan personnel to extract information from it in a variety of ways helpful to bankers, traders, financial advisers, comptrollers and the like. For example, the Bankers Workstation, introduced in New York in 1985, and around the world in 1986, helped focus on client relationships and deal-making potential. The workstation provided access by serving both as a terminal for reports drawn from the bank's main systems and as a research tool to pull data down from large data bases for local modelling at the workstation level. The Global Account Profitability system aggregated information on the volume and value of services and products provided to multinational corporate clients by all branches of the bank, giving the relationship managers a global overview of clients, including subsidiaries and affiliates in different countries operating in diverse currencies. Similarly, the corporate finance system provided a range of services designed to help stimulate new business opportunities, including the broadcasting of swap open positions to facilitate matching of counterparties, access to financial markets and product information, to facilitate the development of customized financing packages and market rate information for deal-making[8].

One result of developing such an integrated data base had been that a number of banks had recognized that the need for data on corporate accounts was different from that for personal customers. The problems of combining both sets of data on a single data base had therefore led them to segregate personal and corporate operations. Once this fundamental decision had been made, it was logical to subdivide the organization of the bank along similar lines and the importance of data base management had therefore begun to have a fundamental effect on bank organization structures, with an increasing number reorganizing to provide different services to retail and corporate customers via specialist internal divisions.

[8]J. P. Morgan, Annual Report, 1985, pp. 8–11.

6.4   NEW PATTERNS IN CORPORATE BANKING STRATEGY

The growing sophistication of the large multinationals had forced the major commercial banks to change their marketing tactics. Increasingly, unless there was a strong probability of achieving a lead or strong secondary position within an account, which established a long-term relationship, commercial banks were questioning the selection of multinationals as key target accounts. Secondly, banks were turning away from straightforward lending and looking either for lead positions in syndications or for collateral business with fee-generating capacity. Thirdly, banks had reduced their asset positions by selling loans and disintermediating from their traditional role. Fourth, the large commercial banks had built their investment banking capabilities in order to gain fee-based income. Fifth, a number of lending institutions had moved rapidly to establish global positions. Sixth, individual banks had specialized into niche strategy positions, focusing upon particular industries, products or geographic areas or some combination of these. Seventh, many banks had begun to refocus on the needs of the 'middle market' in the hope that loan spreads to these companies would remain attractive compared to those available in the large corporate market. Eighth, some banks had identified the importance of electronic banking and had endeavoured to build their position on the provision of electronic services. This had included not only banking services for corporate accounts, but also for other banks, and had included information processing, the sale of software and transaction processing for other banks. Finally, banks had diversified their activities, in particular into all areas of securities dealing, thus accelerating the process of disintermediation.

6.4.1   Revising the Target Account List

During the 1970s, as multinational banking developed, most of the major banks targeted leading multinational corporations as actual or potential key account customers. Many adopted focused organizational units similar to Citibank's success. As a consequence, by the end of the 1970s most of the large commercial banks in Europe and the USA had key target account lists of around 500 names. Given the relatively small numbers of global multinationals most banks were actively chasing the same small group of users.

However, as interest rate margins shrank, despite having inadequate control systems, many banks began to question the wisdom of pursuing large multinational accounts, when the companies themselves could possibly borrow more cheaply than the bank in the growing commercial paper markets. By the mid 1980s, therefore, many banks were reappraising their key account strategies. Account names were being reviewed to reassess their potential in terms of the probability of penetration, given existing bank relationships. Further, collateral services such as foreign exchange and trade finance were especially sought after. Those accounts where the modified potential was considered to be inadequate were being dropped from key account lists and the expensive account executive calling and servicing time was being redeployed onto higher potential accounts.

By contrast, specialist banks such as J. P. Morgan were actually increasing their focus on the large corporate market. Here the strategy was to create deep relationships with key customers, based on understanding the account's financial and strategic needs, to generate innovative 'solutions'. Although these might involve significant levels of lending, they also tended to be based on investment banking skills and the use of the bank's own uniquely strong customer base to identify integrated multi-counterparty transaction opportunities.

6.4.2 The Move to Loan Syndication

During the 1970s the key change in corporate lending was the move away from overdraft in many countries, to some form of medium-term lending. This was pioneered by the major US banks and, by the end of the 1970s, medium-term lending had become an important element in the asset base of all major multinational banks. This appplied to both domestic and international lending. Large loans were increasingly subjected to syndication. Lead banks would package the financial requirements of sovereign borrowers or large corporations, for a fee related to the size of the loan, and sell the bulk of the asset to participants in a syndicate of banks. In addition to syndication, medium-term loans were also effectively created by roll over facilities. As a result, five-year borrowing could be supported by a series of rolled over six-month deposits. Thus a bank would raise a deposit at an agreed interest rate and lend to a borrower at a spread over the cost of funds. This would be repeated every six months, with the actual interest rate potentially changing, but with the bank's spread remaining constant. The successful lead banks were those that demonstrated sophistication in packaging large loans, were aggressive in terms of pricing, and had the placing power to ensure that the borrower was able to obtain the funds required.

While, to some extent, the successful syndicating banks changed during the late 1970s, there was a steady group which consistently did well. These included the leading US money centre banks, some British and French and the leading German banks. Since the end of the 1970s the Japanese banks had also become more important, after an earlier series of entries and exits from the market. The market for syndicated loans tended to be dominated by the major commercial banks. However, as these institutions' ability to raise low-cost funds came under threat, and more creative solutions, based on swaps and options, became a cheaper source of funds, the investment banks had increasingly come to dominate the provision of large-scale funds for major corporations.

Growing competition in the market for large loans thus severely reduced spreads. Unless banks, therefore, obtained a lead position with its corresponding fees, revenue from loan syndication for large corporations and sovereign risk borrowers had become increasingly unattractive. Moreover, as loan losses increased, and the threat of sovereign risk defaults grew, so banks in the 1980s became increasingly reluctant to take extra assets on their own books. Loan growth was further inhibited by the rising cost of deposits and the weakness of bank equities, making it difficult for the banks to support asset growth due to capital adequacy constraints.

6.4.3   Disintermediation and Loan Wholesaling

In addition to the threat of the sovereign risk debt crisis, there had also been a severe increase in bad loan write-offs, caused by problem loans amongst large corporate accounts. In 1982, Chase Manhattan Bank was severely affected when Drysdale Government Securities Inc., a small, but aggressive, New York Securities dealer, defaulted on $106 million owed to other government securities dealers. Chase Manhattan, which acted as the principal intermediary for Drysdale in the government securities market, was forced to cover Drysdale's debts at a cost of $117 million after tax[9].

Chase, together with Continental Illinois and Seattle First National Bank, were also badly hit when US Federal Regulators closed the small, but highly lent, Penn Square Bank in Oklahoma which had outstanding energy loans of some $2 billion. Many of these loans had been syndicated on to leading banks. Penn Square had advanced enormous sums to seriously under-capitalized oil and gas companies and had often failed to perform the legal work necessary to secure its claim on collateral. Continental Illinois had purchased over $1 billion of these loans and was forced to establish a $220 million reserve for likely loan losses[10].

In West Germany the leading domestic banks had been forced to rescue the heavily leveraged AEG Telefunken Company, while in Canada the major banks faced serious loan write-offs at Dome Petroleum and Massey Ferguson. Elsewhere in the world, similar problems were occurring for the banks as high-capital-intensity corporations came into care due to high interest rates, falling sales and cash flows unable to support new investment to cover the effects of inflation, interest and loan payments. Similarly, as oil prices began to decline, aggressive lending to secondary energy producers, oil field equipment and construction firms began to produce loan losses. The lessons of the property market investments of the early 1970s, which had caused the Real Estate Investment Trust write-offs in the United States, the Secondary

---

[9]*Business Week*, August 1982, p. 40.
[10]*Ibid*.

Table 6.1   Loan loss provision trends 1982–86

US Banks $m	1982	1983	1984	1985	1986
J.P. Morgan	114	230	150	335	265
Chase Manhattan	230	254	215	320	475
Citicorp	473	520	619	1243	1825
Chemical NY	117	166	165	113	170
Bank of America Corp.	501	658	860	2180	2004
UK Banks £m					
Barclays Bank	300	442	469	416	416
Lloyds Bank	219	219	269	257	215
National Westminster	116	155	199	255	313
Midland Bank	196	318	616	431	357

Source: Annual Reports

Banking crisis in the United Kingdom, and similar collapses in the property markets of most industrial countries, were being repeated.

On this occasion, however, the problems were more serious. It was not the secondary banks which risked collapse but rather the possible fall of major institutions which threatened the viability of the entire banking system[11]. Chase Manhattan survived in these early loan losses. However, the problem later effectively eliminated Continental Illinois as a major competitor, caused Seattle First to merge with Bank of America (which subsequently came under massive pressure due to severe loan losses in Mexico and California), caused the leading Texas banks to seek merger partners, and rapidly increased the number of bank closures, notably in the USA. These problems also forced the Midland Bank to sell Crocker and other assets. An indication of the decline in bank profitability and rising loan losses is shown in Table 6.1. Following the crash of 1987 these problems seemed likely to be exacerbated.

Banks had therefore sharply reduced their overall asset growth, especially in the corporate and sovereign risk markets. For the high-quality corporates the use of the commercial paper and bond markets had proved increasingly cheaper than stan-

[11]T. Anderson and P. Field, The tremors that threaten the banking system, *Euromoney*, October 1982, pp. 17–27.

dard bank credit lines, as bank credit ratings had suffered as a result of the debt overhang. Amongst the large money centre banks in the USA, therefore, only Morgan Guarantee maintained its triple A credit rating in 1987. Secondly, concerned regulatory authorities had forced the banks to increase their capital adequacy ratios, to strengthen their balance sheets against possible loan write-offs. This had been done in several ways—by retaining earnings, by issuing convertible floating rate notes, and by reducing asset growth or even selling assets.

Citibank's Institutional Banking Group thus reduced its asset position between 1983 and 1986 from $87 billion to $75 billion. In particular, commercial and industrial loans were reduced from $44.6 billion to $39.8 billion as part of a strategic realignment to higher yielding assets. This was accomplished by a mixture of syndications, loan participations and other methods. As a consequence of this revision in policy, while Institutional Banking remained an important contributor to Citicorp profitability, profits from this activity had been virtually static since 1982, and in real terms had shown a substantial decline. Overall corporate profitability had grown sharply, however, due to profit expansion in individual and investment banking. For Citibank, therefore, while the Institutional Banking Group might generate a loan, the Capital Markets Group could also take such a loan and sell it off to other banking customers, so reducing asset exposure and increasing fee income. In making its provisions for sovereign risk debt exposure, in 1987, Citicorp had indicated that it similarly intended to sell on part of its loan portfolio and to convert other parts of it into securitized assets which could be disposed of in the capital markets[12].

Bankers Trust had similarly modified its strategy, moving away from a conventional lending bank perspective of making loans for its own book, towards one of loan wholesaling. The bank's Syndications Group was actively selling loan participations, bringing greater liquidity to the loan portfolio and so freeing the bank's capital and gaining fee-based income. Loan sales also provided other banks with the means to increase their asset positions and increase yields by participating in high-quality loans across a range of industries and maturities. Bankers Trust handled all documentation and bore origination costs of the loans it sold without recourse. In 1984 the bank was the largest seller of such loans in the world, selling participations of over $7 billion. This compared with the position of loan sales of only $200 million in 1980. By 1983 this had reached $2 billion. The customers for such loans included savings and loan associations, foreign central banks and other international lenders. As Bankers Trust President, Charles S. Sanford Jnr, commented: 'One of the bank's long-term goals was to liquefy our loan account'[13].

While loan sales were not the same as securitization they were clearly a short step from this position. They did, however, represent a clear move towards the disintermediation of commercial banking. Instead of collecting deposits and lending these on at a spread, the banks were becoming more like very large investment banks. The new strategy was increasingly to provide a service to large borrowers by arranging loans and then placing them with other banks, rather than placing them in a full, open secondary market. While loan syndication was not new, the active efforts on the part of the large commercial banks not to add to their own asset base, and to even reduce it, was a new strategy, originating in the turbulent market of the mid 1980s.

6.4.4   Building Investment Banking Capability

In conjunction with the development of disintermediation and the efforts to build fee income, major commercial banks were actively building their capabilities in investment banking. Citicorp, for example, began actively to expand its investment banking activities from the beginning of the 1980s. By 1985 it had expanded its presence to cover 36 countries and 16 US cities. Earnings had increased from $100 million in 1980 to $160 million by 1984, 18 per cent of total profits, despite heavy increases in expenses as the global presence was established. Moreover, return on equity was 31.2 per cent, more than double

[13]Bankers Trust Annual Report, 1984.

the average for all Citicorp businesses. Citicorp was a leading dealer in US government securities and had expanded the distribution of these to overseas capital markets in London, Zurich and Tokyo. The bank provided a full range of interest rate risk management tools and was the leader in interest rate and currency swaps, in cross-border mergers and acquisitions, in Swiss franc foreign financings and in the market for yen bonds, issued by non-Japanese companies[14]. Citicorp had continued to build its investment banking capacity and had actively restructured its institutional and investment banking businesses to increase the attention given to new investment banking products while streamlining the number of traditional services. Staff reductions also occurred in the institutional bank while recruitment continued in investment banking. On a revised basis, income from investment banking had risen from $343 million in 1984, to $429 million in 1986, although return on equity had fallen slightly to 27.5 per cent.

Morgan Guarantee was similarly actively developing its investment banking capability. Unable to underwrite equity and bonds in the domestic US market due to the restrictions of Glass–Steagall, Morgan, like Citibank, had concentrated on building its investment banking position based on the Euromarkets. In its coverage it was not emulating Citibank's global approach but rather concentrated initially on Eurobond operations out of New York and London. In 1980, as its Eurobond capabilities were being built up, Morgan ranked number 46 in lead management positions. By 1984, Morgan was responsible for 33 deals totalling $5 billion, making Morgan second only to the specialist joint venture investment bank, Credit Suisse First Boston, the acknowledged Eurobond market leader. Morgan's success in the Eurobond market had come especially from a highly innovative approach to financing which included new concepts such as 'morning to midnight' defeasance deals, to the first insured Eurobond, to $750 million in undated FRNs, convertible into four-year FRNs and $500 million in the first FRNs sold by auction[15].

[14]Citicorp Annual Report, 1984, pp. 22–4.
[15]S. Wittebort, Inside the Morgan machine, *Institutional Investor*, July 1985, pp. 59–74.

All the major commercial banks were similarly endeavouring to increase their merchant banking capabilities. Morgan, Citibank and Bankers Trust had been relatively successful amongst US banks in adding such skills, while Barclays had been most aggressive in the UK. Prior to the 'Big Bang' Barclays purchased, at a cost of over £100 million, one of the six leading London brokers, de Zoete and Bevan, and one of the two leading jobbers, Wedd, Durlacher. The bank also made a number of top-level investment banking appointments of executives, head-hunted from other institutions. All this was done in addition to a substantial capital injection to bolster Barclays Merchant Bank which, for over a decade, had failed to make significant impression on the leading London merchant banks. Initially, the bank focused on the London market, but was also actively developing its position in Paris, Amsterdam and Tokyo, although Glass–Steagall restricitions prevented development in the USA. While Barclays remained weak, compared to the big global investment banks and brokerage houses, after a year of the Big Bang the advantages of scale were beginning to show. While BZW was profitable, albeit with a return on the assets invested which was low by comparison with some, most of the smaller London merchant banks were finding they had difficulty competing in a market where the size of balance sheet had suddenly become critical. As a result, a shakeout seemed inevitable for the smaller, merchant bank players. By late 1987, Guinness Peat and Hill Samuel had already been acquired while others, such as Morgan Grenfell and Kleinwort Benson, had experienced difficulties in attempting to compete with the big players in post-Big Bang market making.

In West Germany the main three banks had traditionally been universal institutions, but in most other countries the development of serious investment banking capabilities was limited except in selected sectors such as the Swiss banks in the bond market. Competition was also emerging in investment banking from the leading securities institutions, notably Merrill Lynch, Shearson Lehrman, Dean Witter and increasingly, the Japanese institutions, especially Nomura, Yamaichi and Daiwa. In addition, the major US investment banks were similarly moving towards a global-dealing-based strategy as US technology forced an increase in the speed of market operations. The large banks such as Salomon Bros, Goldman Sachs, First Boston and Drexel Burnham Lambert had thus all increased their share of new issue underwriting in the USA and increasingly in the Euromarkets, due to their placing power and their ability to innovate. Even these institutions, however, were not immune to the pressures of market share and scale. By late 1987, therefore, major cutbacks in staff had occurred in a number of the major investment banks in response to competitive market forces.

The build-up of investment banking skills inside the commercial banks had proved difficult, however. Firstly, the skills required for successful investment banking tended to include a high level of innovation and individualism. These were difficult to accommodate within the confines of most commercial bank organization structures. Successful investment bankers were also very well paid by comparison with the salary structures usually offered in the commercial banks. For example, a Wall Street dealer with three years' experience in high-growth segments such as interest rate swaps or mortgage-backed securities might be paid some $200,000 per annum, while many partners in leading investment banks earned regularly over $1 million a year. Such salary discrepancies between commercial and investment bankers created great rivalry and jealousy, expecially amongst commercial bankers, whose cultural norm included rigid job grading and commensurate (and much lower) salaries.

Investment bankers had also tended to enjoy substantial freedom to operate and make decisions, compared with the commercial banks where much more reliance was placed on committee systems. Long-term planning was not the rule in the short-term dealing mentality of the investment bank required to live on its wits. Corporate finance units were increasingly thus located close to the dealing floor, rather than in cosy wood-panelled offices, so as to spot just where and when capital could be raised to the best advantage of buyers and sellers. The poaching of successful individuals, and even whole units, was a commonplace event amongst both investment banking and securities industry competitors. As a consequence, it was potentially a serious difficulty for the commercial banks both to hire and to retain good investment bankers, given their very different corporate cultures. This indeed had been the experience of a number of organizations after the Big Bang in London. Citibank and Chase Manhattan, both of which had bought substantial British brokerage houses, had experienced considerable difficulties in retaining staff in their new subsidiaries after attempting to impose American commercial bank style control systems and procedures. Nevertheless, in line with the changes in the capital markets and the trend towards fee income and disintermediation, leading commercial banks were being forced to focus increasingly on building investment banking skills and to accept the organizational upheaval such a strategy might produce.

6.4.5   Niche Strategy Specialization

While a number of major commercial banks and financial institutions had opted to pursue a global strategy, only a small number could expect successfully to achieve such a position. There had been a growing recognition amongst banks that not all could achieve a strong global presence. An increasing number, therefore, had reappraised their strategic positions and opted to concentrate on specific areas where they could achieve and sustain competitive advantage. Such strategies might focus on a specific industry where specialist knowledge or skill allowed a bank to be competitive or a market maker, irrespective of size or global network cover. For example, First Chicago was a specialist lender to transportation industry companies, while First Boston enjoyed a special position in film finance. Such specialist markets offered superior spreads because of their perceived greater risk. However, for those institutions which really understood their markets the risk tended to be reduced due to expert knowledge.

Similarly, many banks had focused on specific geographic territories. Usually in such areas banks held a specific advantage, not only in terms of specialist knowledge, but also in terms of served market coverage. Moreover, there were few scale diseconomies in terms of cost of funds for smaller, national, or even regional banks. Indeed, in the US many regional banks had a higher credit rating than the large commercial banks, due to the exposure of the latter especially to sovereign risk and large corporate borrowers, compared with a preponderance of middle-market and individual borrowers on the part of the smaller banks. Further, despite their smaller size, the regional banks had not necessarily suffered seriously from a lack of economies of scale in operations. While the cost of new technology was heavily volume-dependent, a number of larger banks had built their volume positions by actively promoting the sale of operational services to smaller banks. The future of regional banks was threatened, however, by the entry of the larger banks into their areas of interest, where these were sufficiently large to attract external entry. Nevertheless there were many examples of successful regional banks, both based domestically and in terms of international specialization. In the US regional banks, such as

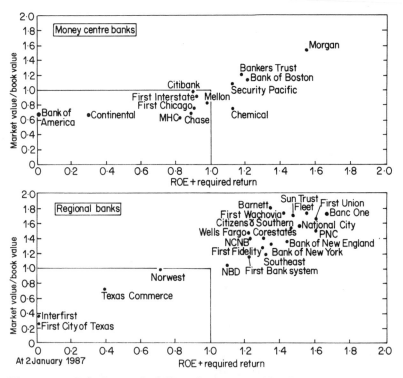

Figure 6.1   Relative profitability of US regional bank
Source: *The Banker*, March 1987, p. 40, Financial Times, London

Banc One, Wachovia, National Bank of North Carolina, and the like, were notably more profitable than their money centre counterparts, as shown in Figure 6.1. Internationally focused successful competitors included organizations, such as Westpac from Australia, which focused on the Antipodes and the Pacific Basin; Security Pacific, which had also opted to focus on the Pacific Rim; and the major banks from the countries of Scandinavia and the like. Provided such banks confined themselves to their chosen local territories and, in international activities, concentrated on serving their domestic customers or trade finance with their specific territories, their future seemed assured. Where substantial geographic deregulation occurred, however, a threat from the entry of new global competitors threatened margins. Niche positions thus seemed to offer the most likely profitable positioning for most banks in the future. The problems were to be expected amongst those with delusions of seeking a global position without the resources to support it, and those regionals which did not establish barriers to the encroachment of the major institutions into their traditional market areas.

6.4.6 The Attack on the Middle Market

By contrast with the margin pressures in the large corporate market, which had forced the banks to reconsider their intermediary role, smaller companies had remained less price-sensitive. Further, such organizations did not enjoy access to the capital markets in the same way as large corporations and still required credit from banks. In all the major developed country markets the banks had therefore turned their attention, and increasingly their marketing efforts, to middle-market companies. This included not only indigenous banks, but also the branches of major multinational banks which had not only been seeking international business but were prepared increasingly to compete for purely domestic business, especially in the main developed country markets.

Middle-market companies had traditionally been more loyal to their banks than large corporations and had fewer bank relationships. To penetrate these accounts, therefore, banks had been forced to increase their calling officer commitments and to redesign and improve services to meet the needs of these concerns more carefully. It had also been found important to demonstrate loyalty to the account and not be identified as a 'fair weather banker', providing credit when times were easy but being quick to withdraw facilities at the first sign of difficulties. To service the middle market, banks had also been actively localizing their operations by creating regional corporate branches from which calling officers could cover specific geographic areas and/or industries where such latter concentration made specialist calling viable. They had also actively been trying to improve their crude definition of the market into more meaningful segments in order to enhance marketing strategy.

While the large commercial banks had been turning their attention to the middle market, so too had other new non-bank competitors such as the securities houses and savings and loan banks which, in the United States, had been freed to make commercial loans. Industrial companies and trading companies had also been active in the market with credit finance, leasing, factoring and trade finance. Merrill Lynch, for example, was selling loans to the middle-market sector by providing its account officers with a simple, standardized, loan-making kit[16]. By packaging groups of such loans, securitization of middle-market credits was also clearly a possible future threat to conventional lending.

The middle market was thus seen as a critical 'killing ground' for conventional credit operations in the late 1980s. For indigenous and regional banks, middle-market accounts represented the core of their profitable asset structure. However, competition was increasing from large commercial money centre banks and foreign banks in the developed economies. New non-bank competitors were also a growing threat. Margins were therefore expected to decline. Bank cost structures were also expected to be under pressure, as to achieve the same overall volume of lending the large banks would need to take on many more small loans by comparison with the former large loans to multinational corporations or participations in international syndications.

---

[16]*Economist*, International Banking Survey, 24 March 1984, p. 58.

For the middle-market companies themselves, the attractive companies were increasingly splitting their banking between two or more banks. In particular those concerns with international activities tended to take on a non-indigenous institution to handle overseas banking needs. This often occurred because the lead bank was poorly organized to provide such services on a local basis, even though they were provided to large multinationals, and such banks did have significant international networks.

6.4.7   The Development of Electronic Banking Services

As the world's financial markets had speeded up, as a result of globalization in the capital and foreign exchange markets, and the growing linkages between them, multinational corporate treasurers had needed to improve the speed of information flows from subsidiary units around the world in order to optimize their cost of funds. As the banks had linked their international branch networks for their own administrative purposes, so some had also diversified into providing direct electronic linkages for their corporate accounts via their own, or other, proprietary networks, such as the interbank cooperative message switching system, Society for Worldwide Interstate Financial Telecommunication (SWIFT). Established in 1973, by 239 banks in 15 countries, as a non-profit bank-owned cooperative, SWIFT had grown to around 2000 banks in 50 countries by 1987, processing almost a million messages each day, and traffic was still expanding at a rate of 20 per cent per annum[17].

The development of SWIFT had established the message text standards for international interbank message transmission. Transactions included international functions such as customer transfers, documentary credits, bank transfers, foreign exchange confirmations and the like. The SWIFT message standards allowed banks around the world to communicate through a common computer-readable language. SWIFT competed directly with bank in-house networks such as those of Citibank, Chase and Chemical, and others operated by third parties like GEISCO

[17]*Euromoney*, Information Technology, August 1987, p. 22.

and ADP, on which many banks operated their proprietary cash management systems.

The pace of change in corporate electronic banking had been extremely rapid. In the early stage of electronic banking development, banks provided corporate treasurers with a balance-reporting facility for the corporation and its subsidiaries reporting into the bank's branches within a country or around the world. This facility did not, however, meet the needs of the treasurer as it provided no details of debits or credits received that day. The second phase of the development provided details of previous day debits and credits. This was followed by the provision of balance history reporting providing statistics on transactions for around the previous 60 days.

In the third phase of electronic development, banks began to provide their customers with interactive facilities. These enabled the treasurer not only to interrogate past history, but also to send messages and initiate payments. In international markets, as such facilities began to be offered, they were initially confined to operations in dollars, but were subsequently expanded to include transactions in other major currencies.

The fourth stage, which began to be introduced around 1983, was the provision of the corporate workstation. This phase provided cheap and easily available microcomputers, notably the IBM-PC, and software to enable the corporate treasurer to interface with the bank's main frame to draw down data about his accounts, manipulate this data with a variety of software tools, and then operate on the accounts by transmitting messages back to the bank from his intelligent terminal[18].

The growth of cash management systems had been dramatic. In the US alone, in 1976, the number of end users of cash management systems was 200; by 1983 this had risen to 27,500[19]. In 1984 Citibank doubled the number of terminals it had installed in customer premises for the second year in a row, bringing the total to 17,000 worldwide[20].

The advantages of balance-reporting systems for the corporate treasurer were that they provided information that allowed the

[18]The electronic treasurer, *The Banker*, March 1983, pp. 77–82.
[19]R. Lipp, Data flow in Utopia, *Euromoney*, October 1983, p. 386.
[20]Citicorp Annual Report, 1984, p. 7.

treasurer to minimize the presence of non-interest balances; to move balances from lower to higher interest-bearing accounts; to avoid mismatches of currency receipts and payments by netting off; and to manage foreign exchange exposure positions. In addition companies could monitor cash receipts and disbursements to check that cash was paid in the right currency, at the right place, at the right time. Bank charges could be more easily equated with transaction levels and the reconciliation process between bank ledger and cash positions could be improved, especially by the identification of the value dates of transactions. An important additional factor was the elimination of float delays. Further bank charges could be minimized and the cost of treasury administration, which tended to be paper-based, could be reduced[21].

In this early period banks provided cash management products in an effort to tie corporations into using the vendor bank for all transaction services. This was resisted by corporations which did not wish to be locked into one bank, nor did they wish any bank to have full knowledge of their transactions. Banks had, therefore, recognized this problem and had modified their systems to permit data to be originated and used from banks other than the bank providing the cash management service.

Citibank, for example, offered a system called Infopool, based on a central main frame computer based in Brussels. Citibank cash management customers could request other banks to provide details of transactions and balances to Infopool using SWIFT message statements or telex. The data collected on Infopool could then, on demand, distribute data on cleared balances, transactions and forward clearings, via Citibank's Global Transaction Network, as shown in Figure 6.2. Chemical Bank provided a similar service, linked to its Chemlink system, and around 100 banks provided data into this system which could be collated and provided in downloaded form to Chemical's customers' main frame or micro. Chase Manhattan, Bank of America and Manufacturers Hanover also operated their own similar networks and from the mid 1980s, many other European and Japanese banks also operated their own systems.

[21]M. Austen and P. Reyniers, Developing software to meet treasurers' needs, *Euromoney*, Corporate Finance, July 1985, p. 13.

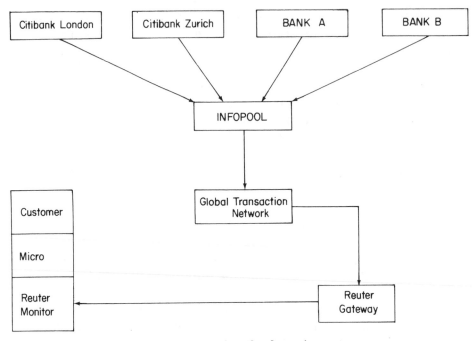

Figure 6.2   Citibank's Infopool and Citibank service system
Source: Citibank, Citicorp Public Affairs Department, New York

Apart from the banks, a number of important non-bank competitors were present in the market place for cash management
and other areas of electronic banking, via the provision of both
hardware and software services. The leading non-bank competitor was GEISCO (General Electric Information Services Co), the
largest global time-sharing system in the world. GEISCO was the
primary data processing conduit for a number of bank and non-
bank software packages, including those of Chemical Bank, Barclays, First Chicago, Morgan Guarantee, National Westminster,
Royal Bank of Canada and National Data Corporation. Automatic Data Processing (ADP) was the other leading non-bank
competitor which both offered its own software and also shared
its network with some banks, including the Midland Bank.

The data provided from pooled systems tended to reflect
previous day positions. For intraday or real-time data it was
necessary for corporations to access those branches which held

their accounts. This factor was important in persuading companies to maximize the number of accounts held with a particular bank rather than with multiple banks. Using CHIPS (the US Clearing House Interbank Payment System), CHAPS (the UK Clearing House Automated Payments System) or SWIFT, such branch information was available on an essentially real-time basis. Some bank proprietary networks were also moving to an on-line real-time basis internationally. Systems of this nature were already in place in Scandinavia but only for the domestic market.

The development of software packages which enhanced the traditional cash management systems was developing strongly by the late 1980s. Instead of using the intelligent terminal to receive and send messages, Corporate Treasury Work Stations (CTWS), were providing integrated software packages to facilitate the treasurers' manipulation of data received from the bank. The key user requirements for treasury systems had been identified as modelling, pre-deal support, and management reporting[22].

Modelling capability enabled treasurers quickly and accurately to test alternative hypotheses by 'what if' questioning. Pre-deal support included controlling the deals that treasurers intended to make. Transaction processing or post-deal support provided records of deals, confirmation letters to counterparties and the registering of investments, financing, currency and banking transactions by division, product group or type of deal. This activity also provided differences in foreign exchange, interest accruals and other accounting information.

Management reporting systems allowed treasurers to communicate to financial management on deals they were undertaking with reports covering, for example, movements, balances, and performances in placing investments, raising finance and executing foreign exchange transactions.

Future workstations were expected to be even more integrated. Inputs would include not only details of bank transactions, but also link in a full range of external information services such as

[22]P. Reyniers and M. Austen, What treasurers can expect from bank balance reporting, *Euromoney*, February 1985, p. 28.

Reuter Monitor. This service was provided by Reuters, which by the late 1980s had emerged as the world's foremost news and financial information organization, providing data in real time from over 110 securities and commodities markets around the world. By 1987 there were over 110,000 Centre Monitor terminals in place throughout the world, giving price information on over 100 currencies, while a considerable share of all foreign exchange transactions took place on Reuters' own dealing service, with over half a million calls a week occurring throughout the world in 1986[23].

Typical of the new type of integrated CTWS was Debt Manager, a second-generation system from Bank America's Micro Treasurer system, illustrated in Figure 6.3. This system focused on four areas of treasury management; foreign exchange and money market, assets, liabilities and administration. These were all internally integrated by the use of common commands and key operations, and a common data base structure designed to allow for a wide range of analyses. In addition, the system linked to external software packages such as Lotus 1-2-3 to permit more sophisticated interpretative modelling. The system also allowed for the integration of future system developments and reporting facilities included a full five-year file per currency; details for up to 300 banks; the full name and address of 300 subsidiaries covered by the system; FX rates for up to 25 years ahead; base currency and local currency interest rate revaluation and performance monitoring[24].

CTWS, in 1987, were still not widely used outside the US but users were generally favourable about their potential. Most treasurers using CTWS, while still seeking further improvements, wondered how they ever managed without it. Administration on data inputs and checking positions was dramatically speeded up. The systems had also allowed companies to undertake faster and more complex management tasks than were possible under previous manual facilities. The available packages were considered to offer excellent reporting and recording facilities, but decision support systems and the integration of

[23]Euromoney Supplement, Information Technology, August 1987, pp. 5–10.
[24]Cash Management News, No. 12, June/July, 1985, p. 1.

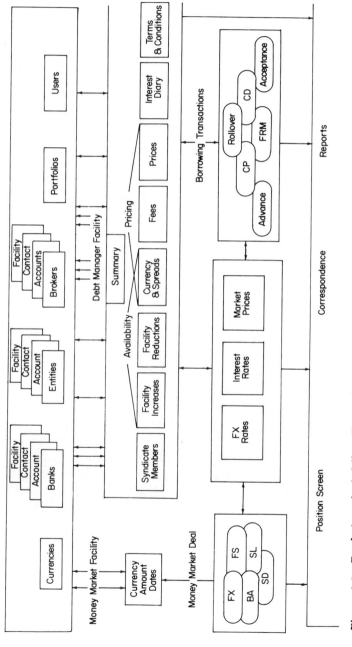

Figure 6.3   Bank America's Micro Treasurer structure
Source: Bank of America, San Francisco, California

non-bank market data were still areas where treasurers expected
improvement. Overall, the probability was very high that CTWS
would become increasingly widely used, these supplied both by
banks and by non-banks. As a result banks seemed likely
increasingly to become conduits for information and processors
of messages received, but would increasingly cede control of the
transaction process to their customers.

Major users of electronic banking services were other banks
and financial service institutions. As a result, the sale of software
and taking in processing for other banks had become a major area
of concentration for high-technology banks. For example, Chase
Manhattan was a leading processor of transactions for other
banks in the New York Area; Mellon Bank undertook a similar
role in the state of Pennsylvania; while Chemical Bank had sold
its software to other banks with its Banklink System. In both
domestic and international correspondent banking, Manufacturers Hanover and Chase Manhattan had been particularly active
in establishing relationships[25].

The New York banks in particular had developed specialist
organizational units to manage correspondent bank relationships. These new business units were usually known as
Financial Institutions units rather than correspondent banking,
and focused on selling services to banks and other financial
institutions, using the relationship management system which
had worked so well in servicing the large corporate market.

In addition they had increased the range and sophistication of
the credit and non-credit services being offered. As a result of the
expansion of foreign banks into one another's territories with
their own branches or subsidiaries, the need for indigenous
correspondent services such as clearing funds transfer and local
currency credits had increased competitor pressures. The provision of banking services in foreign countries also required banks
to obtain a good performance from correspondence[26]. The business was also not asset-intensive and indeed close correspon-

[25]N. Adam, How America rediscovered correspondent banking, Euromoney, February
1982, pp. 81–2.
[26]J. P. Rudy, Correspondent banking comes back into its own. The Banker, February
1982, pp. 49–54.

dent relationships provided excellent distribution channels for the growing trend to loan wholesaling.

A number of niche strategies had also developed in electronic banking and processing services. State Street Bank of Boston, for example, was estimated to generate 40 per cent of its net income from services to the mutual fund industry, credit card transaction processing and other areas of data processing. The Bank of New York was also an important processor of mutual fund transactions, government securities, clearing and providing services for institutional trusts. Core States Financial Corp of Philadelphia also generated around 30 per cent of its income from operating the MAC electronic banking network, payments clearing and trust processing[27]. Niche positions thus tended to focus on providing an efficient service to groups of customers in specific financial service sectors. This strategy was viable for a number of smaller banks or data processing organizations prepared to provide such dedicated services.

However, only a limited number of the major multinational banks seemed likely to gain substantial rewards from electronic banking. Significant economies of scale were available to those banks with high-volume usage, since all competitors faced similar cost of software development and main frame back-up facilities. Because of the high 'experience effect' in the electronic banking market it was therefore seen as important to maximize the number of terminals in operation or transactions processed. Banks were therefore extremely keen to place their terminals in customers' offices or to gain extra volume. Regrettably few banks seemed to realize the fact that profitability would go only to the market leaders and that there was a considerable danger of overinvestment in hardware and transaction processing capacity. As a result, losses could be expected for most participants and damaging price wars might ultimately be expected to lead to shakeouts in undifferentiated, overcapacity sectors of electronic banking including, especially, international funds transfer.

In addition, electronic banking was helping to speed up all the financial markets. It was stimulating the foreign exchange markets by encouraging not only financial institutions but also

[27]Salomon Brothers, *Technology in Banking*, 1987, *op. cit.*

multinational non-financial corporations to take positions, increasing the velocity of money flows, thereby increasing the problems of central bank controls over money supply management and reducing bank float, so shrinking interest rate margins even further.

6.4.8 Entry into Securities Trading

A consequence of the combination of advances in information processing and deregulation meant that the commercial banking industries and securities industries were tending to merge. In 1975, the New York Stock Exchange had initiated the trend when it abandoned fixed rates of commission on securities trading. In a study of the impact of abandoning fixed commissions, the Securities Exchange Commission (SEC) found that, between 1975 and 1980, commission charges, as a percentage of the principal value of securities transactions, fell by 57 per cent for institutional investors and 20 per cent for individual investors. The effect of lower dealing prices tended sharply to increase volumes, which more than tripled between 1974 and 1980, and reduced the volume of trade through off-exchange dealing—the 'third market'—from 7.87 per cent of total volume in 1972 to 2 per cent in 1980. Profitability within the industry also increased[28].

There was, however, a shakeout amongst market participants. The number of firms doing business shrank from 422 in 1974, to 389 in 1980. Industry concentration also increased, the top 25 broker-dealer firms accounting for 53 per cent of gross revenue in 1975, compared with 61 per cent in 1980[29].

The NYSE specialists were often unable to operate effectively as dealers able to offset large block orders. However, block trading grew rapidly and, by 1983, represented some 47 per cent of all requirements. During the early 1970s the SEC moved to encourage the development of a central market in order to take care of the move to block trading. In addition the SEC believed that investors would be better served by more open market

[28]J. Walmsley, New York's 'Big Bang'—10 years after, The Banker, March 1985, 35–9.
[29]Ibid., p. 36.

competition. Next, the SEC believed that a computerized linkage of securities clearance and settlement systems was a logical development of market trends to create a national, electronic market system. Finally, they felt their system was the precedent of NASDAQ (National Association of Securities Dealers Automated Quotations). This started in 1971 and revolutionized the trading basis of the over-the-counter market into an automated share trading system. By 1985, NASDAQ provided bids and offers from some 470 competing market makers in over 4000 stocks to some 125,000 screens. Since December 1984 NASDAQ had offered automatic execution of small orders via interactive terminals. In addition, it was hoped to expand the size of the market for terminal-based deals and to add stock index option trading[30].

As a result of creating NASDAQ, average spreads on the US over the counter market were reduced from 3/8–1/2 per cent on a $20 stock to 1/8–1/4. Volume, however, increased sharply from 1.2 billion shares traded in 1974 to 15 billion in 1984. Liquidity also increased. Productivity improved sharply, with high volume relative to the physical trading market being undertaken by a small trading group.

A second electronic trading system, Instinet (Institutional Networks Corporation), was a screen-based dealing system offering updated market information, automatic execution of deals up to 1000 shares, and on-screen negotiations of other deals by 1987. Instinet allowed the dealer to trade in real time in over 8000 exchange-listed and NASDAQ securities, with two-way communications. Instinet also traded in American Depository Receipts (ADRs). These ADRs allowed non-US equities to trade in the US in the form of receipts, which gave the owner the right to a block of shares registered in the name of an American depository bank. Thus, over half the stock of the multinational chemical company ICI was traded in this way. In addition, Instinet allowed trading in stock options and currency options via the Chicago Board Options Exchange. In 1987 Instinet was acquired by Reuters, which hoped to develop it as a major element in the development of global 24 hours, equities markets.

[30]America's example, City of London survey, *Economist*, 6 July 1985, p. 21.

The main stock exchanges had also invested heavily in technology. After spending $100 million on new systems, the NYSE was able to handle trading volumes ten times higher than in the late 1960s at over 100 million shares per day on average. Over 65 per cent of orders on the NYSE were electronically processed and many discount brokers, making up nearly 10 per cent of the membership, were electronic access only. Regional stock exchanges in the USA were already linked through the Intermarket Trading System (ITS) which provided common price and trading information and allowed orders to move between exchanges when price differences occurred.

As the electronic markets had developed, the securities companies had been forced to wire up and place their dealing rooms on a real-time basis. The range of products handled had increased sharply as the stock markets and other financial markets had begun to be much more closely integrated. The effect had been to shake out the smaller institutions which were unable to afford the cost of investing in the new technology, and those organizations involved in market making without the volume and/or capital base to sustain the loss of commission income and undertake the big deals. Following the crash of 1987, however, trading volumes on the world's stock exchanges slumped dramatically, leading to the collapse of a number of smaller market makers and a major shakeout of dealers even from the major institutions.

As with corporate banking, the electronic integration of the securities market was also being decentralized to provide remote terminal access to distributed brokerage offices and increasingly to customers such as life assurance and pension fund managers. Financial information markets had mushroomed for companies such as Reuters, Telerate and Dun & Bradstreet. This growth had encouraged new entries such as Citicorp, which had purchased Quotron, or the abortive link between Merrill Lynch and IBM, aiming to provide downloaded financial information services to intelligent terminals which could ultimately be used as remote order entry systems, thus allowing clients to make and complete their own share deals. As the volatility of the financial markets had increased, information about money had become as valuable as money itself.

The major investment institutions had thus increasingly been provided with the technological tools to enable them to drastically to speed up their trading positions with much better information services to improve their dealing capacity. Thus, for institutions which previously valued their portfolios only monthly or perhaps weekly, the trend had been to on-line real time and to a dealing mode of management[31]. A major consequence of the securities markets moving to electronic systems had been to breed a fast-dealing mentality. Trading volumes had grown sharply on all the major exchanges and institutional investors and brokers were actively managing portfolios increasingly on a worldwide basis. New risk management techniques had also emerged, linking the equities and future markets, while computer-driven programmed trading had developed. These new techniques, combined with the increase in speed caused by electronic trading, had accentuated the volatility of the markets. However, few would have foretold the speed with which these systems would work on 19 October 1987, when Wall Street fell by more than 500 points, or 25 per cent of its value, and for this to be echoed around the world's stock exchanges during the next few hours, as trade moved onward around the globe.

While the securities market was moving towards an integrated electronic global stock exchange which, like the foreign exchange market, could trade 24 hours a day with individual stock markets increasingly linked to one another, US and Japanese commercial banks within their domestic markets were still restricted from operating in these markets by the Glass–Steagall Act and its Japanese equivalent, Clause 65. The Act had erected a barrier between commercial and investment banks and their subsidiaries or affiliates, preventing them from engaging in underwriting or dealing in corporate bonds, equities and some types of municipal securities. It had been designed to discourage speculation, avoiding conflicts of interest within the banks and promoting the soundness of the banks. The Act was still being maintained in the mid 1980s despite the pattern in Germany and the UK, for example, which did not restrict commercial banks from operating in the securities markets.

---

[31]*Economist*, March 29, 1986, *op. cit.*, p. 22.

In the United States, the commercial banks had endeavoured to change the law and, when this proved difficult, to circumvent it. First, they had become large operators in the market for private placements where the banks acted as an intermediate bridge between corporations interested in selling their securities and institutional investors, rather than acting as 'principals'. In commercial paper the banks also operated as placing agents.

The banks had endeavoured to challenge the Glass–Steagall restrictions directly by seeking legal loopholes. Bank holding companies won the right to acquire discount brokerage firms, offering no-frills brokerage services and not engaging in underwriting. Nevertheless, Glass-Steagall still restricted the development of full service capabilities by major US commercial banks and even affected their international strategies. Thus, while the Canadian market deregulated in 1987 and US banks, such as First Chicago and First Interstate, had acquired stakes in leading Canadian brokerage houses, the US subsidiaries of these concerns were being handled on an arms' length or divorced basis.

Glass–Steagall had also been the foundation of Clause 65 in Japanese banking legislation which similarly maintained a clear division between securities houses and banks. The Japanese authorities, in their move towards deregulation were, however, allowing banks with securities subsidiaries in Europe similarly to operate securities subsidiaries in Japan in some cases. In both the US and Japan, therefore, the breakdown of the traditional barriers between banking and the securities industry was forcing a rethink of historic legislation.

In the United Kingdom, the restrictions of Glass–Steagall did not prevail after the Big Bang in October 1986. There was also no legislation clearly dividing commercial and investment banking. Merchant banking organizations were, however, denied membership of the Stock Exchange and hence confined their activities to developing and underwriting new issues, although after the Big Bang they could purchase brokerage companies as, indeed, most had. While the clearing banks could technically have operated in the same market they chose not to until the mid 1980s.

The run up to the Big Bang started in July 1983 when the British government announced that it was to deregulate the City of London by 1986, in order to enhance its position as an international financial centre. As a result of deregulation, commissions on the London Stock Exchange would no longer be fixed, but would be subject to negotiation. The traditional distinctions between brokers and jobbers were to be eliminated and banks and securities houses would be allowed to enter one another's markets. The new system was scheduled to come into effect with a 'Big Bang' in October 1986. In the interim, banks and other institutions could take up strategic stakes in brokerage companies, which could lead to full ownership from March 1986. At this point the new securities groups would be able to begin to integrate their back office operations, but full integration of sales and trading under one roof would not be allowed until a few months before the Big Bang.

The London Stock Exchange, by comparison with the New York Exchange, Tokyo and NASDAQ, seemed at first sight extremely small, as shown in Figure 6.4. However, London was

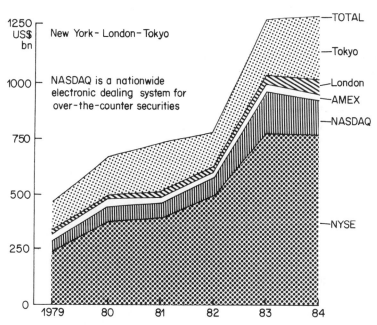

Figure 6.4   Volume of the major Equity trading markets
Source: *The Banker*, March 1985

the centre of the Euromarkets. Moreover, the Big Bang break-down of the Glass–Steagall-type regulatory wall dividing banks and securities houses meant that London would be the first well-regulated, dual-capacity securities and lending centre in the world. Coupling this with its position between the New York and Tokyo time zones, a history of highly active, high-technology foreign exchange and international money market dealing meant that potentially London could become the centre for the first global stock exchange, involving all types of institutional competitor including investment banks, commercial banks, brokerage houses and the like.

After the announcement of the change in regulations in London there was a dramatic scramble to form relationships between traditional brokerage houses and banks and other financial institutions, as shown in Table 6.2. Of 28 London brokers, 27 made links and only Casenove of the large brokers had not linked up by late 1987. Of 12 London jobbers only 3 remained unlinked. Three of the major UK clearing banks, the exception being Lloyds Bank, had joined in the scramble, together with many major US banks, including Chase Manhattan, Citicorp, Security Pacific and North Carolina National Bank. Other banks included Union Bank of Switzerland, Crédit Suisse and Royal Bank of Canada[32]. The US investment banks had initially not entered the market, perferring to see how it would settle, but being prepared to move if deemed necessary. By contrast, nearly all the leading British merchant banks had actively developed alliances. This was to prove of little avail, however, and most seemed destined to be swallowed up by larger institutions.

A year after the start of the Big Bang, the financial institutions were beginning to count the cost. Market volume on the London Stock Exchange had virtually doubled in equities (excluding deals between market makers) and the major increase in trading had come from foreign investors whose share of the total trades had risen from 10.5 per cent to 20 per cent by value. Commission rates on large deals had fallen substantially and some 30 per cent of all deals between large investors and market makers occurred

[32]R. McDougall, London's new securities houses shape up. The Banker, March 1985, pp. 19–34.

Table 6.2 New City of London pre-Big Bang relationships

CLEARERS Bank	Merchant bank subsidiary	Jobber	Broker	Equity market maker	Gilts market maker	Inter-dealer broker	Int'l dealer ship
Barclays	Barclays Merchant Bank	Wedd Durlacher Mordaunt 29.9% £30 million March 1984 (75%) New name: Barclays de Zoete Wedd	de Zoete & Bevan 5% March 1984 (75%)	*	*	–	*Wedd Durlacher Int'l
Lloyds	(new merchant bank)	–	–	*	*	–	–
Midland	Samuel Montagu (60% Midland 40% Aetna Life & Casualty)	–	W. Greenwell 29.9% Mar 1984 (50%)	*	*	–	*Greenwell GIC
National Westminster	County Bank	Bisgood Bishop 29.9% Feb 1984 (100%)	Fielding Newson-Smith 5% Jul 1984 (100%)	*	*	–	*Bisgood Int'l
MERCHANT BANKS Baring Bros	Wilson & Watford 29.9% Dec (100%)		–	*	*	–	–
Guiness Mahon	White & Cheeseman 29.9% Apr 1984		–	*	–	–	–
Hambros	–		Strauss Turnbull 29.9% Mar 1984			–	*SHS Securities International

Table 6.2 New City of London pre-Big Bang relationships (contd)

CLEARERS Bank	Merchant bank subsidiary	Jobber	Broker	Equity market maker	Gilts market maker	Inter-dealer broker	Int'l dealer ship
Hill Samuel	—		Wood Mackenzie 29.9% £5.9m Jun 1984 (100%)	*	*	—	—
Kleinwort Benson	Charlesworth & Co 29.9% £0.24 Jun 1984 (100%)		Grieveson Grant 5% £2.2m Jun 1984 (100%)	*	*	—	*Grieveson
Mercury Securities (SG Warburg)	Akroyd & Smithers 29.9% £41m Nov 1983 [Newco to be owned: MS 73.3%, AS outside shareholders 19.4%, R & P 2.6%, Charter Consolidated 4.2%, M 0.5%]			*	*	—	*
Morgan Grenfell	Pinchin Denny 29.9% Apr 1984 (100%)		Pember & Boyle 5% Oct 1984 (100%)	*	*	—	*
N.M. Rothschild	Smith Bros 29.9% £6.5m Dec 1983		Scott Goff Layton 5% Dec 1984 (100%)	*	—	—	*Smith New Court
FOREIGN BANKS							
Australia and New Zealand Banking Group (Grindlays Holdings)	—		Capel-Cure Myers	*	—	—	*
Banque Bruxelles Lambert	—		William de Broe Hill Chaplin 29.9% Dec 1984 (66.6%)	*	*	—	*

Chase Manhattan	–	Laurie Milbank 1984 Simon & Coates (100%)	*	*	–	–
Citicorp	–	Vickers da Costa 29.9% £20m Nov 1983 Scrimgeour Kemp Geen to Merge with Vickers da Costa: Scrimgeour Vickers (100%)	*	*	–	*
Crédit Suisse	–	Buckmaster & Moore 29.9% Jan 1985 (85%)	*	–	*	–
Hongkong and Shangai Banking Group	–	James Capel 29.9% Aug 1984 (100%)	*	Gerrard & Capel	–	–
North Carolina National Bank (Carolina Bank)	–	Panmure Gordon 29.9% Dec 1984 (29.9%)	*	–	–	*
Royal Bank of Canada (Orion Royal Bank)	–	Kitcat & Aitcen 29.9% Feb 1984 (100%)	*		*	–
Security Pacific Bank	Charles Pulley 5% Apr 1984 (100%)	Hoare Govett 29.9% £8.1m Jun 1982	*	–	* Tullett & Tokyo Securities	* Hoare Govett Int'l Securities
Shearson Lehman American Express	–	L Messel 5% Jul 1984 (100%)	*	*	–	*
Union Bank of Switzerland	–	Philips & Drew 29.9% Nov 1984 (100%)	*	*	–	*UBS Securities

Information on second line: percentage stake agreed in letter of intent, amount paid for that stake, date of announcement, agreed extent of future stake. In the last four columns * indicates 'positive commitment'; — 'no interest'. Others are 'open-minded'.
Source: Derived from *The Banker*, March 1985

Table 6.3   Developing global strategy players

	London		New York		Tokyo	
	SE	GBD	SE	GBD	SE	SL
Citicorp	×	×	×	×	×	×
Chase	×	×	×	×	−	×
Bankers Trust	×	×	×	×	−	
Security Pacific	×	×	×	×	−	×
Morgan Guaranty	×	×	×	−	−	−
Merrill Lynch	×	×	×	×	×	×
Salomon Bros	×	×	×	×	−	×
Morgan Stanley	×	×	×	×	×	×
Goldman Sachs	×	×	×	×	×	×
Amex	×	×	×	×	−	×
Barclays	×	×	−	−	−	−
NatWest	×	×	×	−	−	×
Kleinwort Benson	×	×	×	×	−	×
Mercury (Warburg)	×	×	×	−	×	×
Deutsche Bank	×	×	×	−	−	×
Crédit Suisse First Boston	×	×	×	×	−	×
Nomura	×	−	×	×	×	×
Daiwa	×	−	×	×	×	×
Yamaichi	×	−	×	−	×	×

NB: GBD—Government Bond Dealer.
Source: *Financial Times* World Banking Survey, 7 May, 1987, p. ii, Financial Times, London

on a 'net' basis. Commission rates for small investors had, however, risen sharply. Competition overall had increased in some market sectors, notably gilts, where substantial overcapacity had developed due to a large number of new entrants[33]. By late 1987, therefore, while only the exit of Lloyds Bank had occurred, many others were losing money or holding on in hope. A number of organizations had also begun to shake out very expensive market-making personnel and the survival of the biggest seemed most likely. The market had also become screen-based at a remarkable pace, with use of the physical floor of the London Stock Exchange being reviewed for possible conversion to a theatre or a restaurant. Even the name of the Exchange had been changed to the International Stock Exchange.

[33]*Financial Times*, 27 October 1987, p. 11.

The key result, therefore, was that London had been the catalyst for the rapid globalization of all the securities markets. Global strategy players had emerged quickly, attempting to establish dual-capacity positions, in particular in the three major financial centres of London, Tokyo and New York, irrespective of the existing regulatory restrictions. These new global players are shown in Table 6.3 and included most of the leading US money centres and investment banks, the leading US brokerage houses, many major European banks, and the largest Japanese securities houses. Volume of international trading on the leading stock exchanges for foreign stock transactions was also escalating rapidly as the markets moved towards 24-hour trading for the leading equities as shown in Table 6.4. The real impact of the opening of the London market was therefore not the scene within the domestic market, but rather the putting in place of an essential step in time-zone terms, towards the creation of a global equities market and a major element towards the ultimate demise of the artificial separation between the banking and securities markets in Tokyo and New York.

6.5 CONCLUSION

The scramble for entry into the London securities market and the globalization strategies of the leading financial service institutions emphasized the rapid trend towards the linkage between the financial markets and the traditional boundaries between different groups of financial intermediaries being rapidly eroded. Coupled with the rapid growth in information technology, the market for traditional wholesale and corporate banking was being rapidly transformed by the late 1980s.

In the market for the supply of financial services to large corporations, the role of the banks as suppliers of conventional loans was disappearing as corporations undertook the issue of their own paper or turned to the international capital markets to provide cheaper, more flexible funds. Those banks making such arrangements were also increasingly acting as wholesalers for loans, selling them on to smaller banks or other institutions. With the introduction of electronic banking, corporations were

Table 6.4 Market size of world stock exchanges

		1984			1986		
		Tokyo	New York	London	Tokyo	New York	London
No. of listed companies	Domestic	1444	1490	2171	1499	1516	2101
	Foreign	11	53	582	52	59	584
No. of listed stocks	Domestic	1450	2266	1857	1504	2194	1781
issues	Foreign	11	53	504	52	63	490
Bonds	Domestic	536	3549	3179	742	3384	2917
	Foreign	200	202	1520	237	222	1556
Total market value $bn	Stocks	644.4	1529.5	236.3	1794.3	2128.5	472.9
	Bonds	371.4	1021.8	240.9	772.1	1691.6	447.5
Trading value $bn	Stocks	271.1	764.7	42.3	955.3	1374.3	132.9
	Bonds	150.6	7.0	168.5	836.3	10.5	264.6
No. of member firms		83	628	216	93	611	357

Source: Tokyo Stock Exchange

also increasingly acting as initiators of their own transactions, using the bankers more as information providers and processors than as financial intermediaries.

To maintain their traditional role the banks were turning to the middle market in an attempt to sustain lending margins. Here too, competition was rapidly increasing, and loan spreads were expected to come under pressure. Finally, disintermediation and securitization of assets were forcing the commercial banks to try and build their investment banking capabilities and to enter the securities markets where this was permitted.

By the late 1980s the traditional bank role, as a financial service intermediary in the corporate and wholesale markets, was undergoing dramatic change. Instead, there was the emergence of a series of global players, concerned increasingly with securitized lending and dealing, together with the provision of investment and electronic banking services. Some large multinational corporations, in turn, threatened to themselves become global players, and undertake many of the conventional banking roles in-house. Increased competition for middle-market business; traditionally less price-sensitive, was also reducing historic loyalties. The future for corporate banking strategy thus seemed likely to favour the large global players or the banks occupying product market niches, sustainable against the firepower of the global players.

CHAPTER 7

The Return to Favour of Retail Banking

7.1 INTRODUCTION

At a meeting of US bankers in 1980, Walter Wriston was asked: 'What is your vision of the bank of the future?' He replied: 'It already exists, Don Regan runs it and it's called Merrill Lynch Pierce Fenner and Smith.' Although Citibank had embarked upon its comsumer banking strategy in the mid 1970s, in part to increase its base of low-cost deposits for the banking markets of the 1980s, actual saving deposits had not risen dramatically due to the introduction of money market funds offering much more attractive interest rates. Citibank's success in generating consumer deposits had occurred largely since 1982 when the bank had been able to compete on equal terms with the brokerage houses by offering high money market-related interest rates. By contrast, although technically not a bank, Merrill Lynch, the New York-based brokerage company, had launched its 'Cash Management Account' late in 1978 and by the end of 1983 this had attracted funds in cash and securities of over $70 billion. If treated as bank deposits, these investments would have made the brokerage house the ninth largest bank in the United States.

In 1984 retail deposits still accounted for 56 per cent of US bank deposits. However, in the years since the mid 1970s the development of money market mutual funds had attracted deposits from small savers which amounted to over $200 billion by 1984. These funds had initially grown rapidly by brokerage houses and other non-banks collecting together relatively small deposits from individuals usually via mail or direct response advertising at competitive interest rates. Such deposits were then combined into mutual funds which in turn invested in Federal instruments, bank acceptances and bank certificates of deposit which, for large sums, offered money market rates of interest.

These smaller investments thus offered money market rates of interest rather than the 5.25 per cent interest limit paid by banks for deposits as a result of the anachronistic Regulation Q. From 1982 banks had been able to compete more fairly and had introduced Money Market Deposit Accounts (MMDA) which were liquid, short-term, small-denomination accounts free from interest rate ceilings. The rapid acceptance of this product had halted the growth of money market funds while MMDA deposits had grown to over $450 billion by the end of 1984. This result was not achieved without penalty, however, as banks found the cost of their deposit bases sharply higher. The trend in US consumer deposit instruments is shown in Figure 7.1.

In particular the US Savings and Loan Institutions, similar to the British building societies, the traditional repository for small savings, dramatically lost deposits and were forced to borrow in the market at high interest rates to cover their asset positions. As their primary lending function was to lend long-term for house purchase, traditionally in the form of fixed rate mortgages, the savings and loan banks found themselves in the high-inflation early 1980s with a severe reverse yield gap. As a result, with the tight money policies of the early years of the Reagan administration pushing money market rates to highs of nearly 20 per cent, while the average interest on loans was fixed at around 9 per cent, the Savings and Loan banks rapidly cost their deposit base to the money funds. Many quickly began to get into difficulties, often compounded by a rising default rate on mortgage payments and a deflated housing market caused by the world economic depression following the second oil shock and rising unemployment. In 1980 the Federal Savings and Loan Insurance Corporation (FSLIC) was forced to rescue 11 Savings and Loan Institutions. In 1981 this number rose to 23 and jumped to 47 in 1982, in all costing the FSLIC over $1.5 billion. By 1984 bank failures had reached 130. As a result a series of mergers had occurred

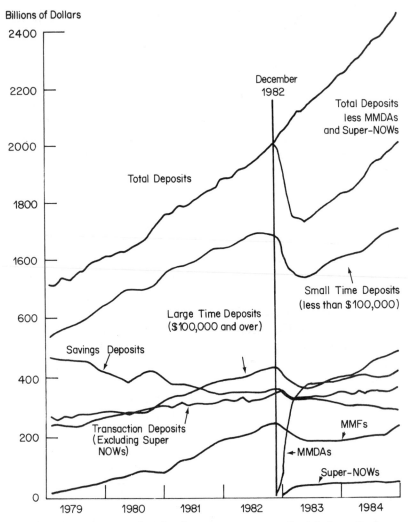

**Figure 7.1   Money market funds vs components of total deposits (com-
bined bank thrift total)**
Source: McKeely and G. C. Zimmerman, competition for money market.
Deposits Accounts, Federal Reserve Bank of San Francisco, *Economic
Review*, Winter 1985, San Francisco, California

within the industry to assist in the rescue of troubled institutions
and at the same time help to break down the barriers to US
interstate banking.
  It was not only the US Savings and Loan Banks that were

affected. Other banks with a strong retail position, and in particular a heavy lending portfolio in fixed rate mortgages, were also hit badly. The large California banks such as Bank of America and Wells Fargo showed severe earnings depression. For example, Bank of America saw its earnings slump dramatically from 1979 to overall losses in 1986. A major factor in this dramatic earnings decline had been Bank of America's increased cost of funds due to a tranformation in its deposit base away from 'free' current-account balances and low-interest deposit rates to bank certificates of deposit MMDAs and super-NOW accounts.

The declining share of the market for retail deposits and the rising cost of these funds to banks that occurred in the USA was a pattern that had been repeated in many other developed countries around the world. In the UK the pattern was similar. Banks lost deposits increasingly to building societies which offered transaction accounts paying interest and they also had longer opening hours. During the 1980s therefore a critical element in retail banking strategy had become the challenge to attract back some of these funds which had been lost, usually to non-commercial banks, either operated by private investment management corporations like Merrill Lynch or to public sector institutions such as local authority bonds, government stocks or savings organizations such as post offices. The problem for banks had been compounded since the mid 1980s by a major move by individuals into equities due to the sustained bull market in the major financial centres of New York, London and Tokyo. After the crash of 1987, banks could look forward to a return of funds from the equity markets as investors returned to cash and what they perceived as safe depositaries.

The main causes of the loss of bank deposits around the world had thus been the offering of superior deposit products by non-bank institutions, a growing sophistication on the part of medium- and high-net-worth depositors and a switch to equities. Historically in most developed countries current account funds paid little or no interest, creating the so called endowment effect of 'free' funds for banks in return for the provision of checking and other payments services. In practice the banks had tended to give back to consumers some return on their funds by offering such services free or at low cost, provided accounts had been maintained with a specified minimum absolute average balance. This balance had usually been low, thus effectively penalizing the account holder with a high current account balance. The funds of such individuals could be used for loans by the banks and the revenues so earned made a contribution to profit and overhead or could cross-subsidize less attractive accounts. Around the world the actual cost of servicing consumer current accounts varied according to the productivity of individual banks. This service charge was largely a result of branch overhead costs, and was found to be between 5 and 9 per cent for banks in different countries. As a result when loan interest rates were high banks enjoyed a substantial spread on current balance funds and this had tended to be a major reason for the high rates of profit enjoyed by many banks such as the large British commercial banks in the early 1980s.

Deposit accounts, by contrast, paid interest although again for small savers in most countries the rates offered had usually been substantially lower than those available for large sums in the capital markets. Again, therefore, although administration costs had been higher, banks with a large retail deposit base had normally enjoyed a lower cost of funds than those such as J. P. Morgan which had to borrow in the interbank market. During the 1980s a major change had taken place, however, in the cost of retail deposits. Almost invariably the change had been brought about by competition for these funds from non-bank competitors which had often made use of technology to break down the traditional barriers imposed by banks on current and deposit accounts, to offer interest-bearing transaction accounts of one kind or another. Moreover increasingly these institutions had also combined the deposits of small savers into larger sums so that they could enjoy the higher rates of interest traditionally confined by the banks to major depositors. At the same time, because of improved effiiciency in the capital markets and high liquidity, the cost of wholesale funds had tended to fall below the overall cost of gathering consumer deposits. A number of the services offered by non-bank competitors are described in the following sections and the response of the banks is then reviewed, together with an assessment of the impact of a higher cost of funds on bank operations.

7.2 THE NON-BANK CHALLENGE

7.2.1 The Growth of Money Market Mutual Funds

In the late 1970s the US mutual fund industry began to offer a new form of mutual fund investing in US treasury funds, bank acceptances and certificates of deposits. These funds were sold to small depositors with each dollar deposited buying a unit in the mutual fund. The interest earned on the investments was returned to investors or could be cumulated and invested in new units. As an additional facility to allow easy access to the investor's funds the mutual funds developed arrangements with a number of banks to offer a cheque book which enabled the investor to write a limited number of checks which would be cleared either by using existing cash balances or by the sale of the equivalent number of units of the mutual fund. The checking facility usually imposed some restriction in terms of the minimum size of the check that could be issued, or the number of checks issued in a given time period. It was not the mutual fund's intention to take over the transaction business of the banks but rather to leave the bulk of this business with the existing bank relationship while encouraging investors to withdraw their deposits which ironically the banks would have to borrow back through the capital market, but at a higher rate of interest.

The money market mutual funds were dramatically successful in attracting deposits. They offered a rate of interest fixed to the money markets. As interest rates escalated in the early 1980s in the face of high inflation following the second oil shock, to nearly 15 per cent higher than deposits left in traditional savings and loan deposit accounts, they proved an attraction too tempting to avoid for many. Although the mutual funds were not insured, neither were they required to place part of their funds with the Federal Reserve in non-interest-earning deposits. Moreover the funds were extremely cheap to operate, making use of telephone and direct mail distribution systems to conduct most of their transactions with investors and not needing any form of branch network. Finally, funds could be collected from anywhere in the USA without the restrictions of state boundaries which artificially constrained the activities of the banks. Not surprisingly the money market funds grew dramatically with most of the funds being withdrawn from the traditional banking industry. This trend eventually forced the regulatory authorities to relax traditional interest rate ceilings and allow the banks to develop more competitive deposit products.

7.2.2 The Development of the CMA[1]

In 1975 Merrill Lynch employed Stanford Research Institute as consultants to assist the company in its search for new, distinctive financial services which Merrill Lynch could offer to supplement its traditional brokerage business. One such service contemplated but initially rejected as being infeasible was a combined brokerage/banking account. When this decision was questioned a joint task force was assigned to review the possibilities of developing such an account.

After over 100 man years of systems design, in late 1978 Merrill Lynch was ready to launch a product that was to change the world of retail banking, the Cash Management Account (CMA). This new account concept was to revolutionize upmarket comsumer banking. The company, prior to launching the CMA, was careful to check and obtain clearance with the Federal Reserve that its new product did not constitute a bank account and therefore could be offered nationwide, would not place Merrill Lynch in contravention of banking law and would not require reserve deposits to be placed with the Federal authorities. In addition, Merrill Lynch cleared with the Securities Exchange Commission that the CMA was still technically a brokerage account, in that any loans granted would be at the brokerage loan rate and 'deposits' would be treated as investments by the brokerage house investing them in mutual funds or securities, according to client instructions. The product was then trickled out with little publicity, in part to avoid provoking the banking industry. By the time the banking industry realized the

---

[1]D. F. Channon, Merrill Lynch Case Study, *Bank Strategic Management and Marketing, Case Book*, Wiley, 1986.

importance of the Merrill Lynch innovation the CMA was rapidly becoming established and the brokerage house had a lead time of several years as banks tried, largely unsuccessfully, to block the CMA while imitators amongst other non-banks struggled to develop the intricate systems technology to offer similar products.

The CMA was designed to appeal to the moderately well off, but not necessarily the rich, since the product was created to provide a mass market service. To open a CMA investors needed to have at least $20,000 of cash or marketable securities to place in the account. They were than charged a low annual fee for the use of the account for which they received the following services. Firstly, account holders were given a cheque book and a Visa card. These two facilities, although cheques were make out as Merrill Lynch, were operated by Banc One of Columbus, Ohio, one of a new breed of high-technology banks and although a small regional bank, one of the largest VISA processors in the USA. Merrill Lynch CMA cheques carried the Banc One clearing house number and were automatically routed to Columbus for processing.

Secondly, holders received a comprehensive monthly statement of all transactions conducted using the CMA. The statement therefore showed the investor's holdings of money market shares, stocks, corporate, treasury and municipal bonds, dividends and interest received, securities and options bought and sold during the month, brokerage charges, checks drawn, Visa debits incurred, and any margin loans taken and paid off and the interest charged. Even the check statement was comprehensive since it not only showed the amount debited but also the date paid, the name of the recipient and the date the check was written. This allowed the investor to see how long it took for a recipient to present his check, realizing that all this time he was still earning daily interest on his funds.

Funds placed in the CMA were in the form of cash, stocks and bonds. All cash was then placed in a money market fund on which interest accumulated daily. The success of the CMA led Merrill Lynch to expand the range of investment instruments which account holders could opt for. By 1985, there were four main choices: the CMA Money Fund, paying current money market yields; a CMA Tax Exempt Fund; the CMA Government Securities Fund; and the Insured Savings Account. The latter was a money market deposit account opened by Merrill Lynch at banks and savings and loan institutions throughout the USA. All dividends or interest received on stocks and bonds or the proceeds from the sale of such securities were computer swept regularly into one of the money market funds unless an account holder had given instructions to the contrary. When checks or Visa debits were incurred, these were first deducted from any cash awaiting computer sweep to the money market fund. Should this be insufficient then a sale of money market funds resources would be automatically triggered. When these funds in turn were inadequate to meet obligations a margin loan was triggered up to a value of 50 per cent of the value of the securities, stocks and bonds held in the account. These loans were charged at the brokerage loan rate.

The effect of the CMA for the investor was to provide a facility to concentrate most of the financial services he required into one comprehensive, cheap and highly convenient account with the attractive feature of having the automatic facility to monetarize fixed assets. At the same time whenever cash funds were not in use they received an attractive rate of interest while still remaining effectively within a free checking account. As with the money market funds, Merrill Lynch did not encourage the use of CMA checks. Instead the company advised account holders that they should maintain existing bank relationships and use these for small checks. Certainly it was the case that CMA holders used only some 5–6 checks per month, with the largest recipient being American Express. Investors used the Amex card for its extended credit, rather than the CMA Visa facility where a debit would lead to an immediate deduction from investment in money market funds.

For the monetary authorities the CMA was also a potential nightmare in that the account was technically invisible since only one transaction occurred each day between Merrill Lynch and Banc One which cleared all the CMA holders' transactions processed that day. The process is shown in Figure 7.2. A CMA holder would initiate a transaction using either a Merrill Lynch check or Visa card. Merchant checks on the Visa transaction

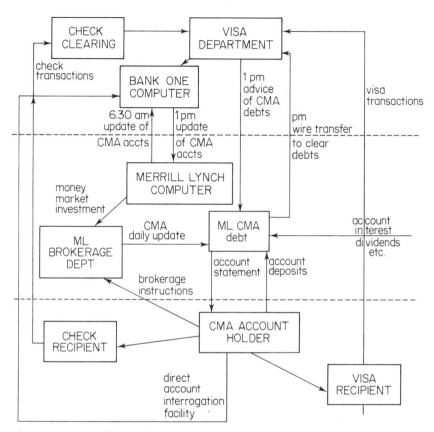

Figure 7.2 **Merrill Lynch Cash Management Account operation**

would be made to the appropriate section of Banc One—not Merrill Lynch—and all checks would be cleared through Banc One.

Each morning the Merrill Lynch computer would update the Banc One computer on the current status of all CMAs. The bank would process all transactions received that day and update the account files which it would then advise to the Merrill Lynch computer by 1 pm. At the same time the bank would advise Merrill Lynch of the total debits incurred by all CMA holders that day and Merrill Lynch would send a bank wire transfer to clear the outstanding debt before the close of the bank clearing house that day. During the night the day's transactions incurred by CMA holders at Merrill Lynch such as stocks and bonds bought and sold, interest and dividends received and the like would be input to update the CMA file before updating the Banc One computer at the start of business the next day.

As a result since Merrill Lynch itself was outside the banking industry and therefore not required to report the activities of CMA holders, the authorities had no knowledge of fixed assets that might be monetarized. Should these loans be large some impact could be made on the monetary supply which would be outside the control of the authorities and the banking system. Later imitators of the CMA had even compounded this problem by permitting account holders automatically to trigger loans against the equity value involved in personal property. The CMA and its imitators thus provided a new, and potentially large, form of consumer credit essentially outside the control of the central authorities.

The success of the CMA was dramatic. By mid 1982, Merrill Lynch had 680,000 accounts and was still adding new ones at the rate of around 1000 a day. By 1984, there were over one million CMA holders and the account was available in 21 countries. Outside the USA holders did not invest in US-based money funds but rather in Merrill Lynch International Bank at a rate of 1.25 per cent below LIBOR. The average account balance after 90 days was $70,000 and 30 per cent of CMA holders were new customers of Merrill Lynch. The average CMA holder was mainly male, over 50 years old and had an annual income of greater than $50,000. Counting CMA funds as deposits made Merrill Lynch the ninth largest bank in the USA. Apart from investments placed under management, however, Merrill Lynch found the CMA provided the brokerage house with a substantial level of interest income. Rather than trading their investments, many CMA holders took advantage of the margin loan facility. As a result the percentage of earnings derived from interest earnings rose rapidly.

The success of the CMA was also being used by Merrill Lynch to spearhead its penetration of the same consumer segment outside the USA. The product was launched in Europe in mid 1981, primarily for expatriate Americans, but it was later extended to provide a similar service to local nationals as well.

There was little doubt that the CMA had a dramatic impact upon the banking and financial services industry in the USA and later around the world. While the money market funds had a major impact in forcing banks to disintermediate and pay realistic market rates on consumer credit balances, the CMA had forced the tecnological development of automatic sweep accounts and integrated multiservice accounts, which provided consumers with the choice of operating on their funds in a variety of ways while still needing only one account. By contrast, the traditional bank approach separated checking funds into a current account, on which no interest was paid, or into deposit accounts on which low interest was paid. This forced consumers to initiate transfers between the two, did not grant automatic loans against securities held probably in bank safe deposit boxes, and required customers to collect and pay in any dividends and interest received. Moreover, Merrill Lynch's success allowed the brokerage firm to gain a large share of the upmarket consumer segment which more and more bank and non-bank institutions recognized was amongst the most profitable sector in the personal financial services market.

Imitators were quick to recognize the potential of the CMA and a spate of mergers occurred within the USA linking major brokerage houses with other financial and non-bank institutions. American Express merged with Shearson to create a package of financial services to a similar market segment to that served by Merrill Lynch. As a result American Express/Shearson offered a range of the leading travel and entertainment cards, a major brokerage account, excellent international coverage and a quality private banking service for its rich clients.

Prudential Insurance made a similar move via its purchase of the brokerage house Bache, but this had been a less integrated strategy. The two organizations still operated separately and there had not been serious moves to link the two client bases or to cross-sell an integrated service package between them.

7.2.3 The Entry of the Retailers

By contrast Sears Roebuck, the leading department and catalogue store retailer, had been actively developing an integrated concept, based less on deposits but rather on the provision of a wide array of financial services. These included brokerage, savings accounts, loans, insurance, and real estate brokerage and all these had been combined with Sears traditional retailing consumer credit and card businesses in a unique composite package.

Up until 1979 the emphasis at Sears was on retailing, although the store group had long issued its own consumer credit card, and was a major provider of insurance services. Seen almost as a US national institution, Sears was especially strong with middle America with over 39 million credit card holders, over 18 million catalogue sales customers and a reach which touched virtually all parts of the USA via its store locations, specialist insurance outlets and insurance agencies[2]. Already by 1981, financial services in the form of consumer credit and insurance produced most of the company's profits. Sears then embarked consciously on building up a position as a supplier of a comprehensive range of financial services to its large established customer base amongst middle-class Americans.

In addition to its consumer credit company and All State Insurance, Sears acquired the brokerage firm of Dean Witter Reynolds and the real estate brokerage company, Coldwell Banker. In California the company also acquired a savings and loan bank, the Sears Savings Bank, which operated branches in 39 store centres. The company had also made efforts to acquire similar institutions in other states but had been thwarted by the regulatory authorities and in 1986 this business was disposed of.

The objective was to develop each of these institutions as both independent and linked deliverers of financial services, operating via their own offices and via Sears Financial Network Centres. Experimental financial centres were established in a number of Sears Stores during 1982. By the end of 1986 more than 600 centres had been established in most of Sears major store outlets throughout the USA, offering a range of services from All State Insurance and Dean Witter and Coldwell Banker. This new distribution channel was positioned to appeal to Sears traditional customers and was sold with an advertising theme stres-

[2]Annual Reports, and R. Gurney, The retailers approach to developing financial services, 1984, *International Retail Banking Conference*, Retail Banking International, London, 1984.

sing a 'one stop' financial centre and Sears traditional reputation for quality and reliability. In addition the message was that there was no such thing as 'bankers' hours', with the financial centres being open for the same hours as the store, 9.30–9.30 Monday to Friday, 9.30–5.30 Saturdays and 11.00–5.00 on Sundays.

The new centres brought together each of the main Sears subsidiaries, in one location within the stores. They were deemed by Sears to have been highly successful with a substantial number of first-time investors for brokerage services in particular. For Dean Witter, 35 to 40 per cent of all new brokerage accounts were being opened through the in-store centres. Some 80 per cent of this business was from new investors or reactivated dormant accounts. Six out of every ten accounts opened at the in-store centres were first-time brokerage accounts with more than half the new account holders being women[3].

These new brokerage accounts indicated to Sears a new and untapped 'middle market' for personal financial services. The account holders tended to be somewhat younger, with moderate family incomes with an average similar to that of Dean Witter account holders from traditional offices. Coldwell Bank was also performing well. By 1986 Dean Witter was opening more than 700,000 new brokerage accounts, many of which were first-time purchases generated from the in-store financial centre.

A further result of Sears strategy of linking together retail financial services had been the rebundling of related, but traditionally unbundled services. For example Sears had created a new home equity loan programme, the Sears Homeowners Resource Account. Under this system Sears Savings Bank underwrote a mortgage, All state Finance handled the processing and Dean Witter sold the mortgage as part of a mortgage-backed security. Similarly new products had been developed which were jointly marketed by Dean Witter and All State executives, while the Sears Homebuyers Savings Programme gave customers buying a house through Coldwell Banker a special discount on a wide range of merchandise at Sears Stores covering items such as appliances, floor coverings and furniture. Sears was also capitalizing upon its extensive card-processing capability. Already the

[3]Gurney, op. cit.

largest retailer card issuer in the USA, Sears in 1985 launched Discover, its own general credit card, to compete directly against Visa and Mastercard. To issue the cards and fund the receivables in an effort to get a larger share of the travel and entertainment markets, Sears purchased Greenwood Trust in Delaware to operate the new card, despite already having adequate transaction processing capacity in its existing operations and indeed undertaking processing for banks and other organizations[4]. By 1987, Sears had issued over 12 million of the new cards and had gained acceptance in some 500,000 merchant locations. In addition to typical credit card features, Discover was also designed as a marketing conduit for selling a range of financial services. For example, the Discover Savers Account was introduced in 1986 as Sears rolled out its new card. This account featured a fixed interest rate structure for deposit and rewarded higher balances with higher yields. Other services were also being developed.

Overall, by 1987 Sears offered a variety of financial services through a number of separate distribution channels to different groups of customers. Apart from the store-based delivery systems by the end of 1986, All State had a full-time agent force of over 14,000 and some 12,000 independent agents and brokers selling its products; Dean Witter had an account force of over 7500; while Coldwell Banker had offices totalling over 1750 throughout the USA and a residential property sales force of over 30,000.

While Sears was seen as the leader amongst retailers in attacking traditional banking markets, around the world many large retailers had been watching Sears progress and had begun to emulate the group. Most major department stores in the USA offered their own in-store card systems to support in-store sales. A number had followed Sears and were introducing a full range of financial services. These included J. C. Penney and K-Mart, while many supermarket groups were important operators of ATM networks and even switching systems such as that of Publix in Florida.

Outside the United States similar trends could be observed. In the UK clothing and department store retailers offered in-store

---

[4]*Retail Banking International*, 25 February 1985, p. 1.

card systems some of which were also offered to other retailers such as Welbeck Finance, owned by the Debenhams Group, and Club 24, owned by Next. A number of retailers were also beginning to offer a full range of financial services in stores, including Storehouse, operating in conjunction with Citibank Savings, while Marks and Spencer, Debenhams and House of Fraser had also established store card customer bases of well over 1 million accounts which were potential customers for loans and other financial services.

In France, Nouvelles Galerie, via its finance company Cefinga, operated a card system for the parent store and other retailers. Similarly, the major hypermarkets operator Carrefour first set up a financial/card subsidiary in 1981 in conjunction with Société Générale. In 1985 the store group split from Société Générale to form a new joint venture with Compagnie Bancaire, a specialist retail bank with other activities in insurance and mutual fund management. Carrefour had also established a significant insurance broking activity in a number of its stores. La Redoubt, the largest French mail order company, was also active in loans, card credit and retail insurance. G. B.-Inno, the leading Belgian retailer, was similarly a leader in the development of non-bank dominated EFTPOS; while in Germany bankers were warily looking at the assembly by Schickendanz, the parent of leading German mail order operator Quelle, of a full range of financial services including insurance and personal banking—the latter via the purchase of the technically advanced Verbraucher Bank. By the end of 1986 Quelle's mail order customers were being offered a full range of retail services and over 50 branches had been established in the group's department stores.

One of the most advanced merchandizing systems by retailers of financial services was offered by the Seibu department store group in Japan. Using an array of advanced interactive terminal-driven systems, Seibu had used advanced information technology capability in its department stores to compete over a wide range of banking and insurance services, real estate brokerage, securities purchases and credit services. By 1987, profits from the supply of financial and related services accounted for some 20 per cent of Seibu's profit and this was estimated to rise to 80 per cent by the turn of the century.

For the main store groups credit was more important than deposits. However, in the case of Sears the offering of a full financial package was something that banks found difficult to compete against since in most countries they were inhibited from operating in all the Sears markets. The provision of in-store credit was a clear threat to the bank's own personal lending especially for high-margin retail revolving or in-store credit finance. By taking such credit directly on to their own books, store groups could take the spread between the rate provided to consumers and that the store could command either direct from banks or from the commercial paper market. As an alternative, some stores, including Sears, were securitizing their debts and selling them in parcels to banks or third parties.

The challenge of a large multisite retailer to traditional branch bankers was clear. The retailer could afford the best sites and space within a large retail outlet could be allocated on a marginal basis for financial services. Moreover, the large retailer such as Sears already had a strong established client base via its own charge card system, catalogue mail order business and natural store traffic for the purchase of merchandise other than financial services. A store group such as Sears, with a strong private label brand image for quality and reliability, could also find it relatively easy to transfer this image to financial services and especially to those where consumers did not feel they had received good service from traditional suppliers. To some extent banks and insurance institutions were not especially popular with their customers and hence could be especially vulnerable to such a competitive threat.

7.2.4   The Building Society Challenge

In the UK the main competition for the banks in the small savings market had occurred from the building societies. Unlike the US Savings and Loans industry, these institutions had been extremely successful in attracting savers, both those with a bank account and those without. In part the success of the British institutions had been due to the fact that they had been able to charge variable rates for mortgage loans, unlike the US institutions. As a result, apart from providing funds for widespread home ownership, the building societies had been able to offer relatively attractive rates to mass market savers. Interest was paid on an after-tax basis following agreement with the Inland Revenue on a composite rate of tax to be paid on building society interest. In practice this had meant that some low-tax-rate investors paid net by the societies had probably been penalized.

Nevertheless the societies had been remarkably successful in appealing to all social classes and age groups throughout the United Kingdom. In 1970 the average penetration of building society accounts amongst adults was 17 per cent, with the highest penetration being amongst 55–64 year olds where 20 per cent of adults held accounts and the lowest amongst 35–44 year olds where only 15 per cent of adults held accounts. By 1979 the average penetration amongst all adults was 43 per cent with the lowest penetration being amongst 45–54 year olds where 39 per cent held accounts. The societies had during the decade been very successful in capturing the young-aged group, who were also a major source of borrowers, and 52 per cent of adults between 25–34 in the UK had building society accounts. Across social classes, while only 15 per cent of all adults held accounts in 1968, 32 per cent of upper-class individuals held accounts compared with only 7 per cent of lower socio-economic categories. By 1979, when 43 per cent of the adult population had accounts, upper-social-class penetration had increased to 61 per cent, almost double the position in 1968, while amongst lower social classes the number holding accounts had risen 400 per cent to 28 per cent of adults.

One result of this success in gaining accounts amongst all sectors of the population was that the building societies' share of all consumer deposits rose from less than 38 per cent in 1973 to around 52 per cent at the end of 1986, a rise of 14 per cent. This rise in deposits was mainly at the expense of the banks, which did not offer deposit products designed to attract consumers until the mid 1980s. There was also little attempt to attract specific segments of savers such as the retired, the high net worth individual and the like. Moreover, even by the late 1980s, most banks still did not offer interest on current account balances or provide sweep facilities to transfer surplus funds automatically into an interest-bearing deposit. By contrast the societies had been very active in trying to attract additional deposit accounts, developing a variety of deposit products including term accounts which offered higher rates of interest in return for longer periods of deposit. As a result, where once the societies tended to have most of their funds at call while lending long for house purchase, by 1981 only 68 per cent of funds were held in ordinary accounts, the balance being in term and regular savings accounts.

The number of building societies had traditionally been large. The movement was originally created as a development from mutual aid house-building groups in the nineteenth century, but later evolved largely as a series of localized organizations collecting funds from depositors to lend for house purchase within the society catchment area. In the post-war period there had been substantial rationalization in the number of societies which had declined from 481 in 1970 to 148 in 1986. The consolidation of the movement had accelerated during the 1980s as deregulation had led to increased competition. In particular a number of large mergers had occurred, increasingly concentrating the share of deposits and advances held by the leading societies. By 1987 some two-thirds of all business handled by the societies was undertaken by the largest six. Moreover, as deregulation of the industry continued the trend towards further consolidation seemed likely to accelerate. In addition, these largest societies had emerged as national organizations. This had been achieved by a series of new branch openings to create nationwide coverage, by extensive media advertising and by the merger of geographically complementary societies.

The building societies had therefore been rapidly expanding their branch coverage at the same time that the banks had been slowly facing up to the rising cost structure of their own systems and stabilizing or marginally reducing their branch numbers. The rate of growth of building society branches is illustrated in Table 7.1, which shows that overall the number of branches operated by the building societies increased sharply from 2016 in 1970 to 7000 by 1986, about half of this increase coming from expansion of the branch networks of the largest ten societies. These ten societies which between them held over 77 per cent of

Table 7.1 The changing pattern of the British building societies

Year	Number of societies (1)	Number of branches (2)	Number of shareholders (000s) (3)	Number of depositors (000s) (4)	Number of borrowers (000s) (5)	Number of staff — Full-time (6)	Number of staff — Part-time (7)	Share balances (£m) (8)	Deposit & loan balances (£m) (9)	Mortgage balances (£m) (10)	Total assets (£m) (11)	Advances during year — Number (000s) (12)	Advances during year — Amount (£m) (13)
1900	2,286		585							46	60		9
1910	1,723		626							60	76		9
1920	1,271		748					64	19	69	87		25
1930	1,026		1,449	428	720			303	45	316	371		89
1940	952		2,088	771	1,503			552	142	678	756	159	21
1950	819		2,256	654	1,508			962	205	1,060	1,256	302	270
1960	726		3,910	571	2,349			2,721	222	2,647	3,166	387	560
1970	481	2,016	10,265	618	3,655	24,116	1,050	9,788	382	8,752	10,819	624	1,954
1971	467	2,261	11,568	655	3,896	26,178	1,238	11,698	490	10,332	12,919	769	2,705
1972	456	2,522	12,874	675	4,126	28,193	1,380	13,821	592	12,546	15,246	893	3,630
1973	447	2,808	14,385	672	4,204	29,682	1,630	16,021	596	14,532	17,545	720	3,513
1974	416	3,099	15,856	641	4,250	30,774	1,911	18,021	633	16,030	20,094	546	2,945
1975	382	3,375	17,916	677	4,397	32,485	2,464	22,134	762	18,802	24,204	798	4,908
1976	364	3,696	19,991	712	4,609	34,673	2,704	25,760	848	22,565	28,202	913	6,183
1977	339	4,130	22,536	760	4,836	37,876	3,213	31,110	1,224	26,427	34,288	946	6,745
1978	316	4,595	24,999	781	5,108	40,870	4,062	36,186	1,254	31,598	39,538	1,184	8,808
1979	287	5,147	27,878	797	5,251	43,963	5,207	42,023	1,281	36,801	45,789	1,040	9,002
1980	273	5,684	30,636	915	5,383	46,418	6,309	48,915	1,762	42,437	53,793	936	9,503
1981	253	6,162	33,388	995	5,490	47,716	7,661	55,463	2,577	48,875	61,815	1,096	12,005
1982	227	6,480	36,607	1,094	5,645	49,102	9,047	64,968	3,532	56,696	73,033	1,322	15,036
1983	206	6,643	37,711	1,200	5,928	50,761	10,431	75,197	5,601	67,474	85,869	1,511	19,347
1984	190	6,816	39,380	1,550	6,314	51,660	11,454	88,087	8,426	81,882	102,689	1,658	23,771
1985	167	6,926	39,996	2,149	6,657	53,172	12,519	102,332	10,752	96,765	120,763	1,682	26,531
1986	149												

Source: Annual Reports of the Chief Registrar of Friendly Societies, except 1986 figure

Notes:
1. The figures are based on annual returns provided by all building societies in Great Britain.
2. The figures are the aggregation of figures for societies' financial years ending between 1st February in the year in question and 31st January of the following year. (Prior to 1930 the figures are the aggregation of figures for societies' financial years ending in the calendar year in question.) Because not all societies have financial years ending on 31st December the figures in the table are not strictly compatible with figures in other tables which relate to calendar years.
3. Before 1930 borrowers who were not also shareholders were included in the number of shareholders.
4. The number of advances include further advances and therefore does not indicate the number of home-buyers.

Source: BSA Bulletin, No. 49, January 1987, p. 18

total society assets in 1987 had emerged as national institutions which were strongly threatening to challenge the oligopoly of the major British commercial banks in most areas of retail banking. Moreover, this concentration was due to increase still further following the merger of the Nationwide and Anglia societies and the Woolwich and Gateway in 1987.

The large societies had also developed nationwide networks of branches which were complemented by even larger numbers of agency branches operated as ancillary businesses by other professional organizations like estate agents and accountants. These networks had been supplemented by the development of automated teller machine (ATM) installations. While not as extensive as bank ATM networks the building societies had pioneered the establishment of cooperative networks. Thus Matrix was a solely building society network linking the machines of 10 societies with some 475 ATMs; while Link, a network of some 700 machines, integrated a mixture of smaller bank networks, the Post Office, the Abbey National and Nationwide building societies and a consortium of societies and other institutions such as American Express and Diners Club. Only the largest building society, the Halifax, operated a proprietary network of some 540 machines[5].

The societies also offered superior convenience to the banks, being open for longer hours on weekdays and also on Saturday mornings. The societies also held the majority of all outstanding housing loans which made up about 80 per cent of total assets, the bulk of the rest being in liquid form. The banks had, however, made substantial progress in penetrating the market for housing loans and by 1987 had reduced the share of new mortgages held by the building societies to under 70 per cent. Moreover, the US trend towards securitized mortgages also appeared to be developing as a new threat to the societies.

In addition, the societies had also since 1984 experienced setbacks to their historic success in attracting consumer deposits. This was due largely to a switch by consumers from interest-bearing accounts of all kinds to equities. As stock mar-

[5]N. Madden, Societies in forefront of technological innovation, *Building Societies Year Book*, 1987, p. 42.

kets around the world climbed sharply upwards, individuals moved funds from building society accounts into unit trusts and equity investments. In the UK in particular this movement was fuelled by the privatization of state-owned industries, where the striking price for such new issues was usually positioned at a substantial discount to opening market prices, so guaranteeing early capital gains for successful subscribers. As a consequence of these changes and as a result of changing legislation which permitted societies to pay interest on Eurobond deposits, gross rather than after tax, many of the larger societies had turned increasingly to the wholesale markets for their funds. As a result, from 1984, the societies had raised substantial sums in the capital markets, and by the end of 1986 such wholesale funds represented 10.3 per cent of the societies' investment bearing liabilities, while for some larger societies wholesale funds exceeded 15 per cent. The crash of 1987 was, however, expected sharply to favour the 'societies' as disenchanted small investors turned back to what they considered to be the relative safely of deposit accounts with the building societies.

In 1986, as part of the process of deregulation of the British financial services industry, new legislation was introduced which largely removed the traditional barriers existing between the societies and commercial banking. As a result of the new legislation, societies were free to offer many banking-type services. These included transmission services where aggressive societies, like the Abbey National, offered an interest-bearing transaction account, while others linked with banks to offer full current accounts and in particular linked with the Bank of Scotland, a bank with no branch network in England and Wales. A number of societies had also successfully applied to join the enlarged bank clearing system. Abbey National was also actively seeking to offer its own credit card as part of the Visa organization.

Most societies had also rapidly expanded their insurance broking activities away from endowment mortgages for house purchase and property insurance to other forms of life and personal lines. Mortgage services, too, were being extended into areas such as secondary mortgages for non-property usage, while many societies were seeking a wider role in property development, estate agency and conveyancing.

On the investment side of a number of societies had introduced personal equity plans and some had linked with stockbrokers to provide retail brokerage services. Some societies were also building investment management expertise so as to provide direct and linked equity investment products under the new legislation. Societies were also allowed to market their own unsecured loans. While some had established links to specific consumer finance companies a number were also determined to undertake this activity themselves.

Overall, as deregulation proceeded in the building society movement, a series of changes was expected. First, the differences between banks and building societies were expected to be sharply reduced with the leading societies becoming members of the Bank Clearing House and offering a wide array of consumer banking services. Second, further rationalization of the movement was expected as large societies merged to create national institutions to compete against the clearing banks. Third, the funding base of the societies would shift to much greater reliance on wholesale deposits in a similar manner to the banks. Fourth, the range of credit products would increase to cover the full range of consumer credit and not merely mortgage or housing-related finance. Fifth, diversification was likely into property-related activities including property development, estate agencies and conveyancing. Sixth, the societies would become a critical delivery system for all forms of retail insurance and investment products and services. Finally, a major shift in corporate culture seemed likely, as the new legislation gave societies with assets over £100 million the opportunity to demutualize. It seemed likely that the largest societies would ultimately do this so as to become profit-seeking full service institutions and direct competitors to banks and insurance companies providing a comprehensive range of retail financial services.

7.2.5   The Postal Savings Banks

The largest deposit-taking organization in the world was the Japanese Postal Savings Bureau (PSB). As in a number of countries, Post Office savings were a major threat to the banking system in the competition for savings. In Japan, the PSB held nearly a third of all personal deposits of 100,086 billion yen at the end of 1985. Originally established in 1875 to channel the funds of small savers into industrial development and modernization, the funds it collected played a significant role in government finance. The PSB was administered by the Ministry of Posts and Telecommunications (MPT) and jealously guarded its independence from the Ministry of Finance, although the ministry made use of the funds generated by the Post Office. It was therefore the MPT which set interest rates for PSB accounts while the MOF, via its guidance system, set interest rates in the banking sector[6]. This freedom of the MPT to set rates was a source of resentment with the private banks and also the MOF, which believed it gave the PSB an unfair trading advantage.

The PSB offered depositors higher interest rates than the private banks and a number of tax advantages. Overall the PSB had some 60 million ordinary deposit accounts—about half the Japanese population—although it was thought that many of these accounts were actually individuals holding multiple accounts in different names[7]. This practice stemmed from Japanese tax law which allowed savers to receive tax-free interest on individual accounts of up to yen 3 million and each person was allowed up to three such accounts, one each in three different types of financial institution. However, the Ministry of Finance estimated that nearly 60 per cent of all individual savings in Japan were tax exempt during the early 1980s. The PSB had traditionally turned a blind eye to the opening of multiple accounts, as had the private banks. Despite the efforts of the MOF over a number of years to introduce tax schemes or to prevent the widespread evasion there was strong resistance to any such moves[8].

The Postal Savings Bureau operated a system of 23,000 nationwide branches and agencies linked by on-line computer. These branches offered a wide array of banking services although they did not provide checking facilities. Some rural offices also

[6]N. Simonson, The postal hydra, *The Banker*, August 1981, p. 101.
[7]*Retail Banking International*, 1 October 1984, pp. 6–7.
[8]See *Retail Banking International*, 10 December 1984. p. 7.

served as a base for the bank's 'Field Canvassers' who went out to collect deposits directly and to sell the bank's services. The bank also supported a large nationwide ATM network installed in post offices and had 3.1 million cards in issue. In 1984 an agreement was reached with a consumer credit company to permit savings investors to apply for a credit card.

The PSB offered a variety of deposit accounts including an ordinary passbook account on which interest was calculated daily; collection deposit accounts offering a higher rate in return for regular monthly deposits over a maximum period of two years; and Teigaku deposit certificates which accounted for 90 per cent of the deposit base. These latter accounts carried an interest rate which compounded every six months for the minimum deposit period of three years. The maximum period over which funds could be left in such accounts was 10 years.

A variation on the Teigaku account was a deposit certificate for wage-earners' property accumulation. It was used mainly by prospective house purchasers. Deposits were involved for a minimum of three years and could not be withdrawn for the first year, again interest rates were compounded every six monthes. Time deposits were also available and were accounts with a maximum duration of one year. The PSB had begun to provide loans connected with specific deposit accounts. Mortgage funds could be made available from the state-owned Housing Loan Corporation based on an account into which the customer agreed to pay a fixed monthly deposit for a period of say five years. A similar system was available for deposits aimed at creating loans for education.

The PSB had also introduced a number of new services for customers. Utility bills could be automatically paid from ordinary deposit accounts into giro accounts held by the utility companies. Stock dividends could also be paid directly into deposit accounts.

The PSB offered an attractive source of funds for government although the MPT was unhappy at having to pass over all the funds it generated to the Trust Fund operated by the MOF. This invested the savings in government bonds at low interest rates and in the MOF's 'national investment and loan programme'. As a result the rates received by the PSB were not market-related although the rates it paid were slightly above market rates. Deregulation of the Japanese market was therefore a potential problem to the PSB. The PSB was in favour of deregulation of interest rates but also wanted the right to place its funds at market rates although this was bitterly resisted by the MOF. Deregulation, however, threatened the historically privileged position of the PSB and after a strong rearguard action the bank was learning to adjust to a new competitive environment.

By 1987, a remarkable change had come over the bureaucrats at the MPT who had traditionally strongly opposed any changes in the tax-exempt position of PSB account holders. As the MOF moved progressively to deregulate interest rate levels of savings, tax reforms were expected which would ultimately remove the tax advantage of the PSB. As a result the bank was preparing to compete more aggressively, having been permitted to add some new services, including the sale of government bonds over the counter and the provision of consumer loans to customers using these bonds as collateral. In addition, the bank was expected to be able to manage a portion of its funds itself rather than handing all of them over to the MOF[9].

Although not as large, state-run institutions such as the Japanese Post Office Savings Bank were important sources of funds for government in a number of countries. A number were also very progressive, especially in operating transmission systems, and were major competitors to the banking system for retail deposits. As with the PSB, the trend to deregulation was also changing such institutions into full service competitors to the banks.

7.3   THE BANK RESPONSE

7.3.1   New Deposit Product Introduction

The challenge for deposits presented by the non-banks had to date largely gone unanswered in many countries. As a result banks had tended to lose market share of consumer deposits. In

[9]Japanese banking & finance, *Financial Times*, 16 February 1987, p. viii.

the United States the threat of the money market funds and brokerage houses had proved so serious, however, that the banks had been forced to respond.

In the early 1970s the concept of paying interest on current account balances was largely pioneered by savings and loan institutions anxious to emulate full service banks. These orga nizations began offering negotiable order of withdrawal (NOW) facilities for conventional savings accounts. Effectively this was the equivalent of a checking account which paid interest. The NOW account, although still tied to Regulation Q, proved very popular in New England where it was initially legalized and within a few years most banks and thrift organizations in the region were paying interest on current account deposits. In 1980 the NOW account became legalized throughout the United States and most banks were forced to offer a similar service.

The rapid rise in interest rates following the advent of the Reagan administration, however, emphasized the advantage of the money market funds which also provided a limited checking facility and paid a substantially higher interest rate than the 5.25 maximum rate allowed under Regulation Q. As a result money continued to flow to the money funds. Not even the direct sale of bank certificates of deposit could hold consumer interest. While most banks began to sell their own certificates of deposit to small investors at roughly money market rates these lacked the flexibility and ease of access of the money funds.

In 1982–3, however, the Federal authorities relented on Regulation Q by granting the banks the right to offer two new types of account. The first of these was like the money market account and offered an interest rate essentially similar to that of the money funds plus limited checking facilities. The second or SuperNow account offered a slightly lower rate of interest but with unlimited checking facilities. Moreover, both of these savings/transaction accounts were fully insured by the Federal government up to $100,000. Another variant, the sweep account, paid a high rate of interest on part of the deposit and a low or nil rate on a specified minimum balance used to compensate for the cost of providing transaction facilities.

The new accounts did much to restore the competitiveness of the banks for consumer deposits, but at a significant cost. Money market accounts offered essentially similar rates to the money funds coupled with limited transaction facilities such as a specified number of checks per month often without penalty with additional checks being charged at full cost. Alternatively there was a minimum value introduced for each individual transaction. As with money funds, interest was paid and compounded daily in many cases, although a few institutions offered less frequent interest calculation. This was largely a factor of how well the bank's back office automation was developed. Funds were also essentially at call with no withdrawal notice required. In an effort to stabilize their funding base and to reduce their maturities mismatch, like the British building societies, the US savings and loan institutions had also begun to offer different, and higher, interest rates for longer period deposits, rising from around half a per cent over the short-term rate for a six months deposit, to around 2.5 per cent for four years and over. The commercial banks had not done this but did still offer period certificates of deposit at a somewhat higher rate than the money market account.

In January 1983, US banks were also freed to offer the Super-Now account with unlimited checking. This account, which was designed to restore the competitiveness of the interest-bearing transaction account, was introduced by all the major banks. Offering an interest rate somewhat lower than the money market account the SuperNows offered these superior rates usually for balances in excess of $2500. Below this level the rate paid fell to the previous 5.25 per cent. Account holders also paid a monthly maintenance fee of around $3.50 plus transaction fees both for checks used and for deposits. Within a specific geographic area, interest rates offered were broadly similar, with most banks setting weekly rates, although some changed the rate of interest offered daily in line with market changes, and a few confined themselves to monthly rates. Although rates were roughly similar within an area, however, they did differ between areas, although such differences were disappearing with the advent of nationwide telemarketing activities.

Banks around the world had all begun to contemplate the introduction of interest-bearing checking accounts or offering sweep systems. In addition there had been increased efforts to segment the market, with specific products being designed to meet the needs of particular market segments. To date such products had tended to fucus on socio-demographics or lifecycle segmentation rather than lifestyle. Thus there had been special service offerings developed and directed at such segments as child savers, students, women, professional and the retired.

In particular there had been a drive to attract the high net worth individual segment focused upon by Merrill Lynch. In New York for example Citibank eventually managed to match the CMA of Merrill Lynch. In 1984, the bank launched its 'Focus' and 'Focus on Line' products which had most of the same features as the CMA. Based largely on electronic technology the bank was, however, subsequently able to produce a slightly downgraded product for customers with only $5000 of deposits. Similarly around the world Citibank began to launch other product variants based on advanced technology and remote access delivery systems. In Hong Kong for example the Citifunds Service was launched for higher income customers.

With a minimum deposit of around $25,000, the account allowed customers to make deposits in US dollars, Hong Kong dollars or yen. These funds could be held on call and accrue interest at between 1 and 2 per cent above the prevailing rate for day-to-day savings. Funds could also be invested in gold or unit trusts or lodged as time deposits in a variety of financial centres. The client could access his account by telephone and issue instructions on the account for immediate action or for execution at the next available opportunity[10]. This type of account was subsequently offered in other financial centres around the world.

Outside the USA innovations also occurred in the development of general accounts. For example as early as 1979 Svenska Handelsbanken introduced its General Account or 'AllKonto' which was designed to replace and integrate all other types of account. The new account was designed both to be simple and to yield a better return for the customer. Although the new account was therefore to be more expensive for the bank, a gain in market share was expected which would improve the bank's overall position. The new account allowed customers immediate access

---

[10]*Retail Banking*, 17 September 1984, p. 7.

to their funds from check, cash dispenser or passbook. It offered overdraft facilities and could accept payments of various kinds. Interest on the balance was paid on a tiered basis, amounts above SK 15,000 paying at a higher rate than those below, the difference reflecting the cost of providing transaction services.

The common feature of these enhanced deposit products with automatic credit facilities and other features was their reliance on advanced systems architecture. This enabled the bank to link together a variety of transaction mechanisms with automatic debit and credit account records. Relatively few banks in the world, however, enjoyed this technical capability and many services were therefore hastily designed to restore competitive position by operating part of the system on a manual or external basis. For example, the software capabilities of a number of retail banks operating in New York had been inadequate to provide the full range of services offered by Citibank's Focus or Merrill Lynch's CMA. To remain competitive, therefore, they had been forced to offer brokerage services, for example, via a third party so adding to expense and a serious loss of efficiency.

While product innovation and the development of comprehensive package products was common for up-market consumers, low-deposit, high-transaction customers were being discouraged or forced to use alternative delivery systems. No-frills banking was also developing, partially in response to consumer pressures as a result of loss-making customers becoming recognized and squeezed out of the bank's customer base. For example, Citibank in New York identified a series of mass market segments and decided it did not wish to do business with those who did not leave adequate funds on deposit or borrow to cover the costs of servicing them. As a result branches were subdivided. High-net-worth individuals with average balances of over $20,000 were provided with a better furnished area of a branch, in which to do business with a personal financial adviser and the like. Accounts with $3000 average balances were provided with conventional counter service, while those with only $1,500 up to $3000 were encouraged to use ATM machines rather than human tellers. Customers with average balances below this level were examined carefully and subdivided into a series of segments according to average balances and transaction rates. The lowest balance, highest transaction balance segments were encouraged to obtain their banking services elsewhere.

Other banks, rather than so 'purifying' their coustomer base, had sorted their branches to provide much more specialized service ranges. Traditionally, most bank branches had theoretically offered all the services of the bank irrespective of cost, quality of service and quality of delivery. To cut costs in terms of both space and staff some banks had subdivided their branches in different ways so as to provide more specialized coverage of the market, as described in Chapter 8.

7.3.2   Pursuit of Consumer Credit

During the late 1970s and early 1980s most major commercial banks directed their attention to lending to large corporate accounts and to sovereign risk borrowers. The problems of debt rescheduling, disintermediation and securitization, coupled with focused attacks by non-banks, had led the banks to rethink their lending strategies to place greater emphasis on loans to consumers.

The main areas for consumer lending had traditionally been mortgage finance, education, automobile loans, home improvements and credit finance for durables purchase. Commercial banks in the USA and many other developed economies were not the primary source of mortgage finance, which tended to be provided by specialist institutions such as savings and loans banks and building societies. In the early 1980s, however, mortgage lending appeared increasingly attractive to commercial banks which traditionally were worried about the funds mismatch of taking in short-term deposits and lending relatively long.

However, the mortgage product was increasingly seen as a high loyalty building service, offering the institution the opportunity to cross-sell other services to customers with established credit records. In the United States, where fixed rate lending for housing was the tradition, serious problems resulted in many savings and loan intitutions and some major commercial banks with large mortgage portfolios such as the major Californian banks, as interest rates soared during the high-inflation period following the second oil shock. Elsewhere, where variable rate lending was the norm, mortgage banking had been found to be attractive by many commercial banks which had been able to gain significant market share from traditional housing finance providers. The trend toward securitization, however, had not bypassed the mortgage market. In the USA there had been spectacular growth in the issuance of mortgage obligations. Whereas in 1970 only 4.9 per cent of US mortgages were resold by primary lenders into the secondary market, by 1982 this proportion had increased to 52.1 per cent[11]. This trend had not developed to anything like the same degree in other countries, but as securitization proceeded similar trends could be expected to appear elsewhere, spearheaded by investment banks and securities houses.

Commercial banks in the USA were the traditional source for automobile loans. However, falling domestic car sales, the rapid increase in interest rates and higher levels of loan default had caused the banks to pull back somewhat from this market and cede share to the in-house captive finance companies operated by the major automobile producers. In the USA commercial banks retained the largest market share with 45 per cent of auto loans outstanding at the end of 1982 but this share had fallen by 15 per cent since 1978. Over the same period the share of loans held by General Motors, Ford and Chrysler had increased by 13 per cent. General Motors Acceptance Corporation (GMAC) alone held over \$33 billion in auto loans or over 25 per cent of the market, the largest bank lender held one-sixteenth that of GMAC. As interest rates stabilized in the mid 1980s, however, banks began to make a comeback and increase their penetration[12]. Similar patterns towards in-house captive finance for automobile loans could be detected outside the USA. Further, auto loans were strong candidates for securitization and by mid 1985 Salomon Brothers had already made several issues of Cars (Certificates for Automobile Receivables)[13]. Other large-scale

[11]J. Walmsley, US debt market ring the changes, *The Banker*, August 1985, p. 23.
[12]H. Rosenblum, Banks and non-banks: Who's in control? *The Bankers Magazine*, September October 1984, pp. 14–15.
[13]Walmsley, *op. cit.*, p. 23.

receivables such as computer leases, truck credit finance and the like were also candidates as possible contenders for issuance as securities.

In other areas of consumer instalment credit the banks had also tended to lose market share during the late 1970s and early 1980s, with large gains being recorded by finance companies. While many of these organizations had been purchased by banks as part of a strategy of diversification, in-house finance companies operated by manufacturers and retailers had grown substantially. In the USA rapid shifts in market share were observed, indicating an increasingly price-sensitive volatile world as deregulation proceeded apace.

One area which banks had concentrated on to build their consumer lending books had been the credit card business. In the United States interest rate ceilings imposed by state usury laws were circumvented by moving the headquarters of card operations to states willing to relax such ceiling constraints. Cards thus not only offered an attractive interest rate spread but they were not constrained by state banking limitations. A number of the major money centre banks, notably Citibank and Chase Manhattan, therefore actively expanded their card coverage nationwide by direct marketing techniques.

The main credit cards, Visa and Mastercard, had their origins in the California retail market. In 1959 Bank of America entered the bank card market and, via its extensive network throughout the state, it quickly built an extensive consumer and merchant franchise. By 1961 Bank Americard had one million cardholders and this had risen to 2.7 million by 1967. In 1966 Bank of America decided to license its card expertise to other banks for a fee. This scheme was successful because bankers did not have to learn to set up their own schemes and cardholders could use their Bank Americard in other states. By 1970, 3300 banks were affiliated[14].

To compete against Bank Americard, other major California banks, led by Wells Fargo Bank, formed the California Bank Card Association as a non-profit organization to issue a common card. The right to use the name 'Master Charge' was purchased from

[14]A. C. Drury and C. W. Ferrier, Credit Cards, Butterworths, London, 1984, p. 20.

First National Bank of Louisville and a joint computer centre established. In other parts of the United States, especially where statewide branching was permitted, other banks developed card schemes and in restricted branching states regional associations formed. In 1976, seven bank card schemes merged to form the International Card Association to allow interchange between the regions. Local bank identities were maintained, however, and merchants were reluctant to accept unfamiliar cards.

As a result, in 1969 the California Bank Card Association conveyed its rights to the Master Charge logo to the Interbank Card Association. Members of the system started reissuing their cards, giving emphasis to the new, standardized logo. By 1970 therefore almost every state in the USA was represented by banks offering either Master Charge or Bank Americards. Processing for these transactions was undertaken by banks which established such facilities or by collectively-owned processing centres. Credit control and computing was maintained by the central organizations. Credit was taken on the books of the individual issuing banks.

In 1958 the American Express company had introduced the American Express Card as a travel and entertainment card. This was soon internationalized as Americans abroad sought to use their cards. The first sterling American Express card was issued in 1963. The bank card groups, too, internationalized. Bank of America first allowed Barclays to issue cards under the Bank Americard Scheme in 1966. The Bank of America sold its interest in Bank America Service Corporation in 1970 and in 1974 a separate international organization, IBANCO, was formed. To improve the internationalization of the card a common global name, VISA, was adopted and in 1977 National Bank Americard Inc. became VISA USA and IBANCO became Visa International. In 1979, Interbank also recognized the need to be more international and announced a change of name and card design. By 1983 the Master Charge name had been changed to Master Card throughout the world. In 1976 the exclusivity of one card for one bank was broken and it then became common for an individual bank to become an issuer of both main cards.

Within the USA much of the development of credit cards came from the issue of cards nationwide by a number of major banks, especially Citibank. Using direct mail marketing, Citibank expanded its card base across the United States and by 1974 was the largest US bank card operator with over 11 million cards in issue. Other major money centre banks similarly used direct marketing techniques to extend their geographic coverage nationwide. An alternative strategy was that adopted by Banc One, which obtained national, and some international, coverage by acting as processor and Visa card issuer for most of the leading brokerage house cash management accounts. Banc One was also prepared to offer cards in conjunction with retailers and other non-banks.

Again outside the United States the development of credit cards was spearheaded by the Visa International and Master Card secretariats. By 1986 each main card had over 100 million cards in issue, about half of which were located in the United States. Visa had some 20,000 participating banks with about $50 billion and around $40 billion turnover[15]. While the spread of credit cards was widespread their progress had not been universally welcomed. In Germany their introduction was bitterly resisted by the Deutsche Bank, led by Dr Eckart Van Hooven who believed that credit cards had an inflationary effect. The Deutsche Bank had favoured the use of a European system. It therefore supported the development of the Eurocheque system—a paper-based check system which provided holders with access to their accounts in any local currency at participating banks throughout Europe. A card system had been subsequently developed but this was a charge card rather than a credit card and primarily intended for travel and businessmen. While the Eurocheque system was highly convenient and had gained widespead acceptance in Europe, it was not a credit product.

By contrast the development of credit cards in North America and other countries could prove an attractive source of new consumer credit business, especially for those banks which had built a substantial card base. While the two main cards were themselves global no single bank was a global issuer. However, those banks that were developing a global consumer presence were beginning to emerge as at least international issuers, Citi-

[15]*Ibid.*, p. 34.

bank, for example, issued Visa or Master Card cards in a variety of countries as did a number of other multinational banks including Bank of America, Chase Manhattan and Barclays.

Travel and entertainment cards were different. They were not credit cards with accounts being cleared each month. Profits were generated from transaction charges to merchants and by the cross-selling of other services to account holders. The two principal cards were those operated by American Express and Diners Club. American Express was owned by American Express and operated on a global basis with some 11 million cards in issue. Diners Club, ownership of which was fragmented, was being developed as a global card by Citibank, which had purchased Diners Club. Unfortunately for Citibank however, the original international development of the card had been franchised to banks in various countries. Citibank had therefore actively bought up franchises when they had become available and by 1985 held most of the main country world rights. As a consequence it was aggressively attempting to develop Diners Club against American Express on a global basis. By 1984 worldwide, Diners Club had some 3 million cards in issue.

The banks dominated the credit card market, although brokerage houses held a position and building societies and savings and loan institutions were of potential importance. In travel and entertainment cards the market was essentially shared between American Express and Citibank. Card-based consumer credit had become an important ingredient in the credit market and seemed likely to remain so with the main competition being between general cards issued mainly by banks and specific cards issued by retailers and oil companies. In addition, the bundling of credit card receivables as another form of security looked a likely prospect for the late 1980s. The future of card-based financial service systems was also expected to show substantial development as a consequence of the introduction of EFTPOS and card technology development to introduce the chip-based or smart card. This latter card would improve security and offer a wider variety of financial services. In particular the introduction of a smart card was likely to encourage the development of debit cards, although initial consumer and retailer reaction to these systems had not been very positive, as discussed in Chapter 8.

7.4 CONCLUSION

Since the late 1970s the banks had faced a major assault on their retail business bases. The assault had been led by non-banks, notably brokerage houses and retailers, which had provided superior product offerings often directed at specific customer segments. These competitive threats had been successful in part as the result of superior technology, which has enabled the competitors both to integrate and to disintegrate a wide array of credit and deposit services. Technology had also been partially responsible for lower delivery system costs.

Retailer competitors, as with building societies, had offered convenience as superior features to conventional banking. In the USA retailer opening hours were dramatically longer than those of banks, while elsewhere longer opening hours were also a distinct advantage for the building societies and/or retailers providing retail financial services.

Postal Savings Banks had also proved to be important competitors in some countries. Again, where the postal system had invested heavily in technology they had come to play important roles in the payments transmission system. Some also held important shares of retail deposits and credit services as in Japan and West Germany.

Banks had been forced to respond to these competitive threats. In general this had resulted in a sharp increase in the cost of funds for those banks which did not adjust to cope with increased delivery system costs and the need to pay money market interest rates on credit balances. Opportunities and threats had also been present in consumer credit markets. Again some banks had adjusted their focus back to consumer markets and away from large corporations and governments. Particular areas of concentration had been the provision of mortgage finance and the development of card-based credit products. The banks had, however, been faced with fierce competition within the consumer credit markets both from other banks and from non-banks, especially in-house manufacturer and retailer finance companies. Disintermediation had also increased the competitive position of investment banks and brokerage houses in the USA where they had acted as intermediaries for the securitization of many forms of consumer credit and especially mortgages and automobile loans. For those banks which had adjusted, however, while the market for retail financial services was fiercely competitive, it provided the largest source of deposit funds in the world with potentially greater stability than over-reliance on the interbank market and attractive credit market opportunities. The 1990s therefore seemed likely to see a strong swing back towards retail banking services by many banks as a core area for stable and attractive profit opportunities.

CHAPTER 8

The Delivery System
Revolution

8.1 INTRODUCTION

In a major review of its strategy, completed in 1980, Citibank concluded that by the end of the decade the customer, whether corporate or personal, would determine the time, the place and the method of the banking transaction. The reason for reaching this conclusion was the development of technology which was providing a series of alternative systems for delivering financial service industry products. In particular the emergence of remote access electronic delivery systems was proving a growing threat to the traditional branch bank. Further, it also threatened the traditional power base of the banking industry—its control over the payments system. While traditional paper-based payments were cleared through the banking system the widespread availability of large linked computer systems offered non-banks the opportunity to process and operate alternative electronic payment systems. This chapter explores the changes in payment systems now emerging around the world, examines the strategies of a number of banks and analyses the implications for future bank strategy.

8.2 TRADITIONAL BRANCH-BASED BANKING

The branch had been the traditional method of distributing banking services. The branch provides a physical location for customers in a given geographic catchment area to conduct banking business. Most branches have traditionally been full service, providing the complete range of services offered by the bank to all kinds of customers including both personal and corporate. The branch played a critical part in the traditional commercial bank role of the financial intermediary. In particular at branch level the bank was a convenient repository for personal savings via deposit accounts and for the provision of current account checking facilities. Where nationwide branching was permitted, as in most countries, banks therefore developed national or regional branch networks in order to provide deposit and payment system transmission facilities. Deposits could be aggregated and lent to commercial and individual borrowers again via the branch network, although large corporate accounts might be handled somewhat differently. Such funds were cheap since in many countries banks traditionally paid no interest on current account balances but rather offered transaction services at below cost as partial compensation to customers. For banks such as the US money centre banks, operating in restricted branching environments, the primary source of funds, however, came largely from the money markets. While these funds had been historically more expensive, the banks concerned did not have to bear the cost of running large branch networks. Nevertheless, the banks with large retail customer bases tended to enjoy a funding advantage up until the early 1980s, when customers became more conscious of the value of their money, due to the growth of alternative deposit products, and began to demand higher interest rates for their funds whilst deregulation removed artifical interest rate ceilings. Since the early 1980s therefore, as the process of deregulation and disintermediation had gathered pace bank branch networks had come to appear an increasingly expensive mechanism for gathering consumer deposits, compared with money market funds or even bank consumer deposits gathered by direct marketing techniques such as off-the-page press advertising and, more recently, telemarketing.

The branch system also played a primary role in providing transaction services. The provision of withdrawal and payments services was an important function, where customers of all kinds demanded convenience thereby encouraging growth in the number of bank branches. The cost of providing these services was also usually covered by the banks' making use of idle funds in current accounts and paying lower than money market rates on money held in deposit accounts. As a result the true costs of transactions were usually hidden from customers who had in many countries become accoustomed to free or highly subsidized transaction services. In particular the system had encouraged the continued strong growth in paper-based transactions and most notably personal checks. Banks, too, often tended to neglect the high cost of transaction services as a result of the effect of bundling these costs with the value of deposits.

As customers had come to demand a realistic return on all their deposits, the unbundling of interest and transaction charges had therefore become an important issue for the banks. In particular the cost of providing full branch-based transaction services had come under increasing scrutiny by comparison with the cost of using alternative delivery systems, notably automated teller machines (ATMS), electronic funds transfer (EFT), telephone and home banking. This had led to the introduction of a variety of new pricing strategies where banks increasingly tried to recover fully the true cost of transactions and used price as a mechanism to encourage a switch from paper-based systems to electronic banking. Such moves tended to meet strong consumer resistance.

In most industrialized countries branch-based banking systems had developed which tended to contain a mixture of a small number of large commercial banks, coupled with many smaller savings or mortgage banks operating often on a regional basis. The large commercial banks were those from whose ranks had developed the leading international and multinational banks. These institutions also tended to have the largest branch networks, usually operating on a national basis. Such organizations had therefore been able to provide transmission services over a wide area and had tended to dominate in the corporate banking market. A few such banks were also emerging as global banks operating branch networks for consumers as well as for the corporate market in a number of different countries.

Savings banks had not, however, been crushed by the large commercial banks in most countries. Operating in local markets, they had offered a level of personal service which had often been superior to that from the more impersonal, large institutions. To provide improved geographic coverage and transmission facilities such banks might also have created cooperative institutions to provide a similar level of overall services such as commercial banking, card operations and ATM network management. In addition, many countries had developed specialist institutions to support particular areas of development, such as agriculture or long-term, regional or industrial investment. Cooperative institutions and mortgage banks were also important in a number of countries. By and large, the more fragmented the banking industry in a country the more likely it was that there was a tendency to excessive branching unless specific regulatory constraints were applied to prevent such development.

The different extent to which branch-based banking had developed in a number of the leading industrialized countries is illustrated in Table 8.1. Some countries such as Belgium and Switzerland appeared to be overbanked, with a branch for around every 1000 inhabitants while Italy and Japan appeared somewhat underbanked with nearly 3000 or more inhabitants per branch. These figures have to be treated cautiously, however, as other organizations, notably post offices, provide a number of banking and transmission services. In the UK for example there were over 19,000 Post Office savings bank branches compared with 24,574 bank and building society branches. A similar situation occurred in Japan, Germany and France. The figures also do not show adequately the degree of industry concentration. In West Germany for example there were 4848 deposit-taking institutions at the end of 1983 of which only 243 were commercial banks, operating 5938 branches. These banks held 21 per cent of sight accounts containing $24.2 billion or 33 per cent of all sight balances. The commercial banks held only a 7 per cent share of total deposit accounts but a 39 per cent share of all deposit account balances. There were also 604 savings banks with 17,333 branches, these institutions overall held 44 per cent of all sight accounts but only 38 per cent of total balances. They also held 31 per cent of time accounts and 32 per cent of balances. The largest group of deposit-taking institutions was the credit cooperatives, of which there were 3763 operating 15,863

Table 8.1 Comparison of the relative importance of the deposit-taking industry

	Number of deposit-taking institutions	Number of branch offices of deposit-taking institutions	Inhabitants per office	Number of transferable deposit accounts at deposit-taking institutions per inhabitant
Belgium	120	10,183	968	0.8
Canada	3,504	12,938	1,934	1.6
France	4,065	35,898	1,524	0.8
Germany	4,848	39,936[a]	1,541	0.9
Italy	1,087	12,913[b]	4,398	0.3
Japan	6,942	42,648[c]	2,780	n.a.
The Netherlands	1,124[d]	6,441	2,222	0.9
Sweden	182	3,581	2,318	3.0
Switzerland	431	4,986	1,300	0.5
United Kingdom	805[e]	24,574	2,283	1.8
United States	38,280	102,000[e,f]	2,310	0.3

[a]Including 13 postal giro offices.
[b]Branches located inside firms or public institutions are not included. The number of such branches was 966 at end-1983.
[c]Including head offices.
[d]This figure includes 965 cooperative banks (1 central cooperative bank and 964 independent member banks), which in fact operate as one institution.
[e]This figure includes 594 recognized banks and licensed deposit-taking institutions, 5 exempted banks and 206 building societies.
[f]Excluding non-bank deposit-taking offices.
Source: BIS

branches. These institutions had 27 per cent of all sight accounts and 20 per cent of balances while they held 62 per cent of deposit accounts but only 25 per cent of balances[1]. The market was therefore much more concentrated in the large commercial banks than would at first sight seem to be the case.

The actual make up of the main industrialized country markets by numbers of accounts and share of deposit volume by type of institution is shown in Tables 8.2 and 8.3. Commercial banks in most countries were the dominant holders of sight deposits but in the United States, West Germany, Switzerland and the United Kingdom, savings banks, thrift institutions and building societies or mortgage banks had a strong position. In these countries the role of such institutions had grown as deregulation had increased the degree of competition between them and the commercial banks. This was also related to the differences in payment systems between countries, with the UK and USA making very heavy use of checks compared with West Germany and Switzerland where credit transfers were much more important. A similar pattern was observable with time deposits, with commercial banks again holding most of the volume of deposits but less of the numbers of accounts. Small savers thus tended to make greater use of savings banks, cooperative institutions and post offices where these competed. Cooperative institutions were especially important in France, Germany and the Netherlands while the post office was important in Belgium, France, Italy, the Netherlands, Japan and Switzerland.

As the banking industry had developed, there had been a tendency in all countries for the range of financial services offered to customers, both corporate and consumer, to increase in range and complexity. Traditional branch architecture in Western Europe had, however, been designed primarily to provide for transactional business. As a result branch layout had been a substantial deterrent to the sale of non-transactional services. A typical branch design is illustrated in Figure 8.1. The majority of space in such a branch was devoted to back office operations. Facing the customers, which could be a broad cross-section from medium to small corporations to all segments of

[1]BIS, *Payment Systems in Eleven Industrialised Countries*, BIS, Basle, 1985.

Table 8.2 Financial institution market share distribution by number of accounts

	Commercial banks		Savings and mortgage banks		Cooperative banks		Post offices		Other	
	Sight	Deposit	Sight	Deposit	Sight	Deposit	Sight	Deposit	Sight	Deposit
Belgium	45.1	52.6	10.5	0	–	–	16.1	0	28.4	41.3
Canada	na		na		na		na		na	
France	36.8	12.7	4.1	39.9	41.5	25.1	17.6	22.3	–	–
Germany	21	7	44	31	27	62	8	0	–	–
Italy	69.1	17.5	27.9	12.4	–	–	3	69.2	–	–
Japan	na		na		na		na		na	
The Netherlands	26.7	15.9	9.2	21.5	26.6	35.1	37.5	27.6	–	–
Sweden	50.3		38.3		6.8		4.6		–	
Switzerland	40		34		1		25		–	
United Kingdom	52		31		0		13		4	
United States	52.3		46.6		0		0		0	

Source: BIS

Table 8.3 Financial institution market share distribution by volume of deposits (%)

	Commercial banks		Savings and mortgage banks		Cooperative banks		Post offices		Other	
	Sight	Deposit	Sight	Deposit	Sight	Deposit	Sight	Deposit	Sight	Deposit
Belgium	67.7	66.3	6.6	13.6	–	–	0	0	13.7	20.1
Canada	75.8	67.8	11.8	17.3	–	–	0	0	12.4	14.8
France	54.3	28.3	1.1	30.0	28.5	24.5	15.0	14.8	1.1	2.4
Germany	33	39	38	32	20	25	6.0	0	2	4
Italy	66.6	54.2	23.2	24.4	2.1	5.8	8	15.5	–	–
Japan	15.3	35.2	2.2	5.2	2.4	10.8	1.4	16.6	2.4	8.5
Netherlands	44.7	26.7	4.1	17.5	22.7	40.5	28.5	15.3	–	–
Sweden	59.8 {		28.8 {		7.2 {		4.2 {		– {	
Switzerland	35	54	37	41	1	5	27	0	–	–
United Kingdom	45 {		50 {		– {		2 {		3 {	
United States[a]	33.1	26.3	17.7	22.9	–	–	0	–	–	–

[a]Shows only total deposits within the Federal supervised system.
Source: BIS

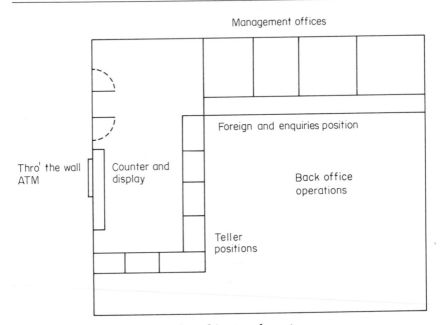

Figure 8.1   Traditional branch architecture layout
Source: D. F. Channon, *Bank Strategic Management and Marketing*, John
Wiley & Sons Ltd, Chichester, 1986, p. 154.

individual consumers, was a range of teller positions. In some
countries these teller positions were undifferentiated and were
expected to conduct all basic transactions. The level of 'personal
service', claimed by many banks to be a highly desirable attribute
for customers, was thus constrained in some countries by security screens and the use of drop trays to inhibit criminal assault.
In such branches, any out of the ordinary transactions such as
loan requests, foreign exchange and the like were normally dealt
with at a special teller position and needed to be customer-rather
than bank-initiated.

While branches were usually graded by size of asset base, their
capability actually to deliver the greatly expanded range of
financial services offered by banks varied considerably. In many
branches, there was only a limited number of managerial or
selling staff, while the task of the branch manager had become
increasingly difficult. As well as administering the branch, the
manager had been asked increasingly to sell the bank's whole

range of services to all customer segments covered by his branch. This could range from being account manager to all the medium and even large corporate customers within the geographic area covered by the branch to selling services offered to all individual personal banking accounts, including insurance and securities management services. As a result the role of the branch manager had become increasingly difficult as customer segments had become more sophisticated and demanded more specialist services while managers had been required to absorb information on an ever growing products and services portfolio. The task had been made more difficult by the lack of integrated data bases in most banks, which made it almost impossible for managers to identify cross-selling opportunities even where they existed with both corporate and retail customer groups.

Further, except in large financial centre branches, there was not usually the level of traffic to justify the presence of service specialists within a branch. As a result many branches had not actually had the trained staff to provide professional knowledge on many of the bank's offerings. Historically, too many branch managers were also hired during the era when the active merchandizing of financial services was neither required nor desired. At this time, in a buyers' market when competition was limited, many branch managers were actively discouraged from aggressively selling the services of the bank. Thus many managers were poorly equipped to take on a proactive selling role. This historical conservatism also led to a somewhat negative attitude by bank managers to customer credit requests and gave banks a poor image in the eyes of many customers, both corporate and individual, as positive providers of financial services.

8.3 NEW MODELS OF BRANCH BANKING

The rationale for the traditional, universal full service branch had come under increasing scrutiny during the 1980s as competitive pressures had built up and different bank and non-bank institutions had turned towards focused customer segment strategies. The universal branch had come to be seen both as expensive in its overall operation and also as not necessarily efficient or effective in providing specific services to particular customer groups. For example, transmission services could be provided by credit cards supplemented with ATMs and telephone banking much more cheaply than via bricks and mortar branches. Thus John Reed, Chairman of Citibank, estimated the cost to service a credit card holder to be $20 a year compared with about $150 to service a bank customer using branches and teller services[2].

Further, new specialist services into which the banks had diversified such as brokerage, trust and investment advice, could not be easily provided except via terminal-based systems in most branches because the human expertise was not available and the cost of providing it could not be justified because of the limited volume of demand.

As a result, the universal full service branch delivery strategy had begun to change. In its place banks were opting for a number of alternative delivery systems with the mixture of systems being used reflecting the specific strategic positioning each individual institution had chosen for itself. This trend towards multiple delivery systems, aimed at providing the effective position of a limited, but related, range of financial services to a particular cluster of actual or potential customers at the lowest possible cost had developed most rapidly in the United States. Deregulation and the intensification of competition, much of which had been targeted at narrow customer and or product market segments, had forced banks to focus much more closely on delivery system cost structures and service quality. As a result, the delivery of a few closely related products through dedicated channels to carefully targeted customer groups had been found to be extremely successful.

The pattern of specialized delivery systems to replace the full service branch had not really developed to the same degree outside the USA. By the late 1980s, except for the large and increasingly the medium corporate market, where many European banks had removed the servicing of such accounts from their branch networks, most branches were still full service operations. There had been variable levels of acceptance of

[2]*Wall Street Journal*, 22 June 1984.

automation and indeed in back office automation, paper truncation and transmission systems some countries in Europe, notably
in Scandinavia, were much more advanced than the USA. The
emergence of global strategies, such as those provided by some of
the major US multinational banks and non-banks had, however,
led a growing number of banks in other countries to look towards
developing specialized delivery system strategies. A number of
different types of delivery system had become clear by the late
1980s and strategic patterns involving mixes of such systems
were also emerging.

8.3.1 Limited Service Branches

A substantial number of traditional full service branches were
being converted to limited service operations. To reduce costs
the existing manager was removed from such a branch and the
range of services offered sharply cut back. Teller positions could
also be substantially reduced by the increased use of ATMs and
cash dispensers, both within the bank and through the external
wall. All middle-market and above corporate accounts were
removed and relocated in a 'Corporate branch' or 'Commercial
Centre', although some banks had retained paying-in facilities
and the like in limited service branches where customer convenience had been an issue. Costs could be further reduced by
the use of on-line till systems, connected either directly to
central mainframes or to local concentrators in key branches.
This could substantially cut the overall level of personnel
needed to run a branch. Security Pacific Bank, for example, had
since 1981 reduced its number of full service branches in the
bank's 600-plus branch network in California to around 50,
while at the same time the average number of employees per
branch had fallen from 14 to 8[3]. Reduced personnel numbers
also had the effect of reducing branch space requirements with
the average square footage of such branches falling from around
4000 square feet to around 2000–2500 square feet[4]. Some pro-

---

[3]Security Pacific Annual Report, 1983.
[4]D. F. Channon, Bank Strategic Management and Marketing, Wiley, 1986, p. 162.

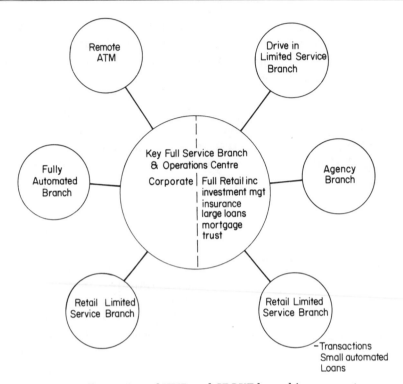

Figure 8.2   Illustration of HUB and SPOKE branching concept

duct diversity could be retained and even enhanced in much smaller locations, however, via the expansion of terminal-delivered services which were customer-initiated. Thus, insurance quotation and policy generation in all forms, loan applications and the like could all be computer terminal-based, customer-driven and deskilled in terms of branch-located personnel for both the retail and corporate market segments.

It had become common to link limited service and full service branches in a key branch and satellite structure, as illustrated in Figure 8.2. Under this system only a limited number of branches operated a full service. The latter tended to be located in urban centres. Around these key branches, suburban branches were converted into limited service branches, concentrating on transmission services. The model for this structure based on market research suggested that certain key services were ones which customers were willing to travel further to obtain. Such services, which were usually credit-based, were used infrequently, but were of a size and scale that required specialist advice, and for this customers were prepared to travel to a central branch. The frequency of use of such services was also insufficient to justify the provision of such specialist advice in all branches. By contrast, customers required local proximity for basic services like cash withdrawal and simple transactions.

The adoption of such an organization had important implications for the cost structure of branch banking systems. For example the Bank of America, in the California retail market, showed that although people would only drive a mile and a half for transaction accounts, they would go six to eight miles for credit services. The bank concluded that it should therefore reconfigure its branch structure to a key branch and satellite system. As a result the bank rationalized its 1050 branch network, closing up to 400 branches and using ATMs and home banking to provide transaction services. By the end of 1984, using a combination of branches and ATMs, Bank of America had a transaction facility within one and a half miles of 80 per cent of its served market[5]. The range of services offered in most of the remaining branches was also being reduced, with only 100 key branches located in urban areas, providing the full array of credit services. Some credit services were still being offered throughout the network, however, but the key branches undertook the processing via computer link-ups, for example in credit scoring for loans and the maintenance of credit administration.

8.3.2   Fully Automated Branches

In a drive to improve productivity and cut costs still further, the fully automated branch had begun to appear in a number of countries. These had been most widely accepted in Japan where branch openings are strictly controlled by the Ministry of Finance. For the two-year period 1985–6, the banks opened some

---

[5]P. Talbot, Overhead management, 1984. International Retail Banking Conference Proceedings, London, *Retail Banker* 1984, p. 40.

1800 new branches—half the number opened in the previous two years. Only 190 of these were full service branches, however.

Of the rest, 1144 were small-scale branches employing up to 15 people and offering a limited range of services but preserving some personal contact and communication with the customer. The remaining 467 branches were 'mini-scale', electronically-automated facilities which made heavy use of ATMs and employed less than six people[6].

A typical fully automated branch is illustrated in Figure 8.3. In such a branch, cash deposits and withdrawals, balance enquiries and interaccount transactions could be conducted by the customer without bank employee intervention. Two employees were present in the branch to assist customers in using the machines and also to provide advice on non-automated services such as loans and investments. Loans too were becoming automated, either by the introduction of universal accounts which included automatic, overdraft or credit line facilities or by computer-based credit scoring. Some of these, such as First Interstates Advance Line revolving credit, provided a credit line of $5000 and gave customers the option of choosing from a series of secured and unsecured credit alternatives.

In Europe, a number of banks had automated branches in operation by the late 1980s. One of the most advanced was the small West German chain, Verbrauche Bank, which operated only automated branches. This bank was acquired early in 1984 by the largest German mail order retail company, Schickendanz, as part of the retailer's strategy to build up a full financial service business[7]. In the United States, automated branches were also becoming more commonplace. The Bank of America, as part of its branch restructuring, increased to 35 the number of its convenience banking centres in California. These centres featured a high degree of automation to facilitate self-service banking with bank employees on the premises to fulfil activities such as loan application processing. Outside the normal banking hours, when no branch personel were present, customers could still gain

[6]*Retail Banker*, 1 July 1985, p. 13.
[7]Channon, *Bank Strategic Management and Marketing*, John Wiley & Sons, Chichester, 1986, p. 164.

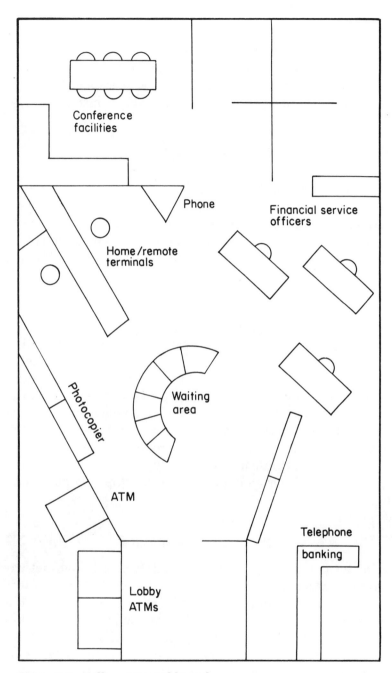

Figure 8.3   Fully automated branch
Source: D. F. Channon, *Bank Strategic Management and Marketing*,
John Wiley & Sons Ltd, Chichester, 1986, p. 161

entry to use the automated facilities by unlocking the door with their ATM cards. The bank also opened 144 fully unmanned sites where automated banking services were available. Other banks had introduced similar automated branch systems.

8.3.3   Speciality Branches

In addition to changing the universalist approach to branch banking many organizations were adopting a boutique approach and opening branches designed to cater for the needs of particular groups of customers. Such branches tended to focus on the needs of specific market segments and included the following:

Real Estate Branches

Centred upon mortgage finance, specialist real estate branches had emerged from conventional savings and loan and building society operations. They had reduced the space devoted to transactions in the branches had focused on the sale of mortgages and personal loans. In addition to providing mortgage finance such branches could offer real estate brokerage services, for both the sale and purchase of properties, personal loans especially for home improvements, personal and property insurance and sales outlets for institution-backed property developments where the bank might be either an equity-based developer or construction financier.

Private Banking Branches

An increasing number of banks had targeted high-net-worth consumers as a priority market segment. Located in appropriate socio-demographic neighbourhoods or inside apartment and condominium complexes, banks had opened special branches to provide a range of financial services for high-net-worth individuals. Based usually on some minimum account balance criterion, such branches offered the services of personal financial advisers. Interiors tended not to have conventional teller windows and had open plan layouts. Bank of America, for example, had designated Personal Financial Services officers to provide such individualized service for its up-market customers. By the end of 1984, 15 private banking offices had been opened in California together with a further 23 overseas offices located in low- or no-tax areas or financial centres. These offices could handle a complete range of investment, real estate, trust and other services[8].

Chase Manhattan had adopted a variant of this strategy, by opening Business Banking Centres on the upper floors of office buildings. These centres, which provided personal banking services to business and professional customers, were not designed to look like conventional branches. Customers entered to be met by a receptionist and each customer had a personal service representative, who sat in a private office with a conference table. A teller window was present but hidden discreetly 'behind the potted palms'. Chase had 20 such centres operating in New York by the end of 1985 and planned to open similar offices in other financial centres around the world[9].

Corporate Branches

In addition to moving to a relationship management approach for large corporate clients, many banks had also changed the way middle-market corporate accounts were serviced. Specialist financial officers had been appointed from regional dedicated corporate branches. Such branches did not normally handle retail banking business but offered a range of services used by medium-sized corporate accounts within a particular geographic area. In addition to domestic services such outlets were being equipped to provide a number of international or even investment banking services such as foreign exchange, trade finance products, letters of credit, asset-based finance, corporate cash management and the like.

[8]Bank of America Annual Report, 1984 p. 4.
[9]*Retail Banker*, 20 May 1985, p. 8.

8.3.4 The Financial Supermarket

As a result of deregulation it had become possible either directly or indirectly to operate a supermarket of retail financial services. Such a concept brought together in a single location a comprehensive range of financial services including those traditionally offered by non-bank specialist institutions such as insurance and brokerage services. In many countries, banks were prohibited from offering such services but had circumvented the authorities by franchising part of their branch space to specialists.

By offering all these services under the same roof, banks had been able to spread overhead costs while at the same time extending the appeal of the branch to users of the various financial services. Conventional financial services were not, however, always sufficiently popular of themselves to generate substantial branch traffic volume. As a result a number of banks had explored a variety of alternative methods of generating greater floor traffic. These devices had included the positioning of transaction services at the back of branches to draw potential customers past open plan displays of other services. A second method had been to add facilities, such as credit finance and travel services, as additional traffic generators. Third, some banks had opened financial centres as components of shopping centres or adjacent to superstores to try and capture part of the financial service business of customers of other retail operators. Finally, some banks had franchised space inside variety and department stores or had formed joint ventures with retailers in order to compete with those retailers such as Sears Roebuck and Seibu which had decided to offer their own range of in-house finance services.

Security Pacific's Financial Centers typified the financial supermarket concept. These units were located adjacent to or inside shopping malls and opened at evenings and weekends to provide customers with financial services at times outside normal banking hours. These hours were also similar to those operated by new retailer competitors such as Sears Roebuck. At the centres, financial counsellors actively endeavoured to sell a range of financial services from interest-bearing checking and savings accounts to consumer and real estate loans, discount brokerage and investment services.

Without doubt, the conventional branch system for delivery financial services seemed increasingly unattractive if banks wished to develop deeper relationships across an array of services with their customers. Further, a much better understanding of retailing concepts and approaches seemed highly desirable if banks were to improve the relative attractiveness of their outlets. Whether financial supermarket concepts were the answer, however, seemed debatable unless such a concept was located adjacent to or within a location which was a primary traffic generator such as a department or superstore or a shopping mall.

8.4   NON-BRANCH-BASED DELIVERY SYSTEMS

8.4.1   Automated Teller Machines

Although most automated teller machines were installed physically in bank branches, technically they could be considered to be an alternative delivery system to the branch. Moreover, the ATM when linked with others was becoming not only a national but a good global transaction system which actually went far beyond the boundaries of any individual bank. ATMs could also potentially deliver a much wider range of financial services than the relatively mundane main task performed in the late 1980s of cash dispensing. Linked ATM networks also formed a significant component in the development of first national and later supra-national electronic payment systems based on credit or debit cards. The installation of automated teller machines had expanded rapidly since the late 1970s. By the end of 1986 in the United States over 67,000 ATMs were in service compared with only 9750 in 1978. Similar figures for other leading industrial countries are shown in Table 8.4. Apart from the United States, extensive ATM penetration had occurred in Japan which with 55,000 machines installed at the end of 1986 had the lowest number of inhabitants per machine. Large networks were also operational in Canada, France and the United Kingdom, with West Germany being noticeably backward in installing ATMs. The most efficient networks were those in Sweden and Canada with 7700 and 7000 transactions per machine per month, respectively.

Table 8.4 Comparison of number and use of ATMS and cash dispensers

	No. of machines installed			Machines per million people	Number of transactions per machine per month
	1978	1983	1987		
Belgium	0	560	703	71	4,700
Canada	250	1,960	3,241	130	7,000
France	1,000	5,100	9,500	174	3,100
Germany	0	1,600	3,400	55	3,900
Italy	0	1,500	2,500	44	1,000
Japan	12,800	37,900	55,000	470	na
Netherlands	15	32	na	na	na
Sweden	483	1,074	1,227	147	7,700
Switzerland	100	1,027	na	na	na
UK	2,189	5,653	10,800	190	4,200
USA	9,750	48,118	67,000	282	5,000

Sources: BIS, Battelle Institute and *American Banker*

The use of ATMs effectively transferred the undertaking of transactions from bank staff to customers or some other intermediary. While such systems were expensive to set up they had the distinct advantage of being volume-sensitive. As a consequence there has been a drive towards increasing transaction volume market share in order to cut costs in electronic banking. This is illustrated in Figure 8.4.

In the United States the use of ATMs had been the primary means of expanding electronic payment services. Traditionally checks were the most frequently used means of payment in the USA and were expected to remain so for some time. In 1983 Americans wrote approximately 40 billion checks of which 55 per cent were written by individuals, 40 per cent by businesses and the rest by state and local governments. The vast amount of paper to be handled and a lack of an efficient truncation or electronic transmission system had encouraged the banks to move to ATMs and to experiment actively with other electronic delivery systems.

Paper-based systems tended to be roughly stable once a bank had reached a moderate size and there were therefore no significant scale advantages. However, with electronic banking a strong volume-related experience effect existed. While capital

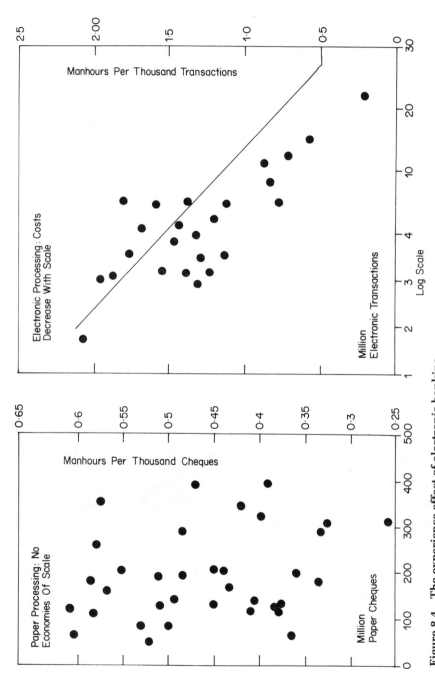

Figure 8.4   The experience effect of electronic banking
Source: Boston Consulting Group

costs were initially high, creating a severe barrier to entry, marginal transaction costs tended to be very low. Further, the greater the volume of transactions that software and systems development could be amortized over, the lower the individual unit cost. For example, the cost of an automatic teller machine (ATM) was between \$25,000 and \$50,000 depending upon the number of tasks it could perform and the location it was placed in. However, the cost of each individual transaction once the machine was installed was substantially lower than a human teller transaction[10]. In the United States for example, in 1982, it was estimated that the cost of a human teller transaction and one done on an ATM were approximately the same. By 1986, however, the average cost of an ATM transaction was substantially less than the cost of one using a human teller. This was because the volume of ATM transactions had grown rapidly with average transactions per machine per month of 4000 in 1978 growing to 6500 in 1983. Thus while wage costs were rising at least in line with inflation the costs of ATMs were falling in real terms by 6–10 per cent per annum.

By 1987, however, the installation of ATMs in the USA appeared to be approaching saturation. While about half US bank customers had been given ATM cards only a third had become frequent users. Moreover, since the early 1980s the number of transactions per installed machine had actually fallen. Few banks had been able to crack the '33 per cent wall'. Citibank in New York by issuing cards to everyone with a checking account and integrating cards into the delivery of virtually all retail services, had managed to convert 80 per cent of its customers into ATM users. Citibank's 600 machines in New York, being expanded to a network of 900 in 1987, was an exclusive network Exchange (NYCE), the ninth largest domestic US network[11].

While both ATMs and cash dispensers were used in the USA, almost 99 per cent of machines installed were ATMs offering a full range of services including cash withdrawal, deposits, transfers between accounts, cash advances from bank credit card accounts, bill payments and balance enquiries. Most of the US

---

[10]*Economist* International Banking Survey, 24 March 1984, p. 73.
[11]*American Banker*, 19 August 1987, p. 22.

Table 8.5   Major US ATM regional networks 1987

Network	No. of ATMS	Interchange use per card per year	Interchange transactions (millions/month)
Mac, Pennsylvania	270	13.5	5.58
Pulse, Texas	4353	5.3	3.02
Exchange, Washington	1300	16.4	3.00
Mpact, Texas	1272	15.6	2.74
Honor, Florida	2382	6.4	2.24
Avail, Georgia	1247	10.8	2.07
Cashstream, Pennsylvania	1844	6.9	2.04
Cash Station, Illinois	1259	15.0	2.00
NYCE, New York	2754	3.0	1.75
Shazam, Iowa	864	16.2	1.62

Source: *American Banker*, 9 August 1987

installed base was located in the lobbies or through the walls of banks and savings and loan institutions. In the past few years, however, there had been a growing trend to instal ATMs in high-customer-traffic locations such as supermarkets, convenience stores, shopping centres, airports, hospitals, office buildings and industrial plants. Further, a growing number of installations were being made by retailers. In particular, food retailers were keen to instal ATMs, since in the USA, because of their much longer opening hours, the supermarket operators had evolved as the main providers of check chasing services.

ATMs in the United States had also provided a major mechanism for developing interstate banking by the creation of shared networks. The two largest networks which had emerged as essentially nationwide were CIRRUS and PLUS. Both originally owned by groups of banks, these systems operated some 15,000 ATMs throughout the USA. In 1987, PLUS formed a strategic alliance with the credit card company VISA while CIRRUS was actually acquired by Mastercard, as discussed below. These two leading national networks were supplemented by a series of regional ATM networks as shown in Table 8.5.

In the most ATM-intensive country, Japan, the use of machines was also more advanced than in other countries. Because many Japanese accounts were passbook, a capacity to read and update passbooks was a necessary feature of Japanese machines. In addition currency recognition and depository facilities were integrated with traditional cash-dispensing functions.

Japanese ATMs therefore had the additional features of depositing cash and automatically recirculating the cash by placing bills into the dispensing cartridges. Called the 'Turnaround System' and invented by Oki Electric in 1983, the recycling deposit of funds had meant that the float needed to stock an ATM had been reduced from around Y10 million to only Y2 million[12].

Passbooks could be automatically updated, including unposted items and automatic page turning. Colour graphic displays and voice assistance encouraged customers to undertake more complicated transactions such as on-line money transfer and bill payments. Some machines could also split account transfers across multiple accounts and receive and dispense coins[13].

The Japanese machines were not available on a 24-hour basis but were generally in operation from 8.45 am to 6 pm on weekdays and from 9 am to 2 pm on Saturdays, which was longer than banking hours. The machines were, however, usually linked on a network basis. A customer could therefore use his own bank's machines and those of any other bank that was part of the same network. There were four such networks run by different categories of financial institution in 1983. A second type of network was operated by the Nippon Cash Service Co. (NCS). Launched in 1975 and jointly owned by 54 banks, NCS had installed some 250 cash dispensers in railway stations, hotels, department stores and supermarkets in the three largest metropolitan areas. These machines were usable by card holders of NCS-participating banks for a small transaction charge[14].

The linkage potential of ATMs was also leading to the globalization of payment systems. This process was being led by the international credit card companies which by a series of arrangements with participating banks were making it possible for cardholders to use ATMs around the world. VISA pioneered the development of international ATM transactions in March 1984

[12]R. Nevans, Banking technology in Japan, *Retailer Banker*, 17 June 1985, p. 11.
[13]R. South, Overhead management in Japanese Banking, 1984, International Retail Banking Conference Proceedings, *Retail Banker*, 1984, p. 50.
[14]BIS, Payment Systems in Eleven Industrialized Countries, p. 215.

Table 8.6   International ATM networks (September 1986)

	VISA	MASTERCARD	AMEX	PLUS
Total ATMs live worldwide	10,795	6,071	8,757	8,500
Total ATMs live in EMEA[a] Region	5,003	0	125	0
Number of countries worldwide	15	3	17	0

[a]EMEA—Europe Middle East and Africa.
Source: *Retail Banker*, 8 September 1986, p. 11, Lafferty Publications Ltd, London

and by mid 1985 over 4400 machines accepted its card in eleven countries.

By late 1986 over 10,000 ATMs in 15 countries around the world accepted VISA cards, as shown in Table 8.6. Mastercard was still largely confined to North America and had singularly failed to penetrate the market in Western Europe. VISA'S main competitor in Europe was Eurocheque which linked over 2000 ATMs in operation in Denmark, Spain, Germany, Portugal and the UK by the end of 1986 and expected to increase this to between 4000 and 6000 by the end of 1987. American Express had also been rapidly building its international coverage, although the number of machines accepting AMEX cards outside the United States remained small. The large US network PLUS was also expanding its international coverage in Europe and Japan where it had linked with JCB, Japan's largest credit card operator[15].

In 1987 both VISA and Mastercard dramatically expanded their ATM network cover by linking with the two leading US ATM networks. In March 1987, VISA linked with the 14,000 strong PLUS system by taking a one-third shareholding in the system and agreeing that PLUS would become the international service logo for VISA's own ATM network. In September 1987 Mastercard purchased the whole of the CIRRUS network from the partnership of banks that owned it. Under this agreement, Mastercard would become the largest debit card organization in the world with 25,362 ATMs in place worldwide. Membership

[15]*Retail Banker*, 9 September 1986, p. 11.

in CIRRUS was also to be extended to all Mastercard-issuing banks, so breaking the exclusivity enjoyed over certain territories for the original bank owners. By contrast VISA expected to have 24,000 worldwide ATMs by the end of 1987.

8.4.2   EFTPOS

Although not strictly an alternative delivery system, Electronic Funds Transfer at Point of Sale (EFTPOS) was seen as an important additional method of consumer payments. Again much experimentation was underway throughout the world as banks were anxious to eliminate expensive paper-based transactions. EFTPOS offered an electronic cashless method of payment to the consumer at the point of purchase. Using a plastic card and a personal identification number, the customer accessed his account in a participating bank via a central switch and the account was then debited and the funds transferred electronically to the retailer's account in another bank, again via the central switch. Once the transaction had been made it was immediately confirmed at the retailer's till.

The range of point of sale services actually covered a wider range of activities than direct electronic fund transfer. They could involve supplementary features to existing services such as check verification and guarantees, on-line credit card authorization and the like. They could also include the use of ATMs at point of sale, and the use of customer-operated direct debits, especially useful for automated petrol stations and for machine-based shopping systems.

Around the world the potential opportunities for banks to eliminate expensive paper-based payment systems had led to substantial experimentation. These experiments had, however, revealed sharp disagreements between bankers and retailers largely as a consequence of bankers trying to pass on the costs of developing such systems to the retailers. In particular, retailers had been incensed at the attempts by some banks, and in particular VISA and its affiliate banks, to try to charge a percentage fee for debit card transactions in a similar manner to credit card charges rather than a flat fee irrespective of transaction value as with checks. In the USA, VISA introduced a debit card, Entree, in the mid 1980s and this flopped badly. In 1987, Barclays Bank, the main VISA operator in the UK, introduced its Connect card to similar howls of protest by retailers and ended up being faced with a Monopolies Commission enquiry into both its new debit card and traditional credit card products.

There were other areas of substantial difference between retailers and bankers which also required resolution before EFTPOS could expect to take off. These conflicts arose from the different objectives of each group. For retailers, EFTPOS offered different advantages or otherwise, dependent upon the sector of the industry in which they operated. Oil companies operating retail gasoline sites were strongly in favour of EFTPOS because it would enable them to automate marginal gasoline stations and, in the USA, to reduce the float costs of money tied up in credit card systems. They also wished to increase customer convenience by providing terminal access for all forms of debit and credit card and to maximize the cardholder base able to utilize their sites. As a result the number of EFTPOS terminals installed in retail gasoline operations was expected to rise sharply, as shown in Table 8.7. Interestingly, however, some of the gasoline companies had opted not to join bank EFTPOS networks and

Table 8.7   Estimated growth in US point of sale debit terminals

	Mid 1986			1990 Estimates		
Merchant type	POS terminals	Share of of total (%)	Monthly trans. per terminal	POS terminals	Share of total	Monthly trans. per terminal
Supermarkets	2,249	13	200	74,760	42	624
Gasoline retail	5,536	32	475	30,260	17	1,764
Convenience	1,384	8	475	12,460	7	1,470
Fast food	nil	–	–	17,800	10	400
Other	8,131	47	60	42,720	24	140
Total	17,300	100	243	178,000	100	734

Source: *American Banker* 1 June 1987, p. 16

Shell Oil and Amoco had connected their stations to the J.C. Penney electronic network.

By contrast most supermarkets were not prepared to welcome debit cards. They argued that instant debits were not popular with their customers and such systems could hold up the speed of check-outs, especially if non-universal card systems were in operation. Grocery retailers were also installing their own POS systems to trap financial and inventory information for their own purposes. They therefore were resistant to any bank-owned terminal systems which were not fully intergrable with their own. Moreover, the attempts by banks to price EFTPOS services on anything other than a flat fee basis were bitterly resisted. In the UK, Asda, a major superstore operator, refused to accept Barclays' Connect card, while in Belgium the leading supermarket retailer, GB-Inno, was charging banks for using their cards in the GB-Inno system rather than the other way round. Nevertheless, there were some signs in the USA that more supermarkets would accept EFTPOS, partly perhaps because they had emerged as the largest handlers of checks. However, as electronic systems developed there a number of the leading retailers were making a strong effort actually to manage EFTPOS switching systems.

Another source of conflict between bankers and retailers concerned neutrality. Retailers did not wish to come between the banks and account holders. They also wanted EFTPOS payments to be irreversible so as to provide a similar level of protection to that of authorized checks. In addition they required simplicity with security in transactions, no more than 25 seconds per transaction and, most of all, a share of any cost savings.

By contrast, banks wished to retain any cost savings for themselves and wanted to make a percentage charge per transaction rather than a flat fee. They also wanted to retain their own customers' loyalty and were resistant to full universality which allowed, in particular, non-bank debit cards to be used in the system. The banks were also anxious to retain control over the payments system and so were very resistant to any non-banks being allowed to operate electronic message-switching systems.

Around the world, however, there was growing competition from non-banks to dominate emerging EFTPOS systems. Large, high-transaction-volume retailers such as Sears Roebuck and J.C.

Penney were clearly contenders, as were organizations such as building societies and credit unions which had built up electronic-transaction processing capabilities. In some countries the PTTs, with well-developed payment systems, were also contenders to manage EFTPOS.

In particular the moves by the major credit card companies, VISA and MASTERCARD, to build international ATM networks capable of accepting debit cards from constituent banks offered a significant advance in the development of EFTPOS. After their early abortive attempts to launch independent debit cards Mastercard, VISA and the PLUS and CIRRUS ATM networks were brought together by the American Bankers Association to set technical standards for debit cards accepted at the point of sale and to try to get some order into the fragmented issuing of cards by individual organizations throughout the United States. A new version of the original VISA debit card, Entree, was to be introduced, which in addition to carrying the common logo would also permit participating banks to display their own identities. As a result the US banking industry was more optimistic about the spread of EFTPOS.

Perhaps the most advanced and ambitious EFTPOS programme was that backed by the French government and the local PTT. The French banks had committed themselves to the use of the 'smart' card. This card contained a microprocessor which could hold far more information than the more common magnetic stripe card and could be constantly updated each time a transaction took place. After experimenting with debit cards the French were moving towards the distribution of smart cards and readers. These could also be connected to a Minitel unit. In 1987 French Télécom began to distribute 50,000 smart card readers while France's Carte Bancaire began the initial distribution of smart cards in 1986. This programme involved the introduction of some 17 million cards to French bank customers by 1989. The French intended that the use of smart cards would thus cut significantly into the volume of payments undertaken by checks.

In many countries, therefore, there remained considerable conflict between bankers and retailers on the installation of EFTPOS systems. While retailers tended to accept that electronic fund transfer would come in, they believed it mainly benefited banks and that consumers were not keen on it. By the late 1980s EFTPOS was therefore still not an important element in payment systems anywhere in the world. Like home banking it was expected to grow in importance, especially as some retail sectors favoured its introduction. The probability was high, however, that EFTPOS would become an important factor in payments systems during the 1990s as bankers everywhere sought to reduce the cost of operating paper-based systems.

8.4.3   *Truncation and Paperless Payments*

Apart from the development of EFTPOS and automated teller machines there was a major effort taking place around the world to substitute electronic payment transfer systems for paper-based methods. Historically, in most countries paper-based systems were the normal method of effecting non-cash payments, as shown in Table 8.8. In terms of volume, paper-based systems and especially checks were the predominant form of non-cash payment in most countries. Great scope therefore existed for cost reductions in cashless payments either by elimination of paper altogether or by truncation.

Truncation had proceeded furthest perhaps in Scandinavia and the elimination of much of the paper from the banking system had enabled the banks to operate with significantly less labour per branch than banks still dominated by paper payment systems.

The predominant payment system in Sweden, as in several other European countries, was the Postal Giro which carried out all kinds of payments ranging from small payments between individuals to the governments' payments. It was administered by the Post Office and cooperated closely with the PK-Bank, a government-owned commercial bank. The savings banks in Sweden also formed a link with the Postal Giro in 1982 and a new system, the Savings Bank Giro, was introduced. The main commercial banks also introduced their own giro system called Private Giro and as a result almost every Swedish household therefore had a giro account. These Giro systems provided a cheap and effective payment system.

Table 8.8   Comparison of the relative importance of payments instruments other than cash

	Checks	Credit transfers[a]	Direct debits	Payments by credit card
	(as a percentage of total volume of transactions in 1983)			
Canada	91.0	(insignificant)	2,0	7.0
France	82.5[b]	9.2	6.2	2.1
Germany	11.0	57.0	32.0	(insignificant)
Italy	85.3[b]	12.7[b]	1.5[c]	0.5
Japan	18.7[d]	14.8	56.3	10.3
The Netherlands	22.3[b]	62.0	15.6	(insignificant)
Sweden	20.0	72.0	1.0	7.0
Switzerland	10.6	88.0	0.8	0.5
United Kingdom	61.0	23.0	6.0	8.0
United States	98.6[e]	0.9	less than 1	7.2

[a] Including interbank transfers.
[b] Including postal checks.
[c] Data are for 31 banks accounting for 70 per cent of the total balance-sheet assets of the banking system.
[d] Including bank checks, bills and promissory notes.
[e] Including payment son credit card accounts.
Source: BIS

The basic transmission services offered were in-payments, out-payments and transfers. A variety of transactions were possible by mixing these services. Payments were made by means of transfers between giro accounts. The book-keeping, crediting and debiting of accounts, and the printing of account statements were all computer-based. Individuals and small businesses initiated transactions manually by sending special giro forms by post instructing the Giro to debit the payer's account and credit the payee. Payment orders from larger companies were usually sent in the form of magnetic tape or by direct computer-to-computer link. For firms receiving large numbers of in-payments, the in-payment cards were printed to enable them to be read optically at the Giro centre. The data were then delivered to the account holder on magnetic tape with the account statement.

While most of the non-cash payments volume used the Postal Giro system, checks were used, mainly by individuals, to effect transactions through banks while corporations tended to use the Bank Giro system. Although the volume of checks grew rapidly during the 1960s, this growth had largely stopped by the mid 1980s, partially by the introduction of discriminatory pricing against small-value checks and by the lower cost of giro transactions.

The Swedish banks had, however, reduced the cost of check handling substantially. This was achieved by all the banks cooperating with one another to redeem each others' checks. As soon as a check was presented at a bank it was automatically truncated by keying in the relevant data in electronic form. All checks were standardized regarding account number, identification, description, layout and the like. The checks were filed by the cashing bank and the issuing bank received only the accounting data plus a code to tell it where the checks were filed. Should the using bank need a particular check it could therefore be produced but this was an extremely rare event[16].

The success of the Scandinavian banks and postal system in reducing check volume by efficient giro systems and by the truncating of checks themselves had probably been more successful and efficient than the very much more expensive EFTPOS experiments. At present consumers tended to prefer checks to card-based operations and it seemed unlikely that paper-based systems would decline in volume substantially until at least the mid 1990s. The introduction of greater efficiency into the existing systems of paper clearing by transaction was therefore seen as an extremely attractive proposition in those countries where checks made up the bulk of cashless payment volume.

8.4.4 Telemarketing and Direct Mail

Manufacturers Hanover Bank's Consumer Convenience Center in Hicksville, Long Island, was the bank's largest 'branch' with retail deposits of $230 million in 1985. Yet not a single customer had ever set foot on the premises. All the deposits were gathered

[16]BIS, op. cit., pp. 238–42.

by direct mail or a nationwide free phone system prompted by rate advertisements placed largely in local press around the United States. The collection of deposits by 'off the page' marketing had become an important method in many countries and much cheaper than utilizing physical branches for many banks.

Similar long-distance marketing methods were being widely adopted in the United States by institutions such as the money centre banks and brokerage houses. Initially such techniques had been adopted to help circumvent the restrictive state banking laws, but they had also developed as low-cost alternatives to traditional branches. Manufacturers Hanover Retail Card Services business unit thus operated telemarketing and direct mail campaigns in 48 US states. The unit offered more than a dozen card-based credit products including both VISA and MASTERCARD credit cards. Calling unsolicited potential customers throughout the United States, Retail Card Services would attempt to sell the call recipient one of its credit services. Commenting, the head of the unit added: 'Our strategy in telemarketing is not just to stop with a credit card. When we telephone a potential customer it's often the first time they've heard from Manufacturers Hanover. We lead with a credit product offering and then try to sell them on the bank's deposit services. We found that if we can sell them on one product, we can usually sell them on any number of others.' As a result of such strategies Manufacturers Hanover had built up a customer base of over 4 million accounts, half of which were located outside New York State, with California being in second place[17].

Similar telemarketing and direct mail tactics were being used increasingly by US banks in the domestic market. Where suitable media facilities were available overseas, those institutions interested in developing international or global consumer strategies had begun to deploy similar methods in other countries. In the main, however, telemarketing had been confined to US corporations but direct mail and the sale of financial services via print media had been adopted by a growing number of financial institutions throughout the world. As integrated data base accounting systems became more widely installed, very

[17]Manufacturers Hanover Corporation 1984 Report, Part 1, p. 10.

carefully targeted direct marketing methods were expected to become increasingly important within the banking industry.

8.4.5   Home Banking

Around the world there had been great interest expressed and many experiments in home-based banking. These utilized a microcomputer or some other form of terminal and a telephone or videotex link to the bank's computer system. Such systems were usually part of wider home interactive systems (HIS) packages which included news, information and shopping facilities. The range of HIS services is illustrated in Figure 8.5. Some banks saw home banking as an alternative delivery system to branch-based banking, thus reducing operating costs. The strategy was therefore especially attractive to banks or financial institutions which had not already established branch banking systems. For example in the United Kingdom, one of the first home banking systems in the world was launched in September 1983 by the Nottinghamshire Building Society. This was also linked to a system operated by the Bank of Scotland. Unlike some societies, the Nottinghamshire had not invested heavily in branches and the society considered that each new account generated via its home banking facility cost only a third of that of a similar account produced from a branch system[18]. Similarly the Bank of Scotland had no branch network in England and Wales. These systems, however, operated through British Telecom Prestel system for which there were only some 80,000 subscribers, thus severely limiting the available audience.

Few home banking systems, however, were profitable by 1987. A critical element in making home banking profitable was likely to be the use of such systems for bill payments rather than using paper- or mail-based systems. In the USA such payments cost retailers, utility companies and the like some three times the estimated cost of making a similar payment via a home banking system[19].

---

[18]*Economist*, 26 January 1985, p. 75.
[19]D. F. Channon, Banc One Corporation Case Study, *Bank Strategic Management and Marketing, Case Book*, Wiley, 1985.

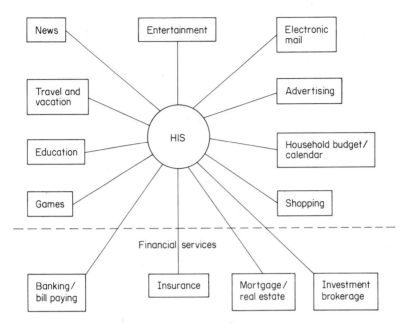

Figure 8.5   The range of 'HIS' services

In the United States only three videotex projects were in operation in 1978 while by 1983, 17 home banking projects were underway and a further 37 were planned or in the course of development, involving some 100 organizations[20]. By 1987, most major US banks offered some form of video banking service. However, the take-up rate for these services had been very poor. Despite the fact that there were some 25 million personal computers in use in the United States only around 100,000 people subscribed to home banking services[21]. The largest system was Covidea, which had some 50,000 subscribers. This was a joint venture formed in 1985 to link the home banking service of the Bank of America with the Pronto system developed by Chemical Bank. Other partners in this venture included AT and T and Time Inc., which offered electronic news and information services[22].

[20]Trans Data Corporation, *A Compendium of Videotext Home Banking Studies*, 1983.
[21]*Financial Times*, Information Technology in Finance Supplement, 16 October 1986, p. iv.
[22]James B. Wiesler, The national strategy of Bank of America, *The Bankers Magazine*, March/April 1985, p. 37.

Home banking services included balance enquiry, account statements, bill payments, bank credit and account status, funds transfers among accounts, and information about certificates of deposit and interest rates. Fees for such services were around $10 per month and users could usually access the systems using a variety of home computers as terminals. The average time spent using home banking services was ten minutes a day and the average number of banking transactions was six per month[23].

In West Germany, the Post Office offered a videotex service enabling the banks to offer home banking initially in two test cities, Berlin and Dusseldorf. In 1984, this was extended to the entire Federal Republic. By the end of 1983 over 10,000 bank customers had TeleKontos (giro accounts) which they could access from their homes. The advent of a nationwide videotex service was expected to lead to a considerable growth in the number of subscribers. In practice the take-up rate had been much less than expected and by the end of 1986 only some 40,000 people had subscribed to the service.

France was the only country to have a large, screen-based, banking service. In France home banking had benefited from the development of the French electronic telephone directory. To access this a Minitel terminal was needed and over 2,500,000 terminals had been supplied by the end of 1986. More than 50 banks provided simple account statements via these terminals. One bank, Crédit Commercial de France, had, like the Nottinghamshire Building Society, endeavoured to build its customer base without adding to its limited 150 branch network. Using the Minitel videotex terminals provided by the French government, the bank offered a range of banking services and had successfully attracted over 110,000 individuals and 7000 business subscribers[24]. In a number of countries computer-driven, voice-response systems utilizing telephones rather than screens had proved more popular than screen-based home banking. They were also much more easily available as they did not require videotex systems. In the United States the first such system was introduced in 1976 and worldwide there were some 5 million

---

[23]Trans Data Corporation, *Test Marketing Videotex/Home Banking Services, Pilot Results*, 1983.
[24]*Financial Times*, op. cit., p. iv.

users of such systems by the end of 1986. The largest in the world was that offered by Banco de Santander in Spain[25].

Such systems were also easier to use than screen-based systems. With the Banco de Santander system, for example, the customer dialled the bank where a computer-generated voice responded asking for the customer's account number, which was entered by punching the telephone keys. Next the voice requested a PIN number which in turn was punched in, after which the bank's services could be accessed.

By the late 1980s home banking had not developed as an important delivery system for financial services. Around the world there was much experimentation but no clear sign of great consumer interest. For screen-based systems this was largely due to the very slow penetration or lack of availability of videotex systems. Telephone-based banking, however, was beginning to emerge as a potentially significant system. Screen-based systems therefore seemed to be a potential distribution channel for the 1990s rather than the 1980s.

8.5   IMPLICATIONS FOR EMPLOYMENT

The main area for employment within the banking system had traditionally been in branch offices. This work had involved substantial numbers of clerical workers involved in back office operations handling paper-based systems. Transactions in the front office had largely been conducted by human tellers. The trends in bank delivery systems described above posed a substantial threat to much of this traditional employment. In Western Europe it was argued strongly by many bankers that radical change in large branch systems was neither necessary nor desirable.

The Deutsche Bank, for example, still insisted that all its branches remained full service and had been reluctant to instal electronic banking. Commented its Chief Executive: 'We always put much more emphasis on human banking, the machines are the same everywhere. As soon as we introduce electronic bank-

[25]*Ibid.*

ing, then we lose our advantage.' One of the major German banks, however, was already installing a new on-line communication system which, when fully operational, would enable the bank to handle the same volume of business with 20 per cent fewer staff[26].

In Canada, however, the number of bank employees fell by 1 per cent in the 12 months to the end of June 1984, while the number of installed ATMs increased by 48 per cent. The Bank of Montreal planned to reduce employee numbers by 6.8 per cent in Ontario and by 10.4 per cent in British Columbia[27]. In Japan, the widespread use of ATMs meant that the number of employees per dollar of deposit was only a quarter of those for banks in other countries. Even with a 300 per cent growth in transaction volumes during the decade to 1984 and a 35 per cent increase in the number of branches, Japanese banks actually recorded a decline in the number of bank employees from 1981. At the same time, the volume of deposits, withdrawals and posting transactions through machines reached 60 per cent and was expected to grow to 80–90 per cent by the end of the 1980s[28]. Amongst major US retail banks the trend was the same: increased automation, more ATMs, specialist branch offices and fewer retail banking employees. One estimate suggested that over 500,000 teller jobs would be eliminated in the USA by 1987[29]. Another bank noted that when considering the opening of a new branch it seriously 'investigated its future potential as a restaurant or a funeral parlour'[30]. The aspirations of the European bankers thus seemed unrealistic and significant reductions in both the number of full service branches and staff seemed likely over the next decade in the main industrialized countries.

Citibank's retail banking strategy in New York City typified the shift in delivery system strategy. Between 1979 and 1984 the bank reduced the number of its branches from 260 to 220. At the same time, however, the bank expanded its number of distribution points by installing over 500 ATMs which, under the slogan

---

[26]*Economist* International banking survey, 24 March 1984, p. 74.
[27]*Retail Banker*, 29 October 1984, p. 10.
[28]South, *op. cit.*, p. 52.
[29]Salomon Bros., *op. cit.*
[30]Channon, *op. cit.*, Banc One Case.

'The Citi never sleeps', were available for transactions 24 hours per day in the lobbies of existing branches. At the same time bank staff were cut from 7000 to 5000. High-net-worth individuals, with a minimum of $25,000, were singled out for special attention with individual financial counsellors and provided with services in superior surroundings. Mass market customers were carefully subdivided into seven segments according to their service needs and relative value to the bank. Customers in the less attractive segments were encouraged to leave and service quality to the remaining customers was upgraded. Customers with low balances were encouraged to use ATMs by discriminatory pricing, resulting in over 70 per cent of Citi's cash withdrawals being made on ATMs. The overall effect of the strategy was to improve profitability substantially by lowering operating costs and the elimination of loss-making customer segments. At the same time Citi's market share in New York doubled from 5 to 10 per cent, the largest shift in share for several decades.

8.6 CONCLUSION

Major changes were taking place in financial service delivery systems in the late 1980s, which substantially threatened the traditional full service bank branch. New electronic systems offered customers the capability of widely distributed transaction processing via machine-based banking. In the United States, where regulatory barriers had traditionally tended to constrain the geographic coverage of banks, linked ATM systems were providing a system of nationwide access to funds. On an international scale the major credit card operators were similary globalizing funds access.

The demand of customers for maximum value on their deposits was also forcing the unbundling of the traditional practice of subsidizing the costs of transaction systems by providing poor deposit products. In future it seemed likely that banks would be forced to pay an economic price for deposits and to charge for transaction services in relation to their cost as well as to look at new ways of providing such services at lower costs. In particular, banks everywhere were expected to endeavour to substitute electronic payments systems for paper-based systems. This substitution, however, would transform the relative strategic advantage of competing institutions since electronic systems were much more cost-sensitive to volume than were paper systems. As a result, for many banks the move to electronic systems represented an expensive investment while for the larger institutions significant potential strategic advantage could be gained. Similar advantages were, however, open to large non-bank competitors, notably retailers who were threatening to take a substantial role in transactions processing and other banking services via cheaper delivery systems. Some new payments systems, notably EFTPOS and home banking, had not yet made a significant impression and seemed unlikely to do so until towards the 1990s when EFTPOS in particular was expected to emerge as an important alternative remote financial service delivery system. Who would dominate these systems, however, remained open to debate and the challenge of non-banks was expected to be fierce.

The reappraisal of the economics of bank branches was causing many banks to reduce the numbers of their networks, to convert most branches from full service to limited service operations and to open specialist branches aimed at specific consumer segments. A further consequence of the transformation of changes in financial service delivery networks was expected to be a decline in the numbers employed in the industry, especially in those routine positions which could be readily automated.

CHAPTER 9

The Strategic Impact of Regulation and Deregulation

9.1 INTRODUCTION

In recent years the election of a number of governments with economic ideologies based on free market competition has accelerated the pace of deregulation. Historically, strong regulatory barriers to entry between the various sectors of the financial services industry had created clear differences between the product ranges offered by institutions based in each sector. Indeed, the institutions within each sector, usually operating in conjunction with official bodies such as a central bank or finance ministry, would act in accord with government policy in such matters as interest rate levels, liquidity management, lending and the like. New entries into specific sectors such as commercial banking, investment banking and insurance were usually closely scrutinized and operating licences were required and available only on a restricted basis. Institutions collecting deposits from small savers were particularly regulated to ensure the protection of depositors.

In the United States specific restrictions preventing commercial banks from participating in securities markets were adopted following the 1929 crash and the subsequent banking crisis in 1933, to protect the safety of the banks, although conflict of interest questions and the fuelling of speculative pressures were additional rationales for the separation. Subsequent US law based on the Bank Holding Company Act of 1956, and its later amendments, was more concerned with preventing the overconcentration of financial power and potential conflicts of interest between, for example, lending and investment management interests. In other countries similar regulatory barriers tended clearly to define the areas of activity available to specific classes of financial service institution.

These regulatory barriers tended to impact on the development of the financial services industry in three main ways. Firstly, they specifically excluded competitors from a particular product market sector from providing services allocated to institutions in another sector, so limiting the level of competition. Secondly, they acted as a severe brake on innovation in service development and delivery systems. Thirdly, they usually placed specific limits on geographic expansion.

In the past decade, however, the regulatory walls have increasingly tumbled. This has occurred for a number of reasons. Firstly, the political will to remove regulatory barriers has been popular with the electorate although in many cases regulations have tended to be changed only after they have been breached by actions of institutions attempting to circumvent the law, thus making the regulation a nonsense. Secondly, the development of financial service industry multinationals and the evolution of the global capital market has tended to lead to a growing similarity in service offerings provided by competitors from traditionally separate sectors within the major industrialized countries. Thirdly, technology has fundamentally transformed industry cost structures and increasingly made regulatory differentiation based on delivery system differences obsolescent.

This chapter explores the effect of deregulation more specifically on the strategies of the major commercial banks and identifies a number of apparent strategic and structural patterns that can be discerned around the world and a number of future trends that seem likely to emerge.

9.2 THE IMPACT OF REGULATION

In virtually all countries regulatory authorities historically imposed strict controls on the activities of financial service institutions in ways not normally found in most manufacturing sectors. In the USA for example, the Federal authorities imposed a series of regulations restricting bank branching across state lines for the purposes of taking deposits (but not for making loans); setting the maximum level of interest to be paid on consumer deposits (but not on commercial deposits in the capital market); preventing commercial banks from dealing in securities underwriting and the issuing of mutual funds as part of trust or investment management activities; stopping the banks from entering the insurance industry; and preventing them from engaging in commercial property development.

Similarly, savings and loan institutions were prevented from offering checking services, issuing credit cards or making instalment loans as well as being subject to many of the same restrictions applied to commercial banks on interest rate ceilings and the like. Insurance institutions were restricted from engaging in any form of 'banking' business, although the provision of savings and investment vehicles such as life insurance, which were clearly meant to be paid out during the policyholder's lifetime, made distinctions increasingly technical. Insurers were also not allowed to participate in lending, apart from mortgages, although they were allowed to invest their clients' money in equity participations such as commercial property development. Investment banks similarly did not engage in retail banking but could and did provide investment advice to wealthy individuals and offered mutual funds for a widespread investment client base. Each type of institution also had its own regulatory body with separate authorities covering banks, savings and loans institutions and insurance at both state and Federal level. There could also be substantial policy differences between these authorities which in turn tended to increase the inconsistencies between and within the discrete sectors.

In the USA, securities companies, while not regulated to the same degree as the banks and insurance, operated under the auspices of the Securities Exchange Commission. Again they could not provide checking facilities or take deposits, although they could take savings and invest them in instruments such as mutual funds which, ironically, were largely invested in bank securities at money market rates of interest. Furthermore, the securities companies were not inhibited from offering their services on an interstate basis. The securities companies could also provide lending lines via the use of margin loans which, although technically short-term in nature, could be rolled over to provide a longer term instrument. As a consequence the securities companies had played a major role in forcing deregulation in the USA due to the use of their greater flexibility to design products such as money market mutual funds and the cash management account which had so seriously affected the deposit bases of the commercial and mortgage banks.

Regulations thus significantly inhibited competition between institutions based in different sectors and also tended to diminish the potential for competition between similar institutions in the same sector. Similar laws operated in most other countries and the regulatory authorities broadly felt that such limits to competition were desirable for stability and the protection of the individual. Ironically, in some countries like West Germany, many of these restrictions did not apply and 'universal' banking for example was quite normal and had not noticeably led to any of the risks feared in the more rigidly controlled financial systems.

The development of multinationality also tended to be tightly constrained. Some degree of internationalization was usually permitted but this again tended to be limited to protect local national institutions or to centralize specific activities within particular institutions. For example, entry into any market by overseas competitor institutions was usually strictly controlled by the necessity to obtain a suitable local licence. In some countries these were strictly controlled with only a few being issued and in some countries such as Australia and Canada entry by foreign banks had not been permitted until the early 1980s. While entry barriers were common in Japan, tight control by the Ministry of Finance had unusually inhibited the international development of indigenous Japanese banks. Moreover, even where foreign institutional entry was more readily available, the multinational banks were usually restricted to operating in narrow areas of the market and/or were denied access to critical facilities or sources of funds. Thus, it was not until 1984 that the Committee of London Clearing Banks allowed access by some building societies and overseas banks to the English central clearing system. Similarly, in Japan, foreign banks were still denied direct access to the Japanese retail deposit market, thus severely constraining their ability to compete on equal funding terms to the domestic institutions.

Similar constraints applied on an international basis in other financial service industry sectors. Thus access to insurance underwriting in many countries was reserved for domestic institutions or multinational securities firms were denied seats on local stock exchanges.

Until the early 1980s, therefore, it was probably correct to refer to the sectors of the financial services industry as a series of separate industries, artificially separated by regulatory barriers which prevented any intermarket penetration. The product market sector separation was also reinforced by geographical barriers which substantially prevented international competition between institutions from different countries engaged in the same business sector. Such geographic barriers could also apply within the same country especially those with an underlying federal state structure such as Australia, Japan and especially, the USA.

Such local state barriers had interesting side-effects on commercial bank strategy evolution. In the USA for example, large money centre banks such as First of Chicago and Continental Illinois, based in Illinois, were severely constrained from branching more than a short distance from the parent bank. As a consequence although these institutions provided some retail services they were severely inhibited from developing a retail business based upon branch banking. They therefore grew by focusing on large corporate business and providing support finance for the local commodities market. Their deposit bases were largely drawn from interbank sources rather than personal savers. In New York, banks were permitted only to branch within the county. Hence most of the major New York banks had developed small retail banking businesses based on local branch networks of perhaps a couple of hundred branches. Again the banks' focus had centred on corporate banking and these institutions had been the primary movers to develop as multinational institutions, in part to follow their customers, but also to some extent to escape the especially severe regulatory constraints imposed by both national and state authorities. In sharp contrast, the state regulatory authorities permitted statewide branching in California. This had led to the development of large, branch-based banks like Bank of America and Wells Fargo, which were much more orientated to retail business and whose funding base until the late 1970s was heavily dependent on local small savers. While such banks provided services to corporate clients, the size of their branch networks led them naturally to tend to organize themselves on a geographic basis. The New York banks by comparison were the pioneers of organizing by customer type, segregating personal and corporate accounts and introducing account officers, based on industry specialization, during the 1970s. Even when they adopted multinational strategies aimed primarily at corporate customers, the California banks still adopted a geographical organization structure and it was not until 1985 that Bank of America made the fundamental move towards separating its retail and corporate banking businesses.

In Europe, most countries permitted nationwide branching for commercial banks, although local geographic-based institutions initially developed. However, these had tended to consolidated to create an oligopoly of major nationwide institutions. Some regional institutions had usually survived in most countries, again often as a result of regulatory barriers which provided them some protection. For example, in the UK, while the major English clearing banks dominated in England and Wales, in Scotland a separate banking system had developed and the English banks had only very limited representation although some had taken significant equity holdings in leading Scottish banks. Indeed, in 1985 the move by Royal Bank of Scotland to rename the small, regionally based English bank, Williams & Glyn's, which it had earlier acquired with what was seen as a counter-invasion by a Scottish bank of the English market.

Where regionalism prevailed, for example in countries like West Germany, Italy and Japan, the system that tended to emerge was one of a small number of large nationwide banks which were largely corporate in their business orientation, together with a series of regional banks which tended to service the retail savings market within their sphere of influence and be less con-

Nation	Branching Regulation	Bank	Branch Strategy	Customer Orientation
USA—Illinois	Strict geographic limit	First Chicago	Nil	Corporate
New York	Limited to county	Citibank	Limited national International	Small retail Largely corporate
California	Statewide	Bank of America	Multibranch	Largely retail
UK—England & Wales	Nationwide	Barclays	Multibranch	Largely retail/ Middle corporate
France	Nationwide	Société Général	Multibranch	Largely retail
W. Germany	National & regional	Deutsche Bank	Urban branches	Largely corporate
		West Deutschelandes Bank	Regional branches	Largely retail
Japan	National & regional	Mitsubishi Bank	Urban branches	Largely corporate
		Bank of Yokohama	Regional branches	Largely retail

Figure 9.1   Impact of geographic regulatory barriers on bank strategy

cerned with the large corporate market. Both in Germany and Japan therefore, the major national commercial banks had extremely close contact with the leading industrial companies, as discussed in Chapter 3. These banks also had a much lower share of retail deposits than in France and the UK but acted as repositories for surplus deposits gathered by the regional banks. The differences in strategy brought about by the impact of geographic regulatory constraint are summarized in Figure 9.1, which indicates the strategies of a number of banks and how these had been affected by the presence or absence of barriers to branching.

Domestic geographic constraints had less impact on other sectors of the financial services industry. In brokerage, credit finance, merchant banking and insurance, constraints on developing nationwide distribution had not been especially restrictive although there had not been a strong trend towards the development of such systems. In the United States brokerage had been distributed due to much greater public involvement in securities trading and a number of major brokerage houses had developed branch distribution systems. Similarly in insurance, national brokerage chains had emerged either on a fully owned or franchised basis. A number of nationwide credit finance companies had also developed. However, by contrast to the large branch bank networks, these distribution chains had tended to be smaller. Moreover, in the other major developed economies such chains had tended to be very small and concentrated on major city centres.

The main geographic regulatory constraint on non-commercial bank financial service companies has been on an international basis. The development of global competition has in many cases been severely restricted by governments preventing the entry of cross-border competitors. In Western Europe for example despite continuous effort, especially by the British, the insurance markets of the individual European Economic Community countries have remained largely closed to competition from companies based in other countries of the community. The integration of the European community in the early 1990s offers significant opportunities for new pan-European strategies to emerge. Similarly, in Japan the brokerage market had largely been constrained to keep out the major US brokerage houses. As a result the development of global competitive markets in many areas of the financial services industry was only just getting under way and further substantial intermarket penetration could be expected.

9.3   DIVERSIFICATION AND INTERPRODUCT MARKET PENETRATION STRATEGIES

The regulatory barriers constraining competitors from entering one another's product market and geographic territories began to erode during the 1970s. The barriers were, however, seldom dismantled by political initiatives but rather as a consequence of service and delivery system innovations by new or existing competitors. These not only circumvented existing regulations but used the constraints, in some cases, to gain strategic advantage over traditional competitors.

Many of the new services were pioneered by non-bank competitors, although banks subsequently often entered these markets when permitted to do so and in many cases used their financial strength to acquire earlier, small innovators. As a consequence therefore, since the late 1960s commercial banks had in many cases adopted a strategy of extensive product market diversification. The speed and direction of such a diversification strategy had varied throughout the world, dependent largely on local regulatory constraints. By and large the looser these had been the faster and further diversification strategies had evolved.

The process is well illustrated by the example of the evolution of domestic product market services by the leading British commercial banks, where deregulation and the injection of a policy of increased competition had been gradually followed since 1968. Up until that time the structure of the British banking industry had remained unchanged for around 50 years, an interest rate cartel was operated in conjunction with the central bank and competition was constrained between the commercial banks, while each type of leading financial service company was engaged in clearly defined product market boundaries.

	Securities Dealing	Securities Underwriting	Merchant Banking	Eurocurrency Lending	Unit Trust Management	Leasing	Insurance Broking	Mortgage Lending	Insurance Underwriting	Credit Finance	Venture Capital	Trade Finance	Counter Trade	Computer Bureau	Travel Service	Channel Island Trustees	Credit Card Operations	Personal Tax & Financial Planning	Estate Agencies	Private Banking	Cash Management	HNWI Bank Account
1968																						
Barclays	—	—	—	W	W	—	—	—	—	A	A	W	—	—	—	W	W	—	—	—	—	—
Lloyds	—	—	—	W	W	A	—	—	—	⌐	?	W	—	—	—	—	—	—	—	—	—	—
Midland	—	A	A	A	—	—	A	—	—	W	⌐	W	—	—	—	W	—	—	—	—	—	—
National Westminster	—	W	W	W	⌐	W	—	—	—	W	?	W	—	W	—	W	A	—	—	?	—	—
1987																						
Barclays	W	W	W	W	W	W	W	W	W	W	W	W	—	A	W¹	W	W	W	—	?	W	?
Lloyds	—	—	W	W	W	W	W	W	W	W	W	W	—	—	—	W	⌐	W	W	—	?	W
Midland	W	W	W	W	W	W	W	W	W	W	W	W	W	W	W	W	⌐	W	—	—	?	?
National Westminster	W	W	W	W	C	W	W	W	W	W	W	W	—	W	—	W	⌐	W	—	?	W	W

W = Wholly owned subsidiary; C = Controlling interest; A = Associate company.
? = Limited engagement in activity. ¹ = Travellers cheques only.

Figure 9.2 Diversification by major British clearing banks 1968–87
Source: Services Guides Annual Report

In 1968, the Bank of England allowed the merger of two leading banks to form the National Westminster, dissolved the interest rate cartel and encouraged competition between the institutions. The subsequent impact of these changes led ultimately to significantly increased competition, rapid service diversification, and a breakdown of traditional institutional product market boundaries. The changing product market scope of the commercial banks is illustrated in Figure 9.2, which shows the degree to which each had diversified their range of service offerings within the domestic market.

In 1968, when the banks were relatively undiversified, their orientation was as retail deposit gatherers who lent their funds primarily on overdraft to commercial borrowers. There was also some personal lending but much consumer credit was provided by credit finance companies in which banks often had a shareholding interest but no managerial control. Mortgage lending similarly was provided by building societies with banks being concerned only with construction finance and short-term bridging loans. Commercial banks were also not concerned with alternative financing methods such as leasing and factoring, other skills introduced mainly by credit finance companies, credit cards, investment management and merchant banking.

Following deregulation which was designed to increase the level of competition between the banks themselves and between other financial institutions, the banks rapidly diversified and the level of competition increased, largely as a result of new market entrants, notably from foreign banks. Some consolidation occurred in markets like credit finance where most of the major independent concerns were acquired by the leading commercial banks. However, new sources of credit finance did emerge from retailers and the entry into the market by a number of US banks. Moreover, building societies also began to provide personal loans for other than house purchase. The overall concentration of the market for personal credit thus actually tended to decline as many new competitors sought to gain a share of it. Moreover, the range of credit instruments similarly increased sharply.

In the market for commercial credit a similar trend occurred. The US banks in particular were especially active in penetrating the market for large corporate credits, causing the UK banks a substantial loss of market share. Again the variety in the number of credit instruments expanded rapidly and in the early 1980s instrument innovation had been a major source of competitive advantage. With the more recent trend to disintermediation in lending products, competition had intensified still further with the entry of brokerage houses and both domestic and foreign investment banks, providing direct access for corporate clients to the capital markets, both within the UK and in some cases overseas.

The commercial banks, too, had attempted to penetrate the markets traditionally reserved to the investment banks. This had occurred both in attempting to gain share in the market for investment banking advice in such areas as financial structuring, mergers and acquisitions, and issues and syndications. While such activities had not always been successful, the banks had slowly begun to gain some synergistic effect from combining new skills with their traditional financial size and strength. In investment management again banks had sought to break into the traditional preserves of specialist investment management groups, insurance companies and merchant banks offering investment portfolio and unit trust management services. Overall in all these sectors, despite many consolidations, the impact had again been one of increasing the number of large direct competitors and a rising level of competitiveness.

In the UK, commercial banks traditionally had not entered the market for mortgage finance. In the late 1970s, however, as government began to dismantle the regulatory differences between banks and building societies to enable both to compete on essentially equal terms, the banks entered this market with considerable success. The societies, too, responded by entering the banks' traditional territory of transaction processing and the provision of checking services as well as beginning to offer non-housing-related personal loans.

Unlike the major US banks, British commercial banks had been less keen to enter the market for brokerage. However, with the deregulation of the securities dealing market in the UK in 1986 and the rapid trend towards disintermediation, this policy had been reversed and some of the banks by 1987 had developed or acquired brokerage houses, gilt securities dealers and/or merchant banks to strengthen the pattern of market interpenetrations.

Finally, in the area of insurance, banks had made early moves to enter into insurance broking and in some cases underwriting. By contrast, the insurance companies had been inhibited from penetrating back into the provision of banking services although future linkages between the insurers and building societies could lead to such interpenetration.

Overall, therefore, in the space of some fifteen years there had been a dramatic increase in the level of product market diversification by the commercial banks in the UK. They had, as regulations had permitted, penetrated many of the sectors traditionally reserved for other specialist institutions which in many cases had reciprocated by attempting to invade the commercial banks' traditional spheres of influence.

In the United States a similar pattern of strategic evolution could be observed. However, in contrast to the British commercial banks, their US counterparts had been subjected to much greater regulatory constraint and therefore their degree of domestic product market diversification was much less than that of the British banks. Instead the trend in the USA had been for non-bank institutions to diversify into traditional areas of activity undertaken by banks. Further, the banks had been inhibited in responding by the regulations, so providing the non-banks with important competitive advantages. The pattern is illustrated in Figure 9.3, which shows that between 1960 and 1984 US commercial banks were much less able to add new financial services in non-traditional product market sectors such as insurance, underwriting, investment management and direct property investment. By contrast the non-bank institutions such as retailers, brokerage houses and insurance companies had been able, by in some cases carefully circumventing regulations or by acquisitions, to enter virtually all the traditional banking markets to a greater or lesser degree.

Such patterns of related product market diversification were not uncommon in large corporations and support the theory of corporation evolution that companies develop from narrow to

Service	Banks		Savings & Loan Assocs		Insurance Companies		Retailers		Securities Dealers	
	1960	1984	1960	1984	1960	1984	1960	1984	1960	1984
Cheque accounts	★	★		★		★		★		★
Savings accounts	★	★	★	★		★		★		★
Time deposits	★	★	★	★		★		★		★
Instalment loans	★	★		★		★		★		★
Business loans	★	★	★	★		★		★		★
Mortgage loans	★	★	★	★	★	★		★		★
Credit cards		★		★		★	★	★		★
Insurance					★	★		★		★
Stocks & bonds brokerage		★		★		★		★	★	★
Underwriting									★	★
Mutual funds						★		★	★	★
Property						★		★		★

Figure 9.3　US intersector deregulation effect

broad product market scopes[1]. However, what is interesting in the context of the banking industry is the speed at which diversification where permitted, had taken place and how in some countries the natural process of evolution had been specifically inhibited by the barriers imposed by regulation. For example in Japan, where traditional product market boundaries had been particularly vigorously enforced, it had been necessary for banks to enter new financial markets by forming specialist subsidiary companies. The banks then held a small minority shareholding in these concerns with other holdings being distributed throughout the industrial groups of which the banks were core members.

[1]See, for example, D. F. Channon, *The Service Industries, Strategy Structure and Financial Performance*, Macmillan, London, 1977, and B. R. Scott, *The Stages of Corporate Development*, Part 1, unpublished paper, Harvard Business School, Boston, 1971.

As a consequence the achievement of any synergistic integration between different financial services had been especially difficult.

Moreover, where such contraints had occurred, in many cases institutions had sought to participate in the process of evolution by diversifying their product market schope in more favourable geographic environments. For example, a bank like Citibank had entered the insurance and securities markets outside the USA where to date it had been prohibited from so doing.

There were some signs that the process of diversification was still continuing but into areas less related to the traditional scope of the financial services industries. For example, Lloyds Bank had acquired a substantial number of real estate brokerage companies to become one of the largest operators of such a business in the UK. The Trustee Savings Bank had acquired a leading car hire company while the Midland Bank had purchased travel agents Thomas Cook. Elsewhere the Deutsche Bank acquired the largest management consultancy company in Germany, Citicorp had acquired Quotron, providers of an automated share quotation system. In the opposite direction, many industrial companies had also begun to develop a comprehensive array of financial service activities. For example, Ford Motor Company had acquired First Nationwide, one of the largest US savings and loan banks and had opened a series of retail branches in K-Mart stores, while US General Electric had acquired investment bankers Kidder Peabody and major interests in insurance to add to its credit finance activities. There were logical reasons for the forging of such alliances, suggesting that in future, while a core set of relationships might well prevail within major commercial banks, areas for differentiation might also emerge with particular institutions seeking to develop specific niches in which they enjoyed some relative uniqueness.

9.4   GEOGRAPHIC DIVERSIFICATION STRATEGIES

Concurrent with the trend towards increased product market diversification banks had adopted geographic expansion strategies. Initially such activities tended to be orientated to corporate business and many banks tended to operate a combination of servicing existing multinational clients and attempting to penetrate local corporate markets. More recently, however, there had been a substantial attempt to develop global strategies which made use of integrated international branch networks for both corporate and retail customers. Both within federal state structures such as the USA and on an international basis, regulatory barriers based on geographic constraints had been severely undermined by the development of alternative electronic delivery systems. In addition, regulatory authorities had found containment of globalization strategies especially difficult because they had no agreed pattern of coordination to handle such approaches. For example, attempts to constrain the development of the Euromarkets led to the development of offshore centres such as those in the Caribbean which emerged to escape the regulatory conditions of New York. Similarly, the intermediation potential of the Euromarkets had made it extremely difficult for individual countries to maintain tight control over enchange rates or even exchange controls. The Euromarkets had also been the first step towards the integration of the world's capital markets, again severely constraining the capability of individual finance ministries to isolate their own capital markets from international forces.

The differences between national regulatory positions had also begun to enable institutions to exploit these to develop global strategies. For example in 1984, when the British authorities permitted the purchase of stakes in brokerage companies by banks as part of the run up to the Big Bang in the City of London, US-based Citicorp purchased a 29.9 per cent stake in the British brokerage house Vickers da Costa. This company was one of the few foreign brokerage companies to occupy a seat on the Tokyo Stock Exchange where historically banks and securities houses had been strictly segregated. As a result of a permitted transaction based in the UK therefore Citicorp was able to further its objective of establishing a worldwide brokerage operation, breaching the regulatory barrier in Japan, and being in a strong competitive position to exploit the development of the global securities dealing market.

Geographic deregulation had, however, seen the emergence of rationalizations as well as expansion strategies. While many banks had expanded their geographical coverage both on an international basis and within countries, modern delivery system strategy made use of alternatives to conventional branch-based systems, especially those which were electronically based. In those states and countries which originally allowed widespread branching, those banks with large physical branch networks had been facing severe difficulties as the result of rapidly rising branch costs for people and premises, while new entrant competitors had been able to exploit new, low-cost delivery systems to reach specific segments of the market. These new systems based on electronics, direct mail and the like were capable of providing low-cost but not necessarily low-quality services to customers, allowing them the freedom to choose the time, place and method of conducting their transactions. The new delivery systems utilizing plastic cards, automated teller machines, interactive home or office terminals, direct mail and telephones did not require the expensive overheads of conventional bank branches, offered significant savings in bank personnel and provided the opportunities to develop experience cost-based strategies. As a consequence, the adoption of new delivery systems had led to major restructuring of conventional branch-based delivery systems, resulting in rationalization, specialization and the adoption of more efficient manning levels. The new delivery systems had also tended to force the deregulation of conventional geographic regulatory constraints. For example in the USA the traditional constraints on interstate banking had been severely undermined by the development of nationwide shared ATM networks, telemarketing and the equivalents of national checking accounts offered by non-banks. These network patterns were also beginning to develop on an international basis in multicountry areas like Western Europe.

The development of worldwide branch networks initiated in the early 1970s was by the mid 1980s largely complete for the leading European and US banks. Finding these networks expensive to operate and not generating the contribution levels expected, many were rationalizing their networks by closures or by seeking to add additional services to generate profitability. Japanese banks, late starters in the development of international networks, were, however, still expanding their branch coverage.

Elsewhere new branches were opening only in attractive, newly deregulated markets such as Australia and Canada.

The late 1980s were also seeing the emergence of new linkages between geographical and product market strategies. For example, some competitors were developing specific services on a global basis which made use of linked networks. Such services as global cash management, foreign exchange and financial information services were being offered to large multinational industrial concerns and to other financial institutions unable to support the cost of developing similar systems. A number of retail services were also being developed on a global scale such as travel and entertainment cards, ATM networks, private banking and travellers cheques.

A second strategy was to offer services on a more limited geographic basis but amortizing the development costs for such services on a global basis. Citibank, for example, thus developed its Citifunds multicurrency investment product on an international basis, but offered the product in a series of different national markets. Other products could be offered on a regional or national basis according to delivery system coverage, volume of demand and regulatory constraints. An indication of alternative geographic competitive strategies for a number of different institutions providing specific services is shown in Figure 9.4.

9.5 SECTOR CONSOLIDATION WITH INCREASED COMPETITION

One result of the increase in competition within the financial services industry had been some consolidation within individual sectors, paradoxically being accompanied by increased competition as a result of intermarket sector penetration due to both product and geographic diversification. Consolidation had occurred as a result of closure and acquisition. In the United States, where deregulation had proceeded rapidly in recent years, the number of bank failures or those in difficulty has risen sharply since 1980. In 1980, 10 banks failed and some 200 were judged to be in difficulty. By 1984 the number of failures had

	Checking Acct.	Savings Acct.	ATMS	Personal Loans	Mortgage Banking	Credit Cards	T&E Cards	Travellers Cheques	Credit Finance	Private Banking	Investment Mgt.	Brokerage	Home Banking	Householdings	Motor Ins.	Fire, Acc. & Marine	Life Ins.	Pension Mgt.	Travel Services	Retailing	Real Estate Brok.	CMA
Citibank	I	I	I	I	I	I	G	G	I	G	G	N	N	I	-	-	I	N	-	-	-	I
Barclays	I	I	I	I	I	I	-	G	I	-	I	N	-	I	-	-	I	I	-	-	-	-
Sears	R	R	-	N	N	N	-	-	N	-	N	N	N	N	N	N	N	-	-	N	N	-
Amex	-	-	I	-	-	-	G	G	-	I	I	N	-	N	-	I	I	N	G	-	-	-
Pru Bache	-	-	-	N	N	N	-	-	-	-	I	N	-	I	I	I	I	I	-	-	-	N
Merrill Lynch	-	-	I	I	N	G	-	-	-	I	G	G	-	-	-	-	-	-	-	-	N	G

- = Not Undertaken.
R = Regional Service.
I = International Service.
N = National Service.
G = Global Service.

Figure 9.4   Alternative geographic/product market strategies

risen to 63 while nearly 800 were considered to be in difficulty[2]. In 1986 145 American banks failed—the most since the 1930s— while 1484 were considered to be in difficulty. At the same time there was a rapid growth in the number of acquisitions of US banks by indigenous and foreign institutions. For example British, Japanese and Canadian banks had emerged as significant competitors in the New York and California markets via the purchase of local operating banks. A substantial number of major acquisitions had also been made by US-based banks of other institutions both within and outside the traditional banking industry. Many of these moves were also allowed to breach the traditional geographic regulatory constraints. Thus, for example, Citibank entered the important California, Illinois and Florida markets by purchasing troubled savings and loan institutions. By the end of 1986 such interstate acquisitions were multiplying rapidly and the early emergence of nationwide banking in the USA seemed certain.

Consolidation had also occurred within the US insurance sector. Industry observers expected that potentially hundreds of the 1900 small and mid-size insurance companies would be eliminated by failure or acquisition in a post-deregulation shakeout within the sector. Similar patterns had been observed in the UK. The Phoenix was acquired by the Sun Alliance, Cornhill by BTR and Eagle Star, and Allied Dunbar by British American Tobacco, two of these acquirers being non-banks seeking to diversify into the financial services industry[3].

The brokerage industry was similarly consolidating on both sides of the Atlantic. Again acquisition, notably by banks but also by other major financial institutions, had led to the absorption of many major national and regional brokerage concerns. Thus Prudential Insurance had acquired Bache, American Express had purchased Shearson Lehman while Sears Roebuck bought Dean Witter Reynolds. Banks, too, had purchased or formed formal alliances with brokerage firms led by the Bank of America's purchase of the leading West Coast discount broker,

[2]*Economist* International Banking Survey, *op. cit.*
[3]In January 1986 BTR sold its Cornhill Insurance subsidiary to the German Insurance company, Allianz, which had previously attempted to break into the UK market by bidding unsuccessfully for Eagle Star.

Charles Schwab. In the UK, no sooner had the decision been taken in 1984 that permission would be provided for banks and other institutions to purchase strategic stakes of 29.9 per cent in brokerage firms prior to opening the British Stock Exchange to foreign owners in 1986, than almost all the major brokers announced linkages with leading British and overseas banks.

As a result of deregulation, therefore, major consolidation was occurring throughout the world in all sectors of the financial services industry largely by the absorption of companies from one sector by new entrants from others, by mergers across geographic boundaries and by closures of failing institutions. However, while consolidation had occurred in the sense that specialist institutions had been shaken out, their place had in large part been taken by new, often large, entrants which had entered new market sectors by some combination of geographic and service diversification.

9.6   INCREASED PRICE COMPETITION

Despite the shakeout of some smaller institutions, the entry of new, powerful competitors as a result of increased market interpenetration had usually led to a sharp increase in industry sector capacity. In addition, the introduction of new technology, together with different cost structures, had meant that previously stable price relationships, based on service bundling and often reinforced by regulations, had become much more flexible. The presence of high experience effects in particular had impacted on volume-sensitive services, while the pricing of services in general had become unbundled. Deregulation had thus tended to lead to the introduction of low-cost service providers which had often stimulated a much greater level of price competition. This form of marketing strategy had thus tended to assume much greater importance while customers, as their general knowledge of the cost of industrial services improved, had become increasing price-sensitive.

In the United States for example, brokerage companies moved into the market for consumer deposits by offering money market funds. Instead of a fixed rate of interest on deposits set by regulation, the money funds consolidated the funds of small savers and used them to purchase money market instruments such as government and local municipal bonds, bank acceptances and certificates of deposit. Further, the brokerage houses attracted these funds by offering superior interest rates, and using low-cost collection systems such as telemarketing, direct mail or press advertising. These systems allowed the institutions concerned to operate both nationwide across state boundaries and with a low-cost overhead structure. The rapid success of the money market funds forced the banks to respond by initially offering bank certificates of deposit direct to small investors and eventually to the removal of the ceiling on interest rates offered for savings deposits. Bank overhead structures were, however, still higher than those of the brokerage houses and the overall cost of bank funds from individuals exhibited a sharp increase.

Similar patterns of low-cost services had also materialized in lending products. Again banks were subjected to competition from lower cost services such as the commercial paper market and the bonds and securities markets which offered funds at a lower cost than those obtained directly from banks. These products were also developed in some cases by banks themselves, generally those without extensive branch network coverage, as well as by investment banks and brokerage houses.

Price competition had also emerged in the insurance and brokerage sectors. In insurance, especially for non-life services, many companies, following the breakdown of cartel-like tariffs, new entrants and non-tariff-based companies, faced with severe overcapacity, had been writing business for cashflow. As a consequence severe underwriting losses had occurred while the companies had been forced to rely on investment income generated from premiums for their profits. In life insurance, as in many areas of banking, the introduction of universal life policies had led effectively to service unbundling. With such policies, the life portion of the policy was uncoupled from the investment element allowing more flexible, but potentially higher risk, investment management policies. In brokerage, by eliminating or unbundling in large part the traditional, but expensive, investment research and advisory services offered by many brokers, discount brokers had developed who competed aggressively on price to gain market volume.

The use of price as a weapon in financial service industry marketing strategy had proved especially difficult to adopt for many traditional competitors. These organizations had frequently not known the cost structure of the specific services they had offered to particular market segments. Rather such institutions had tended historically to operate on a 'bundled' service system, offering a wide range of services to customers for a composite price, usually on an unsegmented basis irrespective of whether customers had needed particular facets of the service offered. Moreover, due to the lack of customer segmentation, different classes of customer had been charged the same, irrespective of their level of service usage. These institutions had also tended to operate universalist delivery systems based on physical branches, which had been shown in some cases to be much more expensive and not necessarily of the quality, of new, alternative delivery systems. Faced with a need to price at market levels due to competitive inroads, many institutions had responded by marketing the offerings of new entrants, without necessarily a full understanding of the effect on corporate profitability. As a result price competition had been ferocious throughout many areas of the finanical services industry, leading to a sharp decline in the profit margins for many services, for many competitors.

9.7 THE NEED FOR COST REDUCTION

Many institutions had endeavoured to reduce the impact of price erosion by attempting to adopt niche or specialization strategies. However, complete insulation from the increased level of competition had not proved easy. As a result, all financial service institutions had been forced to examine ways in which they could increase their efficiency and productivity. One method for improving performance had been heavy investment in back and front office automation. In many cases such investment had not been accompanied by the levels of cost saving, notably by staff reductions, that had been predicted. In a number of such cases reductions had occurred but only when pursued with determination by top management.

The failure by many institutions to achieve the levels in cost reduction anticipated by investment in automation was due in no small part to poor preparation for such exercises. Because of their long history of operating within a regulated environment, few financial service institutions had adequately developed the necessary information systems to provide the data required to make appropriate management decisions. Major investments in suitable cost accounting and management information systems were therefore frequently required to develop integrated accounting and marketing data bases to indentify the profitability of individual services, customers and geographic territories. Further, cost analysis techniques to identify the relative costs of providing specific services via existing and alternative delivery systems to particular customer segments also needed to be introduced. Finally, many institutions were culturally ill-prepared for achieving low-cost operations. Senior management, usually raised in a regulated environment, was often ill-prepared to face a cost-competitive environment. Moreover, salary and fringe benefit policies had also historically been relatively generous due to high levels of profitability achieved relatively easily in the era of regulation.

9.8   ORGANIZATIONAL RESPONSE TO DEREGULATION

The traditional attitude of financial institutions had been to accept the spirit and guidance of the regulatory authorities. As a consequence most institutions had tended to adopt a reactive rather than a proactive stance to deregulation. By contrast, many of the new competitors entering the financial service industry had deliberately sought to gain competititive advantage by circumventing existing regulatory barriers.

One organizational element in a successful deregulation-based strategy had been to adopt a proactive approach deliberately designed to seek gaps in regulatory barriers on both a national and increasingly an international basis. While some non-banks had specifically espoused this model, within the banking industry such an approach was rare. Citicorp had been, amongst banks, especially energetic in adopting a proactive legal approach to deregulation with the assignment of one of its three most senior officers to head its legal unit. Citicorp actively looked for potential weaknesses in regulatory barriers with the intention of breaching these wherever possible. As a consequence Citicorp had successfully developed legal deposit-taking institutions in 17 US states, penetrated the market for securities dealing in a number of markets outside the USA, and similarly entered the insurance industry, avoided the limits on interest rate ceilings for its credit card business by shifting its processing centre to Dakota, and had been actively seeking to develop a full range of financial services throughout the world often in direct conflict with the policies and objectives of individual national regulatory authorities.

Such a confrontationist policy against the regulatory authorities was still uncommon. However, more institutions were beginning to recognize that where regulatory barriers were being maintained yet circumvented by new competitors to gain competitive advantage, a more active approach could be desirable or even essential. The adoption of such a policy nevertheless demanded a change in organizational culture for most financial institutions where senior management had been accustomed willingly to accept the wishes of the authorities.

A further effect of increased diversification on organization structure had been a strong trend towards managing the activities of the bank by a series of customer-segment-based business units, as the range of services offered had expanded beyond the capacity of most managers to service adequately all customer classes through a common delivery system. Moreover, greater competition had forced banks to adopt more proactive marketing and selling stances. Initially this restructuring had tended to separate corporate and retail activities and to organize for geography below the level of the product/customer split.

More recently, rapid growth had occurred in the area of investment banking following the trend towards securitization and the increase in efforts to generate fee-based income. As a result, many large commercial banks were attempting to integrate their investment banking and newly acquired securities trading operations to create major new organizational units. This trend was expected to continue despite the severe difficulties in linking

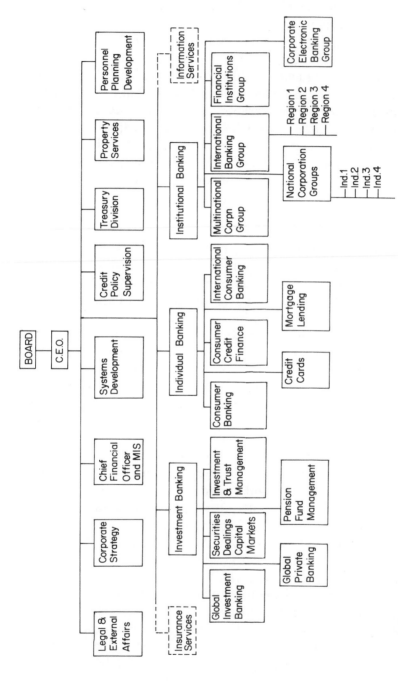

Figure 9.5 Emerging global bank structure

such diverse cultures. Meanwhile further diversifications, especially into the provision of information services and insurance, were likely to create future major new business divisions. At the same time within the macro structure, subdivision of the banks' activities into specialist businesses units was increasing to cope with the skills required to operate effectively in selected market niches and to stimulate subunit profit-seeking. Such units might be organized on a national, regional or global basis dependent upon the nature of the service. An illustration of such a shift in organization structure is shown in Figure 9.5.

9.9   SUCCESSFUL STRATEGIES FOR DEREGULATION

The impact of deregulation on corporate strategies has been investigated by a number of researchers. In a study undertaken by McKinsey, based on the financial services and airlines industries, four specific successful strategies were identified[4]. A more extensive review of the financial services industry has led to an extension to this typology to six potential strategies, as illustrated in Figure 9.6.

Prior to deregulation most firms operating within the financial services industry operated subject to product market and geographic regulatory constraints. Within these constraints, however, many firms provided a wide range of bundled services through a common delivery system to a broad class of customers with competition being limited by the existence of accepted rules. Exceptions to this were those companies operating in a very local geographic area where constraints were self-imposed, and companies which had mutual ownership and as such were not fully subject to the competitive vigour of the equity markets. Such organizations included many savings and mortgage banks and a number of mutual insurance companies.

Following deregulation most competitive institutions moved to adopt one or more of a number of potentially viable strategies. Some institutions have adopted different strategic positions in different international markets and the strategies identified are

[4]Joel A. Bleeke, Deregulation: riding the rapids, *McKinsey Quarterly* Summer 1983, p. 26.

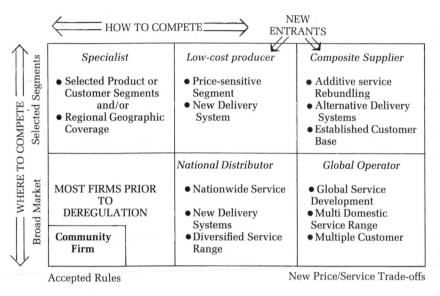

Figure 9.6   Successful strategies for deregulation

therefore not necessarily mutually exclusive. Those left in the original segment serving a broad market have tended to operate a geographic niche strategy as *Community Firms*. Such organizations were rarely attacked by larger competitors because the cost of providing an equivalent level of service for a small geographic market was usually not considered economic although in the long term the strategy was vulnerable. Moreover, such institutions might actually be short-term customers for services provided by larger specialist concerns prevented from developing national strategies, especially for those services utilizing advanced technology which were volume-dependent. These geographic niche specialists could command high levels of customer loyalty based on special local understanding and a high level of service for which many customers were prepared to pay a slight premium. Such community firms remained viable provided they continued to operate on a constrained geographic basis and some geographic regulatory walls remained. Attempts to expand which brought them into direct conflict with large competitors were, however, usually the cause of a serious attrition of profitability.

Many of the 14,000 US banks were community-based institutions. Usually centred upon a small urban or rural area such institutions provided a limited range of transaction and lending services for the local community. In such banks managers tended to know individual customers by sight and loans were made often on a name basis. Outside the USA many such banks remained as local savings institutions with very limited lending capability and/or savings and mortgage banks. An interesting example of such a strategy was that of Banc One of Columbus, Ohio. Not only had this bank been a significant innovator in electronic systems and transaction processing, it had expanded largely by the acquisition of a series of community banks. The institutions so acquired were expected to instal common Banc One control and processing systems in order to capitalize on the parent institution's operating systems. However, the original community bank management was left in place in order to maintain valuable links to each local community, coupled with the addition of strength by putting the Banc One name as an umbrella before each individual community name. In the long term the community firm strategy was not expected to be a significant factor in the financial services industry although many small, local specialists would remain in business.

The second and most commonly successful strategy adopted by a number of small institutions was that of finding a *Specialist Niche*. Such positions tended to be focused upon either product or geography. Amongst product specialists would be banks focused on a specific product or industry such as energy or agriculture. Geographic specialists might include domestic or international banks specializing in specific geographic regions. Such strategies were employed by most banks which were too small to attempt national or global strategies. Niche strategies were effective unless subject to the power of size such as the placement power of large commercial banks versus investment banks. Geographic niches, however, tended to be less defendable than specialized product/customer segment strategies. Both strategies offered potentially both greater risk and reward. For example, the collapse of world energy prices had severely damaged the Texas banks specialized in this sector, while banks like Standard Chartered and Barclays had been affected by political unrest in South Africa where each had a strong market position. At the same time regional banks in the USA enjoyed substantially higher profitability than the money centre institutions.

There are many examples of successful niche strategies. The key to success was to build a defendable position with barriers to competitive entry based on a well-developed skill or market position that customers found more credible than that offered by larger, but perceivably less personal or focused institutions. For example in retail banking, Coutts Bank in the UK, although a subsidiary of the National Westminster, operated a highly personalized service for high-net-worth individuals. Verbrauche Bank in Germany also offered a retail banking service to a narrow market segment, notably the young, upwardly mobile group interested in high-technology-based automated banking, while in the United States, the First Pacific Women's Bank appealed specifically to feminist supporters. Geographically focused institutions were also commonplace. In the UK, many of the building societies stressed their local roots, such as the Halifax, the Woolwich, the Leeds and the Bradford and Bingley; in the Federal Republic of Germany, Sud Deutsche Landes Bank was concentrated in Southern Germany; while on a larger scale Wells Fargo Bank had deliberately abandoned its international ambitions to focus on the middle market and specific segments of the California retail market.

An interesting niche strategy variant were the ethnic banks which deliberately sought out specific communities within countries or on an international basis. Habib Bank, therefore, while strong in Pakistan had also built a limited international retail banking network to service Pakistani expatriot communities around the world; by contrast, Kuwait Finance House was an Islamic bank within Kuwait, aimed at providing Islamic banking services to devout Moslems. Many such banks also were state-owned or enjoyed government protection in providing special services to particular industrial sectors. The long-term credit banks in Japan, for example, had been traditionaly expected to help in the development of Japanese industry structure along the lines agreed between government and industry, while the Bank of Tokyo for many years was the only bank in Japan charged with undertaking foreign exchange transactions. In many developing countries state-owned development banks undertook similar tasks aimed at developing national agricultural or industrial infrastructure.

A third strategy, that of the *National Distributor*, was provided by organizations usually distributing products through broad delivery systems over a wide nationwide or geographic area. Only a few competitors in a deregulated environment tended to operate this type of strategy successfully and such institutions had generally been found to operate three essential components to such a strategy. Firstly, they tended to have developed integrated systems capability to allow them to link their large delivery system networks, although few had developed integrated data bases, in part due to the very large size of their account base. Secondly, such organizations traditionally tended to organize by geography rather then by customer type. In the late 1980s this was changing and a subdivision of such banks into retail and corporate components was occurring. Thirdly, such organizations, as regulations permitted, had developed with a full service perspective, using general branches as the primary mode of service delivery. This, too, was changing as such institutions reappraised the role of the branch within a multiservice delivery environment and new models for the role of branches and alternative delivery systems were being experimented with. While such national distributor strategies were common in Europe they were new in the United States due to regulatory constraints. Within Europe, however, the impact of integration opened the prospect of new supranational (but not global) strategies to emerge.

The National Westminster bank typified the national distributor strategy. The bank, formed originally from a merger between the Westminster and National Provincial banks in 1968, operated until the early 1980s throughout Endland and Wales, with a network of over 3000 full service branches providing a full line of domestic lending and transaction services to all classes of retail and corporate customer. International services for domestic customers and the overseas network of branches built up by the bank group during the 1970s, mainly in the developed countries, were managed via the bank's International Division. Other diversifications, such as credit finance and investment banking, were treated as separate subsidiaries from the main bank and managed via an umbrella structure of a Related Services division.

In the 1980s the competitive threat from foreign, and especially US, banks forced a change in the way services were delivered to different classes of customer. Firstly, the large corporate accounts were removed from the domestically orientated national branch network and became the responsibility of a specialist corporate unit, located within the International Division. Second, middle corporate accounts were gradually being handed over from geographic clusters of branches to special commercial centres which maintained contact with the accounts, although transaction processing remained within the historic branches. Third, efforts were being made to segment retail markets and to modify the service offerings of individual branches to meet the specific needs of their individual customer bases.

A fourth sucessful strategy tended to be utilized often by new entrants to the industry sector. This made use of a competitive advantage gained by being a *Low Cost Producer*. New competitors gained their advantage from operating on a lower cost base by means of using new delivery systems such as direct mail, electronics or in-store operations to provide a narrow, unbundled service range and by expanding this product concept geographically as regulations permitted. Examples of this strategy included discount brokerage houses in the USA which had eliminated expensive stock research facilities or new entrants like Ford Motor company, which had established a network of branches for its First Nationwide subsidiary in K-Mart stores offering a limited range of savings, mortgage loan and transaction service.

Two further successful strategies could also be identified within the financial services industry. The first of these was the *Composite Service Strategy* which deliberately strove for synergistic effects from innovative rebundling of previously separated financial and other services. The successful exponents of the composite strategy tended to have five key characteristics. Firstly, such organizations needed an established customer base, although this need not be associated with the purchase of financial services. Secondly, however, such an organization needed the credibility to offer financial services. Thirdly, it needed an alternative delivery system. Fourthly, it needed to be able to offer extra consumer value added in the form of a package, embracing a comprehensive range of financial services coupled with other consumer benefits, such as product discounts to produce an enhanced composite package of value. Finally, such firms exhibited a low-cost structure relative to traditional suppliers of similar services although the rebundlers were themselves not necessarily price cutters. Sears Roebuck typified the composite service approach to financial services. Building upon its established customer base, Sears had rebundled consumer credit, personal and property insurance property brokerage, securitized mortgages for both home purchases and investors together with its traditional variety/department/catalogue store operations.

The final strategy, which had emerged increasingly in recent times, had been the development of a *Global Service Strategy* for a number of customer segments. This strategy represented a significant extension of the national distributor strategy and provided a range of global services through an integrated global delivery system, again usually electronically linked for specific client bases such as multinational corporations, or carefully selected private banking clients. A growing feature of such a strategy had been the establishment or acquisition of subsidiaries under one set of regulatory conditions in order to penetrate other markets which would otherwise be closed due to local legal constraints. The number of global strategy operators was expected to increase but only a few organizations could expect to be successful in the long term.

9.10 CONCLUSION

The financial services industry had been dramatically affected in a relatively short time by the twin impacts of deregulation and new technology. As a result traditional industry structure dynamics had been breaking down between the historically clearly defined industry sectors as suppliers had integrated forwards and customers had integrated backwards, while industry participants had themselves diversified into a range of related product market segments.

To compete successfully in a much more competitive environment it was becoming imperative for the managements of surviving competitors to examine carefully the consequences of the rapid environmental change that had occurred. As a result of the rapid transformation of financial service industry competitors a number of viable strategy alternatives could be identified. These need not be mutually exclusive and an appropriate mix of suitable strategic options needed to be selected within the resource constraints of each institution's strategic position. Where existing positions were considered to be indefensible appropriate exit strategies or mergers should be contemplated to develop viability.

CHAPTER 10

Implications for Economic Management

10.1   THE PATTERN OF FINANCIAL MARKET CHANGES

In the late 1980s the major commercial banks operating in international markets were undergoing a fundamental shift in strategy and consequently structure. This was transforming them from their traditional role as financial intermediaries concerned with the collection and subsequent lending of deposits usually within a confined geographic market. Rather the major banks were becoming multinational in nature and, by the process of deregulation and securitization, were unbundling their traditional intermediation role and increasingly becoming dealers in securities. At the same time other institutions such as investment banks, brokerage houses, some insurance companies and a number of non-banks were similarly approaching the global market place from their own traditional positions.

As a consequence of the breakdown in traditional barriers a new, global capital market was being created where the savings of a Japanese farmer via a variety of routes could end up financing the channel tunnel. The demarcations between domestic and international capital markets were also blurring, making it difficult for the financial control of any country to remain strictly localized, allowing companies and institutions to bypass exchange controls, interest rate variations and the like. Similarly the differences between traditional, alternative forms of raising capital, namely bonds, loans and equity, were shifting towards a world with an apparently limitless array of alternative financial instruments. By using interest rate and currency swaps borrowers could, in theory, tap any domestic capital market and swap this debt with an overseas based counter-party to obtain funds in another country and another currency. New equity issues could be simultaneously sold by different underwriting syndicates in several stock markets. Major equities could be traded on a global, electronic stock exchange with 24-hour dealing, making individual, physical exchanges obsolete. Dealing possibilities which permitted arbitrage between loans, equities, foreign exchange, futures, commodities and the plethora of new instruments, opened a vast panorama of new opportunities requiring dramatic improvements in hardware and software capabilities, leading ultimately, perhaps, to the intervention of artificial intelligence systems.

These changes which were already present, or in early prospect, by the late 1980s seemed destined to transform the banks and other competitor financial service institutions into new forms of enterprise. These changes could also be expected to have a significant effect on governments and on industry regulators keen to operate a stable monetary system. This chapter briefly explores the implications of the likely changes on those responsible for economic management and financial service industry supervision. In addition the chapter highlights some of the implications for the senior management of banks and their leading corporate customers.

Over the past decade, the trend towards direct financing had actually been encouraged by many governments. The demand for public sector credit had increasingly been met in the developed economies by governments tapping the securities market rather than financing their needs via the banking system. This was because governments, due to their relatively high creditworthiness, found it easy in the case of developed countries to access the capital markets. Moreover, funds could be tied down at low and fixed rates, by comparison with money obtained through the banks. Such funds also did not stimulate inflation by boosting the money supply. Since 1980 public sector financing by most Group of Ten countries made less use of the banking system and in the case of the UK, for example, more securities were sold than were strictly necessary to cover the government's borrowing requirements[1].

Particularly significant had been the huge increase in capital inflows into the USA, to cover the mounting budget deficit. This began in 1983 and was initially made up largely by a change in US-based banks from being capital exporters to becoming capital importers as they reduced in particular their sovereign risk lending. From a net outflow of $42 billion in 1982, banks imported a net $17 billion in 1983, rising to over $30 billion in 1985[2]. While the turnround from capital export to import by the banks was the main contributor to the growth in US capital inflows in early 1980s, there had been a rapid expansion in securities transactions by 1985. These rose from a net $19 billion in 1983 to $50 billion in 1985 due entirely to the sale of US securities to foreigners anxious to invest in the perceived strength of the US economy and for a time the rising value of the dollar. This inward investment was also stimulated by deregulation and the high level of innovation in the US capital markets, which offered investors an ever wider array of flexible financial instruments. In particular, direct investment of the growing Japanese savings surplus was being directed to the USA. Direct purchase of US government securities, for example, more than doubled between 1984 and 1985. Further, even more investment would doubtless have occurred but for the Japanese Ministry of Finance imposing an administrative limit of 10 per cent of total assets being held in foreign investments.

The Japanese trade surplus, therefore, had grown by the mid 1980s to exceed the largest OPEC surpluses enjoyed by Saudi Arabia in the early 1970s, but was not being recirculated via the capital markets as the OPEC surpluses had been. Rather it was being sucked into the USA together with savings from much of the rest of the developed countries to finance the rising US budget deficit. By 1987, when the deficit had grown to an estimated $167 billion, the dollar weakened sharply relative in particular to the yen and the Deutschmark.

---

[1]BIS Annual Report, 1985, p. 54.
[2]Morgan Guaranty Trust Co., *World Financial Markets*, January 1986, p. 7.

As a result Japanese banks and investment institutions became increasingly reluctant to purchase additional US government securities and investment in the equities market was also slowing as Japanese domestic interest rates rose while the value of the dollar continued to fall.

By early 1987 not only had private investors stopped funding the deficit but so too had commercial banks who had also had enough and passed the problem to the Group of Seven of central banks. These institutions effectively funded the US deficit for most of 1987 but with the crash in October, the capital markets effectively recognized that some major adjustment was necessary. The first stage in the possible detonation of the mega debt bomb had arrived.

The funds to support the initial build up in government debt had come in part from the rapid growth in private funds under investment management. This growth in private funds was due to the growth in pension investments, life insurance savings and mutual funds. As a result, savings deposits had tended to shift away from the banking industry into other forms of financial institution. The increase in competition in the securities markets had also led to a sharp reduction in transaction costs, especially for large block trading engaged in by the major investment management institutions. Deregulation also increased the international movement of these investment funds as a result of the removal of exchange controls and the globalization of dealing in all forms of securities.

The changing pattern in the capital markets had also led the banks to rely increasingly on funds gathered in the markets rather than from small depositors. As a result a growing proportion of bank liabilities had been generated from the interbank or other wholesale markets. This trend had been accentuated by the shift in deposits of even small savers towards market-related deposit products. In the USA, UK, Canada and Italy near money market rates for small deposits were by the late 1980s readily available with minimum withdrawal and maturity restrictions.

The deregulation of the financial services industry sectors which had led to widespread market segment interpenetration, both within and between countries, had also been actively encouraged in a growing number of countries. While the primary objective of this pattern had been to stimulate market efficiency and greater competition it had also increased the difficulties of monitoring and regulating the markets. Moreover, the potential for market volatility had been increased dramatically as a result of global trading, new computer-based trading methods and the linkages between markets.

The reduction in distinctiveness between different methods of financing had also helped to transform the markets. Traditionally financial contracts were held until maturity or the transfer or sale of a contract involved the complete transfer of all terms and conditions of the deal. The unbundling of contracts into their constituent elements had allowed institutions to keep those components considered desirable and to sell on those which did not fit their existing portfolio. The rapid growth in the market for swaps, futures contracts, options and the like, illustrated the development of component unbundling. In the main, most innovation in these techniques had occurred in the USA and the Euromarkets, although many other industrialized countries were actively developing financial futures markets.

The trend to disintermediation had also permitted banks and other financial institutions to rid themselves of undesirable elements in financial contracts. Thus interest rate risk could be transferred to other parties, and as a result, the spread on bank transactions between deposit and lending rates had shrunk while the traditional intermediation role of the banks looked more and more similar to direct capital market funds flows. It was not, however, altogether clear what the change towards a securitized market meant for the risk position of banks. By 1987 it was estimated that off-balance-sheet investments had risen to $135 billion of junk bonds; $300 billion of interest rate swaps; $40 billion in currency swaps; and $680 billion of open positions in financial futures and options[3]. In addition there were extensive commitments for back-up credit lines on Euronotes; standby facilities on commercial paper and more conventional instruments such as letters of credit. The securitization of the markets and its impact on bank balance sheets thus also compounded the difficulties of monetary authorities in measuring and controlling

[3]*Economist* International Banking Survey, 21 March 1987, p. 4.

the money supply and in monitoring and evaluating the risk positions of individual banks.

10.2 THE DECLINING ROLE OF THE CENTRAL BANKERS

Historically the major central banks were able to dominate the world financial markets. With the rise of the Euromarkets and the development of the foreign exchange markets the first real sign of the loss of power of the central banks came with the forced move to floating exchange rates. The volume of market transactions until towards the end of the 1970s was still small enough, however, for the combined weight of the central bankers to major industrial nations to be relatively dominant. Moreover, capital markets were still sufficiently closed and different for individual central banks strictly to control domestic financial systems.

The power and influence of the central banks was also enhanced by the strong personalities of many of the leaders of the banks of the major developed economies. Many of these men, such as Paul Volker, Guido Cari, Fritz Leutwieler, Otmar Emminger and Gordon Richardson, had retired by the late 1980s and only Karl Otto Poehl of the German Bundesbank still remained in power of the heavyweight central bankers of the early 1980s.

By the late 1980s, however, the explosive growth of the foreign exchange markets and securitization of traditional bank assets had sharply reduced the power of the central banks. This had also been exacerbated by the adoption of monetarist policies by many governments, which had tended to transfer power from national central banks to ministries of finance. A consequence of monetarism had also been a major switch of capital from the public to the private sector, adding dramatically to the level of investment in securities. This growth was further fuelled by the dramatic expansion in all forms of securities trading on an increasingly global basis.

Even acting in concert in the foreign exchange markets, the central banks found it difficult to have more than a very temporary effect on individual exchange rates. Most central bankers would accept that with the massive expansion in foreign exchange trading volume, their influence over the markets had become very limited and their reserve positions too weak to be powerful players. Indeed some bankers believed that the intervention of central banks in the foreign exchange markets may have been counter-productive as their presence may have added to exchange rate volatilities. The attempts at introducing stability within ranges between currencies after the Plaza Agreement and the Louvre Accord by the end of 1987 were in tatters while the growth in volume continued to rise as dealers continued to play and win against the central banks.

While the central banks' loss of influence over the foreign exchange markets had thus been inevitable, as trading had grown, their declining influence over the banking system could potentially be even more serious. Securitization, unbundling and the rapid growth in new financial instruments meant that central banks had less and less knowledge and control over the exposure positions of banks which they were supposed to supervise. Existing central bank controls were unable to measure effectively the exposure position of banks heavily engaged in off-balance-sheet transactions. Moreover, the pace of change in the capital markets, and the blurring of differences between all forms of financial institutions, meant that the central banks were only supervising a small part of the market place. Again, the increasing complexity of new financial instruments, coupled with the rapid rate of new product introduction and decline, meant that few central bankers had supervisory departments able to understand, much less monitor, these products and their effects on bank risk profiles. Moreover, central banks in general had not traditionally been concerned with the capital markets and trading operations. Their role had rather been concerned with the supply of money, and the supervision and maintenance of stability of the banking system by acting as lender of last resort. They were not, therefore, well equipped to supervise a fully deregulated, trading-dominated market which was expected increasingly to make use of financial instruments which bypassed the need for money at all.

10.3   THE POTENTIAL RISKS OF EXCESS COMPETITION

Deregulation had led to a substantial increase in the level of competition in most areas of the financial services industry. As a consequence there had been a trend to reductions in transaction cost, declining margins, a shakeout of inefficient firms and unbundling of products to modify risk profiles.

However, little was really known or fully understood in many of the institutions participating in the new markets about the medium- and long-term risks associated with this new business. These risks might well also not be understood by most of the top executive managements of the major banks. These individuals grew up in a different era when banking was traditionally an intermediation rather than a trading process, and were not necessarily well equipped to manage the relatively different business of the dealing-orientated, technology-driven modern bank.

In addition, the risks remaining unsecuritized within the banks were quite likely to be of lower quality. The high-quality assets from good-credit-risk borrowers were likely to be those which were most easily marketable, while high-credit-risk assets might be expected to be retained by the banks unless they offered sufficiently high interest rates, such as junk bond securities, to compensate investors for perceived additional risk. As a result many banks could be undercapitalized to support the level of off-balance-sheet transactions they were engaging in, and top management had not sanctioned the level of risk their organizations were exposed to. Moreover, in many countries the new instruments were not subject to prudential controls at all, even assuming central banks understood the risk implications.

Overall, the changing pattern of the financial markets to a trading business therefore almost certainly meant that there had been an increase in risks in many institutions within the system. The shrinking of margins and the trend to high-volume trading for profitability had also surely meant that significant profits would only be generated by institutions taking positions. The potential collapse of a major institution as a result of unmatched risk and inadequate equity could then produce a domino effect throughout not just a national market, but increasingly a global one. The potentially increasing scale of any such collapse, together with the declining role of the central banks and uncertainty about how the role of lender of last resort would operate in a world of trading and complex financial instruments, should be a matter of considerable concern to public policy-makers.

At present, therefore, while efficiency might be increasing as a result of greater competition, risk exposure was also likely to be increasing and prudential authorities seemed ill-equipped either to measure this or to deal with it in the event of a serious collapse. Further, adding to the supervisory requirements imposed on banks did not necessarily improve understanding or management of this risk. Rather it might well be expected to transfer the risk to a less observed area of the financial services markets as a result of unbundling of undesirable contract elements by the banks. In such areas, if a collapse were to occur adjustment and intervention might prove difficult and more costly, as a suitable public sector intervention institution might not be immediately available.

It seemed, therefore, essential that monetary and prudential regulatory systems, on both a national and international scale, should be adequate to ensure that financial institutions participating in major markets had sufficient equity capital and adequate management and information systems to prevent the possibility of them getting out of control. At the end of 1987 this situation still did not prevail despite growing efforts by some central banks to increase cooperation.

10.4   THE DANGERS OF DIVERSIFICATION

The evolution of the capital markets had caused banks to diversify both geographically and especially by product line into new areas of activity. As a generalization, based on the experiences of other industries, most such diversification moves fail. The attempt, for example, by commercial banks to graft on investment banking, insurance and brokerage business to traditional banking seemed likely to result in similar failures in many cases.

There are a number of reasons why such moves usually result in unsatisfactory performance. Firstly, as indicated above, far from reducing risk by spreading it across a broader portfolio of activities, risk can be increased when those new activities are poorly understood by the senior management of the diversifying institutions. Secondly, banks do not tend to have adequate management information systems to measure either the risks or the performance of the new businesses they are embarking upon. Such systems have not been used traditionally within the banking industry and will be required to be both in place and understood by bank management if they are collectively to monitor and control a diversified business. Thirdly, there is almost certainly a misconception about whether or not the new forms of international banking are merely a simple evolution of traditional activity. If, as indicated in previous chapters, the change has been more fundamental, senior management, raised in the previous era and without the foresight to appreciate the strategic shift, may be particularly ill-suited in some cases to manage a period of rapid change. Fourthly, the successful integration of new businesses, many of which have entered the banks as a result of mergers or new alliances and each of which has potentially a different culture and established norms, is an extremely difficult managerial task. It is compounded in the diversification of the banking industry by the extreme differences in salaries and working conditions between sectors and between international financial centres. Few bank managements have probably thought through the implications of these differences or devised strategies for overcoming them. Fifthly, the traditional route to the top management of major commercial banks, especially in Europe, has been through the branch network. The addition of new businesses will require the rapid opening of new succession routes, without which an appropriate managerial balance will not be achieved, but with which it will also be necessary to placate the frustration created amongst the traditional managerial hierarchy. Sixthly, the rapid diversification of so many institutions into one another's territory will lead, in the short term, to serious overcapacity, much of which may well be in the hands of management's adopting poorly understood 'me too' strategies. This will almost inevitably lead to a major shakeout and the creation of casualities which will affect, not only individual institutions, but potentially the total system.

For the top management of banks, therefore, it is extremely important to understand the consequences of rapid diversification and the changing nature of the financial markets. It is essential to devise an appropriate organization structure early on in the process to avoid subsequent revolutionary upheaval which comes with the recognition that the strategy adopted is no longer consistent with the traditional structure. The piecemeal grafting on of new businesses is not an adequate solution. Next, it is important to instal adequate management information systems, appropriate to the new strategy, and to educate conventional bank management to use these to manage a diversified business. Suitable channels of communication must also be installed to create synergies where these are appropriate whilst adequate Chinese walls need to be built to stop inappropriate information transfer. Finally, massive education and guidance is required to modify traditional cultures to the new way of operating a diversified financial service enterprise appropriate to the next century.

10.5   THE IMPACT ON MONETARY POLICY

The development of new financial instruments, the move towards securitization and the globalization of capital markets have also had significant impact on the demand for money. New instruments have substantially enhanced liquidity and monetary velocity. Further, the new instruments have substantially blurred the distinctions between traditional monetary instruments and non-monetary ones. As a result, traditional measures of the money supply, which have often been used as a basis for national financial policy, have become increasingly inaccurate. In a growing number of countries an increasingly complex system of economic aggregates need to be employed to assess economic position. Moreover, traditional relationships between these aggregates might no longer hold and as a result there is a tendency to use aggregates only as guidelines rather than absolute measures.

The move towards securitized credit also affects the use of traditional monetary policy instruments and the way these work within the national financial system. The new system has dramatically increased the flexibility for both borrowers and lenders, opening up substitutes both domestically and overseas, in a way that might be inconsistent with national financial policy. Moreover, administrative control over credit levels, interest rates and investment portfolio composition has become more difficult as greater variety is offered in the financial markets. The adoption of financial policies which are disliked by the international foreign exchange and capital markets also seems to be increasingly difficult. The greater openness of the markets has meant that the foreign exchange market could move rapidly in a direction undesired by national governments but quite outside their ability to control, or governments can be denied access to the capital markets except on terms contrary to national political objectives.

10.6   THE UNCOUPLING OF LONG-TERM AND SHORT-TERM POLICY

The move towards a dealing-orientated financial market place is leading to an increased decoupling between the short-term perspective of the market place and the long-term perspective desired at the level of the firm and national governments for economic development. Foreign exchange trading, for example, has little to do with world trade but rather has become more akin to a giant casino, where each day institutions take positions without responsibility for the economic consequences of their actions on countries, industries, firms and individuals. Similarly, the value of a firm's equity might be subject to forces such as speculation for acquisition, which has little relationship to the organization's long-term economic position.

This short-term orientation of the market has been exacerbated by the development of high real interest rates as monetarist policies have reduced inflation, thus focusing attention on short-term yields. Further, the concentration of investment funds into institutions where active portfolio trading has become the norm has again led to a short-term focus. Deregulation has also made these funds much more internationally mobile as investment managers have sought superior opportunities, increasingly on a global scale.

This short-term focus is not without its positive side. Firstly, it has made many companies much more conscious of the needs of shareholders and has probably resulted in substantial attempts to improve performance. The strategic shock of receiving an uninvited takeover bid has worked wonders in many board-rooms. Secondly, the focus on short-term trading has increased market volume sharply and thereby improved liquidity especially in the New York and Tokyo stock markets.

Nevertheless, continual concentration on short-term performance creates substantial negative effects as well. For the company concerned with the development of new products or services for the future, the need constantly to perform to meet the short-term portfolio needs of institutional investors may well reduce long-term capital investment and research and development. Moreover, the constant threat of an unwelcome takeover reduces managerial concentration on managing the business. In the USA, the need for so many leading companies, not in many cases seen as badly managed, to swallow 'poison pills' to reduce the threat from unwanted suitors cannot be helpful to economic development.

Successful bid and defence tactics have also tended to create unstable corporations, heavily laden with debt as the result of the use of 'junk bonds' and leveraged buy outs, which again reduces the capability of organizations to embark on long-term strategic commitments.

This short-term orientation of the financial markets is also a worrying phenomenon for policy-makers concerned with the longer term issues of changing industry structure, maintaining employment or building social systems. The successful achievement of such longer term policies is usually dependent upon economic performance. However, when the underlying economic achievement of the nation state is perhaps subordinate to the short-term emotional whim of the position trader this has to be a cause for public concern. The effects, for example, of exchange rate manipulation do not affect each industry equally, as MITI has identified. Rather, individual sectors of an economy can be artificially influenced, in a way which defies natural competitive position and in an almost unplannable manner.

It is probably not possible in many industries or countries to shorten lead times for policies or investments to recouple the dealing market and rational economic planning. As a result continued disfunctional behaviour seems likely to occur which can make rational investments, especially for long capital cycle projects, more and more reminiscent of a global poker game.

To counter these undesirable effects governments may wish to direct part of the portfolio of the institutions into longer term investments. In Japan, the policies of MITI and the Ministry of Finance have consistently tended to guide investing institutions into the furtherance of a national economic strategy. In Britain, the Labour Party has recommended the creation of a National Investment Bank to focus similarly on long-term investment. While some such policy seems laudable, and almost certainly would not occur voluntarily, it is important to recognize that it might have the undersirable counter-effect of causing investment managers to focus even more on the short term for that part of their portfolio they were still free to trade. Secondly, such policies may not produce the economic or social effects desired when they are abused to further short-term political aspirations.

In addition a re-examination of public policy guidelines on mergers and acquisitions seems desirable in many countries. This would consider not only the degree to which competition might be reduced by market share combination on a national basis but, where appropriate, on a global one. For example, although a British competitor might enjoy a market share of greater than 25 per cent in the domestic market, it might remain a weak and ineffectual competitor in a global sense. Second, new criteria should be considered, including the effects of merger of conglomerate economic concentrations, and the impact of very high gearing on long-term corporate viability. There should also be closer scrutiny on the role of financial institutions in creating mergers via the use of financial instruments such as junk bonds and the like.

10.7   THE NEED FOR NEW SUPERVISORY CONTROLS

In April 1985, the Bank of England made the first attempt to regulate the new risks to banks from the new financial instruments. The bank imposed a risk asset ratio of 0.5 per cent on the underwriting commitments in RUF and NIF Contracts. At the same time the bank announced its intention to examine the implications of other types of off-balance-sheet risks such as swaps, options and futures and the interest rate risk that maturity transformations created such as a medium-term facility backing a short-term NIF[4].

Other central banks, while not going as far as the Bank of England, had begun to express similar concerns at the potential impact of the new instruments by the end of 1985. The Cooke Committee of banking supervisors, chaired by Bank of England director Peter Cooke and composed of regulators from eleven major industrial countries, identified at least 30 new instruments, the implications of which they wished to examine on the banks under their control.

While the Bank of England's move attempted to impose some caution into banks, other central banks had not made similar moves, partly because they did not understand the potential increase in risk posed by the new instruments, or rather because they hoped these innovations were temporary aberrations which might fade away. The Bank of England was, therefore, conscious of the fact that it could not impose conditions on banks operating in the London market that would make them uncompetitive with those operating in less supervised markets, so constraining the degree to which new prudential controls could be introduced.

The Bank of England's move was also not without criticism. The blanket imposition of a 0.5 per cent weight to NIF and RUF contracts made no allowance for the real differences in credit risk between borrowers. Secondly, the constraint did not apply to investment banks, a factor which annoyed the major commercial banks, who regarded the imposition as unfair competition. Regulators, however, countered by arguing that commercial banks financed their transactions with depositors' money and these had to adequately protected. However, as commercial banks modified their funding base and other financial institutions operated in the same markets, the need to supervise commercial banks, investment banks and equivalent non-banks on a common basis across the entire market on a 'level playing ground' had become an urgent priority.

[4] D. Delamaide, The off-balance-sheet dilemma, *Institutional Investor*, October 1985, p. 136.

The Bank of England's initiative did, however, lead to a growing international recognition of the need to measure off-balance-sheet risk and to the acceptance that it was necessary to harmonize the rules on bank supervision between countries. Under the auspices of the BIS, the central banks of the leading industrial countries were actively working to increase coopera-tion and harmonization between the bank supervisory regula-tions in different countries.

In early 1987, the first major move towards such harmoniza-tion came when the Bank of England and the US Federal banking authorities announced they had reached agreement on common measures of bank capital adequacy. As a first step in covergence the two central banking bodies proposed a common minimum primary capital base. From these beginnings the authorities hoped others, and especially the Japanese Ministry of Finance, would join and so create a common global standard.

Under the two central banks' scheme a common risk-related approach was proposed to the measurement of different types of risk. The new system ranked credit risk by means of a hierarchy of risk weights classified according to the nature of the obligator. The new system included most forms of off-balance-sheet risk in addition to on-balance-sheet transactions.

Under the system a common ratio of primary capital was to be set and published as a minimum requirement which would apply to all British and US banks. In addition the supervisory authorities were to set a minumum, unpublished, primary capital ratio for each individual bank dependent upon its per-ceived relative strength. There were to be five risk weight cate-gories: 0, 10, 25, 50 and 100 per cent dependent upon the nature of the obligator. Two higher ratios applied in the earlier Bank of England initiative were discontinued. The new risk factors did not, however, include country risk differentials which were to be dealt with qualitatively.

Examples of the new system were that cash and claims of the domestic central bank rated a zero risk rating; short-term claims of less than one year maturity on the domestic governments carried a weight of 10 per cent; short-term claims with a maturity of a year or less on domestic depository organizations and foreign banks, together with equivalent off-balance-sheet expo-sures, carried a weighting of 25 per cent; direct claims on multinational development organizations in which the bank's government was a shareholder or member were rated at 50 per cent risk; all other assets carried a 100 per cent weighting. This included open net foreign exchange positions.

To cover the swelling value of off-balance-sheet risk the authorities had devised an approach which endeavoured to convert the credit risk of each instrument into a credit equivalent which could then be the overall risk asset framework.

Thus obligations in the form of financial guarantees, standby LCs, acceptance credits and the like were considered to be unavoidable at the date at which the obligations came due and as a consequence were expected to be converted in risk terms at 100 per cent of the principal value. The risk asset weighting was then determined by the category of the counter-party and, where appropriate, the maturity, with shorter term maturities being treated as less risky. For example RUF/NIFs and the like were to be converted at 10 per cent for maturities of one year or less, 25 per cent for up to five years and at 50 per cent for over five years.

In March 1987, two important gaps left in the original agreement, relating to interest and foreign exchange rate swaps and contracts, were covered in a second agreement. This excluded spot foreign exchange, futures and options marked to market daily but included interest rate swaps, forward rate agreements, purchased interest rate options, cross-currency swaps, forward foreign exchange contracts and purchased currency options. On each such contract the credit equivalent was calculated. This was measured as the sum of the current and potential exposure. For example, for an interest rate swap the current exposure would be the mark-to-market value, positive or negative of a contract on the reporting day. The potential exposure would be an estimate suggested to be between ½–1 per cent per annum of the future credit exposure over the remaining life of the swap.

If the sum of these two exposures was negative the credit equivalent would be set at zero since the bank would not necessarily make a profit if its counter-party failed, as the contract would probably continue. For positive exposures, however, the bank would be required to provide underlying capital support.

These new proposals were, however, extremely complex, especially in the assessment of potential exposure. Nevertheless they did represent a very welcome first step in international harmonization and an attempt to contain the rapidly growing bank risk exposure to off-balance-sheet instruments which had not been tested under adverse market conditions.

The new proposals further did not really handle non-bank players in the new markets. In the United States, for example, investment banks, brokerage houses, insurance companies and industrial corporations, all of whom had become increasingly active in the financial markets, were not subject to the new regulations. Banks were thus to some extent being penalized relative to these players who could both hold down price and add to potential instability of the financial system.

The same effect could also be seen in the securities markets. Again the regulatory authorities in each country were different and different rules applied. Moreover, while some progress had been made in achieving harmonization between the world's leading central banks this was much less developed amongst securities markets regulators. Some progress had been made between the US Securities Exchange Commission and the UK Trade and Industry Department, which was responsible for securities market regulation in Britain. Other quiet agreements covering exchanges of information, especially regarding insider dealing and other criminal activities, had been reached with Canada, Japan and Switzerland but these were wholly inadequate to provide a regulatory framework for a 24-hour global trading environment.

The rapid development of global trading and the interpenetration of one another's traditional markets by banks and non-banks had left a major supervisory problem. Moreover, the growing uncertainty on the measurement of risk exposure and the increased volatility and interdependence of historically separated financial markets meant that major issues in reregulation had to be faced on a global scale. It seemed, therefore, that there was a clear need for bank and securities industry regulators in each of the major centres to develop common methodologies for supervision, risk measurement, capital adequacy and the like to be applied even-handedly to all forms of players in the financial markets. Further, it was important that similar rules be applied globally. While the markets had developed rapidly to become an increasingly integrated global system, the regulators still had a very long way to go.

10.8   CONCLUSION

The rapid diversification of the financial services industry pre-
sents the managements of these institutions with the need to
undertake rapid strategic and structural change. At present probably few such managements appreciate the organizational control system and internal culture issues posed by this change. The
implementational issues raised by the rapid changes in the
financial services industry will thus be the key to success or
failure and senior general managers will need to grasp these
issues if their organizations are to thrive, or in some cases,
survive.

The changing patterns of the international financial services
markets similarly present great challenges to public policy-
makers and regulatory authorities. Unfortunately politicians and
those technocrats concerned with economic management and
financial institutions supervision are, in many countries, lagging
behind the pace of change in the markets.

Some of the more important implications of these changes
include a substantial decline in the power and ability of the
central banks to influence the markets; the increased risks and
volatility of the markets themselves and the implications for the
limitation of individual government powers in economic management, the impact on governmental control of international
monetary policy; and the need for urgent linkages between the
different types of supervisory bodies on a global basis.

It is imperative that these issues be successfully addressed and
with urgency if the world is to maintain a condition of stable
economic and financial equilibrium. If they are not so addressed
the crash of 1987 will not be confined to the world's stock
markets but may spill over into a worldwide banking crisis,
raising again the spectre of a return to the disastrous days of the
1930s.

Index